PARENT–CHILD RELATIONS

PARENT–CHILD RELATIONS
Context, Research, and Application

SECOND EDITION

Phyllis Heath
Central Michigan University

Merrill
is an imprint of

Upper Saddle River, New Jersey
Columbus, Ohio

Library of Congress Cataloging-in-Publication Data
Heath, Phyllis.
Parent-child relations: context, research, and application/Phyllis Heath.-- 2nd ed.
p. cm.
Includes bibliographical references and index.
ISBN-13: 978-0-13-159676-4
1. Child rearing--United States. 2. Parent and child--United States. I. Title.
HQ769.H473 2007
649'.10973--dc22
2009048428

Vice President and Executive Publisher: Jeffery W. Johnston
Publisher: Kevin M. Davis
Acquisitions Editor: Julie Peters
Editorial Assistant: Tiffany Bitzel
Senior Project Manager: Linda Hillis Bayma
Production Coordination: Kelly Ricci/Aptara
Design Coordinator: Diane C. Lorenzo
Photo Coordinator: Shea Davis
Cover Designer: Ali Mohrman
Cover image: Corbis
Operations Specialist: Laura Messerly
Director of Marketing: Quinn Perkson
Marketing Manager: Erica DeLuca
Marketing Coordinator: Brian Mounts

This book was set in Optima by Aptara. It was printed and bound by R.R. Donnelley & Sons Company. The cover was printed by R.R. Donnelley & Sons Company.

Photo Credits for Chapter Openers: Kelly Colson, p. 254; Scott Cunningham/Merrill, pp. 280, 310; Laima Druskis/PH College, p. 142; Phyllis Heath, p. 196; Ken Karp/PH College, p. 48; David Mager/Pearson Learning Photo Studio, p. 2; PCA International, Inc., p. 226; UN/DPI Photo/John Isaac, p. 110; Anne Vega/Merrill, p. 26; Todd Yarrington/Merrill, p. 74; Shirley Zeiberg/PH College, p. 172.

Pearson Education Ltd.
Pearson Education Singapore Pte. Ltd.
Pearson Education Canada, Ltd.
Pearson Education—Japan
Pearson Education Australia Pty. Limited
Pearson Education North Asia Ltd.
Pearson Educación de Mexico, S.A. de C.V.
Pearson Education Malaysia Pte. Ltd.

Merrill
is an imprint of

10 9 8 7 6 5 4 3
ISBN-13: 978-0-13-159676-4
ISBN-10: 0-13-159676-4

To my children Todd, Kelly, and Ken

About the Author

Phyllis Heath is a professor in the Department of Human Environment Studies at Central Michigan University. She has also taught courses for Michigan State University in Okinawa, Japan. She was educated at the University of North Carolina at Asheville (where she earned a BA in Psychology), the University of North Carolina at Charlotte (where she earned a MA in Human Development and Learning), and the University of North Carolina at Greensboro (where she earned a PhD in Child Development and Family Relations). Her research has focused on the ways in which parent–child relationships impact the development of children and adolescents. This research has included the impact of parenting patterns on children's social competence, factors influencing parenting patterns (such as gender role ideology and locus of control), and more recently, the links between parenting patterns and adolescent depression. She has also researched parenting patterns of indigenous people in Oaxaco, Mexico and South Africa. She lives in Mt. Pleasant, Michigan.

Preface

This book was written to acquaint undergraduate students with the study of parent–child relations in the following major areas:

- The history of childrearing in the United States, as well as philosophical and theoretical perspectives that have guided child socialization practices in this country.
- Variations in childrearing patterns, including the childrearing practices of ethnic majority and ethnic minority parents in the United States as well as childrearing practices in other countries.
- Child socialization strategies for guiding children to become increasingly more competent and to have higher self-esteem as well as parenting skills for preventing and responding to problem behaviors and for resolving parent–child conflict.
- Coverage of parent–child relations at each of the following developmental stages: infancy and toddlerhood, preschool and middle childhood, early to late adolescence, and early to late adulthood.
- The changes that occur in the lives of parents who have children with exceptionalities or chronic illness that require specialized care, and recommendations for helping parents to meet these challenges.
- The lives of children who are maltreated and/or exposed to parental violence or parental alcoholism, and suggestions for interventions for these parents and children.
- The challenge faced by parents and children who are dealing with the untimely death of a family member and recommendations for helping children and parents throughout the grieving process.

Contextual Approach to Parenting

The contextual approach to parenting, which is a distinctive feature of this book, is emphasized by the inclusion of both historical and cultural approaches to understanding parent–child relations. Historically, we will examine how these relationships have changed during the past century as well as the ways in which early and contemporary psychological theorists and early childhood educators have shaped these changes. We will also emphasize how recent changes in the family (such as the rising rates of grandparent primary caregivers and teenage parents) have altered caregiver–child relationships. Explorations of parent–child relationships in various ethnic groups within and outside the United States are also an integral part of this textbook. Theory and research in human development and family relations have been interwoven with presentations of cultural and structural variations in the family; this focus is the basis for most of the chapters in the text.

A discussion drawing attention to how cultural beliefs affect parent–child relations is presented early in the text. Because the cultural approach is a central theme of this book, it is essential to understand that there are important differences and similarities in parent–child relationships across cultures. A discussion of the variations in families due to marital status, sexual orientation, and the care of children by adults other than parents, is presented early in the text as well. The purpose of addressing the similarities and differences in various family arrangements is to heighten understanding of the commitment to the care of children that exists in families regardless of the conditions that have brought them together. The early presentations of cultural and structural variations in families are not meant to stand alone but rather to set the stage for discussions throughout the text that will focus on parents and children in the various settings in which their development occurs. This approach allows students to see how culture and family variations, as well as age and gender, are related to parent–child interactions at each stage of life.

Parenting Strategies

Another distinctive feature of this textbook is the in-depth coverage of parenting strategies. An overview of contemporary parenting strategies includes a variety of techniques. Abundant figures in that chapter help explain each technique, and sufficient examples are provided to enhance students' understanding of how to use each of them. Furthermore, the coverage of these strategies early in the book sets the stage for the upcoming chapters that focus on parenting of children at different stages of development and with different developmental needs. The parenting strategies presented in this textbook provide guidance for professionals working with children and their parents or other caregivers. The first part of Chapter 4 includes strategies designed to prevent misbehavior, promote the child's self-esteem, and enhance effective parent–child communication. The second part of that chapter focuses on methods used for providing consequences for behavior and resolving parent–child conflict. The presentation of various childrearing strategies early in the book helps to lay the groundwork for the upcoming chapters. Chapter 4, together with the previous chapters, prepares students to integrate theory, research, and technique while working with children and parents in various family contexts.

Critical Thinking Questions

Each chapter includes a variety of *Critical Thinking Questions* that allow students to pause in their reading to consider how the chapter relates to their life experiences, or how this material might be used in working with parents and children in various contexts. Responses from my students and the students of my colleagues, who also use this textbook, have been that they like the critical thinking questions because they help them to better understand the material. I also have used these critical thinking questions as the basis of an assigned classroom journal, wherein students choose several questions from each chapter and write their responses to the questions in a weekly journal, that is then shared in small classroom groups.

Changes to the Second Edition

In addition to updated references throughout this textbook, this second edition has an increased **emphasis on the various contexts of parenting**, which reviewers and colleagues have cited as a primary strength of the first edition. There are also more personal quotations from parents and children in various family circumstances. This addition is in response to feedback from my own students who said that they thought these examples personalized the material for them.

Some chapters were **reorganized** to add to greater clarification. For example, Chapter 2 became Chapters 2 and 3 in order to allow for an expansion of the discussions of various parenting patterns in Chapter 2 and the diversity of parenting contexts in Chapter 3. This reorganization also allowed for the inclusion of **more examples** and personal commentary. Another change from the first edition is the elimination of a chapter focused exclusively on grief and loss. Although this topic is important, it is now incorporated into other chapters. For example, the chapter that focuses on birth and newborns has a brief discussion related to the loss of a stillborn baby or the death of a baby shortly after birth. In the chapter that discusses elderly parents and their adult children, there is a brief presentation related to the death of an older parent and in the final chapter, along with other challenges in parent–child relationships, is a discussion of the impact of the untimely death of a family member.

Another change to the organization of this book is the **expansion of the discussion of Parents and Their Children Who Have Exceptionalities or Chronic Illnesses**. In the first edition, this material was included in the chapter on Children at Risk and Their Parents. The expansion of this material into a complete chapter allows for more discussion of parents of children with special needs as well as children at risk and their parents, because these topics are now covered in two chapters.

Another change for the second edition is that each chapter begins with a list of **Learning Objectives** and ends with a list of **Useful Web Sites**. These additions provide guidance for focusing on the main points in the chapter and direction for finding additional information on selected topics. Finally, new to the second edition is a **Glossary** of key terms to assist students in understanding unfamiliar terminology.

Supplements to the Textbook

This text is accompanied by PowerPoint slides, an Instructor's Manual, and a Test Bank. The Instructor's Manual, prepared by the author, includes chapter-by-chapter learning objectives, chapter summaries, and recommended audiovisual materials.

Robert Faleer, Central Michigan University, provided suggestions for the audiovisual materials. Dr. Deborah Bailey, Central Michigan University, updated the Test Bank, which contains a variety of test items in multiple-choice, true/false, and essay formats. The supplements can be found in the Instructor's Resource Center at http://www.pearsonhighered.com

ACKNOWLEDGMENTS

Preparing a textbook is an enormous undertaking that involves an entire network of individuals, and I have many people to thank for their contributions. I wish to thank Christina Tawney, my original editor at Pearson/Merrill, who recruited me to write the book; it was her enthusiasm over my new ideas for a parent–child relations textbook that persuaded me to take on the project. Kevin Davis and Martha Flynn, who took over as editors when Christina left for maternity leave and decided to stay home with her new baby, supported the book wholeheartedly and have provided me with the resources I requested to ensure that the book is as good as I could make it.

For the second edition of the book, I have had the privilege of working with editor Julie Peters. I am very grateful for the consistently supportive responses that Julie provided to me during the process of writing this edition. I am also appreciative of the valuable recommendations that Julie has made that I believe strengthen this book in a variety of ways. I also had the opportunity to work with editorial assistant Tiffany Bitzel, who had the demanding task of keeping things organized and providing consistent feedback to me in the production process. I am very grateful for her assistance. Many thanks to both of you.

The reviewers for the first edition were indispensable for the numerous comments and recommendations for improvement they provided. I am very grateful for the time and care spent by the reviewers to give me detailed, well-informed reviews: Susan Bowers, Northern Illinois University; Lane Brigham, Nicholls State University; Martha Bristor, Michigan State University; Patricia Cantor, Plymouth State College; Rena Hallam, University of Kentucky; Arminta Jacobson, University of North Texas; Celeste Matthews, Winona State University; Jacob Mayala, St. Cloud State University; and Sandra J. Wanner, University of Mary Hardin-Baylor.

I wish to thank the reviewers of the second edition for their many useful recommendations: Amanda W. Harrist, Oklahoma State University; Kere Hughes, Iowa State University; Beth Magistad, University of Minnesota; and Mary J. Pickard, East Carolina University.

The production editor for the book was Kelly Ricci, who was exemplary in her competence and professionalism. The photo researcher was Shea Davis, who came up with a wonderful selection of photographs, as you will see.

Brief Contents

Contents

Chapter 2
Parenting Patterns and the Impact of Culture and Context 27

Chapter 3
Parents and Children in Varied Family Structures 49

Chapter 4
Child Socialization Strategies and Techniques 75

Chapter 5
Becoming Parents and Parenting Infants and Toddlers 111

Chapter 7
Parents and Their School-Age Children 173

Chapter 8
Parent–Adolescent Interactions 197

Chapter 9
The Relationships of Young Adults, Their Parents, and Their Children 227

Chapter 10
Middle Age and Older Parenthood and Grandparenthood 255

Chapter 12
Families at Risk and Families Coping with the Death of a Family Member 311

Note: Every effort has been made to provide accurate and current Internet information in this book. However, the Internet and information posted on it are constantly changing; it is inevitable that some of the Internet addresses listed in this textbook will change.

PARENT–CHILD RELATIONS

Historical and Theoretical Influences of Childrearing

Objectives

After completing this chapter, you should be able to

- Summarize the early traditions of childrearing in the United States, as influenced by Hobbes and Calvin.
- Explain how Freud's view of childrearing impacted society's view of the child.
- Describe the methods by which Watson's beliefs regarding childrearing became mainstreamed in the United States.
- Provide examples of ways in which parental responsiveness, or lack of responsiveness, affects the quality of children's attachment, as well as other aspects of development.
- Understand why reinforcement, modeling, and imitation are more effective than punishment for helping children learn certain behaviors.
- Describe the role of parents in the Montessori method.
- Explain how parents use guided participation (Vygotsky) to support their children's learning.
- Use Bronfenbrenner's Ecological Theory to explain the impact of different contexts on childrearing practices.
- Explain the effect of normative and non-normative events on the family system, and the lives of parents and children in the family.

From the beginning of the 20th century to the present, American parents' relationships with their children have undergone considerable change. The way in which parents view children has changed dramatically, and the parental role has undergone considerable redefinition. Child socialization practices of American parents have been scrutinized, criticized, and discussed in writings that have gained increasing public attention. Recommendations for better ways to rear children have been offered by varied sources, including psychologists, educators, and other well-known authorities. In that climate, scientists began to study the interaction patterns of children and their parents, or other caregivers, and the findings of these studies have been widely disseminated. Based on these publications, public policy related to the care and protection of children has changed significantly. All these modifications in the way Americans interact with their children and in how they perceive their roles as parents have not changed overnight. Furthermore, the changes in American childrearing practices have not been uniform. As will be discussed in future chapters, Americans differ in the degree to which they accept professional advice and alter their childrearing practices. These differences can be traced to influences such as the culture in which parents are rearing their children and the parents' educational level as well as a variety of other sources.

AUTOCRATIC PARENTING: A TRADITION OF HARSH, STRICT CHILDREARING

At the beginning of the 20th century, the **autocratic parenting** approach was the prevailing belief guiding early American childrearing. Children were told what to do and expected to respond accordingly without expressing their opinions regarding parental demands. The autocratic approach to child socialization was influenced by two primary sources: the Hobbesian perspective of childrearing that was prevalent throughout Europe for many centuries (Aries, 1962), as well as Calvinist doctrine that influenced the childrearing beliefs of the early Puritans in the United States (Kagan, 1978).

The Hobbesian View: The Willful Child

Thomas Hobbes, who expressed the view that the child's will needs to be tamed, proposed that parental authority, when strictly applied, upholds both a religious mandate and a cultural tradition. It is from Hobbes that we obtained the view of the home as "a man's castle," based on his belief that the family was a miniature monarchy and that the rights and consequences of paternal (he did not mention maternal) and despotic domain were the same. Hobbes equated the status of children with that of household servants, both of whom were expected to have unquestioned obedience to the "master of the house" (Hobbes, 1994). Few questioned the justification for parental authority until the 20th century, and even Jean Jacques Rousseau, who (in the 1700s) romanticized the child and recommended that parents consider the nature of the child in their socialization goals, argued in favor of despotic rule in the family (Baumrind, 1996).

Puritan Beliefs: The Sinful Child

Autocratic parenting views based on Hobbes' idea of the willful child found easy acceptance among early American Puritans whose religious beliefs were shaped by the doctrine of John Calvin. Because Calvinist doctrine emphasized the inherent sinfulness of the child, early American parents believed that to be the cause of children's willfulness. Firm discipline that included a strong belief in corporal punishment rather than parental affection was thought to be necessary for children's development (Kagan, 1978). Parents, therefore, expected strict obedience and submission from their children, not independence or assertiveness. Children who were considered to be disobedient received "correction," which often took the form of a brutal beating (Cleverley & Phillips, 1986).

Thinking Critically

As we begin the study of ways in which to raise children, take a moment to consider your own views regarding the essential nature of the child. In what ways do you think the two views discussed previously regarding the nature of children influence the childrearing approaches that parents use in bringing up their children?

THE QUESTIONING OF AUTOCRATIC PARENTNG

The autocratic approach to child socialization began to be questioned early in the 20th century as the views of early childhood educators and psychologists began to influence childrearing practices in the United States and Europe. As will be shown in the following discussions, autocratic child socialization was challenged from a variety of different perspectives, and these challenges altered Americans' view of the nature of children, the role of the parent, and the appropriate way to bring up children.

The Legacy of G. Stanley Hall: The Child Study Movement

The first of the psychological theorists who influenced American childrearing patterns was G. Stanley Hall, who received the first PhD in psychology in the United States and who began the Child Study Movement in the late 1800s. The goal of the Child Study Movement, according to Hall, was to develop a science of psychology and education that respected the true nature and needs of the child. Hall believed that Americans were slowly awakening to a recognition that "children are not like adults, with all the faculties of maturity on a reduced scale, but unique and very different creatures" (p. 88). Hall believed that "the child's senses, instincts, views of truth, credulity, emotions, and feelings toward objects have very little in common with ours . . ." (Hall, 1965, p. 89).

Sigmund Freud: An Emphasis on Children's Natural Instincts

The next theorist to influence both European and American childrearing beliefs was the Austrian-born founder of psychoanalysis, Sigmund Freud. Freud's view of the nature of the child reflected the philosophical perspective of the French philosopher Jean-Jacques Rousseau—that children are basically good and that under optimal conditions their innate talents would emerge (Synnott, 1988). Reflections of Rousseau's philosophy can be seen in Freud's emphasis on children's innate drives and in his view of the mother as the prototype for all future relationships (Freud, 1931/1961). The beliefs of G. Stanley Hall, that children are different from adults and have their own instincts, also are reflected in Freudian theory. Freud developed the Theory of Psychosexual Development to explain the ways in which the focus of children's sexual energy corresponds to their stage of development (Brill, 1938). Based on that theory, Freud was the first contemporary theorist to propose that parental acceptance of the child's natural instincts should accompany parental attempts to socialize the child to conform to societal norms (Baumrind, 1996).

American parents, who were influenced by Freud during the 1930s, 1940s, and 1950s, rejected the autocratic approach to childrearing in favor of a more relaxed approach to child socialization. Freud's views of childrearing arose in direct opposition to the prevailing overly strict and harsh childrearing approach, and followers of Freud portrayed the child as psychologically fragile and in danger of being made chronically anxious by parental restrictions and demands (Baumrind, 1996). The lenient parenting pattern that developed as a result of Freudian influence reflected Freud's beliefs that (a) early influences are very important for children's development, and (b) harsh parenting methods are detrimental to children's well-being (Freud, 1931/1961).

Thinking Critically

As we began the 20th century, autocratic parenting practices bolstered by fundamental religious beliefs were firmly in place. Then a few decades later, Freud recommended that parents should be less strict with their children but did not address the issue of how parents were to maintain control over their children. How influential do you think Freudian theory was in altering the childrearing behaviors of the typical American parent?

Although the acceptance of Freudian beliefs regarding childrearing loosened the grip of harsh, autocratic parenting in the United States, it did not sufficiently address the issue of limits, boundaries, and guidelines. Because American parents with their Hobbesian–Calvinist legacy still understood discipline from the perspective of autocracy and punitive discipline, not being harsh with children was interpreted as not interfering with children's natural inclinations, thereby not providing limits and guidelines for children. Consequently, most American parents were not influenced by Freudian views of childrearing owing to concerns that they were being asked to relinquish control of their children. Those parents who believed that Freud's advice was a better approach than the familiar autocratic parenting practices tended to develop a lenient childrearing pattern whereby they did not provide sufficient guidelines for their children.

Watson: The Dangers of Parental Affection

Although the study of family socialization during the 1930s and 1940s reflected Freud's view of lenient parenting, this child socialization pattern was never widespread in the United States (Baumrind, 1996). Its reception among better educated parents, nevertheless, opened the door to acceptance of psychological theory as a source of information regarding how to rear children. It was in this climate that behaviorist views espoused by the American psychologist John Watson found easy acceptance. Watson strongly opposed parental expressions of affection for their children. He recommended, instead, that parents use a scientific approach to the rearing of children. Interestingly, Watson's "scientific approach" to childrearing was not supported by scientific evidence. On the contrary, his childrearing advice was based on his fervent personal belief that parents should ignore their natural inclinations to be nurturing and responsive to their children. That recommendation was based on his belief that responsive parenting spoiled children. Based on that conviction, he suggested that (a) parents should not respond to their crying infants and (b) they should feed their infants according to a strict schedule. Those two recommendations, though not supported by research evidence, found widespread acceptance in the American culture at a time when the new psychological theorizing was highly valued (Cohen, 1979; Kagan, 1978).

Watson's Use of the Media. As a uniquely American theory, Watson's "scientific approach to the rearing of children" gained acceptance among American academics as well as Americans at large. The way in which Watson's ideas came to affect so many American parents can be traced to the methods he used to disseminate his controversial views. Throughout 1926 and 1927, he addressed teachers' groups and medical groups on his theories. Then in 1928, he organized his ideas more formally for a set of six articles that appeared in *McCall's* magazine (read by many young mothers) that later came out in a book under the title, *The Psychological Care of the Infant and Child* (Watson & Watson, 1928). In magazine articles published in *Ladies' Home Journal* and *McCall's,* Watson consistently reminded mothers to put their babies on a strict feeding schedule and not spoil their infants by being responsive to their cries. The popularity of Watson's beliefs regarding how parents should rear their children was, therefore, due to his views being broadcast on the radio and published in easily accessible popular magazines at the time. Because Watson's admonitions about parental responsiveness and recommendations regarding scheduled care found their way into the American popular media, they had a much more widespread influence on American childrearing than did Freud's concerns regarding the detrimental effects of harsh parenting on children. In Watson's articles in popular magazines and in his radio broadcasts (before television was available), he said that parenthood is a science and parents should treat childrearing as an experiment. Given the newfound allegiance to science during that historical period, the linking of parenting with science was a very persuasive message to American parents (Cohen, 1979).

Thinking Critically

Which group of parents do you think Watson influenced by publishing his ideas in popular magazines that he would not have reached had he published those ideas in academic journals?

Watson's Ridicule of Mothers. Even though Watson's extreme views were immensely popular at the time, he had his share of dissenters. An example of an objection to Watson's childrearing advice is evident in one mother's statement, "that she was glad she had her children before she had ever heard of John B. Watson and his blasted behaviorism because, that way, she had been able to enjoy them" (p. 210). Instead of respecting that mother's position, her remarks were used by Watson in subsequent lectures to show how parents had used their children selfishly as a means of enjoying themselves. His criticism of American mothers was expanded in a chapter titled "The Dangers of Too Much Mother Love" in his well-known book, wherein he suggested that the reason mothers indulged in baby loving was sexual and that children should not be hugged, kissed, or allowed to sit on the parent's lap. Not only did Watson object to parents showing affection to their children, he frowned also on parental supervision and monitoring of young children. He noted that parents were always keeping an eye on their children, never giving them any freedom. He suggested that if parents could not restrain themselves from watching their children they might use a periscope to observe them, so at least the children would not know they were being watched (Cohen, 1979).

Thinking Critically

How do you feel about the fact that Watson had such a strong influence on mothers whom he consistently criticized for their natural loving behaviors toward their children? How do you think mothers today would react to that type of criticism?

Watson's Impact on American Childrearing. Although there is no question that Watson's views were extreme, the impact of his beliefs on American childrearing and the American child was not negligible. Parents in the 1930s, 1940s, and 1950s were eager for new knowledge, and science seemed to have limitless potential. Given the enthusiasm for scientific discovery that existed during that period of American history, it was plausible to assume that a psychological theory would offer a better way of rearing children (Cohen, 1979). The views of Watson established such a stronghold on parenting patterns during those three decades that we still see his influence on childrearing in the United States today. Concerns regarding the spoiling of children, practices of scheduling infant feeding, and beliefs that parents should let their babies "cry it out," unfortunately, are still considered by some American parents to be the appropriate way to socialize their children.

THEORIES THAT EMPHASIZED PARENTAL UNDERSTANDING OF CHILDREN

Although John Watson's views held center stage in American childrearing beliefs throughout the 1930s, 1940s, and 1950s, other theories that were developed during that period contributed to alternative perspectives regarding the appropriate way to rear children. The development of Attachment Theory by John Bowlby (Bowlby, 1958, 1969) and studies of infant attachment by Bowlby's colleague Mary Ainsworth (Ainsworth, 1973) seriously challenged Watson's recommendation that parents not express affection toward their children. Additionally, the theories of Jean Piaget and Lev Vygotsky contradicted the view of children as passive learners. During the second half of the 20th century, theorists such as Erik Erikson continued to emphasize the importance of parental respect for children's feelings, and the growth-producing effect of parental support for their children. The most recent trends in theory development focusing on parent–child relationships come from Family Systems Theory and Urie Bronfenbrenner's Ecological Theory. These theoretical approaches have drawn attention to the role of context as an influence of childrearing behaviors and children's development. In addition to continued theory development that has increased awareness of the need for parents to incorporate an understanding of children into their childrearing patterns, a number of early childhood educators have spoken out in support of better childrearing practices.

Attachment Theory: A Focus on Parental Responsiveness

Attachment theory was developed by the British psychiatrist John Bowlby in the early 1940s (Bowlby, 1958, 1969). That theory is based on the philosophical view of Rousseau, that children have natural instincts that should be considered when socializing them. Respect for the natural instincts of children served as the foundation for studies of interactions between mothers and infants by Bowlby's colleague Mary Ainsworth. According to Ainsworth (1973), emotionally available caregivers

David Colson

The tender warmth this young mother is expressing toward her contented baby is an excellent example of parental responsiveness—which is the primary predictor of infant attachment.

contribute to the development of **secure attachment**, which is the "affectional tie that one person forms to another specific person, binding them together in space and enduring over time" (p. 33). Ainsworth's perspective emphasizes that (a) socialization begins with personal attachment; (b) the infant is born helpless, requiring care, and (c) parents should respond to the feelings evoked by the child (Elkin & Handel, 1989). Studies of infant attachment during the 1940s awakened the scientific community to how essential parental responsiveness is for the healthy development of infants. These studies documented the following: (a) that infants, whose caregivers are emotionally and physically available to them, develop secure attachment; (b) that having a secure attachment to a parent promotes the infant's exploration of the environment; (c) that the sensitive responsiveness of the caregiver in stressful situations provides reassurance, comfort, and protection for the infant; and (d) that the sensitive responsiveness of the caregiver provides for the child an internalized working model of parental availability (Ainsworth, Blehar, Waters, & Wall, 1978).

Reńe Spitz: The Harmful Effects of Unresponsive Caregiving. Scholars in the areas of developmental psychology were beginning to see the importance of parental responsiveness to infants in the mid-1940s, based on Ainsworth's attachment studies, when the French psychologist Reńe Spitz provided further strong evidence of the crucial importance of parental responsiveness. In his studies of institutionalized infants and children in Europe, Spitz provided indisputable data demonstrating that the responsiveness of the caregiver to infants' cries and other gestures of communication are crucial to infant development. In dramatic film footage that shocked the world, Spitz revealed that infants and children in orphanages who were provided scheduled rather than responsive care showed pained expressions of grief and over time became listless and apathetic. Many of those infants and children lost weight and became ill and some of them died (Spitz, 1954). Concern for the development of children growing up in orphanages led to the appointment by the World Health Organization of other researchers to study orphaned children in countries around the world. These social scientists reported findings similar to those of Spitz and his colleagues and concluded that children who receive minimal maternal responsiveness exhibit delayed development in many areas (Bowlby, 1951).

The Change in Public Policy from Orphanages to Foster Care. Although the views of Watson (that parents should not be responsive to their children) were still basic to American parenting styles, the studies of Bowlby, Ainsworth, and Spitz, as well as findings from other researchers around the world, brought about a change in public policy regarding the institutionalization of children in the United States. Prior to the publication of those studies of orphaned children, American children placed for adoption were typically kept in orphanages until they were around 3 months of age so parents could be assured of adopting a "normal, healthy child." After being confronted with evidence that scheduled care rather than responsive care puts normal children at risk for incurring developmental delays, a significant change in adoption placement policy occurred in the United States during the 1950s. That change resulted in infants and children being placed in foster care, rather than orphanages, until they could be adopted so that they might receive responsive rather than scheduled care (Jones, 1993).

Thinking Critically

Considering the scientific evidence of Ainsworth and Spitz, and the change in public policy based on findings of the harmful effects of scheduled care in orphanages, do you think that unresponsive parenting among American parents is a thing of the past? If not, why not?

Erikson: The Resolution of Psychosocial Crises

In the early 1960s, Erik Erikson, a follower of Freud, developed the theory of psychosocial development that emphasizes that individuals achieve psychosocial maturity by resolving the **psychosocial crises** that emerge at each developmental level. According to Erikson, the quality of the parent–child relationship impacts the individual's ability to resolve psychosocial crises related to each stage of

Stage 1: Infants—Trust versus Mistrust
The task of infants is to learn to trust others. The successful resolution of this stage is the development of a sense of trust. In contrast, the unsuccessful resolution of this stage results in infants developing a sense of mistrust.

Stage 2: Toddlers—Autonomy versus Shame and Doubt
The task of toddlers is to learn to do things for themselves and on their own. The successful resolution of this stage is a sense of autonomy, being able to do things on their own versus the development of a sense of shame and doubt.

Stage 3: Preschoolers—Initiative versus Guilt
The task of preschoolers is to take the initiative in play and playful encounters. The successful resolution of this stage contributes to a sense of initiative. The unsuccessful resolution of this stage contributes to a sense of guilt and feelings of inhibition.

Stage 4: School-Age Children—Industry versus Inferiority
The task of school-age children is to develop a sense of industry, which is related to being able to demonstrate competence in the skills valued by their culture. The unsuccessful resolution of this stage contributes to a sense of inferiority.

Stage 5: Adolescence—Identity versus Identity Confusion
The task of adolescents is to discover who they are and who they are becoming. The successful resolution of this stage is the development of a sense of identity. The unsuccessful resolution of this stage results in the development of identify confusion.

Stage 6: Young Adulthood—Intimacy versus Isolation
The goal of young adults is to join with others in a shared experience. Thus, the successful resolution of this stage is the development of a sense of intimacy. The unsuccessful resolution of this stage is the development of a sense of isolation.

Stage 7: Adulthood—Generativity versus Stagnation
The goal of adulthood is to make a valuable contribution to the next generation. Successful resolution of this stage results in a sense of generativity. Unsuccessful resolution of this stage, however, results in a sense of stagnation.

Stage 8: Old Age—Ego Integrity versus Despair
The goal of older adults is to evaluate their past and establish a sense of integrity. Thus, the successful resolution of this stage is the development of a sense of integrity and the unsuccessful resolution of this stage is the development of a sense of despair.

FIGURE 1.1 Erikson's Stages of Psychosocial Development

Source: Adapted from *Theories of Human Development,* by D. Goldhaber, 2000, Mountain View, CA: Mayfield.

development (see Figure 1.1). For example, the psychosocial crisis of infancy is the development of trust versus mistrust. According to Erikson, by being consistently responsive to their infants' needs during that stage of development, parents contribute to the infant's development of a sense of trust. In turn, being effective in promoting their infants' sense of trust contributes to feelings of satisfaction for parents and those feelings of parental competence promote adults' psychosocial development (Goldhaber, 2000).

L. Morris Nantz/PH College

Responsiveness to the infant's cues is a key factor in the promotion of secure attachment.

Benjamin Spock: Limits Within the Context of Warmth and Affection

During the 1930s, 1940s, and 1950s, the theories of Freud and Erikson emphasized the importance of parental understanding of children's natural instincts. Bowlby's Attachment Theory focused attention on the role of the parent in promoting infant attachment. Researchers using Attachment Theory provided strong evidence refuting the use of scheduled care and demonstrating the importance of responsive care for children's development. It was only after Benjamin Spock's views related to childrearing became well-known, however, that autocratic and unresponsive parenting approaches were challenged in the American public domain. Not only did Spock question autocratic and unresponsive childrearing approaches, he also challenged the lenient approach to parenting adopted by those parents who were influenced by the views of Freud.

Similar to the ways that Watson's views on child socialization became well-known via the popular media, Spock's message regarding childrearing reached large numbers of American mothers who sought childrearing advice from popular magazines and other readily available reading material. Beginning in the 1940s and continuing to the 1970s, Spock's beliefs regarding how parents should rear their children were widely disseminated. During that period of time, in addition to publishing several popular books on childrearing, Spock contributed numerous articles to two popular magazines, *Ladies' Home Journal* and *Redbook*. In those publications, Spock emphasized that children need limits within the context of warmth and affection. He repeatedly emphasized the need for parents to provide their children with firm and consistent but also loving guidance (Spock, 1946, 1985).

The publication of Spock's childrearing advice in popular magazines established him as the new American parenting expert, the role previously held by John Watson (who had earlier gained acceptance as a parenting expert through publications in *McCall's* as well as in radio broadcasts). Spock's advice to parents (that they should be warm and responsive to their children) reflects Freud's position (that children need to experience parental affection). Spock's recommendations also reflect insights regarding the importance of parental responsiveness to children, which was demonstrated by the attachment studies of Bowlby and Ainsworth. Spock did not agree, however, with the lenient style of parenting that had become popular among those American parents who believed they were following the recommendations of Freud. Spock's emphasis on the need to combine reasonable limits alongside warmth and support for children is exemplified in Baumrind's (1971) authoritative parenting pattern. That pattern of parenting will be described in Chapter 2.

Thinking Critically

Since the 1940s, there has continued to be increasing information regarding the dangers of harsh, overly strict parenting and many voices have called for the abolishment of those parenting practices. However, why do you think the autocratic pattern of childrearing still exists in America today?

B. F. Skinner: Reinforcement as a Consequence of Appropriate Behavior

During the same era of the 20th century that the theories of Freud, Adler, Erikson, and Bowlby, and the views of Spock, were influencing childrearing patterns in Europe and in the United States, the American behaviorist, B. F. Skinner, developed his Principles of Operant Conditioning. Skinner stressed that in order for parents to be effective in their childrearing efforts they should have a basic understanding of the role of contingencies in affecting behavior. A **contingency** refers to the relation between a behavior and the events that follow the behavior. According to Skinner, behavioral changes occur when certain consequences are contingent on the performance of desired behavior (Goldhaber, 2000; Skinner, 1950). The use of positive reinforcement to maintain or increase desired behavior in children is an example of the application of that theory to child rearing. Skinner called attention to the fact that the reinforcement of appropriate behavior is more effective than the punishment of inappropriate behavior. Numerous studies have provided scientific evidence of the effectiveness of his reinforcement techniques for producing desirable behavior and lessening undesirable behavior in children (e.g., Hagopian, Wilson, & Wilder, 2001; Manassis & Young, 2001). The use of positive reinforcement as a childrearing strategy will be described and explained in Chapter 3.

Phyllis Heath

In this playful father–child interaction, the young child is mimicking the expression and movements of the father—an example of modeling and imitation.

The Social Learning Theorists: Imitation and Modeling

The behaviorist emphasis on the role of the environment in shaping children's development began to wane in the 1960s as behaviorist views were considered alongside those of theorists who were emphasizing children's needs and the perspective that children are active participants in their own development. In that intellectual climate, Social Learning Theory evolved from Skinner's Principles of Operant Conditioning. The basic premise of Social Learning Theory, developed by Bandura and Walters (1963), is that children do not have to be directly reinforced or punished to learn a behavior. Instead, children learn through **vicarious reinforcement** or punishment that involves two interrelated strategies: imitation and modeling.

There are two ways in which the social learning theorists drew attention to what the child brings to the learning environment. First, by noting children's natural tendency to imitate, the social learning theorists acknowledged the natural instincts of the child. Second, when they pointed out that children learn behaviors that they sometimes perform later, the social learning theorists emphasized the role of children's memory for specific events. By linking children's natural tendency to imitate and remember behaviors that they might or might not perform later (depending on other environmental influences), the social learning theorists de-emphasized the role of the environment and escalated the role of the child (Bandura & Walters, 1963). That direction toward a greater understanding of the nature of the child fit well into the other theorizing of the latter part of the 20th century. The ways in which parents might promote their children's imitation of desired behaviors are outlined in Chapter 3.

The enthusiasm these youngsters are demonstrating in their play reflects the views of Froebel, Pratt, and Montessori.

Anne Vega/Merrill

RESPECTING AND ATTENDING TO CHILDREN'S ENTHUSIASM FOR LEARNING

In addition to the influences of psychological theories, American childrearing patterns during the 20th century were influenced as well by European early childhood educators who speculated on how young children learn. Some of the pioneers of early education who influenced childrearing patterns in the United States and Europe included Marie Montessori and Caroline Pratt. Their views that children have an inborn drive to learn that is expressed in their need to be actively engaged in the learning process led to modifications in school curricula and influenced the cognitive theories of Piaget and Vygotsky.

Caroline Pratt: Children's Play Is Their Work

Caroline Pratt was influenced by the views of Froebel that a child has an inborn drive to learn, and a strong interest in being consistently engaged in activities that promote learning (Froebel, 1909). Pratt published a treatise in 1948, which grew out of her own observations of children and was aptly titled: *I Learn from Children.* As a dramatic departure from the early Puritan belief that children who played were being mischievous, Pratt emphasized just the opposite—that childhood's work is learning and that it is in play that children get their work done. Not only did Pratt elevate children's play to an esteemed position, she emphasized as well the importance of truly seeing children. She believed that to see a child one must be willing to do so from the child's own horizons almost from the day the child is born, "to see how the child's circle of interests widens outward like a stone thrown into a pond" (p. 8). Pratt called attention to the need to observe the urge of the child to learn, an urge that is immediate, practical, and within the scope of the child's learning ability (Pratt, 1970).

Thinking Critically

How do you think the responses of early American parents influenced by Hobbesian philosophy and Calvinist religious doctrine would compare with the responses of parents influenced by Caroline Pratt when their toddlers seem to want to "get into everything" and when their highly energetic preschoolers want to be continuously engaged in play?

Maria Montessori: Children Have Absorbent Minds

Maria Montessori, who became the first woman physician in Italy in 1892, was a pioneer in early childhood education. She challenged parents to allow their children the freedom to explore and learn. Montessori drew on the ideas of Rousseau and Froebel, as well as on her own observations of children, in her development of the Montessori Method of Early Childhood Education. The Montessori Method, which was described in Montessori's first publication in 1909, might be summed up as follows: (a) all children have absorbent minds, (b) all children want to learn, (c) all children pass through several stages of development, (d) all children want to be independent, and (e) all children pass through **sensitive periods of development** (Britton, 1992). A sensitive period of development is a genetically determined timetable during which certain developmental changes occur when normal environmental conditions are present, such as the development of infant attachment, or the early development of language.

The Child's Absorbent Mind. Based on her observations of children, Montessori concluded that the young child's process of learning is active rather than passive and that the child's **absorbent mind** unconsciously soaks up information from the environment resulting in the child's learning at a rapid pace. According to Montessori, the child's capacity to learn at a rapid rate lasts for the first 6 years of life, more or less. Based on the young child's ability to learn so quickly, every early experience of the child is vitally important. During the ages from 3 to 6, while the child's mind is still absorbent, parents will be asked endless questions of *why* and *how*. Therefore, the young child's inborn energies and drives require a say in what experiences they encounter. Montessori believed that the parent's role is to help their children's personality develop during their first 6 years and outlined three golden rules for parents: (a) allow freedom within limits, (b) respect the individuality of the child, and (c) resist imposing their own will and personality on the child. Accordingly, Montessori recommended that parents give their young children as much freedom as possible emphasizing that it is only with that freedom that children are able to develop to their full potential (Britton, 1992).

Through guided participation, this mother is scaffolding the learning experience of her daughter.

Roy Ramsey/PH College

Thinking Critically

Consider a situation in which the parent asks a young child to pick up her toys before coming to lunch and the child responds by asking why. How do you think the autocratic parent would respond to the child's question? How do you think a parent who is influenced by Montessori would answer the child's question?

Jean Piaget: Children Actively Engage Their Environments

We now turn our attention to the contributions of the Swiss psychologist Jean Piaget, who began to influence European views of the child in the 1930s and 1940s. Piaget's view of infants and children is that they are cognitively capable human beings with inborn reflexes that are very quickly altered by their active engagement of the environment. According to that perspective, children (through their active engagement of people and objects in their environment) construct their own cognitive structures (Elkind, 1976). Piaget's view of children as **active participants** in the development of their own mental structures reflect those of Montessori, although Piaget provided more detail regarding what happens as children's minds take in and adapt to information from the environment. Piaget's theory of how children learn also extended beyond the first 6 years that were the focus of Montessori (see Figure 1.2).

The Sensorimotor Stage (from Birth up to the Age of 18 to 24 Months)
This stage consists of a six-step sequence of knowledge construction whereby infants depend on their senses of smell, hearing, touch, and taste to construct concepts of objects, space, and causality. The acquisitions associated with each period of the six-step sequence are specified in chapter 3.

The Preoperational Stage (from 2 to 6 or 7 Years of Age)
This stage can be divided into two phases. Between the ages of 2 and 4 years, the child displays an egocentric use of language and a heavy reliance on perception in problem solving. Between the ages of about 5 to around 7 years, social speech and intuitive thinking emerge.

The Concrete Operational Stage (from 6 or 7 to 11 to 13 Years of Age)
The ability to perform logical operations is reflected in the school-age child's interest in conservation and classification tasks. Development of the ability to conserve matter, volume, length, time, distance, and speed coincides with the development of the ability to understand reversibility and compensation. The development of the ability to classify coincides with the development of the ability to recognize defining properties of objects.

The Formal Operations Stage (Begins from 11 to 13 Years of Age and Is Evident Throughout Adulthood)
The transition to formal operations during adolescence allows the person to consider what is abstract and not immediately present. Thus concrete operations focus on "what is" and formal operations focus on "what if."

FIGURE 1.2 Piaget's Stages of Cognitive Development
Source: Adapted from *Comparing Theories of Child Development,* 5th ed., by R. M. Thomas, 2000, Belmont, CA: Wadsworth/Thomson Learning.

Lev Vygotsky: Guided Participation

Another follower of Froebel and Montessori, Lev Vygotsky developed an alternative theory of children as active participants in the learning process. The views of Vygotsky, a psychologist from the former Soviet Union, have provided valuable insights regarding ways for parents to guide their children. Vygotsky drew attention to the ways in which competencies come about as a result of interactions between novices and more skilled members of a society acting as tutors or mentors. According to that perspective, the implicit goal of the tutor or mentor is to provide the instruction and necessary support to assist the beginner in acquiring the knowledge and capabilities valued by that person's culture. The best means to accomplish that goal is through **guided participation** wherein the teacher engages the learner in joint activities providing instruction as well as direct involvement in the learning process. Vygotsky's theory provides a model of parent–child interactions that emphasizes the important role of the parent in working closely with the child as a partner in the **scaffolding** of child's learning.

Thinking Critically

In traditional cultures, children work with their parents and other older relatives in many activities that benefit the entire family, such as tending farm animals, preparing meals, and taking care of younger children. From the perspective of Vygotsky, how might the performance of these shared tasks contribute to children's cognitive development?

THE ROLE OF CONTEXT IN CHILD SOCIALIZATION

After decades of theorizing on what constitutes the nature of the child and how best to bring up children, it became clear that differences in childrearing patterns are not based simply on variations in individual belief systems. In the latter half of the 20th century, scholars began to turn their attention to the ways in which the family environment impacts the development of children. Adler's Social Discipline Theory introduced the idea of democracy in the family; Bronfenbrenner's Ecological Model called attention to the fact that families influence and are influenced by a number of other systems in which they interact; and Family Systems Theory highlighted ways in which the dynamics of family members influence each other's behaviors. It is now recognized that diversity in child socialization patterns is linked to differences in family context, variation in cultural beliefs, and many other contextual influences.

Adler's Social Discipline Theory: Democracy in the Family

Influenced by theorists who were focusing increasing attention on understanding how children think, learn, and feel, Alfred Adler developed the Social Discipline Theory. Adler's theory increased awareness of the impact of family relationships on children's development and advocated that autocratic parent–child relationships be replaced by democratic parent–child relationships. That position provided the foundation for the Parent Education Movement in the United States, which was led by Rudolf Dreikurs, a follower of Adler. The basic premise of Social Discipline Theory is the recognition of the equal worth of everyone in a group. In families where there are democratic parent–child relationships, all members of a household are allowed to raise issues, and other family members are expected to respect issues raised by any member. According to the **democratic parenting** approach, although parents and children are not equal in terms of responsibility or privilege, both parents and children have equal worth. The attitude of equal worth is played out in valuing the needs and desires of each family member (Dreikurs, 1972; Dreikurs & Grey, 1968, 1970). In articulating his conception of democratic parent–child relationships, Adler provided

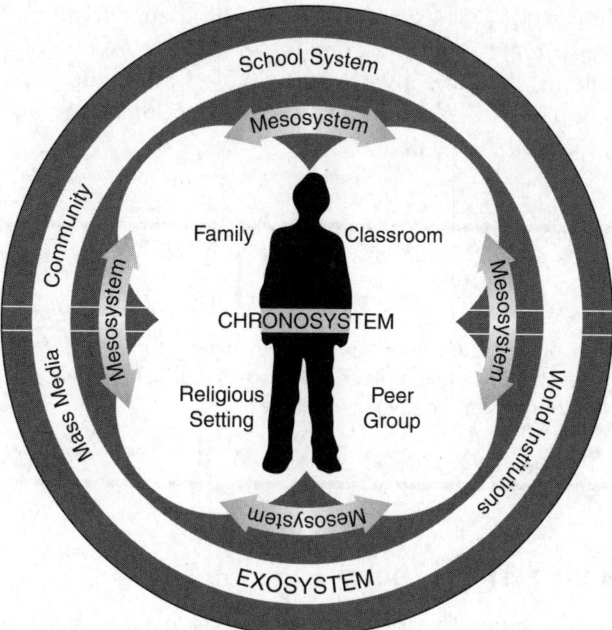

FIGURE 1.3 Bronfenbrenner's Ecological Model

Source: From *The Developing Person Through the Life Span*, 5/e, page 7, by Kathleen Stassen Berger and Ross A. Thompson. © 2001 by Worth Publishers. Used with permission.

specific guidelines for incorporating limits and warmth into the rearing of children. The strategies of parenting described in Chapter 3 are based on democratic parent–child relationships.

Bronfenbrenner's Ecological Model

Urie Bronfenbrenner transformed the way many social and behavioral scientists approached the study of human beings and their environments. His theoretical position is that interpersonal relationships, including parent–child relationships, do not exist in a social vacuum (Ceci, 2006). Bronfenbrenner emphasized that whereas parental behaviors influence the development of children, there are multiple influences on parental childrearing behaviors, including the children themselves, the parents' families of origin, the community in which the family lives, and the culture in which the family is a part. Bronfenbrenner's most recent addition to his ecological model is the **chronosystem**, which highlights the influence of time on the various interacting systems that affect a person's development. The contexts of development, according to Bronfenbrenner (1979, 1989), are described in Figure 1.3. An example of the ways in which ecological theory explains the various influences on parents and children is demonstrated in a study by Meyers and

Miller (2004). These researchers found that features of the neighborhood are directly related to adolescent outcomes (i.e., psychological adjustment and school problems). Specifically, they discovered that although neighborhood characteristics impact adolescents' outcomes, parenting behaviors significantly mediate that association.

Thinking Critically

Which one of the various systems in Bronfenbrenner's Ecological Theory represents the changes that have taken place in the ways that parents rear their children from the beginning of the 20th century to the present time?

Family Systems Theory

Family Systems Theory views families as dynamic systems, characterized by stability and change. According to that theory, family stability contributes to a sense of shared history and a certain degree of predictability. The changes in the family system challenge members to continuously adapt to those changes and to redefine their roles in relation to each other. When children undergo physical, cognitive, and social–emotional development, these changes contribute to alterations in their behaviors that impact other family members' behaviors. The resulting imbalance or disequilibrium in the family system challenges all family members to adjust to these changes, thereby contributing to the reestablishment of family equilibrium (Minuchin, 1974). Parents are undergoing development as well and some of the impact on the dynamics of the family system is related to challenges associated with the parents' stages of development (Steinberg & Steinberg, 1994).

In addition to alterations in the family system brought about by the developmental changes of family members, there are normative and non-normative events that provoke changes in parents, children, and the family system. Examples of normative events are the births of children, the deaths of older family members, or children starting school or going to college. Examples of non-normative events are winning the lottery, the unexpected death of a family member, or learning that a family member has a serious illness. By and large, the events that impact the life of one person in a family affect the lives of all family members, and the behavior of each person in the family has an influence on the behaviors of all other family members. Furthermore, the behaviors of all family members contribute to ongoing alterations in the family system, which in turn impact the lives of the persons who participate in that system. The stability of the family is thereby enhanced if its members are capable of adapting their expectations and behaviors to meet the changing needs of all family members (Beevar & Beevar, 1988).

Thinking Critically

Consider an example of disequilibrium that occurred in your family and was brought about by a normative or non-normative event. In what ways did you, your parents, and other family members adapt to the resulting family imbalance, thereby reestablishing equilibrium in the family?

THE IMPORTANCE OF THE PARENTAL ROLE

In previous discussions, we have considered the historical and contemporary views of the child, advice from various experts regarding ways in which to bring up children, and examined family dynamics from various perspectives. In all these discussions, the parent has been viewed as a significant influence on children's development. Parents play an important role in their children's lives both within their families as well as within their communities.

Galinsky's Six Stages of Parenthood

The importance of the role of the parent is emphasized by Ellen Galinsky who believes that the parental role provides an opportunity and challenge to continually develop new skills and capabilities. She points out that the process of parental role development begins with the anticipation of the arrival of children and is continually adjusted according to the child's ongoing developing needs. Based on her interviews of parents with varying experiences of parenthood, including married, divorced, step-, foster, and adoptive parents, she outlined six stages of how parenthood changes adults (see Figure 1.4). Each of these stages represents ways in which parents invest their emotional and intellectual energy on a particular childrearing task (Galinsky, 1987).

The Reggio Emilia Schools Project: An Example of the Vital Role of Parents

This internationally recognized project, which began in Northern Italy after World War II, illustrates the ways in which theoretical perspectives influence the lives of parents and children. This program is a collaborative effort among parents, educators, and children. The primary objective of the Reggio Emilio Schools is to serve as a resource for educators, and parents to engage in collaboration, communication, and participation to insure the right to quality education for all children according to their individual abilities and specific interests. The view of the actively engaged child found in the theories of Piaget, Vygotsky, and Montessori is central to the philosophy informing the curriculum of those classrooms (Gandini, 1995). Because parents in the project play a vital role in joint decision making with teachers and other community members, the project is also an example of Bronfenbrenner's view that assorted contexts impact the

Stage 1—The Image-Making Stage occurs during pregnancy or preparation for adoption, when adults prepare to become parents by considering what it means to be parents and contemplating the necessary changes in their lives to accommodate the arrival of a child or children (in the case of multiple births).

Stage 2—The Naturing Stage begins at birth and continues to about 18 to 24 months. During this period, parents and infants become attached to each other and parents alter their lives to support their roles as caregivers, balancing the needs of the baby/babies and their own needs. Setting necessary priorities is especially important at this stage.

Stage 3—The Authority Stage begins when children are around 2 and lasts until they are 4 or 5. During this stage, parents become rule markers and enforcers, as they learn to provide structure and order for their children within a loving environment.

Stage 4—The Interpretive Stage begins when children become preschoolers and continues through their adolescent years. During this stage, when children are becoming more independent and skilled, the role of parents is to serve as mediators between their children and other individuals in their children's ever-expanding social world.

Stage 5—The Interdependent Stage occurs when children reach adolescence. During this stage, parents alter their relationships with their adolescent children to allow for shared power. During this stage of shared power, parents still maintain appropriate authority in relation to their adolescent children.

Stage 6—The Departure Stage of parent development begins as their children prepare to leave home. In this stage, parents contemplate not only their success as parents but also how they might have behaved differently.

FIGURE 1.4 Galinksy's Six Stages of Parent Development
Source: Adapted from *Between Generations: The Six Stages of Parenthood,* by E. Galinsky, 1981, New York: Times Books.

socialization process and the ongoing development of the child. Finally, the collaborative role of the parents in the Reggio Emilia Schools Project demonstrates that parents serve as mediators between their children and other individuals in their children's ever-expanding social world, an idea introduced by Galinsky.

SUMMARY

- Over the past 100 years, understanding of the inherent nature of the child has increased substantially, which has altered American childrearing beliefs and behaviors.
- The examination of historical changes in American childrearing beliefs and behaviors called attention to the fact that childrearing beliefs vary historically and are influenced by the "experts of the time."
- At the beginning of the 20th century, the prevailing American childrearing approach was autocratic (strict and harsh) with little thought given to the thoughts and feelings of the child.

- As we begin the 21st century, we have benefitted by many theorists' views as well as research evidence that optimum childrearing approaches take into account the thoughts and feelings of the child.
- Contemporary theories have helped us understand the multiple contextual influences on parent–child relationships and that the family is a dynamic system that impacts and is impacted by each family member.
- Parents not only contribute to their children's ongoing development but the role of the parent also undergoes development as parents of infants become parents of preschoolers, who in turn become parents of school-age children, then parents of adolescents.
- In Chapter 2, you will see that the patterns of childrearing that parents adopt are related to a number of factors, including age, educational level, and cultural beliefs.

KEY TERMS

- absorbent mind
- active participant
- autocratic parenting
- chronosystem
- contingency
- democratic parenting
- guided participation
- psychosocial crisis
- scaffolding
- secure attachment
- sensitive period of development
- vicarious reinforcement

USEFUL WEB SITES

The SUNY Stonybrook and New York Consortium

http://www.psychology.sunysb.edu

This web site is a library of researchers' publication lists and related on-line articles that explain the relationship between Attachment Theory and effective parenting.

The Whole Child

http://www.pbs.org/wholechild/parents/play

The Whole Child emphasizes the importrance of creativity and play, which supports Caroline Pratt's view that children's play is their work. This site provides suggestions for parents regarding opportunities to satisfy the child's need for creativity and self-expression.

The National Council on Family Relations Report

http://www.ces.ncsu.edu/depts/fcs/nepef/build

Excellent examples of the ways in which Bronfenbrenner's view of the family might be used to provide services to children and parents are provided on this site. This site emphasizes the importance of parent educators connecting with other family-supportive professionals to provide services and support networks for parents, children, and families.

The ERIC Web site

http://www.eric.ed.gov/ERICWebPortal/recordDetail?accno=ED441552

The Eric web site provides links to a variety of useful journal articles, including an article entitled "The History of Parenting Practices: An Overview." This article discusses the events, policies, and theories that have influenced parenting practices over the last 100 years. The influences of Freud, Watson, Erikson, Bowlby, and others are also explained.

Parenting Patterns and the Impact of Culture and Context

Objectives

After completing this chapter, you should be able to

- Describe the characteristics of various parenting styles.
- Identify the ways in which parenting patterns differ according to culture, with a particular emphasis on the parenting styles of non-Western cultures as well as ethnic minority cultures in the United States.
- Demonstrate an understanding of the way in which different parenting patterns impact the development of children and adolescents.
- Identify the ways in which family of origin, socioeconomic status, and religiosity impact parenting patterns.

Now that we have taken a historical look at the ways in which various philosophers and theorists have contributed to the evolution of childrearing patterns in the United States, we turn our attention to the role of context in contemporary parent–child relations. We will begin by looking at the current patterns of childrearing in the United States and contrast those to parenting patterns in cultures outside the United States. Next, we will consider the ways in which cultural norms and belief systems contribute to different parenting styles within the various cultures in American society. We then will consider other contextual influences of childrearing, including family of origin, religiosity, and socioeconomic level. Throughout all of these discussions we will be examining the ways in which the lives of children are shaped by the childrearing patterns of their parents and other caregivers.

CHILD SOCIALIZATION PATTERNS OF AMERICAN PARENTS

Studies of childrearing patterns in the United States have resulted in the identification of six distinct parenting styles: **authoritative, authoritarian, permissive** (Baumrind, 1967), **traditional** (Baumrind, 1987), **indulgent**, and **indifferent** (Maccoby & Martin, 1983). Two dimensions distinguish among those parenting patterns: parental responsiveness and parental demandingness. That is, parents differ in the degree to which they demonstrate responsiveness toward their children as well as in the demands and expectations they have of their children. As will be pointed out in the upcoming dialogue, parenting style provides an indicator of parenting functioning that predicts child well-being across a wide spectrum of environments and diverse communities of children.

Parental responsiveness (*love, warmth, nurturance)* is the degree to which parents respond to the child's needs in an accepting, supportive manner. It also refers to the extent to which parents foster their children's individuality, self-regulation, and self-assertion by being attuned to their children and supportive of their needs. Parental warmth is a very influential force in the development of children because it helps children feel loved, secure, and cared about. It also promotes children's acceptance of parental demands (Baumrind, 1991b). Among the indicators of parental warmth are caressing or hugging the child, responding to the child's questions, and inviting the child's participation in conversations with adults (McLoyd & Smith, 2002).

Thinking Critically

Why do you think that parental warmth is such a powerful influence in the lives of children? Why do you suppose children are more accepting of parental demands from parents who are warm and responsive?

Parental demandingness, or parental control, refers to the demands that parents make on children including maturity demands, behavioral monitoring, and the delivery of consequences for inappropriate behavior. By and large, demandingness is the degree to which parents expect and demand responsible behavior from their children. It includes both setting and enforcing rules or limits for children (Baumrind, 1991). When requiring responsible behavior of a child, it is helpful if rules are clear, reasonable, developmentally appropriate, fair and just, and emphasize what the child *should do* rather than just what the child *should not do*. Furthermore, it is best if enforcement of rules does not rely on punishment. In reality, punishment is the least effective of the available alternatives because it tends to increase antisocial

TABLE 2.1 Characteristics of Six Parenting Styles

Style	Parental Support	Parental Control	Expectations of Maturity
Authoritative	High	Moderate Strictness	Moderate
Authoritarian	Low	Strict, often physical	High
Permissive	High	Rare	Low
Traditional	High	Strict	High
Indulgent	High	Rare	Low
Indifferent	Very Low	Very Low	Very Low

Sources: Baumrind, D. (1971). Current patterns of parental authority. *Developmental Psychology Monographs, 4*(1, Pt. 2), 1–103; Baumrind, D. (1987). A developmental perspective on adolescent risk taking in contemporary America. In C. E. Irwin, Jr. (Ed.), *Adolescent social behavior and health. New Directions for Child Development, 37,* 93–125; Maccoby, E. E., & Martin, J. A. (1983). Socialization in the context of the family: Parent–child interaction. In E. M. Hetherington (Ed.), *Handbook of child psychology, Vol. 4: Socialization, personality and social development* (4th ed., pp. 1–102). New York: Wiley.

behavior and only temporarily increases obedience (Gershoff, 2002). Monitoring children's behavior and whereabouts, understanding what motivates children's behavior, preventing misbehavior, rewarding appropriate behavior, and positive guidance are far more effective tools for guiding children and gaining their cooperation.

As you shall see in the upcoming discussions, parents differ on how they balance the two dimensions of warmth and demandingness. Some parents are warm and accepting whereas others are unresponsive or even rejecting. Some parents are demanding and have very high expectations of their children, whereas others demand very little. The six parenting styles shaped by the interplay of high and low parental responsiveness and demandingness are depicted in Table 2.1.

Authoritative Parents

Authoritative parenting, according to Lawrence Steinberg (1990), is the reasonable balance of three key aspects of parents' behavior toward their children–nurturance, discipline, and respect. The balance of these three dimensions is essential for effective parenting. Authoritative parents are controlling and demanding but also nurturing and communicative with their children. In her 1968 article, Baumrind stated that authoritative parents direct their children's activities but in a rational, issue-oriented manner. These parents display firm control at many points of divergence but do not hem their children in with restrictions. An important trait of authoritative parents is that they recognize their children's individual interests and unique personalities. They, therefore, set standards for their children regarding expectations for future conduct but do not expect unquestioned obedience. On the contrary, authoritative parents are willing to explain to their children the reasons for expected behavior. They also are willing to discuss with their children the behavioral guidelines they have set (Steinberg & Levine, 1997). Authoritative parents believe in rational discipline accomplished through parent–child interactions that are friendly as well as tutorial and disciplining. Integration of the needs of the child with those of other family members is, therefore, a high value for authoritative parents (Baumrind, 1996).

Children of Authoritative Parents. One of the advantages of being reared by authoritative parents is that this parenting style has been related to high levels of familial interaction and family cohesiveness (Garg, Levin, & Kauppi, 2005). Additionally, studies of children from authoritative families have consistently demonstrated that these children have more positive outcomes than do children reared by parents who have authoritarian, permissive, indulgent, or indifferent parenting styles. One of the most consistent findings is that children from authoritative families have high levels of academic achievement (e.g., Garg et al., 2005; Jones, Forehand, & Beach, 2000). Children of authoritative parents also tend to be cooperative with peers, siblings, and adults (Jones, Forehand, & Beach, 2000). The authoritative parenting style has been linked as well to children's psychosocial maturity (Mantzipoulos & Oh-Hwang, 1998), reasoning ability, empathy, and altruism (Aunola, Stattin, & Nurmi, 2000). Moreover, children whose parents have an authoritative parenting style are less likely to exhibit behavior problems in comparison with children of parents who use authoritarian, permissive, or indifferent parenting styles (Baumrind, 1996). Finally, children of authoritative parents have the highest levels of **self-actualization** when compared to children of parents who have adopted other styles of child socialization (Carton & Dominguez, 1997). Self-actualization refers to the experience of heightened aesthetic, creative, philosophical, and spiritual understanding (Maslow, 1970).

The encouragement of children's participation in decision making by authoritative parents appears to provide children with the experience needed to engage in thoughtful and responsible behavior. Although some of the competencies promoted by authoritative parenting (e.g., independent thinking) might not be considered as desirable in traditional cultures, authoritative parenting has emerged as the most effective parenting style for the socialization of American children and adolescents. Moreover, the advantages of the authoritative parenting style for American children's development have been found to outweigh factors such as socioeconomic status and ethnic group membership. As a case in point, Mantzipoulos and Oh-Hwang (1998) examined gender, intellectual ability, and parenting practices in a group of 344 Korean American adolescents and 214 European American adolescents. Differences in parenting styles across those two groups were predictive of psychosocial maturity regardless of ethnic group membership. Moreover, compared to all other parenting styles, authoritative parenting was related to significantly higher levels of psychosocial maturity. Finally, parents who use authoritative parenting patterns have more influence with their children and adolescents than do peers. In a study by Bednar and Fisher (2003), adolescents whose parents were authoritative were more likely to refer to their parents when making moral choices and were also more likely to rely on their parents for information on which to base their decisions.

Thinking Critically

Consider the parent–child interactions of a family with whom you are familiar (your own or those of friends or relatives) and see if you can identify a family that fits the authoritative pattern. If so, what are the lives of the children like? See if you can identify some of the positive outcomes of authoritative parenting in those families.

What This Means for Professionals. Because authoritative parenting accomplishes the objectives of demonstrating warmth and support to children while guiding them toward becoming increasingly more responsible and self-reliant, this approach to parenting is an excellent choice. Because authoritative parenting is consistently associated with favorable outcomes for children, this democratic approach to parenting is the basis of the parenting strategies described in Chapter 4.

Authoritarian Parents

Authoritarian-oriented beliefs and attitudes are firmly grounded in early American childrearing patterns in the United States. The disciplinary practices of authoritarian parents are hierarchical and these parents tend to favor punitive, forceful measures to curb what they believe to be their children's willful nature. In addition to punishment and the threat of punishment, authoritarian parents often seek to shame their children into compliance. Authoritarian parents place value on (a) keeping children in their place, (b) restricting children's autonomy, and (c) assigning household responsibilities in order to instill respect for work. A main goal of authoritarian parents is to obtain obedience from their children, and forceful means (including physical punishment) are frequently used to gain their children's compliance to rules (Baumrind, 1967). In addition to the goal of obedience, a secondary goal of authoritarian parents is to emphasize respect for parents, which is demonstrated by their insistence on children's unquestioning acceptance of their parents' word for what is right or wrong. Thus, authoritarian parents discourage their children from freely expressing their feelings (Steinberg, 1996). In authoritarian families, rules are set by the parents without discussion with the child and a child's questioning of the rules is likely to gain the response of "Because I said so."

Children of Authoritarian Parents. The authoritarian style of rearing children is not considered to be conducive to positive outcomes for children. Children reared by authoritarian parents are not encouraged to think for themselves but are expected to look to their parents for approval and answers to problems. Because such parents intimidate their children rather than promote their feelings of self-worth, Alice Miller (1990) labeled authoritarian beliefs as "the **poisonous pedagogy**," charging that such beliefs promote child socialization behaviors that rob children of their human spirit and inhibit their normal emotional development. Children whose parents are authoritarian tend to be dependent, passive, and conforming, less self-assured, less creative, and less socially adept than are other children. In comparison to children of authoritative parents, children of authoritarian parents have been found to have lower psychosocial maturity (Mantzipoulos & Oh-Hwang, 1998) and lower achievement (Aunola et al., 2000). Additionally, children from authoritarian families are more at risk for behavior problems such as substance abuse, crime, and delinquency than are children from authoritative or permissive families (Baumrind, 1991a). The higher vulnerability of children from authoritarian families may be explained by the fact that authoritarian parents restrict their children's interactions and short circuit interpersonal family conflicts by imposing rules intended to prevent conflict from occurring. In this family environment, children are deprived of opportunities to practice the skills of compromise and conflict resolution in relationships. The harsh strictness of authoritarian parents puts them in a position of not having as much influence on their children's decision making in comparison to children's peers (Allès-Jardel, Fourdrinier, Roux, & Schneider, 2002). For example, Bednar and Fisher (2003) found that adolescents with authoritarian parents consulted peers more often than parents when making moral and informational decisions.

What This Means for Professionals. The hierarchical parent–child relationships in authoritarian families reflect the parents' strong beliefs that they must maintain parental control of their children. Intervention in these families, therefore, must address the issue of control. Professionals working with authoritarian parents, therefore, might emphasize parenting techniques that promote children's self-control. If authoritarian parents are assisted in understanding that their parenting is likely to be easier if they use strategies to help the child to become more responsible, they might be willing to consider using such techniques. These parents also need to understand that their influence on their child will be greater and parent–child relationships more satisfactory if children consistently receive expressions of parental warmth.

Thinking Critically

Consider the lives of children you know or have known whose parents are authoritarian. Are you able to identify some of the negative consequences of authoritarian parenting in the lives of those children? If so, what are they?

Permissive Parents

The permissive approach to guiding children is in sharp contrast to the authoritative parenting style, which combines the demonstration of parental warmth with the setting of clear limits, and the encouragement of a reasonable level of independence. Basically, permissive parents are noncontrolling and nondemanding. They do not encourage independence and do not help children internalize limit-setting behavior. Their lenient parenting style involves little restriction of child autonomy and a general lack of routine and consistency. They also engage less in independence training of their children (Baumrind, 1968). An example of permissive parents' lack of demandingness is seen in their giving their children few household responsibilities. Instead of expecting compliance to usual behavioral standards, they by and large allow their children to regulate their own behavior. Permissive parents not only fail to exercise sufficient control of their children, they also appear to have diminished personal self-control. For example, they are not very well organized or effective in running their households. Furthermore, permissive parents tend to be self-effacing individuals who are insecure in their abilities to influence their children (Steinberg & Levine, 1997).

Children of Permissive Parents. Excessive autonomy coupled with insufficient parental monitoring of their activities has been associated with a variety of negative outcomes for children of permissive parents. One of the consequences of being a child of permissive parents is lower academic achievement in comparison to children from authoritative families (Paulson, Marchant, & Rothlisberg, 1998). The children of permissive parents also tend to lack impulse control and to be more immature, less self-reliant, less socially responsible, and less independent in comparison to children of authoritative parents (Baumrind, 1991b). The findings of a study by Mauro and Harris (2000) show that endorsing child-rearing attitudes consistent with permissive parenting interfere with the development of young children's self-regulatory abilities. Another illustration of the relation between permissive parenting and negative outcomes of children was demonstrated by Paschall, Ringwalt, and Flewelling (2003) who examined the effects of different aspects of parenting in a cohort of African American male adolescents. Their findings revealed that mothers' perceived control of their sons' behavior was a deterrent of delinquent behavior.

A consequence for parents who do not provide their children with appropriate limits is that they are not perceived by their children as persons whom they can consult when making important decisions. Bednar and Fisher (2003) found that adolescents with permissive parents were more likely to consult peers than parents in making moral choices. The tendency of children from permissive families to look to their peers for answers does not necessarily mean that children of permissive families have positive peer relationships. Baumrind's (1991a) findings that children of permissive parents are less happy than children whose parents are authoritative or authoritarian) calls attention to the difficulties that children from permissive families have in social relationships.

What This Means for Professionals. Permissive parents do not exercise appropriate levels of control for their children because they think of control as harsh and punitive and thus are reluctant to take that stance. Intervention designed to assist these parents might first make the parents aware of the benefits of parental monitoring, clear rules, and reasonable consequences. Next, these parents are likely to need training in the use of parenting strategies designed to exercise parental authority while continuing to provide warmth and support for their children.

Thinking Critically

Based on children's academic performance, they are typically considered by others to be smart or not so smart. The previous discussions, though, suggest that we look not only at the child's abilities but also at the pattern of childrearing in the child's home. In light of what you have just learned about the effects of childrearing patterns on children's academic performance, what would you recommend to parents regarding ways to promote their children's academic achievement?

Indulgent Parents

The indulgent approach to child socialization represents an excessively lax parenting pattern wherein parents do not exercise control over their children. The pattern of indulgent parenting emphasizes high responsiveness and low demandingness. In comparison to parents with other childrearing patterns, indulgent parents are highest in involvement with their children and lowest in strictness with their children. They have few clear expectations for their children, and they seldom set limits for them or provide consequences for their actions. Indulgent parents view discipline and control as being potentially damaging to children's developing creativity. Therefore, although they provide their children with high levels of support and affection, they do not provide limits and guidelines but grant them instead the freedom to do as they please (Steinberg, 1996).

Children of Indulgent Parents. Children of indulgent parents are likely to be irresponsible and immature. They are more inclined than other children to conform to their peers and more likely than children whose parents are authoritative or permissive to be involved in risk behaviors such as crime and delinquency (Steinberg, 2000). In spite of the fact that their indulgent parents have provided them with responsive care and promoted their autonomy, their parents have not required the kind of responsibility from their children that is associated with healthy development.

What This Means for Professionals. Professionals working with parents who have adopted an indulgent parenting pattern need to understand the thinking that underlies the indulgent parent's childrearing. Indulgent parents are involved in the lives of their children and do not wish their children to have unfulfilled needs. It might be helpful, therefore, to point out that indulgent parenting deprives their children of the necessary guidance they need. Also, it might be useful to share with these parents some of the research findings that show a link between indulgent parenting and negative outcomes for children.

Thinking Critically

Everyone seems to know a child whose parents are indulgent and have noticed the negative effects of that style of parenting on the child's behavior. If you have observed such a relationship and its effects, what are the behaviors of the parent that you would consider indulgent and what examples of negative outcomes have you observed in the child's behaviors?

Indifferent Parents

Indifferent parents have either rejected their children or for various reasons do not expend the necessary time and energy required of the parenting role. They seem uninvolved and even uninterested in their children's development. Their goal appears to be to minimize the amount of time and attention devoted to childrearing. Thus, they require little of their children, rarely bother to discipline them or provide clear guidelines regarding expected behavior, and express little love or concern for their children. In their study of indifferent parents, researchers have found that such parents tend to have life problems and stressors that limit their availability to their children (Steinberg, 1996).

Children of Indifferent Parents. Basic to all effective child socialization patterns is the expression of love and concern. Children from all ethnic groups in all societies benefit if they think they are loved and appreciated. Conversely, they suffer if they feel rejected and unwanted (Khaleque & Rohner, 2002). A general lack of involvement by parents characterized by a lack of affection and/or high levels of criticism and hostility provides the basis for the development of childhood aggressiveness and antisocial behavior problems. As early as preschool, low parental involvement is associated with children's noncompliance. Over time and with ongoing parental difficulties, noncompliance evolves into a behavior pattern characterized by peer rejection, poor academic performance, delinquency, and a dependence syndrome related to alcohol or other drugs (Steinberg, 1996). Adolescent children of indifferent parents tend to have (a) higher rates of delinquency, (b) earlier sexual involvement, and (c) a greater likelihood of using drugs and alcohol. The problem behaviors seen in children of indifferent parents might be partly explained by their tendency toward impulsivity and to some extent by their parents' lack of monitoring of their activities (Jacob, 1997).

What This Means for Professionals. Because Steinberg's (1996) study demonstrated that indifferent parents tend to have life problems and stressors that limit their availability to their children, it is important to address that predicament. If family members, friends, and/or professionals can provide the support that family needs to alleviate their stressful circumstances, their children are likely to benefit. Until parents are able to deal more successfully with their life problems or get the support they require, it is vital that informal support (family members and friends) as well as formal support (social service agencies) provide for the needs of the children to have adult guidance and supervision. Mounts (2002) also suggests that parents who have an uninvolved parenting style might benefit from information that encourages them to guide their children's peer relationships. Mounts recommended that prevention and intervention efforts with uninvolved parents include efforts to show parents ways of being involved in adolescents' peers relationships using appropriate levels of support and control.

Thinking Critically

Of all the childrearing patterns discussed thus far, the indifferent pattern has been associated with the most negative outcomes for children. Generally, we become aware of the high-risk behaviors of the child and are then able to link the child's behaviors to a lack of sufficient involvement of parents. What are some examples you are aware of that demonstrate the ways in which indifferent parents impact their children's lives?

Parents with Inconsistent Child Socialization Patterns

Although in most families, both parents tend to have fairly consistent parenting styles, some parents provide inconsistent messages to their children regarding family rules and expected behavior. Not only do these parents give their children contradictory guidelines concerning how they ought to behave, they tend also to provide differing consequences for misbehavior. In reality, most parents differ from time to time regarding what constitutes appropriate child guidance, but these differences are typically discussed and a consensus is usually reached. Inconsistent parenting, on the other hand, reflects a hidden agenda of parents that aims to undermine each other's parenting efforts and pressures the child to take sides. The reasons behind inconsistent parenting practices have been traced to parental hostility toward the other parent. Researchers have reported direct linkages between marital discord and inconsistent discipline (Gonzales, Pitts, Hill, & Roosa, 2000; Sturge-Apple, Davies, & Cummings, 2006). It has been suggested that preoccupation and distress arising from spousal conflict is particularly likely to disrupt parenting practices that require emotional sensitivity and responsiveness (Grych, 2002).

Children of Inconsistent Parents. Inconsistency between parents in their socialization patterns is linked to negative outcomes for children. Researchers have found that children who perceive inconsistency between their parents' childrearing styles are lower in self-esteem, self-control, and school performance compared with those children who perceive both parents as authoritarian as well as those children who perceive both parents as permissive (Brand, Crous, & Hanekom, 1990). Inconsistent parenting has been found to be related as well to children's and adolescents' deviant peer affiliations (Brody, Ge, & Conger, 2001) and externalizing behaviors (Lindahl & Malik, 1999).

What This Means for Professionals. Because inconsistent parenting has been linked with marital stress, the entire family is likely to benefit if these parents learn to work out the problems they have with each other. Based on their findings, Sturge-Apple et al. (2006) suggested that interventions aimed at strengthening relationships between parents is likely to have a positive impact on their childrearing patterns. They recommend that practitioners help parents to understand that engagement in marital problem-solving, rather than avoidance of anger and hostility, may play a key role in enhancing parenting practices.

CULTURAL VARIATIONS IN PARENTING PATTERNS

In the foregoing discussions, we learned that in studies of American child socialization patterns the authoritative parenting style has been associated most often with positive outcomes for children. It is important to point out, however, that almost all research focused on child socialization patterns has taken place in the United States and that most of this research has focused on European American parents. When we look outside this relatively narrow focus, the most striking finding is how rare authoritative parenting is in other cultural groups. In both non-Western families as well as in American ethnic minority families, we frequently see a style of child socialization that although often labeled as authoritarian actually falls somewhere between authoritarian and authoritative. Not only does the style of child socialization in these families not fit into the classifications discussed thus far, their childrearing approach has other culturally valued traditions that are not found in the childrearing styles of European American parents (Arnett, 2004).

Before continuing, it is important to distinguish between **society** and **culture** and to provide descriptions of the **West**, and **traditional cultures**. *Society* refers to a group of people who live and interact with each other because they share a common geographical area. A culture consists of a variety of customs, religions, family traditions, and economic practices, and is therefore different from a society. The United States, Canada, Japan, Mexico, and South Africa are examples of societies. Within societies, there exists various cultures and members of a culture share a common way of life, although members of a society might not. For example, American society encompasses many diverse cultures such as the African American culture, the Native American culture, the Latino American culture, and the Asian American culture. Members of all these cultures share the common characteristic of being American, are subject to the same laws, and are educated in similar schools. They differ, however, in various customs and beliefs that are related to their unique cultures (Arnett, 2004).

The West includes majority cultures in the United States, Canada, Western Europe, Australia, and New Zealand. In each of these countries, there are cultural groups that do not share the characteristics of the majority culture. These groups are referred to as traditional due to their maintenance of a way of life based on stable traditions passed down from one generation to the next. An example of the stable values of a traditional culture within a Western society is reflected in the following words of a Canadian Cree woman:

> Life was challenging with its physical and emotional demands and discipline but culturally and spiritually rewarding with good values grounded in Cree ways. Values like sharing, interconnectedness among relatives, land, plants, and animal life was an unspoken understanding. . . . I remember the many responsibilities we had as children in our family where we were expected to actively participate in the following work. I have chopped and hauled firewood; hauled water from the lake to our dwellings; helped my mother, sisters, and aunts prepare hides for tanning; preserved and cooked food; made clothes; tended our vegetable garden and; looked after the younger siblings, among many other chores. (Goduka & Kunnie, 2004, p. 14)

In traditional cultures, family life includes adults and children sharing tasks.

Eugene Gordon/PH College

Child Socialization in Non-Western Societies

American scholars studying non-Western parents have consistently attempted to apply Baumrind's original categorizations of parenting styles (authoritative, permissive, and authoritarian) to the approaches non-Western parents use in the rearing of their children. The result has been the labeling of non-Western families as authoritarian because they are typically higher on demandingness than parents who fall into the authoritative pattern. Scholars usually acknowledge, however, that the style they identify as authoritarian among non-Western parents does not have the negative effects typically seen in children of Western parents who are authoritarian. What is not addressed in those comparisons is the possibility that the higher demandingness coupled with higher responsiveness of the non-Western parenting pattern places it outside the original parenting categories identified by Baumrind (1967, 1971).

A key point in understanding child socialization patterns in non-Western societies is that independence in those societies is not the overriding issue that it is for Western parents and their children. The parenting patterns observed in non-Western societies reflect **collectivist cultural beliefs** that differ from the **individualistic cultural beliefs** of the West. Individualistic cultural beliefs tend to give priority to independence, individual freedoms, and individual achievements. Collectivist cultural attitudes, on the other hand, place a higher value on cooperation, mutual respect, maintaining harmonious relationships, and contributing to the well-being of the family and community (Triandis, 1995). In collectivist cultures, explanation and discussion of parental directives is an extremely rare approach and compliance of children is expected without explanation or question. Examples include Asian societies such as China, Japan, Vietnam, and South Korea. In these societies, the role of the parent carries more authority than does the role of the parent in the West (Fuligni, Tseng, & Lam, 1999).

The finding that authoritative parenting is rare outside the West does not mean that the child socialization pattern of non-Western parents is authoritarian. Arnett (2004) emphasizes that although non-Western parents adopt a more noncompromising stance on authority than is seen in the West, their demandingness is most likely to be accompanied by a closeness to children that is rarely observed in Western families. According to McLoyd and Smith (2002), higher levels of parental warmth buffers the potentially negative impact of higher levels of parental strictness. An example of parent–child closeness in non-Western societies is demonstrated by the cultural norm of **amae** in Japan that emphasizes close, affectionate mother–child relationships as the foundation for parenting (Hsai & Scanzoni, 1996). Another example of parent–child intimacy in non-Western families is seen in the findings of Shek and Chen (1999). Those researchers studied Hong Kong Chinese parents' perceptions of the ideal child and found that those parents included "maintaining good parent–child relationships" as being one of their primary goals of childrearing. Although social scientists appear to have misapplied the authoritarian pattern to non-Western families, Baumrind (1987) recognized the difficulty of fitting traditional cultures into her previously identified parenting patterns. In response to that dilemma, she conceptualized the **traditional parenting** style to describe the pattern of parenting usually found in traditional cultures—high in responsiveness accompanied by a type of demandingness that does not encourage discussion or debate.

Michal Heron/PH College

The closeness of non-Western families is supported by many family get-togethers.

Thinking Critically

Similar to the authoritative parenting style, the traditional parenting style has a high level of demandingness as well as high levels of responsiveness toward children. If these are the similarities between the two styles, what distinguishes these patterns from each other? Also, how familiar are you with the traditional parenting style? That is, have you observed that parenting style or does your family practice that type of parenting?

The Traditional Parenting Pattern in the United States

With the exception of Native Americans, all Americans trace their cultural origins to various countries with different beliefs and values. The circumstances associated with being members of various ethnic cultures have influenced the childrearing patterns of those parents. Therefore, each ethnic group in the United States has its own set of values related to differing cultural beliefs. Attempts to distinguish the parenting styles of American ethnic minority parents parallel efforts to demarcate non-Western parenting styles. As in studies of non-Western parenting patterns, the style of child socialization seen in many American ethnic minority families has been most often labeled as authoritarian. It has been pointed out, however, that the labeling of U.S. ethnic minority parenting patterns as authoritarian is a misapplication of the authoritarian style (Chao, 1994). It appears that the traditional childrearing pattern conceptualized by Baumrind in 1987 more appropriately describes the childrearing approaches found among American ethnic minority families as well as the child socialization patterns seen in non-Western cultures.

This scene depicts the family closeness found in many U.S. ethnic minority families.

According to Baumrind, traditional families are characterized by high demandingness as well as high responsiveness and by a strong belief system that has been consistent across generations. Another important component of child socialization in ethnic minority families is **racial socialization**, which acts as a buffer against negative racial messages in the environment (Stevenson, 1995). Racial socialization includes providing a home that is rich in racial culture and socializing children to be proud of their racial heritage. Moreover, Taylor, Chatters, Tucker, and Lewis (1990) suggested that African American parents might have felt it necessary to be stricter with their children because they have had to prepare them for coping with the realities of racism and discrimination. The argument here is that protective factors unique to nonmajority American populations should be contemplated when assessing the effectiveness of parenting patterns in American ethnic minority cultures.

Traditional Cultures and Extended Family Relations. An examination of child socialization patterns in non-Western families and American ethnic-minority families is not accomplished without an acknowledgment of the vital role of other family members in sustaining the childrearing efforts of parents. Throughout the world, the responsibilities of parents in traditional cultures are extended to grandparents and other family members. An example of the viability of the extended family was illustrated by Iuapuni, Donato, and Thompson-Colon (2005) who studied social networks, social support, and child health outcomes in Mexican extended families. The results of that study suggested that networks containing more extended kin and coresident ties offer greater support to mothers with young children, especially among the poorest households.

Similar patterns of closeness have been observed in Asian American families where grandparents typically live in an adult child's house or nearby. In those family arrangements, children and adolescents report that they receive high levels of support and nurturing from their grandparents (Fuligni et al., 1999). Mexican American children also are likely to have grandparents living in their household, and relationships with grandparents are highly valued in the Mexican American culture. The enhanced value of grandparents in Mexican American families was demonstrated in a study by Giarrusso, Feng, and Silverstein (2001), who compared levels of affection for European American and Mexican American grandparents and their adult grandchildren. Their findings revealed that Mexican American grandchildren's affection for their grandparents is substantially higher than European American grandchildren's affection for their grandparents.

The pattern of grandparent involvement is seen likewise in the African American family, which has a tradition of extended family households (Fuller-Thomson, Minkler, & Driver, 1997). Most African American families have a large network of extended family and upward mobility does not seem to erase the African American family's sense of reciprocal family obligation. The extended family network in the African American community, therefore, appears to be a cultural rather than a financial phenomenon. One of the clearest examples of the importance of extended families in that community is the role of the African American grandmother. African American grandmothers often assume some child care responsibilities and in low-income, single-parent families they frequently become **surrogate parents** (Gibson, 2002). Surrogate parents are individuals who have taken on the role and responsibilities of the parents. Grandparents in the role of surrogate parents will be discussed more fully in Chapter 10.

Martin Lueders, Insight Photos/U.S. Census Bureau

The presence of a grandparent in the home is not unusual in ethnic minority families in the United States.

Children of Traditional Parents. Because stricter parenting is balanced by greater closeness, the traditional parenting pattern in American ethnic minority families does not contribute to negative outcomes for children reared in these families (Chao, 2001). An example of traditional parent–child relations in an ethnic minority culture is in Latino American families wherein children generally accept the authority of the parents and also express a strong sense of attachment to their families (Harwood, Leyendecker, Carlson, Ascencio, & Miller, 2002). An illustration of the benefit of racial socialization for American ethnic minority children is that children whose parents provide racial socialization have higher levels of factual knowledge about their culture and better problem-solving skills (O'Brien-Caughu, O'Campo, & Randolph, 2002). Racial socialization contributes also to racial identity, which has been linked to the development of competencies among African American adolescents (Arroyo & Zigler, 1995). Finally, the involvment of extended family members, especially grandparents, provide children in traditional cultures with opportunities for guidance and closeness from parents as well as from other adult family members (Fuligni et al., 1999).

THE INFLUENCE OF FAMILIES OF ORIGIN ON CHILDREARING PATTERNS

Closely linked to the effect of family structure on childrearing is the influence of the family of origin (the family in which a parent grew up). Although adults might not acknowledge the link between their child socialization patterns and the childrearing behaviors of their parents, the research confirms that parents draw on their own childhood experiences in rearing their children. In Chapter 1, we focused on the growth-producing effects of children's attachments to their parents. In that discussion, it was emphasized that secure attachment promotes (among other things) the infant's internalization of a working model of parental availability (Ainsworth et al., 1978). Based on their experiences as children, adults also internalize a working model of their parents' socialization patterns. Those parenting examples influence how parents view their own children and how they interact with them. Social learning theory, also discussed in Chapter 1 (Bandura & Walters, 1963), provides another theoretical basis for understanding intergenerational influences on parental roles because children have many opportunities to observe the ways in which their parents behaved in their parenting roles.

In a classic study that related parents' child socialization patterns with their own childhood experiences, Grusec, Hastings, and Mammone (1994) conducted interviews with parents and discovered that quality of attachment to their parents predicted the way in which those parents interacted with their children. Parents who had a continuously secure attachment to their own parents were emotionally supportive and responsive to their children while setting clear and consistent limits. Parents with an insecure dismissive attachment to their own parents tended to emphasize their own independence and were likely to remain cool and remote from their children. Parents who had an insecure preoccupied attachment to their own parents exhibited a confusing and inconsistent pattern of behavior toward their children. Another example of the influence of their family of origin on adults' childrearing patterns was shown in a study of three-generation families by Delsing, Oud, and Bruyn (2003). Those researchers provided empirical evidence that current-family and (mother's) family-of-origin attitudes were similar on the parental dimension of restrictiveness. In a recent study of young fathers, Shears, Summers, and Boller (2006) demonstrated that men's relationships with their fathers as children influence the ways in which they feel about themselves as fathers. In their study, they asked fathers of Head Start children how their relationships with their own fathers impacted their parenting behaviors. Many of those fathers expressed regrets that their own fathers had been unavailable to them and wanted to be more available to their own children. The following quote from a father in that study shows that one's own parents might serve as models that younger parents do not wish to emulate.

> I think my father thought of himself as mainly the provider. He wasn't really a warm person . . . And I would not like that to be my only role in the family. (p. 264)

THE IMPACT OF SOCIOECONOMIC STATUS ON PARENTING PATTERNS

Because American parents are ethnically diverse, their parenting patterns fluctuate considerably across those cultural contexts. Variations in Americans' socioeconomic status further alter their child socialization patterns. A family's **socioeconomic status (SES)** influences the settings in which children live and the childrearing patterns their parents adopt. The term *socioeconomic status* refers to social status, which includes educational level, income level, and occupational status. A comprehensive review of the research focused on the influence of SES on parenting patterns points to two significant findings. First, SES distinguishes between a parent-centered and a child-centered approach to child socialization. Second, family SES correlates with differences in verbal and nonverbal interactions between parents and children. The link between SES and child versus parent orientation shows a tendency of higher SES parents to adopt a child-centered approach to parenting, which seeks to understand children's feelings and motivations and to use reasoning and negotiation to solve problems. By contrast, the childrearing behaviors of lower SES parents reflect a more parent-centered approach that emphasizes children's obedience and conformity to parental rules without discussion or explanation (Hoff-Ginsberg & Tardif, 1995).

Not only do low SES parents spend less time reading with their chidren, they also spend less time in other verbal interactions with them. Parents with lower levels of SES talk less with their children and elicit less speech from them than do parents with higher levels of SES. The profound impact of the differences in verbal interactions between high and low SES parents was documented in a study by Hart and Risley (1995) who found that professional parents speak about three times as much to their children as do low-income parents. Those researchers also reported that children in lower SES families hear mostly negative parental comments, whereas children in higher SES families hear mostly positive ones. Low SES mothers also frequently punish their children for misbehavior and have a tendency to expect behaviors that their children are developmentally incapable of performing. Whereas low SES mothers have unrealistic expectations from their children, they spend relatively little time in positive nurturing behaviors such as reading to their children (Bluestone & Tamis-LeMonda, 1999; Brenner & Fox, 1999).

The parental behaviors observed in low SES mothers have been found to be similar in low SES fathers. In a recent study of fathers of young children in lower SES circumstances, Burbach, Fox, and Nicholson (2004) found that those fathers reported more frequent use of verbal and corporal punishment as discipline than did higher SES fathers. That finding had been reported for lower SES mothers in an earlier study by Fox, Platz, and Bentley (1995). In the Burbach et al. study, lower SES fathers reported experiencing more parenting stress than did higher SES fathers. The fathers with lower SES also tended to depend more on television to entertain their young children in comparison to higher SES fathers.

THE EFFECT OF RELIGIOSITY ON PARENTING PATTERNS

Imbedded in cultural influences on childrearing patterns is the influence of **religiosity**. Religiosity refers to the extent to which religious beliefs manifest themselves in a person's daily life. In the case of parent–child relationships, religiosity refers to whether and how often parents provide religion to children at home (prayers at meals, family devotions), how much the family's social activities include the church and its members, and whether religious beliefs affect the way parents interact with their children (Gunnoe, Hetherington, & Reiss, 1999). As in the past, religiosity continues to influence parenting styles in contemporary America, although the authority of religion in the daily lives of families today is somewhat weaker than in past generations. In contrast to the historical association between authoritarian childrearing behaviors and fundamental religious beliefs, Gunnoe et al. examined the influence of religiosity on childrearing patterns today and provide a more positive picture. Those researchers concluded that religiosity might be a better predictor of authoritative than authoritarian parenting (Brody, Stoneman, Flor, & McCrary, 1997). In their study of mothers, fathers, and adolescents, Gunnoe et al. found that religiosity is associated positively with authoritative parenting for both parents and that mothers' religiosity is negatively related to authoritarian parenting. An example of the link between family religiosity and positive child outcomes was also demonstrated in a recent study by Caputo (2004) who analyzed data from the 1997 National Longitudinal Survey of Youth. The results of these analyses showed that parent religiosity was positively related to adolescents' good health and higher levels of education and inversely related to substance abuse.

SUMMARY

- This chapter provides a foundation for discussing the parent–child relationships to be covered in the upcoming chapters. The contemporary parenting styles of American parents have been distinguished and consideration has been given to the traditional parenting pattern found in non-Western societies and ethnic minority cultures within the United States.
- Research findings demonstrating the impact of parenting patterns on children's outcome have been presented. In these discussions, we considered the ways in which cultural norms and belief systems contribute to different parenting styles within the various cultures in American society and throughout the world.
- We have seen that parenting patterns reflect parental belief systems that are shaped and altered according to cultural norms, age, marital status, socioeconomic status, religiosity, and parents' families of origin.

KEY TERMS

- amae
- authoritarian parenting
- authoritative parenting
- collectivist cultural beliefs
- culture
- democratic parenting
- indifferent parenting
- individualist cultural beliefs
- indulgent parenting style
- parental demandedness
- parental responsiveness
- permissive parenting style
- poisonous pedagogy
- racial socialization
- religiosity
- society
- socioeconomic status (SES)
- surrogate parents
- traditional cultures
- traditional parenting style
- the West

USEFUL WEB SITES

Positive Parenting Tips

http://positiveparenting.com/resources/resources.html

This Web site has a "Team of Experts" that provide parenting tips, articles, Web links, and multimedia to help enrich individuals' parenting experiences. Their Dial-A-Discipline, based on Adlerian Psychology, helps parents learn new ways to identify and redirect their child's misbehavior.

Parenting Matters

http://www.lifematters.com/parentn.asp

This Web site includes a wide range of topics and promotes a democratic style of parenting that is firm, yet fair, as well as mutually respectful.

Child and Family Canada

http://www.cfc-efc.ca/

This Web site has lots of information about child care, child development, parenting, and family life; in French and English. From the Vanier Institute of the Family.

Parents and Children in Varied Family Structures

Objectives

After completing this chapter, you should be able to

- Identify the strengths and challenges of various families, with special attention to families affected by divorce, or headed by adolescent single parents, gay or lesbian parents, or custodial grandparents.
- Discuss the role of extended family relationships in American ethnic minority families and traditional families in other countries.
- Demonstrate an understanding of which family types have recently increased in numbers, including the societal factors related to these changes.
- Identify the ways in which societal and intergenerational family support varies depending on family structure.

In this chapter, we turn our attention to the lives of parents and children in various family structures. **Family structure** refers to the way in which a family is constructed and how family members are connected (Berger, 2005). At any given time, there are more two-parent families than one-parent families in the United States. The most prevalent two-parent family is the **nuclear family**, which is named after the nucleus (the tightly connected core) of an atom. Whereas the nuclear family was idealized as the only acceptable family arrangement through most of our history, within the past few decades, other family structures have been accepted. Although most children continue to live in households with two adults, those two adults might be their parents, a parent and a stepparent, or their grandparents. A large number of other children live with single, divorced, or never-married parents (U. S. Bureau of the Census, 1999). Furthermore, although most families are headed by at least one biological parent, many children have come to their families by means of adoption.

Although 100% of American children live in one or another of the family structures previously mentioned, many live in variations within these structures. Approximately 7% of school-age children live in their grandparents' home with their parents and often other relatives. In contrast to that extended family arrangement, about 2% of American children live with grandparents alone, who are acting as surrogates for parents who are unable to care for their children for various reasons. Approximately 2% of children live in a family headed by gay fathers or lesbian mothers, and about 1% of children reside with foster parents (Berger, 2005). As you will see, societal and intergenerational family support varies depending on family structure. You will also learn the ways in which the presence or absence of societal and family support impacts the relationships of parents and children within these families.

FAMILIES IN WHICH CHILDREN HAVE BEEN ADOPTED

Adoption in the United States has changed considerably over the last century. In the early 1900s, adoption was closely related to child welfare, many children were available for adoption, and adoptive parents were selective. With the image of the biological family as an example, adoptive families were expected to parallel biological kinship. Thus, children were placed with adoptive parents according to race, religion, and predicted physical and intellectual characteristics. The goal of adoption, at that time, was to make it appear as if the children's lives had begun the day that they joined their adoptive families. Records were sealed, which cut adopted children off from their biological past, and older, nonwhite, and disabled children as well as sibling groups were considered unadoptable. In contrast to those earlier times, much fewer children are available for adoption today and the foster care system has become the source of many adoptions. International adoptions also have increased and other nontraditional arrangements such as single-parent, kinship, and gay adoptions have become more common. Additionally, open communication between adoptees and birth families is now more prevalent, and reunions between late-adolescent or adult adoptees and their birth parents have become widespread. Furthermore, birth parents have become empowered, especially in private adoptions in which a birth parent often chooses among several prospective adoptive couples (Nickman et al., 2005).

The Experiences of Adoptive Parents

Now that we have examined the ways in which adoption has changed over the years as well as a contemporary view of adoption, we will look at the lives of the parents who have adopted children. As you will see, adoptive parents have a number of similar experiences. In their study of adoptive parents, Daniluk and Hurtig-Mitchell (2003) found that these parents tend to have little preparation for, or support in coping with, the realities of immediate parenthood. Thus, it was recommended that they might benefit from suggestions on how to access information on infant and child care. These researchers also suggested that new adoptive parents might be helped by understanding that the stresses they are experiencing are common for other individuals making the transition to parenthood. Adoptive parents, in the study, also reported considerable distress at the thought that their child might be taken from them during the first several months. It was suggested that these parents might benefit from assistance in dealing with the uncertainties of their ambiguous legal status, especially in the early months of parenting. Another important finding of the study was related to the shift that occurred for couples once their child entered their lives. Whereas many had at first expressed concerns about their ability to love and parent a nonbiological child, these concerns were quickly laid to rest. Quite the contrary, after becoming parents, these parents expressed a deep level of attachment to, and love for, their adopted children. Also, they reported that they came to believe that their child or children were destined to be a part of their lives and they were destined to be their parents.

The Lives of Children Who Are Adopted

Although adoptive parents have similar reactions to becoming parents, their lives are as different from each other as are the lives of parents with biological children. Furthermore, children who have been adopted do not have uniform life experiences. Some adopted children have lives that are virtually identical to those of children raised by their biological parents; others have endured harsh deprivation and multiple disruptions of their caretaking environment before adoption. Whether children have favorable outcomes after being adopted depends on their preplacement experiences as well as the age at which they are adopted. Those who are placed with their families as infants show consistently positive outcomes. In contrast, children adopted at older ages, and boys, are more likely to have their placements disrupted (Nickman et al., 2005). This difference is typically attributed to the later-adopted children having experienced earlier trauma. For example, children adopted at older ages have often suffered losses of biological or foster parents, social instability, and stigmatization (Rosenfeld et al., 1997). For those children who are placed at an older age and/or in open adoptions, they tend to fare better if their biological parents support their attachment to the adoptive family and when their adoptive parents show consideration for their biological family (Shapiro, Shapiro, & Parer, 2001). For children who have been adopted by gay or lesbian parents, the research generally shows positive outcomes. This research does not indicate that children raised by homosexual parents are at risk in any way, nor that they are more likely to develop same-sex orientations than are children raised by heterosexual couples (James, 2004).

DIVORCED PARENTS AND THEIR CHILDREN

Due to high levels of divorce in the United States, about half of today's children will go through a marital dissolution of their parents at some time before reaching adulthood. The experience of parental divorce is a major family alteration that is typically viewed as a negative event and is upsetting to children. In addition to the difficulties of coping with their parents' divorce, children have the additional trauma of making a transition from residing in a household headed by two parents to living in a household headed by only one parent. A consequence of parental divorce for children is that they are at greater risk for maladjustment than are children who have not experienced parental divorce (Amato & Sobolewski, 2003). As is the case for their parents, most children experience emotional adjustments for 1 to 2 years during the period leading up to, and immediately following, parental separation and divorce. This is typically the period during which family conflict intensifies, legal battles are fought, and relationships with residential and nonresidential parents are renegotiated (Owusu-Bempah, 1995).

Postdivorce Family Systems

In Chapter 1, you learned about Family Systems Theory, which emphasizes that family members adapt to changes in the family system by redefining their roles in relation to each other (Minuchin, 1974). According to that perspective, in the aftermath of divorce, parents and children become members of various family subsystems, and the roles of parents and children are modified. These changes in family structure and family roles alter family interaction patterns that, in turn, impact the lives of parents and children in these families. Although family roles are modified following parental divorce, both mothers and fathers continue to play important roles in their children's lives. The significance of these relationships to children is supported by Rosenberg and Guttman (2001), who found that the majority of children of divorced parents include both the father and mother as members of their family systems.

The Different Lives of Custodial and Noncustodial Parents. Over the past several decades, the percentage of children living in mother-headed households has increased dramatically (Grossman & Okum, 2003). The rise in the number of mother-headed families is related to a high divorce rate combined with the much greater likelihood that divorced mothers will maintain custody of their children in comparison to divorced fathers. For women who retain custody of children after marital dissolution, their income levels are only about 56% of those of their former husbands. These statistics emphasize that women heads of households can expect to have financial difficulties. Whereas custodial mothers tend to have low incomes, the picture is different with father custody. First of all, there are fewer custodial fathers than custodial mothers because father-headed households constitute only 17% of all single-parent families. Second, men who gain custody of their children are more likely than are custodial mothers or noncustodial fathers to have significantly higher incomes (U.S. Bureau of the Census, 1999). Thus, those fathers who gain custody of their children are a very small minority group of better-educated men with higher incomes in comparison to men who do not gain custody of their children. Consequently, single custodial fathers do not suffer financially in the same way as do single custodial mothers.

The Childrearing Behaviors of Divorced Mothers and Fathers. Researchers have shown that as fathers make the transition from the role of married parent to the role of divorced parent, they become less authoritarian and thereby less strict with their children, more concerned with the quality of care their children receive, and more protective toward their children. Divorced mothers, on the other hand, have been found to rely more on authoritarian patterns of interacting with their children following divorce. When examining the childrearing patterns of divorced parents, it is worthwhile to consider the context in which they occur. For example, divorced mothers of young children are typically younger, have lower income levels, and have lower levels of education compared with young mothers who are married. Furthermore, divorced mothers of young children report higher levels of stress, depression, conflict with their children's fathers, and a greater need for social support (Nair & Murray, 2005). Because divorced mothers have more struggles and less support than married mothers, stress is likely to play a role in their choice of authoritarian parenting.

Research findings showing that divorced mothers become more authoritarian and divorced fathers become more authoritative following divorce might also reflect necessary alterations of the role from married to single parent. Divorced mothers might find it necessary to establish greater authority following divorce, and divorced fathers might find that they need to increase their responsiveness toward their children. Given that the findings showing changes in parental behavior have typically focused on the transition period following divorce, it would be useful to understand the ways in which divorced parents socialize their children after the transition has been accomplished. With this goal in mind, we will now consider the relationships that divorced mothers and fathers establish and maintain with their children in the months and years following divorce.

Custodial Parents and Their Children. As noted earlier, most children of divorced parents live with their mothers (U. S. Bureau of the Census, 1999). Researchers investigating the relationships of custodial mothers and their children have consistently found that children in single-parent households experience a decrease in behavioral control and parental warmth immediately following the marital disruption (Hetherington & Stanley-Hagan, 1999). Surprisingly, many studies show that adolescents whose parents are divorcing do not report lower responsiveness in comparison to adolescents in long-term single-parent households (Freeman & Newland, 2002). It seems that the lower responsiveness of parents immediately following divorce impacts younger children more than adolescents. These findings might reflect the greater need for parental support for young children in comparison to adolescents. An alternative explanation might be that adolescents tend to lean more on peer support than parental support, especially at times when parents are less emotionally available.

Whereas parental sensitivity appears to be compromised in the transitional phase following divorce, when researchers have followed children of divorce across several years, they have acknowledged improvements in parental responsiveness over time. On the other hand, little change in behavioral control across time has been found. Whether we are looking at the transitional period following divorce or in the months and years following divorce, the evidence suggests that divorced custodial parents tend to exercise less parental control of their children in comparison to parents from never-divorced families (Wallerstein, Lewis, & Blakeslee, 2001). An interesting finding by Freeman and Newland (2002) was that lower control of the custodial parent does not have expected negative effects on their adolescent children. It was speculated that the reasons for better adjustment among adolescents might be attributed to their more advanced reasoning ability as well as their access to a larger and more intimate social support network. Moreover, because parents naturally relinquish control to their adolescent children, loosening control during that developmental stage might have little or no negative impact upon the child's level of autonomy.

Noncustodial Parents and Their Children. Because most children whose parents have divorced are in the custody of their mothers, the majority of noncustodial parents are fathers. Living apart from their children creates unique challenges for those fathers. Opportunities for nurturance and involvement in their children's lives clearly are fewer for nonresident fathers than for fathers in intact families or custodial fathers (Amato & Gilbreth, 1999; Fabricius, 2003). Children of divorced parents also experience difficulties in maintaining relationships with their nonresident fathers. The challenge of sustaining children's relationships with their noncustodial fathers is further compounded if either parent makes a geographical move. A residential move by either parent is likely to negatively impact children's access to their fathers. Furthermore, increased distance between fathers and their children is related to decreased contact, with some nonresident parents becoming considerably less involved in their children's lives following geographical separation from them (Stewart, 1999). These compound alterations in children's lives are stressful, require substantial adjustment, and are likely to have a detrimental effect on their ongoing development. Recognizing the value of

Larry Fleming/PH College

The availability and support of their parents aid children's adjustment to parental divorce.

both parents' involvement in their children's lives, recent federal legislation encourages states to support noncustodial parents' access and visitation with their children after separation or divorce (Keoughan, Joanning, & Sudak-Allison, 2001).

THE POSTDIVORCE ADJUSTMENT OF CHILDREN

Despite the many adjustments in family system and lifestyle that are required of children whose parents divorce, the adjustment of children and adolescents in postdivorce families is only marginally lower than for children in continuously intact two-parent families (Amato, 2000). Most important to children's postdivorce adjustment are economic resources, positive nurturing relationships with both parents, low levels of parental and family conflict (Gindes, 1998), relationship quality between divorced parents, and age, sex, and personality characteristics of the child (Hetherington & Stanley-Hagan, 1999). Researchers have particularly emphasized the role of social support in promoting positive child adjustment in response to parental divorce. Supportive parenting has been found to ease children's adjustment in the aftermath of parental divorce (Hetherington & Stanley-Hagan, 1999).

Because the large majority of children live with their mothers postdivorce (U.S. Bureau of the Census, 1999), supportive parenting is especially salient to the mother–child relationship. Clarke-Stewart and Hayward (1996) documented that following divorce, children who have close, supportive relationships with their mothers fare better than those with mothers who are less supportive. By communicating a strong sense of warmth, concern, and caring to their children, highly accepting mothers mediate the relation between divorce stressors and adjustment problems (Wolchik, Wilcox, Tein, & Sandler, 2000). Theoretically, mother–child relationships characterized by high levels of acceptance might promote a sense of security (Ainsworth et al., 1978), which is likely to reduce the threat of divorce stressors. In addition to expressing parental warmth, divorced parents need to provide adequate monitoring, discipline authoritatively, maintain age-appropriate expectations, and avoid coercive discipline (Amato, 2000; Krishnakumar & Buehler, 2000). It is beneficial as well if children of divorced parents have positive events in their lives. Doyle, Wolchik, Dawson-McClure, and Sandler (2003) found that positive events act as buffers against stress for children and adolescents in families in transition.

The Supportive Role of Extended Family Members

Members of the **extended family** (grandparents, aunts, uncles, or other relatives) are frequently valuable sources of social support for children experiencing stress. Unfortunately, these relationships have received little attention in the divorce literature. For example, research on divorce and grandparent–grandchild relationships has rarely focused on children's views of the importance of these relationships when dealing with stress related to parental divorce. In a recent study, however, Wolchik et al. (2000) examined both parents' and children's reports of their relationships with grandparents. The findings from their study were that greater closeness to grandparents is associated with fewer adjustment problems following parental divorce.

Thinking Critically

Based on the previous discussions of children and their divorced parents, what are your conclusions regarding the ways in which to alleviate the stress for children whose parents have divorced?

PARENTS AND CHILDREN IN STEPFAMILIES

Most children of divorced parents will live in a household headed by one parent for about 5 years, and a small majority of children who have experienced divorce will end up living in a stepfamily. This newly-configured family arrangement would seem to be a reasonably good solution for re-establishing the family system following divorce. The stepfamily has two adults present to provide parental guidance and care and one of those adults is the children's biological or adoptive parent. Furthermore, stepfamilies typically do not suffer the obvious economic disadvantages of mother-headed households. Nonetheless, there are a number of stressors for parents and children in stepfamilies.

Stresses in Stepfamilies

The establishment of a stepfamily brings unique challenges for which most couples are generally unprepared. The nuclear family is still viewed as ideal and stepfamilies are frequently compared negatively to that conception of family (Lynch, 2004). Expectations that the stepfamily will function like the intact family are unrealistic given the differences between these two families. Unlike the intact family, the stepfamily is created following the disruption of a previous family, the joining of an additional family member, and the inclusion of nonresidential family members (Erera & Fredrickson, 1999). Furthermore, because remarriage or cohabitation usually occurs within months after the start of a relationship, many couples are concurrently developing couple relationships and negotiating stepparent–stepchild relationships (Coleman, Ganong, & Fine, 2000). Additionally, remarriage represents still another transition in the lives of parents and children who have already undergone adjustments related to parental divorce and the restructuring of their family system. A primary challenge remarried parents face in the establishment of the stepfamily is that they are confronted with negative or idealistic views of the stepfamily. Cultural beliefs perpetuated by media and folk tales either stigmatize stepfamilies (e. g., the wicked stepmother) or promote unrealistic expectations, such as the myth of instant love exemplified in

The Brady Bunch television show. These cultural beliefs tend to affect perceptions and expectations related to stepfamily relationships (Segrin & Nabi, 2002).

Lack of Clarity of the Role of Stepparent. The challenge of assuming the role of stepparent is that stepfamily members frequently do not agree on what role the stepparent should play. Beyond a general consensus that, in comparison to stepparents, parents are expected to exhibit more warmth toward their children and more carefully monitor their children's behavior, there is little consistency in perceptions of the content of the stepparent role. Furthermore, stepparents are less certain about their role in the stepfamily than are other family members. Some stepfathers deal with the issue of role confusion and stepparent identity by assuming a parental role. In contrast, most stepmothers and many stepfathers (especially nonresidential ones) see themselves as a friend to their stepchildren or in some role between a friend and a parent (Erera-Weatherly, 1996).

Children's Expectations and Loyalty Issues. Most studies of stepfamily relationships and processes have focused on stepfathers' relationships with children because most stepfamily households consist of the mother, her children from a previous marriage, and a stepfather. These findings suggest that stepchildren tend to reject stepfathers who engage in discipline and control early in the relationship (Bray & Kelly, 1998; Ganong, Coleman, & Fine, 1999). Children and adolescents expect their biological mothers to maintain primary parental responsibilities and their stepfathers to play a minor parenting role. Particularly, children in stepfamilies expect their custodial parents to provide love, reassurance, support, time, and attention as well as discipline behaviors (Moore & Cartwright, 2005). Parental loyalty is also an issue for children in stepfamilies. Findings from a study by Cartwright (2003) suggest that children and adolescents in stepfamilies want demonstrations of support and commitment from their parents. These expectations extend to beliefs that parents should intervene or support them during conflicts with stepparents.

Stepfamilies That Work

Although there are multiple challenges in stepfamilies, and children in stepfamilies are at greater risk for problems than are children in first-married families, many stepfamilies provide a positive environment for children. Furthermore, researchers have noted that the differences between stepchildren and children living in first-marriage families are small. Most stepchildren do well in school and do not have emotional or behavioral problems (Coleman et al., 2000). The research shows that in stepfamilies where custodial parents maintain supportive relationships with their children and continue to play the role of disciplinarian, family relationships are less conflicted. There is also evidence that children in stepfamilies benefit from demonstrations of support from their stepparents. For example, the expression of mutual affection more often characterizes stepparent–stepchild relationships when stepfathers initially engage in supportive behaviors with stepchildren. Moreover, stepparents who make efforts to maintain a close relationship with stepchildren have closer bonds with them in comparison to stepparents who do not make those efforts (Bray & Kelly, 1998).

The most effective relationship-building strategies for stepparents are dyadic activities chosen by the stepchildren. When stepchildren recognize that their stepparents are trying to do things with them that the stepchildren like, they generally respond with their own affinity-seeking efforts (Ganong et al., 1999). The ways in which stepfamily members communicate with each other also has been found to strengthen the relationships of family members. In a comparison of strong stepfamilies and stepfamilies that were experiencing difficulties, Golish (2003) found that strong stepfamilies use communication strategies that include daily discussions, openness, spending time together as a family, family problem solving, and the communication of clear boundaries and rules.

When Stepfamilies Break Up

Because more than one-third of stepfamilies end in divorce, many children endure the extra trauma of seeing their parents' subsequent marriages break up (Zinsmeister, 1996). When children experience multiple life transitions, they are at greater risk for developmental difficulties. Across samples, gender, and measures of adjustment, children who have experienced multiple parental transitions have been found to have the most behavior problems. Conversely, children of mothers who have experienced no partner change (i.e., married mothers who have remained married or single mothers who have remained single) have been found to have the fewest behavior problems (Hetherington & Stanley-Hagan, 1999). The association between increased risk for behavior problems and multiple family transitions was also reported by Keller, Catalano, and Hagerty (2002). These researchers found that a greater number of parenting disruptions are associated with a higher probability of delinquent behavior in children and adolescents of both sexes.

Thinking Critically

Based on the previous discussion, what would you recommend to parents and stepparents who wish to create a harmonious stepfamily?

ADOLESCENT SINGLE PARENTS

Births to teenage mothers declined as sharply in the 1990s as they had escalated in the preceding two decades. It is worth remembering, though, that teenage pregnancy rates in the United States are still at least twice as high as in other industrialized countries.

Furthermore, the percentage of unmarried teens having babies is over 50% in many of our largest cities and close to that in some states (e.g., Louisiana and Mississippi). Also, teenage parenthood is most prevalent among already-disadvantaged youth (Sawhill, 2000). Teenage parents tend to function less effectively in several realms in comparison to their peers, including low educational achievement and poverty that precede rather than stem from early parenthood. Adolescent parenthood also further reduces the future prospects of underprivileged teenagers, including poorer psychological functioning, lower rates of high school graduation, lower levels of marital stability, and an increased number of nonmarital births (Coley & Chase-Lansdale, 1998).

The Children of Adolescent Parents

Not only does teenage parenthood present tremendous challenges to disadvantaged youth, their children are at heightened risk for suffering a variety of health, social, and economic problems as compared with children born to older parents (Hofferth & Reid, 2002). Whereas differences are indistinguishable during infancy, they begin to emerge during preschool. Young children of parents who were teenagers when they were born are more aggressive and less controlled in comparison to other preschoolers (Chase-Lansdale, Mott, & Brooks-Gunn, 1991). Children of adolescent parents are also at greater risk for cognitive impairment, psychological and behavioral problems, as well as early and persistent school failure (Belle, Doucet, Miller, & Tan, 2000; Sawhill, 2000).

The Challenges of Teenage Mothers and Fathers

The negative outcomes consistently seen in children of teenagers reflect the tremendous challenges faced by their young parents. When a teenager becomes a parent,

Shirley Zeiberg/PH College

This adolescent mother is beginning her parenting career with many disadvantages and will require more extended family and social support than will the typical adult parent.

the role of the adolescent must be reorganized to accommodate the role of parenthood. The reality is that the requirements of these two roles often conflict. For example, body image is a common concern of adolescent females and is likely to influence the choice of whether to breast-feed or bottle-feed. Other developmental tasks of adolescents that might clash with the demands of parenthood include the development of a self-identity, the need for peer acceptance, the desire for relationships with romantic partners, and the struggle for independence (Leitch, 1998).

Adolescent Mothers. An essential aspect of planning for the birth of a child is to prioritize one's health habits and obtain prenatal care. Unfortunately, in comparison to peers who postpone childrearing, pregnant teens are less inclined to have those priorities. They are less likely to gain adequate weight during pregnancy, less inclined to get prenatal care, less likely to receive adequate nutrition, and more likely to smoke and ingest unhealthy substances. The failure to prioritize health habits and get prenatal care puts adolescent mothers at heightened risk for developing health problems such as anemia and pregnancy-related high blood pressure. Consequently, they are more likely to give birth to preterm, underweight infants, who are at greater risk for birth defects, or early death (Shiono, Rauh, Park, Lederman, & Zuskar, 1997). After the arrival of their babies, adolescent mothers are clearly in need of support and are able to function more effectively in their parenting role when they receive assistance (Hess, Papas, & Black, 2002). Nonetheless, there is a downside related to reliance on the support of others. As young mothers' dependence on others increases, so does their susceptibility to the problematic aspects of social relationships. Disagreements, focused on appropriate parenting and the young mother's lifestyle, frequently occur when teenagers share childrearing responsibilities with their mothers (Davis, 2002). Additionally, adolescent mothers commonly mention problems with the father of their children ranging from dissatisfaction over unmet expectations for financial and child care assistance to serious conflicts, problematical break-ups, and physical assault (Leadbeater & Way, 2001).

Adolescent Fathers. In comparison to their peers who do not become fathers during adolescence, teenage fathers tend to have financial difficulties, educational barriers, relationship instability, and a greater likelihood of involvement in high-risk behavior (Marsiglio, Amato, Day, & Lamb, 2000). The Fragile Families Study by Garfinkel, McLanahan, Tienda, and Brooks-Gunn (2001) provides more insight into the lives of young fathers than had been heretofore provided. Whereas about half of young fathers are involved in their babies' lives during the first year of life, contact declines thereafter and there is much less frequent contact for school-age and adolescent children. The difficulties that teenage fathers have in taking on the responsibilities of fatherhood might be attributed to the fact that young fathers tend to be disadvantaged educationally and financially (Lansdale & Oropesa 2001). Furthermore, contact with his children is tied to the relationship the adolescent father has with the mother and might be further complicated by the mother's family where the child resides, especially if the young father is not seen as a good enough provider (Erkut, Szalacha, & Coll, 2005).

Increasing the Parenting Competence of Teenage Parents

Adolescent parenthood negatively impacts the lives of youth who are already disadvantaged teenagers. Consequently, their children are more at risk for developmental problems in comparison to children of older parents. For these reasons, much attention must be given to increasing the resiliency of adolescent parents.

Ways to Assist Adolescent Mothers. Although numerous disadvantages are associated with adolescent parenthood and their children are at increased risk for negative outcomes, many teen mothers become capable parents. Researchers have identified an array of factors that increases the competence levels of these young mothers. Secure attachment to parents, social support from the family or community, father involvement, and graduating from high school all increase the resiliency of teenage mothers (Weed, Keogh, & Borkowski, 2000). Of those sources of support, family support is the most influential basis of informal support for teenage mothers. Within the family, the mothers of adolescent mothers are usually the most reliable source of assistance in the early phases of childrearing. The types of assistance mothers of adolescents typically provide are (a) nurturance of their daughters, (b) help with childrearing responsibilities, and (c) financial aid. Young mothers who have these types of support are in a better position to continue their education or receive job training (Hess et al., 2002).

Ways to Assist Teenage Fathers. In recognition of the difficulty that young fathers encounter in meeting their parental obligations, researchers have provided a number of suggestions. First, it is recommended that services be directed toward strengthening young fathers' earning power through the provision of education and job training (Rozie-Battle, 2003). It also has been suggested that young fathers' participation in the lives of their children might be facilitated by encouraging a positive relationship with the mothers of their children. For example, Coley and Chase-Lansdale (1999) found that, whether or not there is a continuing romantic involvement, a harmonious relationship with mothers increases the likelihood of fathers' involvement with their children. Other sources of support for young fathers include their own families, their current partners if different from the mothers, their peers, and the social institutions that impinge on their lives.

Thinking Critically

Now that we have examined the lives of teenage parents and their children, what are some of the ways you would recommend that families and the community support adolescent mothers? What family and community supports would you suggest for adolescent fathers?

UNMARRIED PARENTS WHO ARE NOT DIVORCED, WIDOWED, OR ADOLESCENTS

Births to unmarried adult females (ages 20 to 34) increased during the last two decades, with the largest increase occurring for females in their early 20s. The increase of births for that age group suggests that adults in contemporary America feel freer to take on single parenthood even when they have no immediate plans to marry and might not be in committed relationships. Furthermore, a small (but increasing) number of unmarried adult women are financially capable individuals. Recent census data indicates that 8.3% of never-married women in managerial or professional positions fit that description (U. S. Bureau of the Census, 1999). Unmarried young adults in well-paying careers who choose to become parents differ considerably from other unmarried parents. Besides being better off financially than unmarried adolescent parents, divorced custodial mothers, or divorced noncustodial fathers, unmarried young adults in professional careers are not simultaneously coping with single parenting and the stresses of losing a spouse through divorce or death. Next, single parenthood for that group represents more of a choice of single parenthood in comparison to single parenthood that results from divorce, death of a spouse, or an unplanned pregnancy. Although unique challenges are to be found in the unmarried young adult parent–child relationship, these challenges must be considered alongside advantages related to maturity, higher income, and a high level of commitment to parenthood as reflected by the deliberate choice to become a single parent.

GAY AND LESBIAN PARENTS AND THEIR CHILDREN

The number of openly gay and lesbian families has been increasing, especially in major urban settings (Vanfrussen, 2003). Families headed by gay fathers are relatively rare but families headed by lesbian mothers occur more frequently. In many respects, families headed by gay or lesbian parents often are indistinguishable from those headed by heterosexual couples. Both sets of parents have similar hopes and dreams for their children as well as the typical challenges of childrearing. Moreover, researchers have found few differences in the way that heterosexual and homosexual parents rear their children. Furthermore, children in households where parents are gay or lesbian fare as well as those where parents are heterosexual. Despite the similarities in families headed by heterosexual or homosexual parents, there are unique challenges encountered by gay or lesbian parents and their children.

Pathways to Parenthood for Gay Men and Lesbian Women. There are several routes to parenthood for lesbian mothers and gay fathers. A common path to lesbian parenthood has been and continues to be through lesbian stepfamilies wherein a lesbian mother has custody of her children from a previous heterosexual marriage. Because custody proceedings tend to favor female and heterosexual parents, only a minority of divorced gay fathers live in the same households as their children. In contrast to the route to parenthood just described, both men and women are increasingly undertaking parenthood in the context of pre-existing lesbian and gay identities. In these situations, parenthood is achieved through donor insemination or adoption. Although gay men sometimes choose to build a family through insemination or surrogacy, that route is much easier for lesbian mothers than for gay fathers (Patterson, 2000). Adoption is another avenue for both gay men and lesbian women who wish to become parents but who cannot or choose not to rear a biological child (Vanfrussen, 2003).

Challenges for Gay and Lesbian Parents and Their Children. Although specific challenges are linked with the way in which gay and lesbian persons become parents, other challenges are common to all families headed by gay fathers or lesbian mothers. For example, all of these families face prejudice, have fewer legal rights, and are less likely than heterosexual parents to have intergenerational support.

Societal prejudice related to sexual orientation. The main differences between gay or lesbian parents and heterosexual parents are that gay or lesbian parents are confronted with prejudices related to their sexual orientation. In contrast, the sexual orientation of heterosexual parents is not questioned. There are two realities regarding gay and lesbian parents: (a) the universal reality of ordinary persons working together to create intimate bonds that permit both individual freedom and family cohesion, and (b) the reality of public prejudice such that at any moment, a gay or lesbian family can become the object of ridicule that negatively impacts family members' self-esteem and raises the level of stress within the family. As noted by Vanfrussen (2003), the increased visibilty of gay and lesbian families in the United States has resulted in a powerful backlash from part of the conservative religious right and right-wing organizations. Both gay and lesbian parents are targeted as undesirable by those groups because they are viewed as threatening the structure of "family life," which has included only married heterosexual couples and their children.

An example of the prejudices that gay or lesbian parents confront is exemplified by a parent who reported that her 9-year-old son came home and told her that his friend's father had said to him that his mother would burn in hell "because she loves women and that is against the rule of nature" (Shapiro, 1996, p. 504). An aspect of the prejudice that gay men and lesbian women face is related specifically to gay or lesbian parenthood. As noted by a lesbian mother: "Ten years ago . . . when I would say I have a daughter, people would sigh and say 'and we thought you were gay, but obviously you are not . . . you are a mother'" (Shapiro, 1996, p. 504). Even when others are not expressing overt prejudice, their insensitive questioning about the lifestyles of gay or lesbian parents might be viewed as intrusive and offensive by parents and children in those families. A case in point is the experience of the gay fathers of an adopted daughter whom they had reared since birth. These parents were financially comfortable and open about their sexual orientation to friends, family, neighbors, and at work. As they searched for a school for their daughter, who was soon to be 5 years old, however, a theme of isolation surfaced. First of all, most parents on the school tours and interviews were mothers, and fathers were a minority. In their interviews with school personnel, they were confronted with numerous stereotyping and offensive questions that were not asked of the heterosexual parents. Those questions consisted of the following: "Who cooks?"; "Who is she?"; "Which one stays at home?"; and "How did you get her?" These fathers said they were tired of hearing the "Excuse me for asking, but . . . " questions. These reactions of school personnel to their sexual orientation were unpleasant and made it difficult for these parents to choose a school that would provide their daughter with a good education while also respecting their family (Ariel, 2000).

Lack of or diminished intergenerational support. In most families, intergenerational relationships are important sources of support for parents and that familial support extends the childrearing efforts of parents. Whereas heterosexual parents are usually able to take intergenerational support for granted, that is not the case for gay or lesbian parents. Rather than being able to benefit from parental support, gay or lesbian parents tend to experience moderate to strong parental disapproval of their homosexual lifestyle, which might create stress in their relationships with their partners and/or impact the lives of their children (Berger, 2000). An example of the effect of diminished parental support for gay or lesbian parents is evident in the following statement made by a biological parent in a lesbian stepfamily composed of herself, her partner, and her adolescent son. The statement was made in response to the question, "To what extent do you and your partner experience parental support of your family?" The names used in the quote are fictitious.

> Well, my own parents do not support my lifestyle and are no longer involved in my life. Therefore, it means a lot to me that Barbara's parents welcome Tommy (the son) and me in their home. Since Tommy and I don't have contact with my parents, that gives us a family. They are nice to Tommy and always remember to give him a present at Christmas. When referring to their grandchildren, however, they don't mention Tommy which means they don't consider Tommy as one of the grandchildren. That hurts because he really wants to be included as a part of the family. (Anonymous)

Denial of basic civil rights. The basic civil rights that extend to other family forms generally do not support gay and lesbian parents and their children (Shapiro, 1996). For example, gay or lesbian parents who wish to adopt children confront many difficult issues. Adoption by lesbians and gay men is permitted in fewer than half the states in the United States. Thus, gay men and lesbians seeking to adopt children have often felt it necessary to hide their sexual orientation and adopt initially as single parents, then attempt to gain parental rights or second-parent adoptions in courts (Vanfrussen, 2003). As stated earlier, legal issues related to parenthood are even more problematic for gay men due to the commonly held beliefs that men are not as nurturing as are women or that gay men are more involved in promiscuous sex or more apt to sexually abuse their children. None of these beliefs have been supported by research; as a matter of fact, the research data that is available suggest just the opposite.

Although basic civil rights and legal difficulties continue to exist, and we have a long way to go, there have been some important changes. Gays and lesbians in recent years have been awarded some rights in several parts of the country. These include joint dental and health insurance, disability and retirement benefits, bereavement or parenting leave, and various family assistance benefits and discount opportunities. They have also been welcomed by a growing number of churches and synagogues, as well as by other organizations specifically created to serve them (Vanfrussen, 2003). Even though gay and lesbian lifestyles are more acceptable today than several decades ago, there continues to be strong opposition to gay men and lesbians becoming parents. Furthermore, the acceptance of this family is not uniform. For example, there is less prejudice in urban settings than in rural areas and some companies offer comparable health benefit to all employees whereas others do not. At the end of the day, the effects of societal prejudices, lack of family support, and not having legal recognition of their family structure are that gay and lesbian parents must establish protective boundaries around their family when confronted with these challenges (LaSala, 2002).

Gay or Lesbian Stepfamilies and Donor-Inseminated Mothers

So far, we have considered the negative societal beliefs, legal difficulties, and lower levels of intergenerational suport that confront all families headed by gay fathers or lesbian mothers. We will now turn our attention to the unique challenges encountered by parents and children in gay and lesbian stepfamilies. Then, we will examine the lives of lesbian women who become parents as a result of donor insemination.

Gay and Lesbian Stepfamilies. Families formed by gay or lesbian parents from previous heterosexual unions have many characteristics in common with stepfamilies created by heterosexual parents. That is especially true of lesbian mothers who frequently have custody of their children from former heterosexual partnerships. The similarities between heterosexual stepfamilies and gay or lesbian stepfamilies are that both families: (a) are created after the disruption of previous families, (b) are formed by the joining of an additional family member, and (c) have nonresidential family members (Erera & Fredrickson, 1999).

The loss associated with previous family disruption. Although all stepfamilies are founded after the disruption of previous families, this loss sets gay or lesbian stepfamilies apart from heterosexual stepfamilies. Whereas studies of heterosexual stepfamilies have dealt with the issue of loss associated with family disruption, the literature on gay or lesbian stepfamilies does not address the loss issue. It is likely that the issue of loss is overlooked by family scholars because the gay or lesbian stepfamily is perceived as a cohabiting couple rather than as a family (Erera & Fredrickson, 1999).

Family roles. In reality, both gay or lesbian and heterosexual stepfamilies are family systems created by the same circumstances and composed of the same family roles. The birth or adoptive parent and children are joined by a stepparent. Sometimes the stepparent brings to the new family system his or her children as well. Both the joining stepparent and the "absorbing" family have their own family connections, rituals, and habits. In the beginning stages, stepfamilies are composed of two distinct subsystems: the absorbing or "veteran" family members and the "newcomer(s)." In addition to the two residential parents and the children and stepchildren, heterosexual and gay or lesbian stepfamilies generally include nonresident members. The nonresidential members are the noncustodial parent and at times an additional stepparent (the spouse or partner of the noncustodial parent) (Erera & Fredrickson, 1999).

Shared parental responsibilities. In both heterosexual and gay or lesbian stepfamilies, residential parents might share parental responsibilities and authority with the nonresidential parents. This interdependence sometimes leads to conflict in situations where the residential and nonresidential parents have different goals or priorities. Lesbian mothers with children from a previous heterosexual union, however, tend to have more congenial relations with their previous husbands or partners than do heterosexual mothers. Additionally, research has demonstrated that lesbian mothers are likely to "adopt" male friends as male role models for their children and usually have more men participating in the lives of their children in comparison to single, heterosexual mothers (Hare, 1994).

The Gay or Lesbian Stepfamily as a Unique Family Form. Even though heterosexual and gay or lesbian stepfamilies share a number of characteristics and face similar challenges, parents and children in gay or lesbian stepfamilies are confronted with a number of challenges that are unique to their family form. According to Lynch (2004), the assumption of a gay/lesbian identity is perhaps the most difficult parenting role in our society. The nuclear family is still viewed as ideal and stepfamilies are frequently compared negatively to that conception of family. When considering families from that perspective, the combination of a gay/lesbian identity with parenthood is considered by many as a contradiction. For gay and lesbian parents who did not initially choose to be parents and biological parents who come out after becoming parents, family relationships must be created with few guidelines. This is especially difficult for the gay/lesbian stepparent who is not acknowledged as a parent and might be unable to count on previous sources of support. Finally, an important difference between stepfamilies headed by heterosexual parents and those headed by gay or lesbian parents is the marital status of the parents. Because gay men and lesbian women are not permitted to marry in most states, it is doubtful that the parents in this household will be married. Consequently, children's coverage on health and dental insurance is likely to be a problem for those families in which the parent with better health and dental coverage is the stepparent whose relationship to the other parent and the children is not recognized.

The Family Created by Lesbian Parents Through Donor Insemination. Greater access to donor insemination in the past two decades has resulted in what has been termed a "**gayby boom**" among North American and European lesbian women (Gartrell et al., 2000; Grossman & Okum, 2003). In interviews with prospective birth mothers and **co-mothers** during insemination or pregnancy, Gartrell et al. (1996) found that having children for these women was highly desirable and that their decisions were thoughtfully considered. The women choosing donor insemination were also well educated regarding the potential challenges of rearing children in a homophobic society. Investigators who have examined the family life of lesbians who have chosen donor insemination have found that the decision usually strengthens the relationships of couples and ties to their families of origin (Dunne, 2000). These mothers tend to be honest with their children about donor insemination and about their own lesbianism, and many believe it is important for them to educate the community as well (Mitchell, 1998). Interviews of these mothers when their children were toddlers suggest that mother–child bonding is as closely aligned with nurture as with biology. According to Vanfrussen (2003), the relationship between social mothers and their children are characterized by a level of acceptance, openness, and authority that is comparable to the children's relationships with their biological mothers. Likewise, the literature on elementary-age children who were conceived by donor insemination and have two lesbian mothers has shown that they are as well adjusted as the children of heterosexual parents (Chan, Raboy, & Patterson, 1998).

Thinking Critically

As you can see, children in the United States are being reared in a variety of family structures. Nevertheless, there are stereotypes and prejudices about which family type is considered to be "normal and appropriate." How do you think negative beliefs concerning varied family structures affect the lives of parents and children who are living in these family arrangements?

Children of Gay or Lesbian Parents

Now that we have considered the various ways that gay men and lesbian women become families and the challenges they encounter in these families, we will examine the lives of the children growing up in these families. The findings of a recent investigation by Golombok, Perry, Murray, and Burton (2003) are in line with those of earlier studies of lesbian–mother families that pointed to positive parent–child relationships and well-adjusted children. In their study, no significant differences were identified between lesbian mothers and heterosexual mothers for most of the parenting variables. Regarding the children, no significant differences in psychological probems were identified. Despite the lack of societal, family, and legal support of their lifestyle, the vast majority of research has demonstrated that the sexual orientation of gay or lesbian parents affects neither their ability to parent nor the outcomes of their children. In a review of the research findings focusing on that topic, Fredrickson (1999) reported that a parent's sexual orientation is not related to the child's emotional health, interpersonal relationships, social adjustment, or sexual orientation. These findings indicate that gay and lesbian parents generally find creative and healthy ways for responding to the challenges they face.

One explanation for the positive adjustment of children in gay and lesbian families is that both lesbian women and gay men are more likely than are heterosexual men and women to form **egalitarian relationships** based on the principle of equality of partners. In these families, household responsibilities are generally shared, reflecting the egalitarian principle. It has been speculated that the reason why gay and lesbian couples tend to develop egalitarian relationships is because they create their relationships without reference to traditional gender roles (Kurdek, 2001). These relationships differ considerably from heterosexual relationships where gender is often used as a determinant for dividing household responsibilities. It should be noted that in all famililes, egalitarian parental relationships have a postive effect on children. Children have been found to be better adjusted when parents divide the child care responsibilities equally (Patterson, 1995). Children of parents who adopt egalitarian roles also are less likely to adopt traditional gender roles. In a review of studies on gay and lesbian families, Stacey and Biblarz (2001) found that both boys and girls of gay or lesbian parents were less constrained by gender roles in comparison to boys and girls in heterosexual families. Girls were less traditional in dress, activities, and career aspirations and boys were less aggressive than boys with heterosexual parents.

SURROGATE PARENTS

Even though the majority of children in the United States and Canada are being reared by one or both of their parents, large numbers of children are being brought up by **surrogate parents**. Surrogate parents are persons who have stepped into the

Anne Vega/Merrill

After rearing their own children, and at a time when many of their contemporaries have retired, these grandparents have taken on the responsibilities of rearing their grandchildren.

parental role to ensure that children have homes in which to live and caring adults to guide and protect them. An increasing number of children are being reared by their grandparents (Grossman & Okum, 2003) and growing numbers of children are being reared by foster parents (Swann, 2006).

Grandfamilies: Grandparents Rearing Their Grandchildren

In the past several decades, there has been a dramatic upsurge in the number of grandparent-headed households. Circumstances resulting in grandparents becoming surrogate parents include parental death, parental physical or mental illness, parental substance abuse, parental imprisonment, or parental abuse and/or neglect of children (Grossman & Okum, 2003). In previous research, grandparent caregivers have most often been African American females living in the inner city, raising their daughters' children. That picture of the **grandfamily** has recently shifted. In the late 1990s, 13% of African American children, 6.5% of Hispanic American children, and 4.1% of European American children were being raised by their grandparents (U.S. Bureau of the Census, 1999).

Most researchers studying grandfamilies have highlighted the risk factors for grandmothers who are bringing up their grandchildren. Consistent findings are that rearing their grandchildren places older women at risk for heightened psychological stress, physical health problems, social isolation, and inadequate resources (Bullock, 2004; Edwards, 2003; Goodman & Silverstein, 2002). Although most studies of grandparents rearing their grandchildren have focused on grandmothers, many grandfathers also are involved in rearing grandchildren. Grandfathers, who take on that responsibility, often feel a sense of powerlessness that grandmothers do not experience. Grandfathers in the surrogate parent role report feeling powerless in the transition to the role, in the activities of everyday parenting, and in their capacity to continue parenting long-term. These grandfathers also are likely to experience caregiver stress including financial worries, social isolation, and poor health (Bullock, 2004).

The Positive Impact of Grandparent Caregivers. Although taking on the caregiver role as older adults places grandparents at risk for jeopardizing their own physical or psychological health, they nevertheless provide a tremendous service to their grandchildren who might otherwise be placed in foster care (Fuller-Thomson & Minkler, 2001). As with any family system, the success of the grandfamily household can be viewed in terms of stresses and resources. A number of stressors in the parent-headed household contribute to grandparents becoming primary caregivers for their grandchildren. On the other hand, the availability of grandparents to step in when parents cannot fulfill their parental responsibilities represents a family resource. Moreover, grandparents who offer a home for their grandchildren provide one of the most valuable resources necessary for the optimum development of children—the availability of caring adults. In research of at-risk children, it has been documented that the presence in one's life of at least one adult the child can depend on to be emotionally supportive promotes resilience in the face of other hardships

(Baldwin, Baldwin, & Cole, 1990). There are also benefits for grandparents who provide a home for children whose parents are unavailable. A primary benefit for grandparents who make that decision is that it alleviates concerns regarding their grandchildren's welfare. For many grandparents, stepping into the parental role, when needed, contributes to satisfaction derived from stabilizing the life of a child (Waldrup & Weber, 2001).

Formal Support for Grandparents Raising Their Grandchildren. It is important to remember that taking on the responsibility of caregiver of one's grandchildren is not as simple as transferring residences. Grandparents who assume parental responsibilities for their grandchildren face a host of legal problems. In recognition of the legal vulnerability associated with kinship caregiving, local support groups, statewide coalitions, policymakers, and legislators began to seek solutions to these difficulties. Some examples of developments include (a) legal authority to make caregiving decisions, (b) financial support for kinship care, (c) resolution of housing problems, and (d) options for permanent care (Takas, 1995). In addition to needing solutions to legal problems, grandfamilies have various needs that require the attention of social and health care providers. Because they differ in levels of financial security, health problems, employment issues, and family conflict, they benefit from varied kinds of social services. In developing social services designed to assist grandparents in their roles of surrogate parents, it is important to include both grandmothers as well as grandfathers. Information regarding the ways in which each grandparent functions in the parenting role should be incorporated into the planning and development of services (Kramer & Thompson, 2002).

Informal Support for Grandparents Raising Grandchildren. A potential source of support for the grandfamily household is from the extended family system. Based on their study of grandparents who are rearing their grandchildren, Waldrup and Weber (2001) identified several ways in which extended family members sometimes assist those grandparents. First, those family members might provide emotional assistance such as advice and encouragement. Second, they might offer practical help, such as transportation and financial assistance. Grandparents benefit as well from respite care whether it is provided by family members, friends, or coworkers, or by a social service agency. In the case of grandparents caring for their grandchildren, respite care refers to the temporary care of those children to provide grandparents with the opportunity to relax, take care of errands, or participate in leisurely activities. The ways in which family, friends, and coworkers might offer assistance to grandparents who are raising their grandchildren are exemplified in the following anecdote from a 50-year-old grandmother, who is raising her two grandchildren and a nephew, in response to the question, "How do you cope with the situation?"

> I have faith. I have lots of faith. My family supports each other. People that I work with are wonderful. They are just marvelous. They work with me; they support me and say, "Sarah, is there anything that I can do to help you, and stuff like that." It makes a difference—100% difference. . . . (Waldrup & Weber, 2001, 467)

Thinking Critically

If you were a professional working with a grandfamily, what recommendations would you give those grandparents regarding social supports that they might access for their families?

Foster Parents and Foster Children

Each year, thousands of children are taken from their biological families and placed in foster care. The number of children placed in foster care at the end of 1999 was over 550,000, which was approximately twice as many as were in foster care a decade earlier (Roche, 2000). The rise in foster care placement coincides with an increase of reported cases of child abuse and neglect in the United States. Unfortunately, predictions are that the numbers of children placed in foster care will continue to grow in the next decade. Not only has the number of children needing foster care become overwhelming, it has turned out to be problematic to find families capable of meeting the complex emotional, behavioral, psychological, and medical needs of those children (Baum, Crase, & Crase, 2001).

The Lives of Children in Foster Care. In a recent study of adolescents in households with no biological parents, Sun (2003) found a number of disadvantages of living with neither parent. Among adolescents from six family types, those in nonbiological-parent families rank the lowest in academic performance, educational aspiration, and locus of control. Whether the problems of foster children are due to foster care placement or to the circumstances that led to foster care placement is debatable. Some research suggests that the circumstances of foster care are more positive than is typically portrayed in the media. Recent studies indicate that children's well-being often improves in foster care (Horwitz, Balestracci, & Simms, 2001). Furthermore, those who remain in foster care for at least 6 years display fewer problem behaviors than those reunited with their parents, despite having multiple placement moves (Taussig, Clyman, & Landsver, 2001). In addition to the everyday care, being in foster care allows children who need mental health services to acquire them (Farmer et al., 2001).

Problems Associated with Finding Foster Parents. Due to the vast need for foster care placement of children and adolescents, one of the primary challenges of foster care professionals includes finding individuals who are willing to become foster care providers. Findings of Baum et al. (2001) indicate that "awareness of the need for foster care" is the most influential factor related to the decision of whether or not to become foster parents. This finding emphasizes the importance of educating the community regarding the crucial need for foster homes. Other motivations that individuals have given for wanting to become foster parents vary but "enjoying and wanting to help children" is a common response.

Goals for Effective Foster Care. One of the major concerns for placing children in foster care is the risk that the placement will not be successful (Baum et al., 2001). Foster home breakdowns or the unplanned removal of children from foster homes can be traumatic for children and might interfere with the child's later formation of intimate relationships (Rosenfeld et al., 1997). To lessen the likelihood that those breakdowns will occur, Daly and Dowd (1992) called for a "harm-free, effective environment," that is free from abuse and neglect and in compliance with legal licensing guidelines. Daly and Dowd emphasized that effective foster parents provide care that promotes spiritual, emotional, intellectual, and physical development. Ways to meet the goals of effective foster care have been suggested by Morrisette (1996), who stresses that two important attributes of effective foster parents are emotional stability and a genuine liking for children. Morrisette points out that it is important for foster parents to show respect for the children in their care as well as to set clear limits and follow through with consequences.

Thinking Critically

In consideration of children's varied living arrangements, how do you think others (teachers, other professionals, friends, and acquaintances) can be thoughtful and considerate in discussing family life, sending notes home, or writing about children and their families so that all children can take pride in themselves and their family life?

SUMMARY

- In this chapter we examined the family structures where children are growing up, including those headed by married, divorced, never-married, and widowed parents as well as those headed by grandparents and foster parents.
- We learned that although there has been a decrease in the number of adolescent parents in the United States, that there continues to be over twice as many adolescent births in the United States when compared to other industrialized countries. We also learned that the birth rates for adolescents are even higher in many urban areas and in some states.
- We discovered that three of the fastest growing families in the United States are those headed by unmarried women in their twenties, lesbian women who used donor insemination, and grandparents who are taking on the role of surrogate parents.
- We examined the ways in which societal and intergenerational family support varies depending on family structure. Relatedly, we increased our awareness of the ways in which the presence or absence of societal and family support impacts the lives of parents and children within families.

- Throughout all the discussions of family life in various family structures, we considered the challenges of parents or surrogate parents as they attempt to provide a positive environment for children. We considered the outcomes of children living in various family arrangements and contemplated ways in which relatives and the community might support the efforts of these parents, foster parents, and grandparents.
- In the next chapter, we will become familiar with a variety of child socialization strategies of parenting specifically chosen to assist parents or surrogate parents in meeting their child-rearing goals.

KEY TERMS

- co-mother
- egalitarian relationships
- extended family
- family structure
- gayby boom
- grandfamily
- nuclear family
- surrogate parents

USEFUL WEB SITES

Promoting Family Resiliency

http://www.glue.umd.edu/-fraz/nnfr.html

This national network for family resiliency is an interactive network that provides leadership for the acquisition, development, and analysis of resources that foster resiliency (defined as the family's ability to cultivate strengths to positively meet the challenges of life).

Support for Adoptive Parents

http://www.adoption.org/

This site is intended to improve the dissemination of information about adoption. It provides information about federal programs that provide assistance for adoptions, state adoption laws, and resources for adoptive parents.

Assistance for Grandfamilies

http://www.grandparentagain.com/

This site provides listings of support groups, legal support, related organizations, and on *Grandparents-US*, *Off Our Rockers*, and *Rocking Chair Gazette* publications for grandparents raising their grandchildren.

Child Socialization Strategies and Techniques

Objectives

After completing of this chapter, you should be able to

- Demonstrate an understanding of a number of child socialization strategies that are useful for preventing children's misbehavior from occurring, while also helping children to meet their goals, and promoting their self-esteem.
- Describe and use strategies designed to assist parents in reinforcing their children's appropriate behaviors, and serving as effective models for their children.
- Demonstrate the ability to use effective parent–child communication.
- Describe and use a variety of childrearing methods, designed to help parents to (a) establish boundaries, (b) set limits, and (c) provide consequences that are developmentally appropriate and growth-producing for the child.
- Demonstrate the ability to use a conflict resolution model, which is intended to help parents and children to resolve conflicts with each other.

As we have seen in previous chapters, the everyday experiences of parents and children are influenced by their social surroundings. Within all family structures and cultural groups, parents are better prepared to be successful in their important parenting career when they have effective child socialization skills. We learned in Chapter 2 that both authoritative and traditional parenting patterns are associated with positive outcomes for children. Both of these parenting styles emphasize parental support as well as parental guidelines, boundaries, and appropriate consequences. The child socialization strategies presented in this chapter also are based on the combination of parental warmth with parental control that is neither lax nor overly strict.

The parenting strategies explained in the first part of the chapter reflect a prevention-of-problems approach, which includes a variety of strategies designed to assist children in meeting their goals and to motivate them toward cooperative behavior. Following the discussion of strategies intended to prevent problems from occurring is a clarification of the ways in which parents might reinforce their children's appropriate behaviors and serve as effective models for their children. After that discussion is a presentation of strategies designed to foster effective parent–child communication. Then, several childrearing methods are explained to assist parents in (a) establishing boundaries, (b) setting limits, and (c) providing consequences that are developmentally appropriate and growth-producing for the child. These socialization strategies are followed by a step-by-step description of a conflict resolution model that is designed to assist parents in resolving conflicts with their children.

GUIDANCE AS PREVENTION OF PROBLEMS

A number of parenting strategies are effective for preventing children's misbehavior. These include (a) a method for establishing *an atmosphere of psychological safety* for children, which stresses the importance of instilling a strong self-esteem in children; (b) the technique of *encouragement* which shifts parents' focus from children's mistakes to what they appreciate about their children; (c) an approach called *four pluses and a wish,* which explains the ways in which parents might motivate children toward cooperation; (d) a technique called *the four goals of misbehavior,* which calls attention to children's feelings and goals underlying their behavior and misbehavior; and (e) a method for improving parent–child communication skills, which includes *problem ownership, active listening, and I-messages.* Those parents who are likely to embrace the prevention of problem techniques are parents who have higher levels of child acceptance and parent involvement. Thus, we will discuss the growth-producing aspect of parent involvement before examining the guidance strategies focused on the prevention of problems.

The Positive Influence of Parental Involvement

Parental involvement might be conceptualized as emotional availability that includes structuring, sensitivity, nonhostility, and nonintrusiveness, as well as responsiveness. Birengen (2000) found that parental emotional availability predicts attachment, positive child development, and the quality of the parent–child relationship. Further support for the positive influence of parental involvement was demonstrated by Juang and Silbereisen (1999) who found that children and adolescents who report their parents as consistently more supportive have lower levels of depression, higher levels of self-efficacy, and higher levels of achievement than do children and adolescents who report that their parents are inconsistently supportive. Moreover, there is evidence that parental involvement is related to children's anger regulation and coping strategies. For example, Clark, Novak, and Dupree (2002) found that children who perceived their parents as involved were more likely to seek diversions rather than acting out their anger.

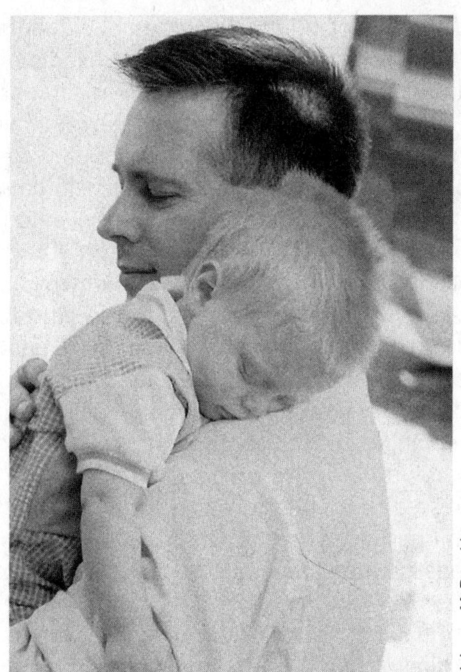
JoLynne McDonald.

When children experience their parent's unconditional love, they develop a positive sense of self.

Establishing an Atmosphere of Psychological Safety

Dorothy Briggs (1975) developed a prevention-of-problems approach to guidance wherein parents are enjoined to create an **atmosphere of psychological safety** for their children. This model is based on Briggs' position that the chief goal of parenting is to build a strong sense of self-worth in children. According to Briggs, there are three levels of **self-esteem**, each of which reflects children's ongoing interactions with their parents. Children with high self-esteem have experienced unconditional love from their parents. Children with low self-esteem have had interactions with parents that have contributed to questions regarding their lovability. Children with middle-level self-esteem have had interactions with their parents that have resulted in the belief that their lovability derives from performance that pleases others.

The House of Self. Briggs uses the analogy of "house of self" to explain how each level of self-esteem is built. According to that perspective, the **house of self** is constructed by developing children from the words, body language, and treatment by important others in their environment, particularly parents. Every day, children are asking, "Who am I?" The answer to that question consists of the collection of messages reflected back to them. Accordingly, the self-image of children matches how they are treated regardless of their actual potential. In determining how parent–child interactions impact a child's self-esteem, the issue is not "Does the parent love the child?" but "Does the child feel and experience the parent's love?" Briggs' emphasis on the promotion of the child's self-esteem highlights the belief that technique and love must be interwoven. Briggs recommends that parents examine all guidance decisions in light of two questions, (a) "Does this approach encourage or discourage a child's sense of self-worth?" and (b) "Would I like to be my own child?"

Because a child's house of self is constructed during everyday interactions with parents and others, it is important that parents attend to their children's feelings as they are instructing them and as they are responding to their behavioral challenges. In these interactions, children need to receive messages that contribute to beliefs that they are competent and lovable. Briggs outlined several ways in which parents might foster their children's self-esteem. She emphasized first and foremost that, in all of their interactions with their children, parents should express unconditional love. Children are more likely to develop a high self-esteem when they feel cherished. For children to feel cherished, they need to be able to get their parents' focused attention, to be really seen (not just looked at). According to Briggs, to truly see a child, the parent must connect to each child with fresh eyes, to attend to that child's *particularness*. She further stressed that children need to know they can trust the adults around them. Briggs emphasized as well that children are able to trust their parents when (a) their real needs are met, (b) parental promises are kept, and (c) parents are not afraid to apologize or to say "no" when a refusal is necessary. Finally, Briggs highlighted the value of having humor in the parent–child relationship. She noted that children are more likely to trust parents who are capable of having fun with them. Laughing, joking, and playing with children dissolve the barriers between parents and children and helps to foster a trusting relationship.

Research Findings That Demonstrate the Value of Promoting Children's Self-Esteem. The importance of using socialization strategies that promote children's self-esteem cannot be overemphasized. The self-acceptance that children gain during the early years reflects the degree to which they feel that they are valued by their parents (Bigner, 1998). Furthermore, high self-esteem helps children to view the rest of their lives from a more optimistic perspective. They are able to believe, for example, that even when their efforts are not successful in certain academic, athletic, or social situations, they are still worthwhile individuals (Harter, 1998). Moreover, children with supportive families develop both higher self-esteem and more positive social relationships. Higher self-esteem also mediates a variety of negative outcomes for children, including eating disorders, depression, and antisocial behavior (Colarossi & Eccles, 2000; Harter, 1998). Finally, parental evaluations of their children's behaviors impact the self-esteem of children much more than does the judgment of others. As noted by Harter (1999), the more important the person is to the child, the more influential are the judgments of that person on the child's attitude toward self.

Guidance as Encouragement of Children

Encouragement is one of the most beneficial skills that parents might use for assisting children in meeting their goals and for boosting their children's self-esteem. Parental encouragement helps children to believe in themselves and their abilities

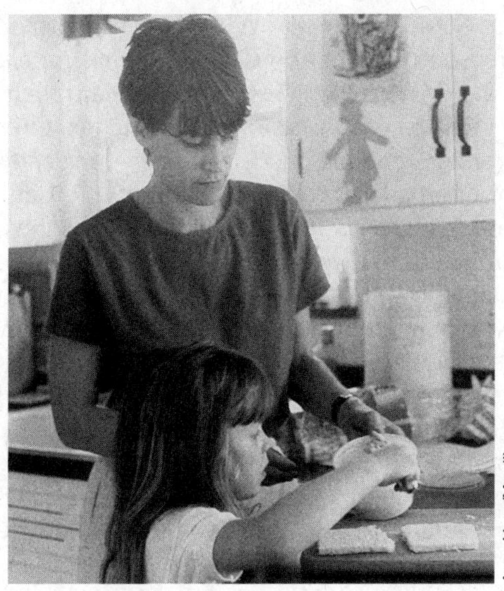

This mother is encouraging her child's self-reliance.

and motivates them to try new things. By and large, parental encouragement of children helps them to have the courage not to be perfect. The strategy of encouragement fits into the democratic model of parenting by shifting the parental focus from children's mistakes to what parents like and appreciate about their children. Parents encourage their children when they (a) avoid placing value judgments on them, (b) focus on their feelings, (c) concentrate on process rather than outcome, and (d) separate children's worth from their accomplishments or their mistakes (Dinkmeyer & McKay, 1989).

Avoiding Value Judgments of Children. The most beneficial effect of encouragement is that it does not place value judgments on children. Too often, when parents make positive comments about their children, those comments are laden with negative values and opinions and as such do not assist their children in believing in themselves. When parents use the technique of encouragement, value-laden words are replaced by nonevaluative phrases designed to assist children to continue trying when things are difficult and to feel proud of their efforts as well as their achievements.

Focusing on the Feelings of Children. To help children feel encouraged, parents need to value how children feel about what they do and who they are. Instead of sending messages of encouragement that focus on a child's feelings and beliefs, parents frequently convey messages of **praise** that emphasize the parents' feelings. If, for example, a child has achieved a particular goal, parents often praise the child by saying: "I'm proud of you." To convert that statement of praise into a statement of encouragement, the focus must shift to a focus on the feelings of the child. Examples of statements of encouragement are, "You must feel proud of yourself," or "Well, I guess you feel pretty good about that," or "How do you feel about that?"

Focusing on Process Rather Than Outcome. When parents wait until their children have achieved a desired outcome before noticing their efforts, they miss out on the opportunity to motivate them as they are working toward their objective. To reach an established goal requires ability and effort, and excellence develops along many steps. Encouragement is, thus, more valuable along the way than it is after the child has already attained success. A statement such as "Look at the progress you've made in putting together that model" focuses on the process rather than the outcome and encourages children to persevere in the face of a challenge. Even when children have achieved a goal, it is more encouraging for them when parents focus on the process that led to the realization of that objective rather than focusing only on the outcome. After a child has completed a project, an encouraging statement (which focuses on process), such as "You really worked hard on that science project, and your hard work paid off," is better than words of praise (that focus on outcome) such as "Good job." Finally, as recommended by Popkin (1987), parents should provide encouragement for children's efforts regardless of whether or not these efforts result in success. An example of a statement of encouragement that concentrates on improvement, rather than perfection, is something like this: "James, you are really improving in your reading. I can tell a big difference in the last few weeks."

Separating Children's Worth from Their Accomplishments. Although it is important to admire children's accomplishments and to encourage the steps along the way to success, it is essential that parents make it clear that they love and appreciate their children independent of what they do. Suggested ways for parents to separate their children's worth from their accomplishments include: (a) taking the time to sit and talk with their children, (b) listening to their children's funny stories as well as their tales of woe, and (c) telling their children (in words and behaviors) that they are loved and fun to be with (Popkin, 1987).

Separating Children's Worth from Their Mistakes. Just as children's worth is different from their accomplishments, their worth is unrelated to their mistakes or failures. Mistakes, such as misbehavior, do not reflect a lack of worth but are actually an aspect of growth and development. An error or a slipup by a child might show that child what not to do in the future, which is a valuable lesson (Popkin, 1987). An example of a way to respond to children's mistakes includes the following statements. "Don't worry about having made a mistake. Making mistakes is how we learn. Instead of blaming yourself, let's see how we can correct it."

Attitudes and Behaviors That Discourage Children. To assist parents in becoming more encouraging to their children, Dinkmeyer and McKay (1989) described several attitudes and behaviors that parents need to eliminate because these behaviors discourage children: (a) negative expectations of their children, (b) unreasonably high demands of their children, (c) competition between or among their children, (d) being overly ambitious, and (e) the double standard (see Figure 4.1).

Negative Expectations
One of the most powerful forces in human relationships is expectations, and parents sometimes express negative expectations of their children in their day-to-day relationships with them (by word and by gesture). When parents do not believe a child will succeed at something, they subtly (and sometimes not so subtly) communicate that belief to the child. The typical result of negative parental expectations is that the child behaves in the manner expected (a self-fulfilling prophecy).

Unusually High Standards
Parents sometimes fail to recognize the positive qualities in their children and communicate to their children that, whatever they do, they should do better. That type of communication sends a message to children that their accomplishments are never quite good enough. Furthermore, parents sometimes expect performance beyond the ages and abilities of their children.

Promoting Competition Between or Among Siblings
Children are discouraged when parents promote competition between or among them by praising one child's success while ignoring another child's efforts. Also, parental gestures or facial expressions can generate competition as much as parental comments. If parents practice the use of encouragement with all their children, however, competition among children decreases and cooperation increases.

Overly Ambitious Parents
Overly ambitious parents expect their children to demonstrate a high level of excellence but that parental goal actually inhibits children from boldly trying new experiences. Because they have come to understand that their parents' standards are very high regarding their accomplishments, children of overly ambitious parents might not try things unless they feel confident of their success.

The Double Standard
Some parents practice a double standard by expressing the belief that it is okay to deny their children the rights and privileges they themselves enjoy. Some ways of avoiding the double standard consist of having rules that affect all family members such as, "family members do not yell at or hit each other," or "cursing or swearing is not practiced in this house."

FIGURE 4.1 Parental Attitudes and Behaviors That Discourage Children
Source: Adapted from *Systematic Training for Effective Parenting: The Parent's Handbook* (3rd ed.), by D. Dinkmeyer and G. McKay, 1989, American Guidance Services, Circle Pines, MN.

Attitudes and Behaviors That Encourage Children. Avoiding attitudes and behaviors that discourage children is an essential first step toward the encouragement of children. The next step is to replace discouraging patterns of interactions with encouraging ones. Attitudes and behaviors of parents that encourage children include (a) appreciating each of their children's uniqueness, (b) showing confidence in their children, (c) building on their children's strengths, (d) avoiding sending mixed messages to their children, and (e) using humor in their parent–child interactions (Popkin, 1987; see Figure 4.2).

Appreciate Each Child's Uniqueness

It is encouraging for children when their parents take an interest in each child's activities, get to know what is interesting to each child, and show an awareness of what each child thinks about things, including favorite foods, colors, and so on. Examples: "Grace, we're having your favorite food tonight—spaghetti," and "Philip, you seem to enjoy that activity."

Show Confidence in Children by Giving Them Responsibility

Parents show confidence in their children when they give them responsibility. When assigning responsibilities to children, though, the parent needs to be aware of the child's level of ability and mindful of the goal the parent wants to accomplish in assigning the child certain responsibilities. Example: Allowing children to have a puppy, provided they assume some of the duties associated with feeding and caring for the pet.

Show Confidence in Children by Asking for Their Advice

When parents seek their children's advice, they send the message that they have assurance in their children's knowledge and judgment. Consulting children on their opinion bolsters their children's sense of self-worth and encourages them to speak up to parents regarding their ideas and beliefs. Example: "Brandon, come look at this map with us and help us decide which route would be best for us to take on our trip."

Show Confidence in Children by Avoiding Rescuing Them

It is discouraging for children when parents do things for them on a regular basis that they are capable of doing by themselves. Parents encourage their children by demonstrating confidence in their ability to complete a task. Example: "I have confidence in your ability to make that decision for yourself," or "I think you can do it on your own but if you'd like a little help, let me know."

Build on a Child's Strengths to Promote Positive Behaviors

A way to focus attention on a child's strengths is to acknowledge those things that the child does well. An example of building on the child's strengths is included in the following request: "Kenny, how about showing your brother, Todd, how to tie his Cub Scout tie." In that example, the parent fosters cooperation between the brothers while promoting the self-esteem of the older child.

Build on a Child's Strengths While Disapproving of Behaviors

Even when a child misbehaves, parents can focus on the child's strength while expressing disapproval of the child's misbehavior. Example: "Nicole, I'm glad that you want to be able to stand up for yourself; that is an important strength but hitting is not acceptable behavior. Let's talk about how you could stand up for yourself without resorting to fighting."

Avoid Sending Mixed Messages

Children receive mixed messages when parents make qualifying or moralizing comments to them, such as "So, why don't you clean your room like this all the time," or "Well, it's about time," or "See what you can do when you try." These qualifying or demoralizing statements do not fall into the realm of encouragement and are actually discouraging to children.

Continued

Use Humor
Parents who can see things from a humorous point of view encourage children to reconsider rigid perceptions of themselves and other persons. The use of humor helps parents and children to relate to the challenges of life in a more relaxed manner. When humor is present in families, there are fewer catastrophes because both parents and children are aware of other ways to look at each situation.

FIGURE 4.2 Parental Attitudes and Behaviors That Encourage Children

Source: Adapted from *Systematic Training for Effective Parenting: The Parent's Handbook* (3rd ed.), by D. Dinkmeyer and G. McKay, 1989, American Guidance Services, Circle Pines, MN; *New Beginnings: Skills for Single Parents. Parent's Manual*, by D. Dinkmeyer, G. McKay, and J. McKay, 1987, Champaign, IL: Research Press; and *Active Parenting: Teaching Cooperation, Courage, and Responsibility*, 1987, San Francisco: Perennial Library.

Thinking Critically

Suppose your 4-year-old child had made his bed for the first time, and, because this was his first time, it was not as neat as it is when you make it. How might you compose a response to the child that represents an example of encouragement?

Research Findings Linking the Use of Encouragement to Positive Outcomes. Harter (1999) recommends that parents use the language of encouragement to promote children's sense of pride in their accomplishments, thereby nurturing their success. The link between parental encouragement and children's success has been observed in various settings. An illustration of the relation between parental encouragement and children's attainment of success is when parents encourage their children's involvement in sports programs. The findings of Green and Chalip (1997) demonstrate that children's level of performance and feelings of success are related to their parents' satisfaction with and encouragement of their performance. Parental encouragement has also been associated with higher college entrance examination scores for adolescents (Furr, 1998). In a more recent study, Hill, Kondryn, and Mackie (2003) found that, for children with cancer, parental encouragement plays a distinctive role in the promotion of social relationships outside the family.

Four Pluses and a Wish—A Strategy for Motivating Children's Compliance

From picking up toys to studying for homework, parents are highly interested in gaining their children's cooperation. When attempting to get a child to comply with parental requests, it is helpful to determine if the behavior being asked of the child is within the child's capability to perform. It is valuable as well for parents to know how to make a request of a child that is designed to gain the child's cooperation while respecting the child's feelings. A technique developed by William Purkey (Purkey, Schmidt, & Benedict, 1990) known as **Four Pluses and a Wish** is an excellent choice for motivating children's cooperation because it contains an affirming exchange that is far more likely to inspire cooperation than is the typical parental command (see Figure 4.3).

In using Four Pluses and a Wish, parents should be certain that their voice tone, facial expression, and body language convey friendliness toward the child. They, then, must take a moment to generate a request that acknowledges and affirms the child before making their request. The effectiveness of the strategy of Four Pluses and a Wish is that children who feel respected are far more motivated to comply with parental wishes than are children who do not feel valued. Using this strategy benefits parents by assisting them in becoming aware of the ways in which their facial expressions, body language, tone of voice, and verbal statements impact their children's willingness to comply with parental wishes.

Four pluses and a wish might be used to inspire the cooperation of a child in the following ways.

Plus 1—Smile

The parent approaches the child with a smiling face (Plus 1). Plus 1 might sound very elementary but it is exceedingly powerful. Children monitor facial expressions from birth and are keenly attuned to parental moods.

Plus 2—Relaxed Body Language

When making a request of a child, it is also important to use relaxed body language that minimizes the psychological distance between the parent and the child (Plus 2). Stiff body language, such as crossed arms or crossed legs, are examples of ways that parents sometimes establish barriers between themselves and their children and communicate a lack of acceptance toward the child.

Plus 3—Say the Child's Name

When making a request of a child, saying that child's name while using an approving voice tone (Plus 3) personalizes the request and conveys respect for the child.

Plus 4—Pay a Compliment to the Child

Then, before making a request from the child, it is important for parents to affirm the child by paying a compliment to the child (Plus 4). At that point, the parent might say something nice about the child or what the child is presently involved in.

The Wish

Only after providing four pluses for the child, does the parent make the request (The Wish).

FIGURE 4.3 Four Pluses and a Wish

Source: Adapted from *Invitational Learning for Counseling and Development*, by W. Purkey, J. J. Schmidt, and G. C. Benedict, 1990, Ann Arbor, MI: ERIC Counseling & Personnel Services Clearinghouse.

Three examples of the use of Four Pluses and a Wish are as follows: Five-year-old Mario is busy playing with his toys and Dad wants him to put his toys away and get ready for bed. Commands such as "Mario, put your toys away and get ready for bed" or "Time for bed, Mario" are not likely to be highly motivating for a 5-year-old boy who is highly focused on playing with his toys. First of all, Mario is less interested in going to bed than he is in playing. Second, a transition from one activity to another is often difficult for children and particularly problematic for preschool children. Using Four Pluses and a Wish, Dad might walk over to Mario with a smile on his face (Plus 1), stoop down (Plus 2), and (in a friendly voice) say "Hi Mario" (Plus 3). Then Dad might compliment Mario by saying "Wow, you've built a great fort; tell me about it" (Plus 4). At that point, Mario is likely to tell his Dad about his project because his Dad has shown an interest in what Mario is doing. After a brief friendly exchange, Dad states the request (A Wish) as follows: "Mario, in a little while (or about 10 minutes), it will be time for you to put your toys away and start getting ready for bed. I will tell you when it is time." Although this example is of a parent and a preschool boy, the technique is effective with children (and adults) of all ages.

Thinking Critically

Suppose you want your school-age children to help you rake the leaves in the fall. Using the technique of Four Pluses and a Wish, how might you request their assistance?

Research Findings Emphasizing Respectful Treatment of Children. Parents use different types of speech when interacting with their children: supportive, directive, and negative. Supportive speech consists of respectful ways of speaking to children as well as giving children the time and opportunity to reply to parental requests (Leaper, Anderson, & Sanders, 1998). The technique of Four Pluses and a Wish represents an example of a way in which parents use respectful speech in making requests of their children. In exploring the links between parent, child, and peer communication patterns, Black and Logan (1995) found a significant difference in supportive speech between parents of peer-rejected children in comparison to parents of popular children. They reported that parents of rejected children use less supportive speech in making requests of their children. Specifically, those parents make significantly more requests of their children and do not give their children time to reply to their requests.

The Concept of Belongingness and Children's Goals of Misbehavior

Children's behavior is labeled misbehavior when it is found to be unacceptable by parents or other adults; however, parents and other adults are more or less tolerant of a wide range of children's behavior (Heath, 1993). For example, one parent might label as *misbehavior* the young child's inability to sit still or stand in line for an extended period of time. Another parent might not require the same behavior from the young child due to the realization that young children are, by nature, very active and curious. Furthermore, some parents regard noncompliance and defiance as misbehavior without consideration of the child's ability or motivation to comply with stated expectations. Dreikurs (1972) provided an approach for understanding the feelings and goals that underlie children's misbehavior by emphasizing the ways in which the socialization process frequently contributes to children's misconduct. He maintained that the chief human goal is belongingness and that in order to achieve a sense of belongingness, children often pursue four secondary goals of misbehavior: attention, power, revenge, and a display of inadequacy (see Figure 4.4). The belief of children that

Goal 1—Misbehavior Designed to Gain Attention

Children feel they have a place in the family, belongingness, when they receive sufficient attention from other members of the family, especially their parents. Based on their high needs for attention, children behave in a variety of ways to gain their parents attention and much of that behavior is appropriate. When parents and/or other family members fail to provide children with sufficient attention, however, children are likely to engage in misbehavior that is designed to attract parental attention.

Goal 2—Misbehavior Designed to Gain Power

To achieve a sense of belongingness in one's family, children need to feel as if they have influence and choices regarding matters pertaining to themselves, such as what they wear, what they eat, and what behaviors they will engage in. Furthermore, children need to feel that they are able to have influence on the interactions of the family group, such as being included in activities the family is engaged in as well as having a say as to how and when those activities are carried out. When children are not consulted or given a say regarding matters that affect them directly and/or what is going on in the family, they tend to feel powerless and might misbehave to regain a sense of control.

Goal 3—Misbehavior Related to the Goal of Revenge

The goal of revenge emerges from frustrated attempts to seek attention and power. Children misbehaving with the goal of revenge are hurt due to past reactions to their behaviors seeking attention and power. Out of their hurt feelings, they engage in misbehavior clearly recognized as vengeful, because their goal is to take revenge on others who have hurt them.

Goal 4—Misbehavior That Reflects a Display of Inadequacy

Children whose behaviors reflect a display of inadequacy are those who are no longer engaging in behavior with the goals of seeking attention or power. Those children are convinced of their lack of belongingness based on their inability to get the attention and power they need in their lives. They have, therefore, given up trying to gain attention and/or power and feel powerless to seek revenge. Attitudes of despair and a stance of "What's the use?" are displayed in various areas of those children's lives. Children who exhibit a display of inadequacy are often viewed as lazy, unkempt, or unmotivated.

FIGURE 4.4 The Four Goals of Misbehavior

Source: Adapted from *Discipline without Tears,* by R. Dreikurs, 1972, New York: Hawthorne.

belongingness and acceptance within the family will be attained through their misbehavior is not realized, though, because unacceptable behavior generally alienates one from others. In recognition of that dilemma, Dreikurs and Soltz (1964) pointed out that children's **four goals of misbehavior** are mistaken goals whereby events are often misinterpreted, mistaken conclusions are drawn, and faulty decisions are made.

Recognizing the Underlying Goals of Children's Misbehavior. Whereas children are generally unaware of the mistaken goals underlying their misbehavior, parents might learn to recognize those underlying goals by the effects of the misbehavior on others. As noted by Dreikurs and Soltz (1964), what a parent is inclined to do in response to a child's behavior is generally consistent with the child's goal underlying that behavior. Parental reactions that correspond to children's goals of misbehavior include giving attention, engaging in power struggles, seeking retaliation, or giving up in despair. Although the method for recognizing the goals of misbehavior is clear and simple, it requires that parents observe carefully not only their children's undesirable behavior but also their own responses to that behavior.

If the parent's typical response to a particular infraction is to provide attention (positive or negative), then a bid for attention is probably the underlying goal behind the child's misbehavior. If the parent becomes angry and loses control, or is inclined to become angry and lose control in relation to unacceptable behavior, the underlying goal of the child is most likely to gain or regain power. When a child's actions result in a parent losing control, then the child gains control or power. If a parent feels hurt by a child's words or other deliberate acts designed to hurt others (such as damaging property), the parent's reaction reflects an attempt by the child to hurt others (revenge). The child's motivation to seek revenge is due to the child's feelings of hurt, born of a perceived lack of attention or power. When a parent sees the child as generally unmotivated (not doing homework, not keeping up personal hygiene, or showing little interest in activities), the child is probably expressing a belief that efforts will not be noticed, appreciated, or rewarded (Dreikurs & Soltz, 1964).

Thinking Critically

Daylon and Dakota, who are brothers, generally get along pretty well. The older brother, Daylon, has recently made the softball team, looks great in his new uniform, is playing well on the team, and has been the main topic of conversation in the family for a couple of weeks. One day, Dakota unexpectedly throws Daylon's baseball cap in the trash. Upon learning of the incident, the parents are disappointed with Dakota's behavior. What do you think was the goal of Dakota's misbehavior? Explain your answer.

Parental Goals for Prevention of Children's Misbehavior. After recognizing the underlying goals of children's misbehavior, parents are in the position to assist their children to achieve a sense of belongingness without resorting to misbehavior. As recommended by Dreikurs and Soltz (1964), the strategy for preventing misbehavior consists of three parental objectives: (a) changing one's responses to the child's unacceptable behavior so that the action does not achieve the goal it is designed to achieve, (b) assisting the child in becoming aware of the underlying goal motivating the misbehavior, and (c) helping children who are prone to misbehavior to achieve a sense of belongingness through appropriate means, so that they do not resort to misconduct to achieve attention or power.

Changing One's Response to a Child's Misbehavior. To prevent their children's misbehavior, parents need to be certain that their responses to their children do not contribute to unacceptable behavior. Specifically, the parent should not (a) give attention to their children's misbehavior designed to attract parental attention, (b) react angrily or lose control in response to their children's behavior that typically contributes to parental anger or a loss of control, (c) focus on or expose hurt feelings in response to their children's misbehavior based on the goal of revenge, and (d) give up in despair when their children seem unmotivated.

Thinking Critically

Suppose you observed a child who repeatedly knocked over her sister's blocks even though that action gained a lot of negative responses from others. Which of the goals of misbehavior do you think the child is using and how would you recommend that the parent deal with this misbehavior based on the preceding paragraph?

Helping Children to Become Aware of Their Goals of Misbehavior. Assisting the misbehaving child in becoming aware of the underlying goal of misbehavior is sometimes accomplished by calling the child's attention to what seems to be the objective of the child's behavior. Dreikurs and Soltz (1964) referred to children's awareness of their goal of misbehavior as the **recognition reflex**. An example of that approach might be to say to the child, "Josephine, do you think you knock over Gabriel's blocks to get my attention?" When parents help children to become aware of the underlying goals of their misbehavior, they prompt them to realize why they act in ways that parents and others consider unacceptable. If the technique is to be successful, though, it must be expressed in a manner that does not communicate a value judgment of the child nor sound reproachful to the child. If children are not smarting from the sting of disapproval, they might be helped to understand the reasons behind their misbehavior (which typically troubles them as well as their parents).

Helping Children to Achieve Belongingness Without Resorting to Misconduct. When parents realize that their children need to be able to get their parents' attention and to have a sense of power in order to feel that they have a place in the family, they are in a position to help their children meet those needs without resorting to misbehavior. To assist children in their quest for belongingness, parents should provide sufficient attention to their children while ensuring that children feel as if they have a say in what is happening in their lives.

Prevention of Children's Misbehavior Designed to Gain Attention. To prevent their children's misbehavior that is designed to gain attention, parents should look for opportunities to give their children positive attention for behaviors that meet parental standards. Sometimes, parents wait until their children behave in unacceptable ways to notice what they are saying or doing. The child thus learns that misconduct will capture the attention of the parent. Although it is beneficial when parents respond favorably to a child's appropriate behavior, it is not necessary to wait for desired behavior to occur before giving attention to the child. When providing attention to their children to prevent them from resorting to misbehavior, parents should remember that attention might be given to their children at any time those children are not misbehaving. It is important for children to know that parents are interested in them, not only when they are doing what parents expect but also just *for being*. Examples of giving attention to a child *for being* include talking with children about what they are feeling or doing and acknowledging children when they come into a room (Heath, 1993).

Prevention of Children's Misbehavior Designed to Gain a Sense of Power. To prevent children's acts of misbehavior designed to achieve a sense of power, parents should provide children with experiences that endow them with a feeling of empowerment. Giving choices to children is one way in which to empower them. For small children, a parent might ask, "Do you want to wear your red shirt or your yellow shirt?" For older children, a parent might solicit their input regarding what to have for dinner by saying, "What do you want for dinner tonight, chicken or spaghetti?" There are a variety of ways to empower children and every opportunity to make choices, or to be heard on their views of things, boosts their self-esteem. Empowering experiences help children to feel a sense of belongingness, thereby preventing misbehavior designed to gain power.

Empowering Children: What the Research Shows. Empowerment of children consists of granting them autonomy, and autonomy granting by parents has been consistently related to positive outcomes for children. It has been shown that when parents are highly supportive of their children's drives toward autonomy, their children become bolder and more competent individuals (Deater-Deckard, 2000). Parental empowerment has been linked as well with children's ability to regulate their behavior. For example, Clark et al. (2002) found that autonomy granting by parents was negatively related to the acting out of anger by adolescents.

Mike Peters/Silver Burdett Ginn.

Finding the time to talk and listen to children is an extremely effective parenting strategy.

EFFECTIVE PARENT–CHILD COMMUNICATION AS A PARENTING STRATEGY

In addition to having a variety of strategies that are designed to motivate children toward appropriate behavior, parents are best equipped to foster the healthy development of their children when they are able to create an atmosphere of healthy dialogue. Effective parent–child communication is the basis of positive parent–child interactions and high self-esteem in children. Furthermore, effective communication between parents and children prevents problematic behavior and helps children understand how to interact effectively with others. Thomas Gordon (1975) developed a valuable model for parent–child communication that has been used in various parenting programs for over 30 years. This approach consists of the strategies of problem ownership, active listening, I-messages, and conflict negotiation. The first three approaches focus on prevention of and discussion of problems and will be presented in this part of the chapter. The fourth approach, which focuses on the resolution of conflict in the parent–child relationship, will be explained later in the chapter.

Problem Ownership

Knowing when to use the techniques of active listening or I-messages depends on the ability to sort out "who has the problem" when a problem has arisen in a relationship. The ability to identify **problem ownership** prevents parents from blaming their children for problems that have arisen in the parent–child relationship or from believing that parents must assume responsibility for solving their children's troubles. To establish who owns the problem, one needs to determine who is distressed by the situation. If the child is troubled by events that have occurred or are occurring in a relationship, the child owns the problem. When the child has the problem, it is appropriate for the parent to use the technique of active listening to respond to the child's feelings. In situations in which the behaviors of the child or events in the parent–child relationship are bothersome to the parent, then the parent owns the problem. In that situation, the most effective technique to use for communicating the parent's feelings to the child is a three-part I-message.

Thinking Critically

Travis and Nicole have been told that they may have no more than three friends in the house after school and that they and their friends must clean up after themselves if they have a snack. For several days in a row, their parents have come home and found that Travis, Nicole, and their friends have made snacks and left a mess in the kitchen. Their parents are feeling irritated with the situation. In this example, who do you think has the problem? Is it Travis and Nicole, their friends, or their parents? Why?

Active Listening

Active listening is a compelling communication strategy that consists of a verbal response containing no actual message from the parent but rather a mirroring back of the child's previous expression. Basically, the parent listens for, paraphrases, and feeds back the child's previous message but the feedback is not merely a tape recording of actual words bouncing back. Instead, the parent listens to and reflects back (in the parent's own words) the feelings of the child as well as the content of the child's message the parent thinks is being expressed. It takes practice and commitment to be able to effectively use the skill of active listening. To actively listen to a child, a parent needs to listen carefully (actively) to the words the child is speaking while attending to the child's voice tone and body language. For example, a child might burst into a room, with tears in his eyes, and exclaim, "I hate my teacher!" Although the child's verbal statement, in that example, does not convey that he is upset or what happened with the teacher, the child's voice tone, body language, and tears unmistakably express both feelings and content. A parental rejoinder that reflects having actively listened to the child might be "Something happened with Mrs. Smith that made you very upset."

There are two main challenges involved in learning to use the strategy of active listening. The first challenge is the development of an affective vocabulary, which includes a range of feeling words. "Boy, you're upset or angry" might be a helpful response to a child in some instances but a child has a varied assortment of emotions that need parental responses. For example, these might be: aggravated, irritated, embarrassed, left out, proud, happy, great, and so on. The biggest hurdle to being effective in the use of active listening, though, lies in the parent's tendency to use **communication roadblocks** (see Figure 4.5) instead of active listening. Communication roadblocks bring to a halt the free flow of problem sharing, whereas active listening communicates to children that the parent hears what has happened as well as how children feel about what has happened.

To develop skills in active listening, it is essential that parents become aware of communication roadblocks and avoid using them when the child is attempting to

1. **Ordering, Directing, Commanding**
   "Stop whining"
   "Don't play with that boy anymore."
2. **Warning, Admonishing, Threatening**
   "If you can't play without arguing, you will have to be separated."
3. **Moralizing, Preaching**
   "You shouldn't complain so much."
4. **Advising, Giving Suggestions or Solutions**
   "If I were you, I would . . ."
   "Why don't you play with someone else."
5. **Teaching, Instructing**
   "Let me tell you how to handle this."
6. **Judging, Criticizing, Blaming**
   "You're being very careless."
   "What did you do to Tommy to make him mad at you?"
7. **Praising, Buttering Up**
   "You're usually very nice to your friends."
   "You're such a nice person. I'm sure you can handle this."
8. **Name Calling, Ridiculing**
   "Shame on you for being so naughty."
   "Boy, you are getting to be such a whiner."
9. **Interpreting, Diagnosing, Psychoanalyzing**
   "You're just jealous of your brother."
   "You always want to bother me when I'm tired.
10. **Reassuring, Sympathizing, Supporting**
    "Don't worry, I'm sure it's going to be alright."
    "Cheer up, why don't you. Lots of people have bigger problems than that."
11. **Probing, Questioning**
    "Where (or when) did that happen?
    "Why did your friend say that to you?
12. **Diverting, Distracting, Humoring**
    Walking away, checking the time, or changing the subject when the child is talking.

FIGURE 4.5 Roadblocks to Communication

Source: Adapted from *Parent Effectiveness Training,* by T. Gordon, 1976, New York: New American Library.

communicate a problem. The use of communication roadblocks by a parent results in the child feeling as if the parent has not heard, is not interested in hearing, or does not care about the child's feelings. Even when the parent avoids each of the communication roadblocks and provides accurate verbal feedback related to the child's feelings and the content of the message, the child might not feel heard if the parent's facial expression, body stance, and voice tone do not communicate warmth and understanding.

Using Active Listening to Respond to Nonproblematic Behavior. Even though active listening is a valuable strategy for letting children know that parents hear and care about the problems they express, this approach is equally effective for responding to children's efforts to convey their feelings related to positive experiences in their lives. In response to the child who runs into the room and says, "Dad, I hit a home run, today!" the parent can send the following active listening response. "Wow, you're pretty excited about hitting a home run. Good for you!"

I-Messages

As previously explained, when the parent owns the problem, an **" I-message"** is used for the purpose of expressing the parent's feelings regarding the child's behavior. *I* messages are not blameful; hence, they are not *you* messages. This is the main objective of the strategy, not to blame the child for the feelings the parent is having regarding a particular action or lack of action of the child. I-messages have three parts: (a) the feelings of the sender, (b) the unacceptable behavior of the recipient, and (c) the tangible effect of the recipient's behavior on the sender. An example of an effective three-part I-message goes something like this: "Kelly, I have a problem I would like to discuss with you" (problem ownership). "When I went into the kitchen and saw the peanut butter and jelly jars with the lids off, and the bread and milk not put away (unacceptable behavior of the recipient), I felt frustrated (feelings of the sender) because I knew that I would have to either clean up the clutter myself or ask you to do it" (tangible effect of the recipient's behavior on the sender).

Notice that the parent in this case has not sent a blameful you-message such as: "Kelly, you never clean up after yourself. Get in there and clean up that mess you made." Children and adolescents are much more likely to respond favorably to a parental I-message delivered in a warm, nonthreatening manner than to an angry-sounding, blameful you-message. When children and adolescents feel parents are criticizing their personalities (you-messages), they feel put down and misunderstood by their parents. In these cases, they are likely to respond defensively. The purpose of using I-messages is to express dissatisfaction with a child's behavior, not to attack the child. Sending a three-part I-message to inform a child of how that child's behavior affects the parent might sound as if the parent is telling the child what the child already should know. People in relationships often believe that others ought to be more considerate without being told, should know how some behavior would affect them, and so on. Even though it would be wonderful if all family members could guess how other family members feel and act accordingly, that simply does not occur in real life. People in close relationships are continuously affected by each other's behavior and do all sorts of things without considering the ways in which their actions affect the people they care about.

Although children's behavior is sometimes unacceptable to parents, the behaviors of parents (as well as siblings) often cause difficulties for children. Thus, it is important that both parents and children learn to use effective communication skills. One of the positive outcomes of the parental use of I-messages is that parents model for their children ways in which to express their feelings related to others' behaviors that their children find bothersome. When children learn to use I-messages, they have a skill that makes it easier for dealing with the annoying behaviors of other family members as well as the behaviors of peers.

Preventive I-Messages. Gordon devised the strategy of the I-message to provide parents with an effective way to address problems that arise in the parent–child relationship because these problems are often challenging for parents and are sometimes handled in ways that are hurtful to both parents and their children. I-messages are useful as well for preventing difficulties in the relationship. As a prevention technique, parents can use I-messages to communicate their positive feelings regarding behaviors of the child that they appreciate.

Let us revisit 12-year-old Kelly and her Mom on the day after Mom used an effective I-message to tell Kelly how she felt about things being left out in the kitchen. The next day, Kelly is sitting in the living room eating her usual after-school peanut butter and jelly sandwich and drinking a glass of milk. Mom comes in the door and Kelly, who has a big smile on her face, says "Hi, Mom." Kelly watches as Mom goes into the kitchen, because she has cleaned up after herself and is hoping Mom will notice. When Mom enters the kitchen and sees that the bread, peanut butter, jelly, and milk have all been put away, she goes back into the living room. With a warm smile, she sends her daughter a positive three-part I-message: "Kelly, when I went into the kitchen, I noticed that you had put away all the things you used to make your snack, and that you cleaned the counter as well (behaviors on the part of the recipient that have not caused a problem), I was so pleased (feelings of the sender). I really appreciate your cleaning up after yourself because that makes things easier for me" (tangible effect of child's behavior on the mother).

As a final point, when parents use I-messages to address or prevent problems, it is important that they have a friendly facial expression, a warm voice tone, and nonthreatening body language. Furthermore, it is essential that the message be specific regarding the behavior in question. Children and adolescents are often confused about what parents are trying to tell them because parents sometimes talk in generalities to their children with statements such as, "I want you to clean up after yourself," which could mean a variety of things. An effective I-message, on the other hand, does not threaten or attack the child nor does it confuse the child. In the case of the preventive I-message, the parent actually affirms the child. Even when no problem has occurred in a particular area, parents might send I-messages to prevent unacceptable behavior in the future. An example of a preventive I-message is, "I like to know where you are when school is out so that I know that you are okay."

Research Findings Showing the Value of Effective Parent–Child Communication. Effective parent–child communication impacts the development of children in a variety of ways at all developmental levels. An interesting illustration of the influence of parent–child communication patterns is that these verbal patterns are often reflected in the dialogues their children have with siblings and friends (Woodward & Markman, 1998). The quality of parent–child verbal exchanges also affects children's developmental outcomes. For instance, open versus problem parent–child communication has been found to be related to children's higher self-esteem and more positive coping strategies (Jackson, Bijstra, Oostra, & Bosnia, 1998). Just as effective parent–child communication is linked to positive child outcomes, ineffective parent–child communication is associated with problems in the parent–child relationship. For instance, Arnett (2004) suggests that some of the arguments that occur between parents and their adolescent children might stem from unexpressed parental concerns. Furthermore, researchers have found that when given the opportunity, children and adolescents are willing to talk to parents. As a case in point, Richardson (2004) found that most young adolescents were able to identify topics they would like to discuss with their parents including their unhappiness with parental conflict, desire for more closeness to their parents, and struggles with autonomy.

GUIDANCE AS REINFORCEMENT AND MODELING

In addition to having skills for encouraging and motivating children toward desirable behavior, being able to understand the goals underlying children's misbehavior, and having effective communication skills, parents also benefit from understanding ways in which to reinforce children for appropriate behavior and being aware of their roles as models for their children's behavior.

Reinforcement of Approved Behavior

Parents benefit from knowing the ways in which **positive reinforcement** influences children's behavioral choices. Theoretically, Skinner (1974) explained that any consequence that increases the likelihood that the behavior will be repeated is reinforcing. Reinforcements might include special treats or desired activities or various forms of social approval. The primary value of using reinforcement as a socialization strategy is because it is far more effective to reinforce approved behavior than punishing disapproved behavior. In using the technique of reinforcement, parents need to be aware of the conditions that facilitate learning. First, the reinforcing consequences must be noticeable to the child, which requires that the child is paying attention to the reinforcement being presented. For instance, if a parent uses social approval in the form of a smile and a comment after the young child has picked up her toys, it is helpful if the parent stoops down in front of the child so that the child can see the parent's smiling face and hear the parent's reinforcing comment. When a parent says, "Wow, nice job" to a child who is flying out the back door, the positive comment is not an effective reinforcement because it is not noticeable. Second, reinforcements of specific behaviors must be consistent to be successful. Parents who are attempting to help their children to develop the habit of wiping their feet on a mat when coming into the house, for instance, should consistently reinforce their children after feet wiping (by making an approving remark) until that behavior becomes habitual. Reinforcing once or twice and then resorting to the commonly used parental phrase of "I told you to wipe your feet when you come into the house" is not nearly as effective as gentle reminders and consistent reinforcement.

Effective use of reinforcement requires that parents understand that the consequence of reinforcement always maintains or increases the frequency of the occurrence of a behavior. An example of a positive reinforcement would be Mom saying to her very young children in an approving voice, "Kenny and Christopher, I see that you are cooperating with each other by sharing your toys." The fact that the parent made the remark does not tell us if the response was reinforcing for the children. To determine if the remark was reinforcing, we need to observe its effect on the children's subsequent behavior. If, after hearing that remark, Kenny and Christopher continue to share and play even more cooperatively, the remark was a positive reinforcement.

To use positive reinforcement to maintain or increase desired behavior, it is important to bear in mind that what is reinforcing varies from one individual to another and from one time to another. An illustration of what is reinforcing being individually determined is apparent in the following example: Two young children, Jangjie and Maho, are offered chocolate bars for picking up papers along the side of a street. Jangjie loves chocolate and, consequently, finds this treat reinforcing as shown by her offering to pick up papers again the next week. Maho, however, does not like sweets and certainly does not like chocolate. Maho does not offer to pick up papers again, and when it is suggested that she do so, she replies that she would rather not. An example of how reinforcement varies from one time to another is provided by the next illustration: Twelve-year-old Christine knocks on her neighbor's door and offers to cut the neighbor's grass for $20. She does a great job, gets her $20, and comes back the following week to ask if she can cut the neighbor's grass again. That $20 is reinforcing to Christine is evident by her returning to ask to cut the grass again. A few years pass and Christine, now 16, has a part-time job and a very busy social life. The neighbor sees her on the street and offers her $20 to cut the grass. Christine answers that she is sorry but just does not have the time—same consequence, same girl, different time, and changed circumstances. What was reinforcing for Christine as a 12-years-old is not reinforcing at 16.

Despite the fact that what is reinforcing varies from one individual to another and from one time to another, a consequence that is reinforcing for most children, most of the time, is social approval. Social approval, which consists of providing positive attention, approval and affection, is the most successful type of reinforcement a parent might use. Guidelines for using social approval as a means of reinforcement include using eye contact, being physically close, smiling, focusing on the behavior of the child, and immediate delivery.

Research Findings Demonstrating the Effectiveness of Reinforcement. The relation between parental reinforcement and children's behavior is seen in a number of ways in which parents might encourage young children's self-reliance. For example, Mauro and Harris (2000) found that young children's ability to delay gratification is enhanced when parents use an authoritative parenting approach. The conclusion reached by these researchers was that the behaviors associated with authoritative parenting serve as a reinforcement of children's positive behavior. The value of the use of social reinforcement in the parent–child relationship is not limited to the effects of parents on children. For example, Hyun, Lee, and Yoo (2002) demonstrated that when family members perform helpful activities for new mothers, including assistance in child care, these behaviors serve as social reinforcement of the new mother and enhance her competence in caring for her infant.

Imitation and Modeling

We will now consider a parenting approach that involves two interrelated strategies, **imitation** and **modeling,** the two key concepts of Social Learning Theory, developed by Bandura and Walters (1963) to demonstrate that many of the behaviors children pick up daily are products of **vicarious learning.** Although parents are not generally aware of the ramifications of their behavioral examples on their children, the reality is that parental modeling might produce significant change in children.

Parental Modeling. Parental modeling is a process of observational learning in which the behavior of the parent serves as an example for similar behaviors of the child. According to Tibbs et al. (2001), parental modeling involves four functions. The first of these functions is **observational learning,** which occurs when the parent exhibits a new behavior, and the child learns that behavior for the first time. For example, a child sees the parent eating a certain food, then tastes the food. The

As shown in this scene, parents have many opportunities to serve as positive models for their children's behavior.

second function of parental modeling is **disinhibiting** or **inhibiting behavior**, which occurs when the child observes negative or positive consequences of a parent's behaviors. If the child observes positive consequences to the parent, they are more likely to mimic the behavior. If, on the other hand, the child notices that negative consequences are linked to the parent's behavior, the child is likely to avoid that behavior. For example, if a child sees a parent making leaf raking a fun family activity by making a big pile of leaves and then encouraging the children to jump in, the child is likely to be eager to take part in leaf raking. On the other hand, if a child observes a parent complaining about the need to rake leaves and not having any fun doing it, the child is likely to develop a negative view of leaf raking and seek to avoid that activity. The third function is **facilitating similar responses,** which occurs when parental behavior serves as a cue for the child's behavior. In this situation, no new behavior is learned but parental actions affect the timing or frequency of the child's behavior. For example, a child who frequently observes a parent eating healthful snacks might consistently choose healthy snacks as well. Finally, **setting cognitive standards for self-regulation** is defined as the parent providing standards for the observing child to emulate. For instance, parents may decide to set an example of hanging up their coats after coming inside while being certain that their children are watching. If children have been instructed to hang up their jackets when coming inside, watching their parents perform that same behavior might influence them to follow the example modeled by their parents.

Parental Qualities that Influence Children's Imitative Behaviors. Due to close proximity and the endurance of time, parents and other family members have many more opportunities to influence their children's behavior than do people outside the family. Nevertheless, as observed by Bandura (1986), children select the persons in their environment to serve as models for their own behavior based on several criteria. First, children are more inclined to imitate parents who are perceived as warm and approachable and less motivated to emulate parents who do not display these qualities. Second, children are more likely to mimic the behaviors of parents whom they consider to have prestige or competence. From a child's perspective, being influential means controlling resources, being able to make major decisions, and having the respect of significant others. Third, children tend to try to be like parents whom they perceive to be similar to themselves. For example, a girl who is told by her father that she is athletic like her mother is more likely to think of herself as capable of playing sports. On the other hand, a father who tells his daughter that she is just like her mother, not good at sports, is unwittingly likely to discourage his daughter's athletic motivation.

Four Ways for Parents to Increase Imitation. Parents are in the position to increase the imitation of certain desired behaviors in their children by understanding the circumstances that promote imitative behavior. Bandura (1977) identified the following conditions under which imitation is most likely to occur. First, the parent must gain the attention of the child, and the target behavior should be observable to the child. Second, the parent might increase the imitation of the desired behavior by using language to call attention to the behavior being demonstrated. By using language, the parent is able to (a) explain what behavior is expected (including the various steps included in the performance of the behavior), (b) clarify instructions, and (c) reinforce the child for performance of the behavior. Third, the likelihood that children will imitate modeled behavior is further enhanced when parents encourage them to practice or rehearse the target behavior. Fourth, when parents are modeling new behaviors for the child to imitate, that goal is best achieved when the modeled behavior builds on behavior already learned. This is achieved by the integration of previously learned behaviors into new patterns. It should be noted that once children have imitated the behavior of a model, they might or might not repeat the behavior depending on whether or not these actions are reinforced by their parents. Especially when the parent–child relationship is close, parental reactions to a child's behavior are a strong determinant of whether or not that behavior will be repeated.

Thinking Critically

Suppose a parent of a young child is aware that the child is able to pick up objects and put them in a box. With the goal of building on that previously learned behavior, what behaviors might the parent model for the child to imitate that would be beneficial in helping the young child to become more self-sufficient?

Research Findings Demonstrating the Effectiveness of Modeling and Imitation. Researchers have demonstrated numerous examples of the effectiveness of modeling and imitation as parenting strategies. Parents use modeling techniques to demonstrate appropriate behaviors that range from promoting their children's language development to reminding them of appropriate social responses (Woodward & Markman, 1998). Furthermore, parents serve as primary identification models for children (Facio & Batistuta, 1998). For example, Markiewicz, Doyle, and Brendgen (2001) found that the friendship networks of mothers were related to their adolescent children's friendship networks. These researchers found that mothers' close peer relationships served as models of warmth and prosocial behavior in their adolescents' peer groups.

GUIDANCE AS LIMITS, CONSEQUENCES, AND CONFLICT RESOLUTION

In this section, we will examine strategies that parents might use for explaining to their children the ways in which certain behaviors result in predictable outcomes (induction), and choosing consequences for their children that are logically related to their children's misbehavior (logical consequences). Parents who adopt the strategies presented in the upcoming discussion must be willing to consider the use of consequences in child guidance as a learning process for the child rather than a mandate for punishment. Understanding that being exposed to any guidance technique is a learning experience for the child, and that many undesirable lessons are learned from punitive consequences, helps parents to evaluate their guidance choices. A relevant question for parents to ask themselves is: "What responses to disapproved behavior will be most valuable in motivating my children to act responsibly?" In choosing the appropriate socialization strategy, Dinkmeyer and McKay (1989) suggest that parents deal with their personal issues of control. The issue of control comes from the mistaken view that the role of the parent is a way to be in control of others. In actuality, if child guidance is to be a valuable learning experience, it cannot be concerned primarily with control. When parents intentionally and consistently adopt strategies that assist children in their efforts to feel good about themselves and that increase children's self-esteem, there is less resistance and less need for parenting strategies designed to punish and control (Colarossi & Eccles, 2000).

Although it is generally understood that the consequences children experience influence their future behavior, what is often overlooked is that these consequences also impact how children feel about themselves, and how they feel about their parents. With those concerns in mind, the guidance techniques presented in this portion of the chapter are designed for parents who wish to help their children to understand the link between their behaviors and the consequences of these behaviors. These methods are valuable for assisting parents in setting limits, establishing boundaries, and providing consequences for their children. A strategy that parents and children might use for resolving conflict is presented as well.

The Technique of Induction

Induction is a parenting strategy designed to promote desirable behavior and reduce undesirable behavior in children by increasing their awareness of the likely consequences of their actions for themselves as well as for others. Induction is a valuable technique for encouraging children's prosocial behavior, helping them to take responsibility for their actions, and promoting the development of their perspective-taking ability. There are two types of induction: self-oriented and other-oriented, depending on who is likely to experience consequences related to the child's behavior. Self-oriented induction involves pointing out to the child what the consequences of the child's behavior are likely to be for the child. Other-oriented induction consists of an explanation to the child regarding how the child's actions affect other persons or animals (Maccoby & Martin, 1983). An example of self-oriented induction is shown in the following example: "Patty, you should walk on the sidewalk because if you run you might fall down and get hurt." The next example demonstrates the use of other-oriented induction: "Philip and Steven, it is important to feed your puppy when you get home from school because when you forget to feed your puppy, he gets hungry." Note that, in both of these examples, the parent emphasized what the children *should do* rather than what they *should not do*. These examples emphasize the importance of stating directives or rules in the positive. According to Marion

(2003), children are most successful in following directives when they are told what they *should do* rather than what they *should not do.* Also, young children have difficulty understanding negative commands because they focus on the verb in the directive as a guide as to what to do. Thus, the young child who is told "Don't play with your food," hears "Play with your food."

Induction Versus Producing Guilt. The appropriate use of the induction technique is to convey to the child the probable consequences of the child's behavior, not to suggest that parental approval of the child is being withdrawn. Furthermore, parents do not have to wait until an act has occurred to use this strategy. Induction might be used in a discussion of anticipated actions of the child or to point out the likely consequences of others' behaviors (Maccoby & Martin, 1983). Examples include: "Katerina, when you want to go visit your friend, be sure to let me know. If you leave and don't tell me, I won't know where to find you." Or "Jose needs to check with his grandmother before he comes over here so that his grandmother will not be worried about where he is."

The previous examples of how to use self-oriented and other-oriented induction demonstrates ways to make children aware of possible negative consequences. Another benefit of this strategy is that it might be used to let children know how their positive and/or helpful behavior benefits others or brings about positive results (Maccoby & Martin, 1983). In the case of self-oriented induction, a child might be told, "If you share your toys with your sister, she will probably feel more like sharing her toys with you." In the case of other-oriented induction, the child might be informed that, "When you picked those flowers and gave them to your grandmother, she was very pleased. You put a big smile on her face."

Why Induction Is Effective. The effectiveness of induction is based on the premise that children: (a) need to engage in prosocial behavior, (b) are motivated toward behaving more maturely, (c) have the ability to understand cause and effect, and (d) have the capability of understanding others' points of view (Maccoby & Martin, 1983). Induction is an effective parenting strategy for a number of reasons. First, because induction is concerned with action, attention is directed away from a personal evaluation of the child. For example, induction teaches the child how to produce actions such as sharing or apologizing. Second, induction motivates children toward more mature reasoning regarding the behavioral choices they make. Third, induction communicates to children that they have the ability to behave in ways that contribute to better consequences for themselves and others. Finally, induction fosters the development of empathy and understanding of others, thereby promoting children's prosocial behavior while inhibiting their antisocial behavior.

Research Findings Supporting the Use of Inductive Parenting. Barnett, Quackenbush, and Sinisi (1996) reviewed the research focused on the behavioral correlates of the parental use of induction when contrasted with the parental use of power assertion. These researchers reported that the parental use of induction is associated with children's and adolescents' heightened empathy and prosocial behavior, lower levels of antisocial behavior, more mature moral judgment, and greater popularity. The link between inductive parenting and children's prosocial behavior was demonstrated also by Krevans and Gibbs (1996) who found that children of inductive parents are more empathic and more prosocial. In a recent study, Kerr, Lopez, and Olsen (2004) found that parental induction, warm responsiveness, and less frequent use of physical punishment were associated with children's higher levels of moral regulation and fewer externalizing problems.

Thinking Critically

Given the many positive outcomes associated with the use of induction, why do you think more parents do not use this technique with their children? In your professional life, do you think you would teach this technique to parents? If a child in your care was hitting another child, how would you use the technique of induction to intervene in this situation?

Natural and Logical Consequences

In recognition that children need to be guided by warm, caring parents to make appropriate choices in their behaviors and to accept responsibility for their actions, Dinkmeyer and McKay (1989) developed the parenting strategy known as logical consequences. This socialization technique addresses the need of parents for guidelines to: (a) develop relationships with their children that emphasize a balance between children's rights and responsibilities, (b) provide children with an opportunity to make decisions regarding their behavior and to be accountable for their choices, and (c) communicate respect for children while teaching them to respect others. Closely aligned with logical consequences are natural consequences. As will be explained, a natural consequence "occurs naturally" and as such is not a socialization technique. Dinkmeyer and McKay, nevertheless, identified the concept of natural consequences to demonstrate its cohort, logical consequences. The idea behind natural or logical consequences is that children learn from consequences when their parents allow them to experience the results of their own actions.

Natural Consequences. When we make hasty or naive choices in our everyday lives, and we learn from them, we experience **natural consequences** (Dinkmeyer & McKay, 1989). A very young child who is running down the sidewalk does not usually consider the suitability of the sidewalk for running. Taking a nasty spill while running on the sidewalk and getting a scraped knee is a natural consequence of running. Taking a spill while running on the grass and discovering that it is not so bad is also a natural consequence. If parents do not interfere with their children's natural consequences, they will undoubtedly learn from these experiences. This approach to child socialization, though, would be dangerous and ill-advised in many instances. Take the case of the child running down the sidewalk. Yes, the child would learn from the consequence of getting a skinned knee but this accident could be prevented by closely supervising the young child and using the technique of induction to warn the child of the problems of running on the sidewalk. Similarly, the parent might use induction to suggest that the child run on the grass instead of the sidewalk.

Logical Consequences. Closely related to natural consequences are **logical consequences** that are appropriate choices when parents want to avoid punitive approaches to guiding their children but would like their children to experience consequences that are logically related to their actions (Dinkmeyer & McKay, 1989). An example of the use of logical consequences is when a mother tells her young children that they may play outdoors, inside the fence, or that they will have to come inside to play. The mother might combine the use of logical consequences with the use of induction to explain to her children why it is important for them to play within the confined area. Children could be informed that the parent needs to keep an eye on them while they play to be sure they are all right and will not be able to do so if they go outside the fence. If, while playing inside the fence, the children see a puppy, open the gate, and start running after the puppy toward the road, the mother might bring the children inside and explain to them that they will have to play inside the house today because they went outside the fence.

In the situation just described, the children are assisted by the parent to make the connection between their actions and the consequences much better than if the parent had used a punitive consequence, such as yelling at or striking them. Another example of the use of logical consequences is when parents expect a child to get a paper towel and wipe up the milk the child has spilled. Still another example of a logical consequence is when, after breaking a sibling's toy, a child is given the responsibility for paying for the replacement of the toy. Finally, in using logical consequences, parents need to use logic in assigning responsibility to the child. For example, a 4-year-old who accidentally breaks a sibling's toy might not be expected to replace that toy, whereas a 12-year-old might be given that logical consequence if she deliberately damages a sibling's possession.

The Problems Associated with Using Punishment

Parents are encouraged to use logical consequences rather than relying on punishment as a consequence of children's misbehavior due to the negative side effects associated with the use of punitive methods. First of all, attempts at punishment of an undesirable behavior might actually serve as a reinforcement of that behavior. An example of that problem is when the child is misbehaving for attention and the parent provides attention while attempting to punish the child. Even though the parental attention might be negative, some children are likely to repeat the misbehavior to gain parental attention. A second reason for parents to avoid the use of punishment is that in most cases punishment is not logically related to the child's problematic behavior. If the child who spills milk is calmly asked to get a cloth and wipe it up, the accident and the consequence are logically related. A punitive consequence of that child's behavior, on the other hand, is not a logical choice.

Research Findings Linking Corporal Punishment to Children's Negative Outcomes. A side effect of the use of punishment is that punishment of the child compromises the parent–child relationship. Children who are subjected to repeated punishment from parents learn to avoid their parents, fight back, or lie about their behavior to avoid punishment. Another drawback related to the use of punishment as a child socialization technique is that children who receive frequent punishment from parents are more likely than are other children to be punitive toward others as well as toward themselves (Grusec & Goodnow, 1994). The parental use of power assertion strategies has been shown to be associated also with children's and adolescents' lowered empathy, higher levels of antisocial behavior, less mature moral judgment, and decreased popularity with peers (Barnett et al., 1996).

What This Means for Professionals. For professionals working with children and families, it is useful to understand which groups of parents are most likely to rely on corporal punishment as a disciplinary choice. To answer that question, Dietz (2000) studied parents' disciplinary practices and found that parents who were more likely to use corporal punishment were those with fewer resources and/or those who had been socialized into the use of violence. The conclusion of Dietz was that efforts should be made to provide these parents with the resources they need to implement alternative discipline strategies. These findings support the views of Dinkmeyer and McKay (1989) that parents who rely on punishment are at a disadvantage when presented with a situation wherein children might benefit from experiencing consequences for their behavior. Their first thought is typically how to punish the child to regain control over the child. That choice, however, has many drawbacks because power-assertive control tactics do not motivate children to become more independent or guide them to behave more responsibly. Instead, it leaves children in a dependent or power-oriented relationship, with their parents in authority. The impact on children in these types of parent-child relationships was demonstrated by Simons, Wu, and Lin (2000) who found that adolescents feel angry and unjustly treated, defy parental authority, and engage in antisocial behavior when their parents use physical punishment.

RESOLVING PARENT–CHILD CONFLICT

Explained earlier in this chapter were ways in which parents might send I-messages to their children when they found their children's behavior unacceptable. There are times, however, when I-messages are not effective due to the child's desire to engage in a particular behavior even when the child knows that the parent disapproves, or the child's reluctance to participate in behaviors that the parent wishes to encourage. In that situation, a conflict exists in the relationship that calls for the employment of methods of conflict resolution.

Step I. Defining the problem. Mommy: "Gabriel, what's wrong? You're not eating your vegetables?" Gabriel: "Mommy, I don't wike dese widdle twees (broccoli)."

Step II. Generating possible solutions. Mommy: "Gabriel, you need to eat green vegetables to grow big and strong. Why don't I put some cheese sauce on the little trees? By the way, they are called broccoli."

Step III. Evaluating the possible solutions. "Here, I will put some cheese sauce on your broccoli and let you try it. Well, Gabriel, what do you think?"

Step IV. Deciding on the best solution. Gabriel: "Mommy, I wike bwockwey wif jees saws! Dis is weally good!"

Step V. Implementing the decision. Mommy: "Now we've worked out a great plan to help you eat your green vegetables so you will grow big and strong."

Step VI. Follow-up evaluation. Daddy: "Gabriel, I see you are eating your green vegetables and growing big and strong." Gabriel: "Yep, me and Mommy sided to put jees saws on all my gween vegdubbles. Now, dey taste weally good!"

FIGURE 4.6 A No-Lose Method of Conflict Resolution

Note: Adapted from *Parent Effectiveness Training,* by T. Gordon, 1976, New York: New American Library.

A problem associated with getting parents to consider using a conflict resolution technique is that many parents are committed to either an authoritarian or permissive approach to conflict management. When conflict occurs, these parents typically rely on two win–lose methods of conflict resolution: strict or lenient. Authoritarian parents believe that in the case of conflict, they should step in to regain control and exert authority over the child. In these situations, the parents win at the expense of the child. Permissive parents, on the other hand, back off from their positions when the child objects, which results in the child winning and the parent losing. In contrast to either the strict or lenient approaches, the **No-Lose Method of Conflict Resolution** that was developed by Thomas Gordon (1975) is a democratic approach to the resolution of parent–child conflict. The No-Lose Method of Conflict Resolution is a win–win approach where both parents and children win. That method consists of the six steps outlined in Figure 4.6.

The Advantages of Using the No-Lose Method of Conflict Resolution

Because the no-lose method of conflict resolution engages both parents and children in a discussion that requires both to think about the feelings and wishes of the other, it represents the democratic process in action. Numerous advantages are associated with the use of this method of conflict management. First, when both parents and children freely express their views relating to an issue, mutual respect is more likely to occur, which promotes parent–child closeness. Second, in contrast to the win–lose approaches to conflict resolution often used by authoritarian or permissive parents, the No-Lose Method of Conflict Resolution requires that both parent and child be satisfied with the outcome. Finally, both parents and children are more motivated to carry out plans based on decisions in which they feel they have had sufficient input. In the example provided in Figure 4.6, the parent's goal was to have the child eat green vegetables and the child's objective was to eat food that tasted good to him. When the parent listened to and accepted the child's evaluation of the broccoli, considered a creative solution for resolving the dilemma, and invited feedback from the child, the parent and child were able to resolve their conflict with a solution that was pleasing to both of them. Parents do not lose when they are able to work out mutually satisfactory solutions to problems they are having with their children. On the contrary, effective conflict resolution enhances the parent–child relationship, fosters the development of the child's self-esteem, and results in a more equitable outcome than does power-assertive techniques.

At this point, some readers might think that the example of conflict resolution illustrated in Figure 4.6 is too easy or that it would not work with older children. Even though the problem seems simple because of the child's age, many parents will not take the time to attempt a creative solution to parent–child conflict, especially when their children are very young. Children are often forced to eat food they do not like or do a number of other things they would prefer not to do because parents do not empathize with the child's feelings and are unaware of a better way of handling a situation like the one in Figure 4.6. The underlying problem behind the parental resistance statement of "It won't work in real life, with older kids, with my kids, and so on" is due to some parents' lack of trust in their children, coupled with their reluctance to allow children to be heard when parent–child conflict emerges. For parents invested in a strict way of handling conflict, the no-lose method seems so unfamiliar to them that they will not even try it. Another reason parents resist attempting the No-Lose Conflict Resolution Method is due to the time investment. Many parents are unwilling to invest the time to learn the skills required for effective conflict management (Gordon, 1975).

Research Support for the Parental Use of Conflict Management. According to Chapman and McBride (1995), when children encounter viewpoints different from their own, being able to discuss these differing perspectives contributes to the child's development of rational thinking. Another benefit of parents and children engaging in conflict resolution was reported by Tucker, McHale, and Crouter (2003) who found that adolescents who participated in conflict resolution with their parents were better adjusted. The conclusions of these researchers were that parents and children with more positive relationships are better able to resolve their conflicts.

SUMMARY

- The parenting skills described in the first part of this chapter emphasize a prevention-of-problems approach, explain a variety of ways that parents might assist their children in meeting their goals, and show parents ways in which to motivate their children toward cooperative behavior.
- The techniques presented in the prevention of problems section emphasize the significance of understanding children's feelings, the role of parents in the promotion of children's self-esteem, and the value of enhancing parental effectiveness through the development of positive communication skills.
- In the discussion of positive reinforcement as a child socialization technique, we learned that any consequence that increases the likelihood that the behavior will be repeated is reinforcing. We also learned that, although reinforcements might include special treats or desired activities, the most effective reinforcement for most children, most of the time, is social approval. That discussion was followed by an exploration of the important role that parents play as models of their children's behavior.
- We then looked at a diversity of effective approaches for setting limits, establishing boundaries, and providing consequences for children, including the technique of induction, and the strategies of natural and logical consequences. The dangers of using punishment as a method of rearing children also were emphasized in that section.
- Finally, a method for resolving parent–child conflict was discussed. All of the socialization strategies presented in this chapter are based on values of democratic parent–child relations.

KEY TERMS

- active listening
- atmosphere of psychological safety
- communication roadblocks
- encouragement
- four goals of misbehavior
- facilitating similar responses
- four pluses and a wish
- house of self
- I-messages
- imitation
- induction
- logical consequences
- modeling
- natural consequences
- no-lose method of conflict resolution
- observational learning
- positve reinforcement
- praise
- problem ownership
- recognition reflex
- self-esteem
- setting cognitive standards for self-regulation
- vicarious learning

USEFUL WEB SITES

Family-First

http://www.family-first.org

At http://www.family-first.org are parenting articles on all facets of parenting under "programs and services". The general parenting section includes a variety of parenting advice and tips on such topics as showing love and affection to children, being a hands-on parent, and more. It also has a number of links to specific parenting information.

The International Network for Children and Families

http://www.incaf.com

The International Network for Children and Families site provides links to articles written or approved by certified parent education facilitators. Under parents, click on "Online Parenting Articles." Parent advice and information is provided in both English and Spanish.

Tufts University also has a Web guide

http://www.cfw.tufts.edu

This guide evaluates, describes, and provides links to websites containing parent-friendly practical advice and information on child development. The content on this site is carefully screened by experts from Tufts University.

Becoming Parents and Parenting Infants and Toddlers

Objectives

After completing this chapter, you should be able to

- Describe the steps expectant parents might take to increase the likelihood that their babies will be carried to full term, have a healthy weight, and have a lower risk of birth defects.
- Discuss the risk factors for low birth weight that are linked with poverty.
- Define kangaroo care and describe its benefits for premature and/or low-birth-weight babies.
- Describe the challenges of parenting low-birth-weight infants.
- Demonstrate an understanding of the factors associated with the satisfaction of parents during the transition to parenthood.
- Describe several ways in which parents might promote the physical health of their infants and toddlers, including the advantages of breast-feeding, and the provision of nutritious food after weaning.
- Demonstrate an understanding of the ways in which parents promote the development of secure attachment of their infants, including the developmental implications of secure attachment.
- Describe several ways in which parents might promote the fine and gross motor skills of their toddlers.
- Discuss the ways in which parents might promote their toddlers' autonomy and exploratory behavior.
- Show an understanding of the critical role that parents play in their infants' and toddlers cognitive development, including the development of language.
- Identify the challenges that parents of infants and toddlers face in rearranging family life so that they are able to care for their children, while also carrying out their occupational responsibilities.

To quote what the king told Alice in Lewis Carroll's *Through the Looking Glass,* let us "begin at the beginning" (Tripp, 1970). This chapter is about beginnings, with all the excitement and trepidation that accompany new adventures. The first beginning is the momentous decision to become parents; next there is the anticipation of parenthood. Then, the arrival of a child confers onto adults the adult role of parent and in marriages or committed partnerships extends the couple relationship into a family. These alterations in adult roles and responsibilities as well as changes in family definition set into motion numerous changes and new beginnings for the child, the parents, the immediate and extended family, and the community.

To appreciate the impact of these various beginnings on the lives of children and their parents, we will start by examining the ways in which expectant parents might take steps to optimize the chances of giving birth to healthy, full-term babies. Next, we will focus on the experience of birth as a universal occurrence that differentially impacts parents according to the nature of the birth or births (in the case of multiple births) and the resources available to the parents. Following the discussion of the birth, we will take a look at the important transition to parenthood. Then, we will consider the ways in which parents' interactions with their infants and toddlers impact their children's development. Finally, we will consider the various ways in which parents coordinate their parental responsibilities with their occupational demands.

OPTIMIZING THE CHANCES OF HAVING HEALTHY BABIES

Although birth is a significant event in all families and the arrival of infants is usually a joyous occasion, the circumstances surrounding babies coming into the world vary considerably. Geographical location, socioeconomic conditions, and the behaviors of expectant parents all impact the health and survival of newborns. Complications of pregnancy that contribute to birth defects, premature births, or low-birth-weight infants are sometimes beyond the control of parents. For the majority of pregnancies, however, there are steps that parents might take to increase the likelihood that their babies will be carried to full term, have a healthy weight, and have a lower risk of birth defects. These include maintaining adequate nutrition, avoiding **teratogens**, and seeking early prenatal care. Teratogens are agents and conditions, including malnutrition, viruses, drugs, chemicals, and stressors that can interfere with prenatal development and contribute to birth defects or death (see Figure 5.1) (Conley & Bennett, 2001; Yonkers, Wisner, & Stowe, 2004).

Maintaining a Nutritious Diet and Avoiding Harmful Substances

The key components of a healthy lifestyle during pregnancy include appropriate weight gain; eating a variety of nutritious foods; vitamin and mineral supplementation; avoidance of alcohol, tobacco, and other harmful substances; as well as safe food handling (Kaiser, 2003). It is imperative that women have a nutritious diet

Diseases
Most viruses
Virtually all sexually transmitted diseases
Rubella measles—one of the first diseases identified as a teratogen
Pediatric AIDS
Mothers who are HIV positive

Many other maternal conditions
RH-negative blood (a recessive genetic trait, not a disease)
Infection
Bacterial vaginosis—a minor vaginal infection, which is easily cured with standard antibiotics
Minor infections—such as gum disease in a pregnant woman

Many widely used medicinal drugs used to treat real or potential problems
These include tetracycline, anticoagulants, bromides, anticonvulsants, phenobarbital, retinoic acid (a common treatment for acne, found in Accutane), and most hormones.

Nonprescription drugs
These include aspirin, antacids, and diet pills

Psychoactive drugs
These include beer and wine, liquor, cigarettes and smokeless tobacco, heroin and methadone, LSD, marijuana, heroin, cocaine in any form, inhalants, and antidepressant pills. Babies born to narcotics addicts are not only more likely to be premature or to have low birth weight, but they are themselves addicted and suffer withdrawal symptoms labeled *neonatal abstinence syndrome*, including tremors, restlessness, hyperactive reflexes, high-pitched cries, vomiting, fevers, sweating, rapid respirations, seizures, and sometimes death.

Nicotine
Every psychoactive drug slows growth but tobacco is the most prevalent culprit. Cigarettes are implicated in 25% of all low-birth-weight births in the United States and in 50% of low-birth-weight births in Europe (where more people smoke).

Alcohol
The numerous effects of alcohol consumption by pregnant women have been collectively labeled as **fetal alcohol syndrome** (FAS). Not only are the children afflicted with FAS more likely to be born dead, those who survive their births will display facial and skull deformities characteristic of that syndrome.

FIGURE 5.1 Common Teratogens

Source: Adapted from *The Developing Person Through the Life Span,* 5th ed., by Kathleen Stassen Berger and Ross A. Thompson, 2001, New York: Worth Publishers.

throughout their pregnancies because maternal malnutrition is correlated with low birth weight. Low birth weight has been linked with inadequate nutrition that results from fasting or starvation (even for 1 day) or the lack of specific nutrients, including vitamin A, folic acid, iron, magnesium, calcium, and zinc. The avoidance of harmful

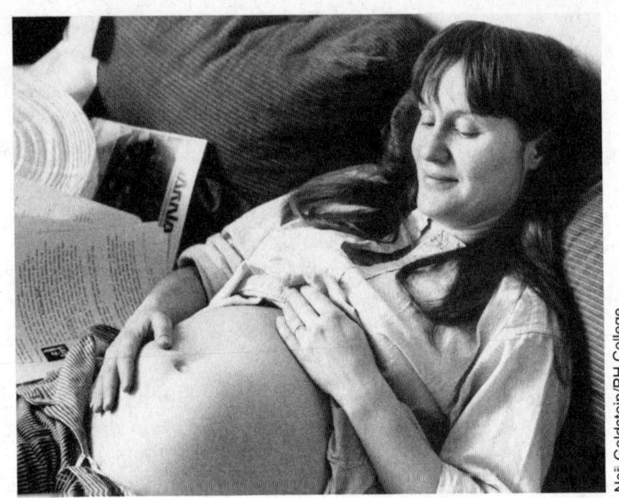

Neil Goldstein/PH College.

This scene captures the feelings of joyful anticipation of birth and motherhood.

substances is equally important. One of the most commonly used substances that compromises the health of the developing fetus is prenatal exposure to nicotine. Despite abundant adverse publicity, tobacco use occurs in about 25% of all pregnancies in the United States. Several reports have established that maternal smoking during pregnancy adversely affects prenatal and postnatal growth and increases the risk of fetal mortality, low birth weight, and infant mortality. Furthermore, cognitive deficits and behavior problems of children and adolescents have been traced to their prenatal nicotine exposure (Ernst, Moolchan, & Robinson, 2001). The use of caffeine during pregnancy should be monitored as well. Some research indicates that the probability of premature delivery is lower among women who do not consume caffeine (Eskenazi, Stapleton, Kharrazi, & Chee, 1999). Finally, in order to protect the developing fetus, pregnant women need to avoid the use of harmful drugs. Profound birth defects, fetal death, low birth weight, and infant mortality have been consistently related to the use of legal and illegal drugs (Laditka, Laditka, & Mastanduno, 2005). All illegal drugs should be avoided during pregnancy and pregnant women should consult their physicians regarding the use of prescribed drugs. For example, some mood stabilizers are teratogens but the treatment of mood disorders or any symptomology can be managed most effectively if pregnancy is planned and the pregnant woman has early and consistent prenatal care (Yonkers et al., 2004).

The Importance of Early Prenatal Care

When pregnancy is confirmed, prenatal care plans must be discussed and the initial visit to a physician should occur during the first trimester. The reason for early prenatal care is because the first 12 weeks of pregnancy are a time of heightened fetal vulnerability to teratogens. Part of the prenatal visit includes counseling about risk behaviors. Therefore, education is an essential component of prenatal care, particularly for women who are pregnant for the first time. Information about the physical changes that occur during pregnancy and preparation for the birthing process are key themes around which to discuss care issues and choices such as breast-feeding (Kirkham, Harris, & Grzybowski, 2005). Early prenatal care also helps the pregnant woman to understand the changes in her body and is vital for optimizing the chances of having a healthy baby or babies (in the case of multiple births). In a review of the research on the link between prenatal care and the health and size of the newborn, Abel (1997) reported that (a) women without prenatal care are three times more likely to have low-birth-weight infants than are women with early and adequate care, and that (b) mothers who are younger, less educated, unmarried, economically disadvantaged, and/or from a minority group are less likely to receive adequate prenatal care and more likely to give birth to low-birth-weight infants. The findings of Laditka et al. (2005) also confirm the link between preventable pregnancy complications and obstacles to receiving prenatal care.

Poverty as a Risk Factor for Low-Birth-Weight Infants

Lack of prenatal care and poor diet during pregnancy are two of the leading causes of preterm deliveries and these two factors are primarily associated with poverty. Furthermore, all of the risk factors for low birth weight correlate with poverty. Compared with women of higher socioeconomic status, poor women are more likely to be ill, malnourished, teenaged, and stressed. Moreover, if they are working during their pregnancies, their jobs frequently consist of physically stressful work, which has been associated with preterm deliveries and low-birth-weight infants (Ceron-Mireles, Harlow, & Sanchez-Carrillo, 1996). Additionally, mothers who are poor often receive late or inadequate prenatal care, breathe polluted air, live in overcrowded conditions, move from place to place, and ingest unhealthy substances from psychoactive drugs to spoiled food (Shiono et al., 1997). Poverty is part of the reason for differences in birth weight and infant survival between nations, and within the United States, ethnic and historical differences in birth weight and infant mortality have been found to be associated with differences in socioeconomic levels (U.S. Bureau of the Census, 1999). For example, Laditka et al. (2005) found that two major risk factors for avoidable pregnancy complications are being uninsured or covered by Medicaid. Even though Medicaid is available for poor women in the United States, doctors who accept Medicaid payments often have so many patients that it takes several months to get an appointment.

Thinking Critically

You might know young women who, during their pregnancies, did not or do not prioritize their health habits and/or get early prenatal care. Are you able to determine some of the reasons why these young women are making these choices during their pregnancies?

What This Means for Professionals. Individuals need to be informed about the importance of adequate nutrition, early prenatal care, and the avoidance of harmful substances during pregnancy. It is important, however, that information of such vital importance to the health and survival of infants be disseminated early and from a variety of professionals who have access to adolescents and adults before and during pregnancy. One might also consider prenatal care as a concept that occurs before pregnancy from a host of caring individuals, such as parents, teachers, and physicians. For example, physicians might routinely inquire about the smoking habits of their adolescent and young adult patients and warn them about the harmful effects of smoking on their future pregnancies. Once a pregnancy has occurred, it is of utmost importance that the expectant parent be made aware of the necessity of early prenatal care, good nutrition, and the avoidance of teratogens. Furthermore, family members, the community, and society should work together to ensure early access to prenatal care for all pregnant women.

BIRTH AND NEWBORNS

Birth is a significant event in the lives of families everywhere whether it is the first baby born to a couple, the birth of a baby to teenage parents, or the birth of a child who has one or more siblings. The primary goal of expectant parents is to have full-term, healthy babies and most parents get that wish because the majority of babies are carried to full gestational term and are born healthy (Munch & Levick, 2001). In the United States, most of these babies are born in hospitals and taken home by their birth or adoptive parents after a brief two-day hospital stay (Lubic, 1997). The arrival of a new baby (or new babies in the case of twins or other multiple births) is an occasion in which the parents, siblings, and extended family members usually rejoice. The feeling of elation that accompanies the birth of an infant is summed up in the following description by a new father whose wife had been in labor for a number of hours before having a Caesarian birth:

> 1:56 a.m. A few minutes later we hear a tiny, muffled cry. Dr. L. asks me if I want to see our baby. I expect to see him holding the child in his arms, but as I emerge from our side of the curtain, I see one of the doctors still pulling the baby out. I don't have the stomach for scenes like this on TV, but here I can't look away. At first, all that's visible is the head, but then the whole body comes out. Dr. L. says, "You have a daughter." Then someone asks her name. As I say "Dayna," I'm filled with a sense of bliss. Before any of this happened, people told me how life-changing it was to have a child. Only now do I understand. Dayna has only been here for a few minutes, but she's already the most precious thing to us in the world (Beatty, 2000).

When Infants Are Born Early and/or Small

In all societies, there are individuals who have been trained in various ways to assist in the delivery of newborns. Nevertheless, there is a major difference in the survival rates of infants born in industrialized and nonindustrialized countries. In some places in the world, hospitals are not available, and even in places where hospitals are accessible they might not have the advanced medical technology and trained medical staff to meet the needs of at-risk babies. Without the assistance of medical technology, parents in developing countries whose babies are considered to be at risk are more likely to suffer the loss of their infants shortly after birth than are parents of at-risk newborns born in industrialized countries (UNICEF, 1998). As an illustration, of the 10.6 million children who died each year between 2000 and 2003 in four developing countries, 37% of those deaths occurred shortly after birth (Bryce, Boshi-Pinto, Shibaya, & Black, 2005).

Whereas parents who live in industrialized countries have greater access to medical care for their at-risk newborns, most traditional cultures also have infant care designed to maximize infant survival. Typical features of infant care in traditional cultures include intensive physical nurturance of the infant, breast-feeding on demand, immediate response to the crying of infants, close parent–infant body contact, keeping the baby beside the mother at night, and consistent care by parents, siblings, and other relatives. These caregiving behaviors have been found to be beneficial for normal-weight infants and particularly important for the survival of at-risk infants (Levine et al., 1994). Furthermore, the skin-to-skin contact so common in many traditional cultures has recently been found to increase the chances of survival of preterm and low-birth-weight babies in intensive care units of modern hospitals throughout the world (Feldman, Weller, & Siroto, 2002).

Kangaroo care was first used in hospital intensive care units in Bogota, Colombia, due to a shortage of incubators. Premature infants were placed naked between their mother's breasts for long periods of time so that the mother's body heat could help these very small infants to regulate their body temperatures (Whitelaw & Sleath, 1985). Today, kangaroo care is used in many infant intensive care units in Western societies to promote the survival of at-risk infants. Although the procedure is practiced in intensive care units of hospitals, it is not the medical professionals who use kangaroo care; instead, they teach parents of at-risk infants the way to hold their infants skin to skin. The infant (wearing only a diaper) is placed on the parent's bare chest (skin to skin). The infant's head is then turned to the side so that the baby's ear is against the parent's heart and any tubes or wires that are attached to the baby are taped to the parent's clothing.

The advantages of using kangaroo care are impressive. Preterm infants, whose parents use kangaroo care, cry less, sleep for longer periods, gain more weight, have more coordinated breathing and heartbeat patterns, and need less supplemental oxygen than preterm infants who do not receive kangaroo care. Kangaroo care of preterm infants also has been found to promote infants' self-regulation, including the regulation of sleep–wake cycles and arousal states (Feldman et al., 2002). In addition to the health benefits of kangaroo care for the infant, Feldman, Weller, and Fidelman (2003) found that kangaroo care early in life is related to later positive interactions between infants and their mothers and fathers. Those researchers found that these infant–parent interactions are characterized by greater sensitivity, lower intrusiveness, higher parent–infant synchrony, and lower infant negative emotionality.

The following quote is from the author's son, Ken, who practiced kangaroo care with his newborn twin son Gabriel, who weighed in at 4.5 pounds (1 pound lighter than his twin sister Josephine) and had to be placed in intensive care. (Note: The hospital in which the twins were born did not teach kangaroo care to parents of at-risk infants but the author taught her son and daughter-in-law about the procedure during the pregnancy because there was a good chance that the babies would be premature and have a low birth weight.)

> At first, we had both the babies in the room. Then the doctor said they would have to take Gabriel to intensive care and I said I was going with him. I stayed there with him holding him skin to skin as much as possible, even with all the tubes. I also talked with him in a soothing voice because I knew he would recognize my voice from my talking to him before birth. Then, when he would sleep, I would lay my head next to his so he could hear me breathing. We developed a special bond between us because of this experience, which I wouldn't trade for the world.

Thinking Critically

Were you surprised to learn that the skin-to-skin holding of preterm infants (kangaroo care) promotes their ability to survive and also has a positive effect on later parent–infant interactions? How do you account for the fact that parents in traditional societies instinctively provide that type of care, whereas parents in industrialized societies have to be taught to hold their preterm infants in that fashion?

The Challenges of Parenting Low-Birth-Weight Infants. The primary challenges accompanying the births of full-term healthy babies are whether to breast-feed or bottle-feed them and how to rearrange family life so that parents can fit the care of their new baby, or babies, into their other family and occupational responsibilities. In comparison to the experiences of parents of full-term, healthy newborns, the parents of babies who receive intensive medical care and/or intensive physical care anxiously watch their newborns' struggles for survival. For high-risk infants who survive, there are frequently complications. These infants are often late to smile, to hold objects, and to communicate. Over time, both short-term as well as long-term cognitive deficits might emerge (Hack et al., 2002). Despite the fact that preterm infants are more at risk for not surviving during their first days or weeks of life, and often have short-term complications, most of these infants make it and are later free from even minor problems. Furthermore, the majority of preterm infants show normal development. Other babies who are born prematurely have physical and cognitive exceptionalities that will require specialized care. For example, by the end of the first year, only 10% of prematurely born infants display significant developmental challenges and only 5% are seriously disabled. By the age of 6, however, 38% of children who were born prematurely have mild problems that call for special education interventions (Hack, Klein, & Taylor, 1995). The challenges of parenting children with special needs are discussed in Chapter 11.

When At-Risk Newborns Do Not Survive. The greatest concern for parents of at-risk newborns is that their babies will not survive. In a study of mothers of high-risk infants, DeMier, Hynan, and Hatfield (2002) found that the baby's birth weight, length of hospital stay, and postnatal complications are significant predictors of anxiety and distress of parents. The joy that accompanies the birth of a newborn is tragically overturned when a baby dies, and the relative rarity of that event makes the loss even harder for parents to accept. Whether the death is a stillbirth or occurs shortly after the baby is born, the loss of a child within hours or days of that child's new life is particularly heartbreaking. Moreover, the merciless combination of the first dawning of life and an unnaturally early death makes the loss of a child incredibly difficult to cope with and the depression of parents whose infants die is a traumatic experience (Murphy, Johnson, Gupta, & Das, 1998). For these reasons, it is beneficial for grieving parents to have a social support group to insure that their natural processes of mourning are able to proceed without interruption (Murray, Terry, & Vance, 2000). A description of an intervention program designed to help parents identify a social support system to help them cope with the death of their newborns is discussed in Chapter 12.

THE TRANSITION TO PARENTHOOD: A MAJOR DEVELOPMENTAL MILESTONE

After having accomplished a successful pregnancy and experienced the birth of one's children or after having completed the adoption process, new parents then engage in a process of welcoming their children into their homes and lives. At this point, parents take on the responsibilities that come with the highly significant role of parent. Whether one becomes a parent during adolescence or adulthood, the transition to parenthood is a major developmental milestone, accompanied by the opportunities and demands for personal reorganization and growth that characterize such major changes. The level of satisfaction parents experience during the transition to parenthood is related to (a) whether the pregnancy was planned (in situations where parenthood results from the birth of a child), (b) the level of support parents receive from spouses, partners, and/or extended family, and (c) the availability and access to medical care (Monahan, 2001; Pancer, Pratt, & Hunsberger, 2000).

Contentment related to the transition to parenthood also has been found to be influenced by men's and women's level of complexity related to thinking about that transition. For instance, Pancer et al. (2000) found that parents who engage in more complex thinking about impending parenthood are better adjusted than those with less complex thinking about that transition. Parents who demonstrate more complex thinking about the transition to parenthood have higher self-esteem, less depression, and improved marital satisfaction. Specific circumstances contribute to more

The joyfulness and pride on the faces of these young parents reflect a high level of satisfaction with the transition to parenthood.

Portraits by Deborah.

complex thinking about parenthood. The findings of Pancer and colleagues were that caring for infants belonging to other family members prior to having one's own children contributes to more complex thinking about parenthood as does discussions and consultations with others about what is involved in being a new parent.

Support for New Parents

Although there are many unmarried adolescent parents today, and there has been an increase in single parenthood among women over 20 years of age, most new parents are in marriages or committed relationships. For parents sharing the same household, the primary sources of support tend to come from each other, although extended family members are typically involved in helping inexperienced parents to make that transition. Even though parents usually cooperate in the care of their infants, there is evidence that new parenthood takes a toll on the relationship of those parents. The challenges that new parents face is that they must rearrange family life so that they can fit the care of their new baby, or babies, into their other family and occupational responsibilities. In that situation, they either work out a plan for dividing up those multiple tasks or one person carries the bulk of household responsibilities. The fact that many new parents have difficulties coming up with a strategy that works for both of them is evident from research that shows that the transition to parenthood has a segregating influence on the division of household labor. Researchers have found that the division of household labor and child care following the arrival of children typically violates the couple's (especially the mother's) expectations of how child care and household responsibilities will be accomplished (Kluwer, Heesink, & van de Vliert, 2002).

Whether married or single, new parents benefit greatly if they have the support of family members and the community in making the transition to parenthood. Nevertheless, the assistance of new parents by extended family members varies across families and across cultures. In the United States, the nuclear family arrangement typically limits the involvement of extended family members and leaves the parental couple more reliant on each other for support in their new roles. That the new parents might benefit from greater assistance from their families and/or the community is evident from the findings of Kluwer et al. (2002) that new parents' satisfaction with their relationship declines during the first 9 months postpartum. Another indication that new parents often need additional support from others during those early months of adjustment to parenthood is the finding that new mothers often turn to their own parents for advice and help in childrearing. Moreover, mothers in the United States frequently receive informational support from community-based programs, such as prenatal classes, hospital visitations, and programs aimed at helping new parents cope with the transition to parenthood. In contrast to the pattern in the United States, wherein new parents rely primarily on each other for support, new mothers in Asian cultures tend to receive considerable assistance primarily from extended family members. In many Asian cultures, a common cultural expectation is that after childbirth, a new mother will need help with day-to-day activities for a prolonged period of time. Consequently, family members often perform many helpful activities for new mothers, including assistance in child care, social reinforcement, physical comfort, appreciation, and giving advice (Hyun et al., 2002).

What This Means for Professionals. The findings that the division of child care and household responsibilities following the birth or adoption of children usually violates the anticipations of many parents (especially mothers), and contributes to less satisfaction with their relationship with each other, emphasizes the need for family and community support of new parents. There are numerous opportunities for family members and friends to sustain the childrearing efforts of those parents and the types of support provided by extended family members in Asian cultures are excellent examples of ways in which family members and friends might offer assistance.

Thinking Critically

Consider young parents whom you have observed at home with their infants or toddlers. What examples of support for each other's childrearing efforts were you able to discern between those two parents. Also, what examples of assistance from family members and friends have you observed?

THE ROLE OF PARENTS IN INFANT/TODDLER PHYSICAL, SOCIAL–EMOTIONAL, AND COGNITIVE DEVELOPMENT

As parents and children begin their lives together as a family, parents embark on a significant new challenge—that of promoting their babies' healthy growth and development. As you will see, the care that parents provide for their babies impacts all areas of their early and later development. We will begin this discussion by focusing on the important role that parents play in promoting their infants and toddlers' social–emotional develoment. We will then look at the ways in which parents influence their babies' physical and cognitive development. Throughout all these deliberations, we will pause to consider the implications for professionals.

Promoting the Social–Emotional Development of Infants and Toddlers

The relationships that parents establish with their infants and toddlers provide the basis for their children's social and emotional development. These early parent–child relationships also set the stage for their children's emotional well-being and social relationships in later stages of life. As will be emphasized in the forthcoming discussion, parents who are consistently sensitive and responsive to their infants contribute to the development of infant trust and attachment that in turn promotes **parent–infant synchrony** and is later expressed in toddler autonomy and exploratory behavior.

Infant Trust and Attachment. Probably the most important goal of parenting infants is to endow them with a sense of trust. You might recall from Chapter 1 that Erik Erikson theorized that the quality of parent–infant interactions influences whether infants develop a sense of trust or a sense of mistrust (Goldhaber, 2000). Infants'

This young parent is showing support for the toddler's strong urge to become increasingly independent.

Anthony Magnacca/Merrill.

development of a sense of trust parallels their development of secure attachment. Parents of securely attached infants have been described as more sensitive, more contingently responsive, more consistent, more likely to hold their infants, less intrusive, less tense, and less irritable (Ainsworth, 1973). The process by which babies develop secure attachment depends on whether or not they experience **contingent responsiveness** from their parents and other caregivers. Parents provide contingent responsiveness to their infants when they allow them to be actively engaged in the roles of elicitor as well as receiver of parental attention. Thus, infants play an active role in providing signals, such as crying and smiling, that guide their parents in understanding when and how to care for them. When parents reliably respond to these signals, their infants learn to trust that their needs will be met (Erikson, 1963, 1982) and also develop secure attachment. Furthermore, consistent with earlier research by Ainsworth and her colleagues (1973, 1978), recent research also links secure attachment to parents' responsiveness to infants' distress signals, such as crying (McElwain & Booth-LaForce, 2006; Posada, Carbonelle, & Alzate, 2004). Contemporary research shows that parental sensitivity contributes to infant security in diverse cultures around the world, which demonstrates that the relation between parental responsiveness and infant security is a universal phenomenon (Posada, Jacobs, & Richmond, 2002).

Short- and Long-Term Effects of Parental Sensitivity and Infant Attachment. The beneficial short- and long-term outcomes for securely attached infants are impressive. Short-range benefits are that securely attached infants are more responsive than insecure infants in face-to-face play. Furthermore, they have more varied means of communication, cry less, and quiet more easily when picked up (Ainsworth et al., 1978; Isabella & Belsky, 1991). Also, securely attached infants usually become toddlers who demonstrate more exploratory behavior than infants who do not demonstrate secure attachment (Ainsworth, 1973), and they tend to become children who are competent in a wide array of social and cognitive skills (Fagot, 1997). For example, Bakel and Riksen-Walveren (2002) found that securely attached children are notably more compliant than children who are not securely attached. Conversely, infants with avoidant and disorganized attachment demonstrate significantly more negative behaviors than do securely attached children. Finally, Hobson, Patrick, and Crandell (2004) demonstrated that infants whose mothers respond to them in a sensitive manner have a propensity to share experiences with their mother and also are more likely to engage with others in their environment.

Demand Feeding: An Example of Responsive Caregiving. An illustration of child care in which parental responsiveness to infants has developmental implications can be observed in how and when parents feed their infants. Whether to feed the baby on demand is an important decision for parents, ranking alongside the choice to breastfeed or bottle-feed. Throughout the world and all through history, babies have been fed when they cried to be fed. As noted by Nelson (1998), crying is an inborn behavior that is primarily an appeal for the protective presence of a parent. Thus, infant crying triggers corresponding caretaking behavior in the parents. Because the cry of the infant is an inborn behavior, the natural response of the parent to feed the hungry baby is an appropriate one. Furthermore, ample research evidence supports demand feeding. In their classic 1969 study, linking parental responsiveness to infant attachment, Ainsworth and Bell reported relationships between mothers' feeding styles during the first 3 months of their infants' lives and the patterns of attachment behavior exhibited at age 12 months. Infants who were fed on demand were more likely to have secure attachment to their mothers than infants who received scheduled feeding.

A Cross-Cultural Perspective of Parental Sensitivity. Parental sensitivity to infants is a global phenomenon and can be seen in parent–infant interactions throughout the world. In traditional cultures such as Bali and many African cultures, parents maintain physical closeness to their babies by continuously carrying them, and by practicing cosleeping (Ainsworth, 1967; Ball, Hooker, & Kelly, 1999). Studies of the effects of infant carrying and cosleeping have been positively related to the physical and social–emotional development of infants. As a case in point, infant carrying by Ugandan mothers was found by Ainsworth (1967) to be correlated with secure attachment as well as advanced gross motor development. An advantage of cosleeping is that it is beneficial for helping to regulate the infant's physiological functioning and for promoting closeness to the parents (Feldman et al., 2002). Recent research also supports the link between parental care and infant security in non-Western cultures. Posada et al. (2004) found that the maternal sensitivity of Colombian mothers is significantly related to their infants' secure attachment. Cross-cultural findings supporting the link between parental sensitivity and infant security suggest that differences in the way parental sensitivity is expressed do not challenge the sensitivity–security link. From an infant's perspective, what matters most is that their signals are responded to appropriately by their parents and other caregivers.

What This Means for Professionals. The importance of parental sensitivity to leave infants, which is demonstrated by parents maintaining close proximity to their babies and being consistently responsive to them, cannot be overemphasized. When parents provide a consistency of care of their infants by being reliably available to them and not ignoring their cries and other bids for attention, babies learn to trust that their needs will be met. When interaction with a parent inspires trust and security, the infant develops secure attachment to the parent and gains confidence in engaging and exploring the world. Furthermore, both short- and long-term benefits of parental sensitivity illustrate the value of parental responsiveness to infants and toddlers.

Parental Support of Self-Regulatory Behavior

Besides providing a responsive environment that helps babies trust that their needs will be met, parents play an important role in supporting their infants' development of self regulation (Weinberg, Tronick, & Cohn, 1999). A principal focus of self-regulation for infants relates to the adjustment of their bodies to regular wake and sleep patterns. How much and when a newborn sleeps is an issue of concern for most parents. Infants spend much of their first 2 weeks sleeping (an average of 16 to 20 hours in each 24-hour period), although there is considerable variability from one baby to another. As infants get older, they tend to sleep for longer periods of time and remain awake for more extended intervals. By 6 months, many babies begin sleeping through the night but all infants are not aware that this is how they are to behave. It is not until age 3 or 4 months that infants sleep more at night than during the day; waking up during the night, though, is a common occurrence during infancy as well as early childhood (Gaylor, Goodlin-Jones, & Anders, 2001).

By the time of their second birthday, although wake and sleep patterns have been established for some time, toddlers sometimes resist going to bed or taking a nap. This behavior might be an expression of their developing autonomy needs, a reluctance to separate from their parents, or a fear of the dark. Toddlers whose parents handle this phase of bedtime resistance with kindness and understanding are better able to make the transition than those whose parents are unsympathetic to their feelings. According to Bigner (1998), American parents are perhaps the only parents in the world who expect their children to develop self-regulated behavior early in life with little guidance from their parents. As noted by Bigner, American parents are likely to simply place an infant or toddler in a crib and close the door, whereas parents in many other cultures typically sing a short, soft lullaby to their infant or rock the infant to sleep. Interestingly, preparing their babies for bedtime by singing to them, rocking them to sleep, or reading a book with them, contributes to their self-regulatory behavior. In turns out that the face-to-face reciprocity found in these kinds of rituals increases toddlers' self-regulatory behavior. For example, the findings of Feldman, Greenbaum, and Yirmiya (1999) were among the first to support the relation between the face-to-face reciprocity between parents and their infants and the later emergence of self-regulatory behavior during the toddler years.

What This Means for Professionals. It is recommended that parents prepare their infants and toddlers for bedtime by means of regular rituals (such as rocking or singing) designed to assist their children in relaxing and settling down. Besides providing a calming and reassuring ritual to support their infants and toddlers in making the transition to going to bed, it is helpful for parents to monitor how much time their children are sleeping during the day. Whereas infants should not be roused from their sleep, toddlers who sleep for as many as 6 hours during the day might have trouble sleeping through the night. In these cases, parents might alleviate this problem by waking a toddler from a long daytime nap.

Thinking Critically

How do you feel about the fact that parents around the world prepare their babies for bedtime by rocking and singing to them and many American parents put their babies to bed without these kinds of preparation?

PARENT–INFANT PLAY

Now we turn our attention to the highly significant role of parent–infant play in the development of **parent–infant synchrony**. The development of parent–infant synchrony depends on the abilities of the parent and infant to accurately read and respond to each other's cues. Interactive play between parents and their infants and toddlers is sometimes initiated by the parents and at other times by the infant. One of the benefits of parent–infant synchrony is that these interactions contribute to the development of infant self-control. Even though most parents accurately read infant cues and respond accordingly, there are two main impediments to the initiation and repair of parent–infant synchrony: Either the parent ignores the infant's invitation to interact or the parent overstimulates the baby who wants to pause and rest. Therefore, when engaging in interactive play with their infants, parents should respond not only to their babies' gestures that are designed to engage parents but also to their signals that they are feeling overstimulated and need a short break. The gesture from infants that signals their need for a brief pause is seen when babies turn their heads away—the first gesture for "No." After these brief pauses, babies will turn back to look at the parent, usually with a smile to indicate they are ready to continue playing (Feldman et al., 1999).

What This Means for Professionals. It is beneficial for parent–infant play to occur simply for the joy of it, and play can be introduced into bathing, dressing, and a variety of everyday caregiving activities. When parents make a game out of giving the baby a bath or playing peek-a-boo as they are putting on a shirt, these activities become more enjoyable for babies as well as for their parents. One of the benefits of interactive play for infants and toddlers is that it increases their overall sense of predictability. For infants and toddlers, gaining a sense of predictability regarding what is likely to happen in certain situations increases their self-control.

PARENTAL INFLUENCES ON TODDLERS' AUTONOMY AND EXPLORATORY BEHAVIOR

Parental responsiveness contributes to infant trust which impacts the development of the toddler's autonomy and exploratory behavior. According to Erikson (1963, 1982), infants who learn to trust their parents become more autonomous during toddlerhood than infants who do not trust that their parents will be consistently available to them. Recent research supports the link between parental sensitivity and infant autonomy. Deater-Deckard (2000) demonstrated that when parents are highly supportive of their toddlers' drives to explore their environment and to try out new things, their toddlers become bolder and more competent individuals. Furthermore, toddlers are highly attuned to the responses of their parents. They continuously check their parent's gaze or facial expressions as well as verbal responses of pleasure or displeasure to guide their behavior (Baldwin, 2000). This behavior on the part of the toddler is called **social referencing.** An example of social referencing is a toddler's typical willingness to comply with their parents' requests (Kochanski, Coy, & Murray, 2001). Most everyday displays of social referencing by infants and toddlers occur with mothers due to infants and toddlers spending more time with their mothers than their fathers. Even though toddlers' social referencing occurs most often with mothers, when both parents are present, toddlers use fathers as social references as much as mothers. In active play, however, fathers tend to be more encouraging than mothers, who tend to be more protective. Thus, when they begin exploring, toddlers often look for approval from their fathers to support their curiosity (Parke, 1996).

What This Means for Professionals. Parents should respond to their toddlers' autonomy needs by being patient with their quest for greater independence and providing assistance as they attempt new tasks without taking over. Parents might remember that, although toddlers often overestimate their abilities and frequently require parental backing, they nevertheless need to continually challenge themselves to become increasingly more self-sufficient. Therefore, even though it takes longer to allow toddlers to attempt autonomous activities (such as putting their shoes on by themselves), it is helpful when their parents take the time to provide the required assistance whenever possible. Parents might keep in mind that, with each endeavor to do things for themselves, toddlers become progressively more independent, and more and more confident of their capabilities.

Autonomy and Independent Toileting

An important milestone in the development of autonomy occurs when toddlers become independent in their toileting. To help their toddlers accomplish this goal, parents should not push them to achieve toilet training before they are ready nor hold them back when they are ready. Assessing readiness is, therefore, one of the key components of successful toilet training. The average age of readiness for toilet training is 22 months, although some toddlers will not be ready at that time and others will be ready slightly earlier. Physical readiness depends on the maturation of the toddler's bladder and sphincter muscles and this maturation varies from one toddler to another. Other considerations of independent toileting include taking preliminary steps to prepare toddlers for toilet training, being ready and willing to devote the necessary time to the training process, and being patient with them as they attempt to achieve that objective. Three ways to assess whether toddlers are ready for toilet training is by determining whether they are (a) staying dryer for longer periods of time (especially overnight), (b) expressing discomfort with wet diapers, and (c) showing an interest in using the toilet (Edwards & Liu, 2002). In assisting their toddlers to become independent in their toileting, parents should be patient and not punitive. In the case of wet pants, a parent might respond to the mishap with a friendly statement that recognizes the accident but does not condemn the child. For example, the parent might say to the child, "Oh, we don't like wet pants, do we?" This type of response to the child's failure to stay dry is not punitive and sends the important message that the parent is there to assist the toddler in the achievement of toilet training. As a partner in the toddler's efforts to accomplish independent toileting, it is imperative that parents not pressure the child to go to the toilet but to make potty visits a natural part of a day in which a number of other interesting activities are also taking place.

THE PROMOTION OF INFANT–TODDLER PHYSICAL DEVELOPMENT

At the same time that parents are influencing the social–emotional development of their infants and toddlers, they are also contributing to their physical development. Parents impact the physical development of their infants and toddlers by the decisions they make regarding their nutrition, their health care, and the experiences they provide to support the development of their motor skills.

Meeting Nutritional Needs

Just as nutrition plays a crucial role in prenatal development, it plays a major part in the physical development of the infant and toddler. The choices parents make regarding breast-feeding or bottle-feeding, when to wean their infants, and when to introduce them to solid foods, will have a significant impact on their children's health and development.

Breast-Feeding in Comparison to Bottle-Feeding. The first choice parents must make related to meeting the nutritional needs of their infants is whether to breast-feed or bottle-feed them. Of these two choices, the rewards of breast-feeding outweigh those of bottle-feeding. The first breast milk of the new mother is called **colostrum,** which is a thick high-caloric fluid secreted by the woman's breast at the birth of her child. Colostrum has many benefits for the newborn, including the fact that it is high in carbohydrates, protein, and antibodies. It is also low in fat, which newborns often have difficulty digesting. Another benefit of colostrum is that it has a mild laxative effect, which encourages the passing of the baby's first stool. This first stool clears excess waste products of dead red blood cells from the infant's body and helps prevent jaundice. Colostrum also contains large numbers of antibodies that help protect the mucous membranes in the throat, lungs, and intestines of the infant. A further advantage of colostrum is that it contains antibodies that protect the infant from harmful viruses and bacteria while establishing beneficial bacteria in the newborn's digestive tract (Davidson, 1999).

After 3 days, mothers produce less-concentrated milk, which is the ideal nutrition for babies for many reasons. Human breast milk is always sterile and at body temperature; it contains more iron, vitamin C, and vitamin A than cow's or goat's milk; and it provides antibodies to protect the infant against any disease the mother is immunized against through vaccination or having had the illness herself. Furthermore, the specific fats and sugars in breast milk make it more digestible than any prepared baby formula, resulting in breast-fed babies having fewer allergies and stomachaches than bottle-fed babies (Talukder, 2000). Also, breast-feeding decreases the frequency of almost every common infectious disease, especially diarrhea, which is one of the primary causes of infant death in developing countries (Isolauri, Sutas, Salo, Isosonppi, & Kaila, 1998). Based on the benefits of breast milk, doctors worldwide recommend breast-feeding. The World Health Association (the WHO), American Academy of Pediatrics (AAP), Canadian Paediatric Society, and American Dietetic Association all strongly encourage breast-feeding for all babies unless the mother is an active drug user (including alcohol and tobacco), HIV positive, or severely malnourished. In those circumstances, bottle-feeding is the better choice (Boyle & Morris, 1999).

Weaning and the Introduction to Solid Foods. The AAP recommends that breast-feeding continue for at least 12 months with exclusive breastfeeeding for the first 4 to 6 months of life. At that point, they recommend that other foods be added, especially cereal and fruit because breast milk does not have adequate iron, vitamin D, or vitamin K for older babies. Also, at that age, foods such as cereal and fruits are easier to digest (Talukder, 2000). For babies who are weaned before 12 months of age, the AAP recommends iron-supplemented infant formula rather than whole milk (Boyle & Morris, 1999). After they have weaned their infants, it is imperative that parents provide an adequate amount of protein and iron to meet the infant's growth requirements because the most rapid growth of the entire life span occurs in the first 3 years. Furthermore, the lack of adequate sources of these nutrients can lead to malnutrition.

Thus, the decisions parents make regarding the timing of weaning and the choice of solid foods provided afterward impact the health and growth of their infants. After infants are weaned, it is of utmost importance that they are fed a highly nutritious diet that consists of foods containing calcium, protein, fruits, vegetables, and whole grains. Unfortunately, many infants do not receive adequate nutrition, and the socioeconomic status and geographical location of the family make a big difference. For example, infants and toddlers in industrialized countries are far more likely to receive adequate nutrition than babies in developing countries. Furthermore, the primary cause of malnutrition in developing countries is early termination of breast-feeding. In many of those countries, breast-feeding used to continue for at least 2 years, as recommended by the WHO. Now, it is stopped much earlier in favor of bottle-feeding, usually with powdered formulas that are very often overdiluted with unsafe water (Berger, 2001). The long-term effects of malnutrition during infancy have been well documented. Longitudinal research on children in Kenya, Egypt, Jamaica, Indonesia, and Barbados reveals that children who are underfed in infancy tend to display impaired learning abilities (especially in their ability to concentrate) and impairment in their language skills through childhood and adolescence. Even in wealthy countries, isolated cases of severe protein–calorie malnutrition during infancy (failure to thrive) still occur. Typically, that happens due to parental emotional or physical stress, or the debilitating effects of parental drug addiction, that are so overwhelming that parents either ignore their infants' feeding needs or prepare food improperly (Kerr, Black, & Krishnakumar, 2000).

Thinking Critically

Given the distressing effects of malnutrition during infancy, to what extent do you think the community should be involved in providing expectant and new parents with information regarding the recommendations of the AAP and WHO about breast-feeding, timing of weaning, and the choice of nutritious foods after infants are weaned?

Providing Health Care

To ensure optimum physical development of their infants and toddlers, it is important for parents to make arrangements for their health care. When parents access available health care for their infants and toddlers, they allow medical professionals to determine if their babies are growing and developing according to expected rates and to respond to health problems (such as ear infections) that periodically arise during infancy. One of the most important aspects of medical intervention that parents need to be certain that their babies receive is immunization against communicable diseases. Today, deadly childhood epidemics are rare and an infant's chance of dying from infectious disease in industrialized countries is less than 1 in 500, down from 1 in 20 fifty years ago. The single most important cause of the dramatic improvement in child survival is immunization. Worldwide, immunization has reached more children every decade, and currently more than 90% of all infants in the world are immunized against the childhood diseases of diptheria, pertussis, tetanus, measles, polio, and mumps (Baker, 2000). In industrialized nations, many infants also are immunized against hepatitis B, influenza, rubella, and chicken pox.

What This Means for Professionals. Parental attentiveness to the nutrition and health needs of infants and toddlers cannot be overemphasized. Child development (including brain development) proceeds more rapidly during the first 3 years (particularly the first year) than during any other stage of development. Consequently, parents' decisions concerning infant feeding and health care have critical implications for the growth and development of their children. Furthermore, community programs designed to promote infants' and toddlers' health are likely to be more effective if they educate parents regarding these important links.

The Promotion of Fine and Gross Motor Skills

In addition to promoting their infants' and toddlers' health and social and emotional development, parents must provide a safe and stimulating environment to encourage the development of their babies' gross and **fine motor skills**. As they are promoting their babies' motor skills, parents tend to overestimate the motor capabilities of their boy babies and underestimate the motor capabilities of their girl babies. In reality, according to developmental norms, infant girls and boys achieve early milestones, such as reaching, sitting, crawling, and walking, at approximately the same ages. Parental gender biases related to their infants' motor capabilities most likely derive from observations of differences in the physical growth and activity levels of infant girls and boys. Even though baby boys have faster physical growth and higher activity levels than baby girls, boys and girls do not differ in motor development during the infancy period (Mondschein, Adolph, & Tamis-LeMonda, 2000).

To promote their babies' fine and gross motor skills, parents must take two important steps. The first step is to provide a stimulating environment and select playthings and experiences that are developmentally appropriate. The second (but equally important) step is to make safety a high priority. By and large, infants and toddlers need a clean, safe environment in which they are able to freely move about and also benefit from having a variety of objects that they can manipulate. Furthermore, parents need to be alert to cues provided by their infants and toddlers regarding readiness to attempt various motor skills. For example, when a toddler shows a strong interest in climbing stairs, that curiosity reflects the child's readiness to master that particular step in gross motor skill development. An example of readiness in the area of fine motor skill development is the baby's attempt to grab the spoon when being fed. In fact, the best example of an early fine motor skill is successful grabbing (McCarty & Ashmead, 1999). Information related to infants' and toddlers' behavioral norms might also assist parents in taking precautions designed to keep their babies safe. For instance, when infants begin to turn over (which typically occurs at about 3 months), it is very important that they not be placed on elevated surfaces without sides. A sudden, unexpected turn might land the infant on the floor and might result in head or bodily injury. Likewise, as infants and toddlers become increasingly more ambulatory (creeping, crawling, and walking), their home environments should be "baby-proofed" to remove hazardous materials such as cleaning products, poisonous plants, and small objects on which an infant or toddler might choke. Electrical plugs should be covered as well and low cabinets should have childproof closures. Finally, parents should continuously monitor their infants and toddlers to ensure their safety. Parents should also be careful in distinguishing between safe and unsafe objects because infants and toddlers indiscriminately pick up and put any small object into their mouths and tug on a number of objects (such as plants) that can be toppled over.

What This Means for Professionals. When parents are aware that their babies' attempts to climb stairs or grab the feeding spoon are actually demonstrations of motor skill readiness, they can assist them in reaching these goals, thereby promoting the advancement of their motor skills. For instance, parents might allocate time for assisted stair climbing by walking behind their toddlers while steadying and encouraging them as they mount each step. Similarly, when babies are trying to master self-feeding, parents might support that goal by being tolerant of the necessary untidiness that accompanies these early feeding attempts. Of course, the parent should supplement the infant's early feeding efforts with a second spoon until the infant's mastery of that goal has been sufficiently refined to the point that the food in the baby's spoon actually reaches the baby's mouth. Other ways to assist babies in self-feeding is by giving them small pieces of cut-up food that can be easily picked up. The spoon grabbing of infants and toddlers' strong interest in stair climbing are examples of the many cues that infants and toddlers provide their parents and other caregivers regarding their readiness to engage in activities related to fine and gross motor skill development.

PROMOTING THE COGNITIVE DEVELOPMENT OF INFANTS AND TODDLERS

Parents play a vital role in promoting their infants' and toddlers' cognitive development. When they engage their babies in frequent interactions and also provide a stimulating environment for them, parents sustain their babies' ability to think and reason. Furthermore, the parent–child verbal exchanges that accompany these interactions promote infants' and toddlers' language development (Moerk, 2000).

Insights from Piaget

As you might recall from reading Chapter 1, Jean Piaget theorized that children are active participants in the development of their own cognitive abilities. Piaget referred to the intelligence of infants as **sensorimotor intelligence** based on the view that infants think exclusively with their senses and motor skills during that stage of development (Piaget & Inhelder, 1969). It is helpful if parents understand that their infants' and toddlers' curiosity about objects in their environment and their strong interest in looking, listening, touching, biting, and tasting is normal and necessary for their cognitive advancement. In the discussion that focused on ways in which parents

This mother understands the toddler's readiness to learn and is providing intellectual stimulation for the child.

Anne Vega/Merrill.

promote their infants' and toddlers' fine motor skills, it was recommended that parents provide their babies with a variety of toys and other objects to be manipulated. These same toys and activities also contribute to advances in cognition.

Contributions from Vygotsky

As discussed in Chapter 1, Lev Vygotsky also viewed children's intellectual development as a product of their active exploration of the environment but placed greater emphasis than did Piaget on the role of parents, older siblings, or other adults in aiding that process (**guided participation**) (Rogoff, 1990). Following Vygotsky's views, parents ought to be actively engaged with guiding and instructing their infants and toddlers as they interact with the persons and objects in their environment. For example, if a toddler is attempting to put an object into a container, the parent is in the position to help the child figure out how to reach that goal sooner by using language to instruct the toddler and demonstrating the procedure. Whether following the views of Piaget or Vygotsky, parents should be aware of the importance of providing infants and toddlers with a safe, stimulating environment in which their natural curiosity is respected and their active exploration is supported.

Findings from Recent Brain Research

Recent brain research takes the idea of the child as an active participant in cognitive development a step further than did Piaget and Vygotsky by demonstrating that babies and young children participate in the building of their own brains. The research that links the development of the infant's brain to emerging cognitive abilities emphasizes that everything the baby sees, hears, tastes, touches, and smells influences the way the brain connections get hooked up. After birth, as experience floods in from all the senses, the baby's brain cells are continuously attempting to make connections to each other (Gopnik, Meltzoff, & Kuhl, 1999).

Thinking Critically

Drawing on the views of Piaget, consider how a parent might design an activity for a toddler with the goal of promoting the toddler's cognitive development. Then, using Vygotsky's idea of guided participation, how might the parent alter the design of that activity?

PARENTS' UNDERSTANDING OF INFANT PERCEPTION

In order to promote infant cognition, it is beneficial if parents are aware of the perceptual capabilities their newborns bring into the world. Infants' perceptual skills of hearing, smell, and touch are very keen at birth and their visual perception is clearest at a range of about 10 to 20 inches, the distance between the baby held in the parent's arms and the face of the parent holding the infant (Morrongiello, Fenwick, & Chance, 1998). Furthermore, infants show clear perceptual preferences, examples of which are seen in their visual preferences, which include (a) the human face; (b) dynamic, moving patterns over static ones (Teller, 1997); (c) sharp-contrast in comparison to low-contrast objects; and (d) primary colors rather than softer pastels (Bornstein & Lamb, 1992). It is helpful if parents understand the ways in which their infants' perceptual preferences guide them in seeking the information they need to know about their environment. An obvious example is the infant's fondness for looking at the human face, which dominates any other visual preference (Valenza, Simion, & Cassia, 1996). The **mutual gazing** of parents and infants has been found to be a central aspect of the infant–parent interactive process. It has been demonstrated that when either the parent or infant looks at the other, the probability of infant–parent interaction is increased. By contrast, when either the parent or baby looks away, the behavior in which they are engaged is likely to subside. It has been suggested that the gaze of the parent or infant acts as a magnet for the other and that the mutual gazing of parents and infants then spreads to interactive parent–infant behaviors. These interactions include parent–infant turn-taking vocalizations, mutual touching, and mutual imitation. Thus, mutual gazing appears to provide a context for promoting and sustaining a complex set of parent–infant interactive behaviors (Weinberg & Tronick, 1996).

In addition to understanding that their infants are highly attuned to perceive parental actions, it is helpful, as well, if parents are aware of their infant's other perceptual preferences. For example, the irresistible allure of sharp contrasts, such as stripes, checkerboards, corners, and other highly contrasting objects, helps babies learn where objects begin and end. Also, infants' fascination with moving objects provides information that helps them to distinguish between objects. Furthermore, through observing movement, babies learn how different objects characteristically move and how they are likely to move in the future. As a case in point, when a parent rolls a ball to a baby, the baby quickly learns to roll the ball back. With more experience with the ball, the baby discovers that it will bounce when dropped on a hard surface. Similarly, infants' keen hearing abilities, coupled with their experience with sounds, help them to learn which sounds are associated with particular objects or events. For example, they learn that the opening of the front door or the sound of the car pulling into the driveway signals the arrival of a family member or visitor (Gopnik et al., 1999).

Based on the neurological and psychological evidence, it is apparent that nature has designed parents to teach babies what they need to learn as much as it has designed babies' brains to rapidly learn from their experiences. In fact, it is the normal, spontaneous interactions between parents and their infants that are the most beneficial. Accordingly, the parental actions that nurture babies are the same behaviors that give infants the information they need, and the nurturing care that parents are naturally motivated to provide their infants is spontaneous, automatic, and unpremeditated. The scientific evidence suggests, therefore, that parents should do just what they normally are inclined to do when they are with their babies—talk, play, make funny faces, and (most important) pay attention to their babies' interests (Gopnik et al., 1999).

Thinking Critically

Were you surprised to learn that infant perception is related to what infants need to learn about the environment and that parents instinctively understand infant perception? Which type of infant perception have you perceived? What type of parent behavior have you observed that demonstrated a knowledge of infant perception?

What This Means for Professionals. Knowing that infants show a preference for the human face, and that their clearest focus is in the range between the caregiver's arms and the caregiver's face, informs parents of the significance of having frequent face-to-face interactions with their infants while holding them in their arms. The understanding that infants prefer dynamic, moving patterns over static ones influences parents to provide their babies with objects that move, such as mobiles. Parents seem to intuitively understand that they must keep in mind the infant's 10- to 20-inch range of visual focus when hanging a mobile. Parental awareness of their babies' preference for dynamic, moving patterns is also frequently observed in parent–infant playful interactions. As an illustration, to call the baby's attention to a ball, the parent is more likely to pick up the ball and roll it toward the baby. Finally, the knowledge that babies prefer sharp-contrast rather than low-contrast objects, and are more attracted to primary colors than softer pastels, is increasingly reflected in parents' selection of their babies' toys and in the choices they make when painting and/or furnishing the bedrooms of their infants and toddlers.

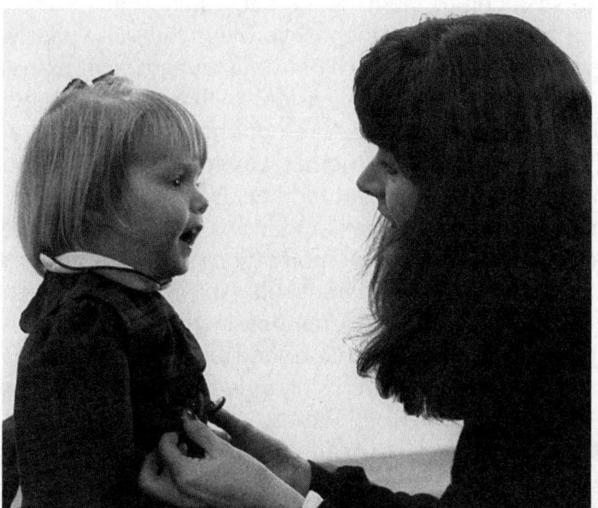

Anne Vega/Merrill.

This young mother is playing an important role in assisting her child's language development by engaging the child in a face-to-face verbal exchange.

PARENT–INFANT/TODDLER VERBAL INTERACTIONS

In addition to being aware of their infants' perceptual capabilities, parents also appear to be conscious of the critical role they play in their infants' development of language. There are several ways in which infants' predisposition to learn language is matched by parents' motivation to promote their infants' language capabilities. First, the hearing of infants is extremely well developed at birth, and it has been demonstrated that babies hear and begin to recognize voices even before birth (Morrongiello et al., 1998). Their pronounced hearing ability provides infants with the capability of being able to immediately benefit from verbal exchanges. Second, for young infants, the sound of the human voice (whether it comes from a parent, sibling, or stranger) evokes special interest and curiosity. Third, parents, grandparents, older siblings, and others use a special language called **parentese** when talking to babies that is intended to gain and maintain the attention of infants. Parentese is a form of adult-to-infant speech that is seen in all language communities throughout the world and infants prefer listening to parentese over ordinary speech. In comparison to ordinary language, parentese is higher pitched; has more low-to-high fluctuations; has a simpler, more concrete vocabulary; and its sentence length is shorter (Jaffe, Beebe, Feldstein, Crown, & Jasnow, 2001). When using parentese to speak with their babies, it is helpful if parents clearly pronounce words such as *Mama* and *Dada*, and it is beneficial as well for infants to be able to see their mouths as they form these words. Singing to their infants is another way that parents promote their infant's language development, given that singing has some of the same features of parentese (rhythmic and higher pitched).

At the same time that infants are learning the sounds of their particular language, they are simultaneously developing the ability to use **linguistic turn taking**. In response to their infants' need to learn turn taking, parents typically provide very brief pauses when speaking to them. These pauses allow them the opportunity to respond; interestingly, infants spontaneously provide the same pauses for parents to react to their utterances. The importance of live language in comparison to recorded language (as heard on the radio or television) is that live language is interactive. Thus, infants and toddlers are afforded the opportunity to play an active role in a verbal exchange (Jaffe et al., 2001). Another way in which parents support the language development of their infants and toddlers is through the use of labeling and gesturing. According to McNeil, Alibali, and Evans (2000), parents' reinforcing gestures are especially helpful when new information is being conveyed or new skills are being taught. The valuable role parents play in promoting the language development of their babies cannot be overemphasized. By consistently talking with them in the special language of parentese, and building in brief pauses to allow them the opportunity to respond, parents provide the ideal conditions for language development to occur. Furthermore, the most verbal babies—first to speak, first to utter sentences, first to use abstract vocabulary—are raised by baby-talking parents (Bruer, 1999).

The Importance of Reading Books with Infants and Toddlers

An auspicious activity related to early language development is parent–child book reading. In fact, a robust and consistent finding regarding early language skills is that parent–child book reading is linked with the early onset of language. Consistently, researchers have found that the younger the child when parents begin shared reading, the better the child's later language abilities. Furthermore, among 2-year-old children, the age that their parents engage them in shared reading is the strongest predictor of language skills. In considering the way in which early shared reading supports language development, it has been suggested that the mechanism through which early reading influences language development is **joint attention**. Thus, whenever their parents read with them, infants or toddlers are engaging in joint attention interactions with their parents. Furthermore, these interactions become predictable to the infant. As a result of these reading episodes, infants and toddlers find it easier to associate words with objects. Because these interactions typically recur over and over again, the infant or toddler is provided multiple opportunities to match words with objects (Karass, VanDeventer, & Braungart-Reiker, 2003).

THE CARE OF INFANTS AND TODDLERS WHEN PARENTS WORK

A primary challenge facing parents of infants and toddlers is how to rearrange family life to fit the care of their children into their other family and occupational responsibilities. Parents coordinate the care of their infants and toddlers with parental occupations in a variety of different ways. For parents who are married or living with their partners, one parent sometimes works while the other parent provides child care, at least in the early weeks or months after the arrival of a child or children. In other two-parent households, both parents work but they coordinate schedules in such a way that each parent takes care of the child, or children, while the other parent is working. Also, grandparents are frequently called-on sources of child care for married or single parents. Although working parents are sometimes able to rely on each other or their own parents to care for their children, most American parents place their children in child care centers while they work.

Center-Based Child Care

As previously stated, the majority of working American parents place their infants and toddlers in center-based child care. More than half of all infants and toddlers in the United States spend at least 20 hours each week being cared for in child care centers. Although the typical age of a baby's first placement in a child care center is 33 months, the age of first placement varies by family income, the marital status and educational level of the parents, family size, and the presence or absence of nonparental adults in the household (Singer, Fuller, & Keiley, 1998).

Factors Influencing Infant–Toddler Placement in Center-Based Care. A primary factor influencing placement in center-based child care is family income, and there is a skewed picture of the effect of income on the selection of center-based care. Both high-income and impoverished families are more likely to place their infants and toddlers in center-based child care than are working-class families. Parents with high incomes can afford the private costs and many low income and working poor families receive subsidies that offset the cost. Working-class families, on the other hand, are least likely to use child care centers inasmuch as they cannot afford the private fees and do not receive child care subsidies. In addition to cost, family size and composition affect whether infants and toddlers are placed in child care centers. Infants and toddlers from smaller families, particularly single-parent families, are more likely to be placed in center-based child care. Also, the presence of a kin member or nonparent adult in the family lessens the likelihood of center placement. Finally, the parents' level of education influences their choice of whether or not to use center-based child care. Better-educated parents are more inclined to place children in center-based care than are parents with less education (Singer et al., 1998).

Assessing the Quality of Center-Based Care. Evidence is mounting that certain features of child care settings are associated with positive outcomes in children and it is precisely these features that reflect the quality of these programs. First among these findings is that center care, family child care, nor father care compromises mother–infant attachment so long as the infant or toddler does not simultaneously experience inattentive parenting while in poor-quality child care. Moreover, infants and toddlers in higher quality child care settings are more securely attached to their caregivers than are infants and toddlers in poor or minimally adequate care. In addition to earlier concerns regarding the impact of child care placement on infant–parent attachment (which has been laid to rest), traditional assessments of child care quality focused on caregiver–child ratio and the safety of the environment (and these features continue to be important). What is missing in those evaluations is reflected in the new directions for studying child care quality. The contemporary assessments of child care quality emphasize the significance of relationships, continuity of care, culture, and context (Love, Raikes, Paulsell, & Kisker, 2000).

In terms of relationships, it is important for parents to choose child care programs that address the developmental needs of their children. Because a major task of infants and toddlers is to establish secure relationships with their caregivers, parents should take into account the nature of caregiver–child relationships. In examining continuity of care, it should be emphasized that to form relationships, infants and toddlers need to experience consistency of care from caregivers that remain in their lives over a period of time. Therefore, parents should be aware that frequently entering into new child care arrangements, or having to get used to the repeated turnover of child care providers, is likely to be detrimental to the developing relationships of their infants and toddlers. Evaluating child care quality in terms of culture emphasizes the need to understand the role of **cultural congruence** on children's development. Children's development is more likely to be enhanced by caregivers who can speak their language and who look and act in ways that are somewhat familiar.

Finally, an assessment of quality child care in terms of context emphasizes such contextual features as the type of setting, staff stability, structural features of the program (such as group composition), staff qualifications and turnover, and parent involvement (Love et al., 2000).

Tag-Team Parenting

Nonoverlapping shift patterns of employment that allow parents to practice **tag-team parenting** are preferred by some dual-earner families for a variety of reasons. For example, in her study of nurses who work the night shift, Garey (1999) found that the night shift was selected specifically to allow those mothers to stay at home with their children during the day. Besides saving on child care costs, parents who coordinate child care with nonstandard shift work are more likely, than are other parents, to share other household responsibilities. In dual-earner families, in which one spouse or partner works a nonday shift, fathers tend to contribute more in household labor when the mother is unavailable (Presser, 1994). Additionally, infants and toddlers in these families are given the opportunity to be cared for exclusively by their fathers, an arrangement that is not practiced in any of the other child care arrangements. Furthermore, mothers who rely on their spouses to care for their children while they work often have acknowledged that father solo care is beneficial for the fathers as well as for the children. The drawbacks for families when parents have different shifts for working and parenting is that each parent is responsible for all the child care while the other parent is working and parents have less time to spend with each other (Hattery, 2001).

Grandparents Caring for Grandchildren While Parents Work

Although grandparents are no longer the primary source of child care for working parents in the United States, many grandparents continue to care for their grandchildren on a regular basis. A number of circumstances influence the likelihood that grandparents will take on the role of caregiver of their grandchildren in order to assist working parents. These factors include the age of the grandchildren, and the age, marital status, ethnicity, socioeconomic status, educational level, and gender of the grandparents. Of these various factors, the age of the grandchildren plays the most significant role in influencing grandparent care, with 9% of all grandparents providing extensive care to grandchildren who are under 5 years of age. In comparison to grandparents who do not provide extensive care for their grandchildren, those who do are significantly younger, and are more likely to be married, African American, and female. Grandparents who care for their grandchildren while the parents of those children work also are more likely to have lower incomes, less likely to have graduated from high school, and more likely to have co-resident children. The clearest advantage of grandparent child care for working parents is the knowledge that their children are being cared for by caregivers who have a close relationship with the children. The closeness of the relationship to the grandparent is an advantage for the child as well, who does not experience disruptions in the attachments they form with their caregivers. Furthermore, grandparents who provide extensive care for their grandchildren report that they have closer relationships with their grandchildren than do grandparents who do not care for their grandchildren on a regular basis (Fuller-Thomson & Minkler, 2001).

SUMMARY

- This chapter focused on the preparation for and transition to parenthood, the role of parents in promoting the development of their infants and toddlers, and the challenges of coordinating occupational demands with parental responsibilities.
- We began the chapter by considering ways in which parents might optimize their chances for having healthy, full-term babies. The focus of that discussion was the nutritional needs of pregnant mothers, the harmful effects of teratogens on the unborn child, and the importance of early prenatal care.
- Next, there was a discussion of the experience of birth as a universal occurrence that differentially impacts parents according to the nature of the birth and the resources of the family and community. We then looked at the ways in which parents, grandparents, and the community work together to accommodate the arrival of babies into the family.
- Much of the remainder of the chapter was devoted to an exploration of the ways in which parent–child interactions promote the social–emotional, physical, and cognitive development of infants and toddlers. Throughout that discussion, we were consistently reminded of the central role that parents play in promoting the health and well-being of their babies.
- Following the discussion of the ways in which parents impact the development of their infants and toddlers, we explored the importance of parent–infant play. We also examined the varied ways in which working parents arrange for the care of their children, and provided guidelines for parents to consider in assessing quality child care.

KEY TERMS

- affective synchrony
- neonatal abstinence syndrome
- colostrum
- contingent responsiveness
- cultural congruence
- fetal alcohol syndrome
- fine motor skills
- gross motor skills
- guided participation
- joint attention
- kangaroo care
- linguistic turn taking
- mutual gazing
- parentese
- parent–infant synchrony
- self-regulation
- sensorimotor intelligence
- social referencng
- tag-team parenting
- teratogens

USEFUL WEB SITES

The American Pregnancy Association

http://www.americanpregnancy.org/links/

This association's site provides multiple resources for getting pregnant, dealing with issues of infertility, and adoption, as well as planning and preparing for the birth of a child. It also provides information related to pregnancy wellness. Additionally, it has numerous links to pregnancy-related topics.

Tips for Parents of Infants and Toddlers

http://www.parenttime.com/

Pregnancy and parenting tips, as well as short articles about babies, written by parenting experts are found on this site.

Expecting parents might also access information from the U.S. government at the following website

http://www.usa.gov/

Here links to "parents expecting" and Expecting Parents: USA.gov can be found. These links provide information related to alcohol and pregnancy, breast-feeding, healthy pregnancy, newborn care, popular baby names, and postpartum depression.

Parent–Preschooler Interactions

Objectives

After completing this chapter, you should be able to

- Identify the ways in which the attachment preschoolers have with their parents impacts their social–emotional development.
- Demonstrate an understanding of the parental behaviors that support preschoolers' curiosity and sense of initiative.
- Explain how parents might assist their preschool children in mastering new skills.
- Describe ways in which parents might promote their preschoolers' self-esteem and self-reliance.
- Identify the reasons why preschoolers need boundaries, regulations, and at times redirection, and show an understanding of how parents might help their young children to understand which behaviors are safe and/or acceptable.
- Explain how parents might meet the nutritional needs of their preschool children.
- Show an understanding of the ways in which the brain development of preschool children makes it easier for them to understand parental instructions.
- Explain the role of parents in promoting young children's cognitive development.
- Demonstrate an understanding of how parents might take into account children's understanding of language as they speak with them, including providing instructions for them.
- Identify the ways in which parents might promote their preschool children's fine and gross motor skills.
- Identify the primary challenges and concerns related to parenting the preschool child and explain ways in which parents might address these challenges.

Children are entitled in their otherness, as anyone is; and when we reach them, as we sometimes do, it is generally on a point of sheer delight, to us so astonishing, but to them so natural.

—Alastaire Reid (Tripp, 1970)

Sheer delight, exuberance, curiosity, and magical thinking are all ways that describe how preschool children engage and react to their world (Leach, 1997). Because preschoolers require assistance, guidance, and care from their caregivers, parents have numerous opportunities to join them in their lively adventures. Furthermore, the level of support that preschool children receive as they enthusiastically challenge themselves, the environment, and their parents, affects their social–emotional, physical, and cognitive development.

THE PARENTAL ROLE IN PROMOTING PRESCHOOLERS' SOCIAL–EMOTIONAL DEVELOPMENT

Consider how different a 2-year-old is from a 6-year-old, emotionally and socially. Whereas the 2-year-old is still vacillating between dependence and self-determination and cannot be left alone even for a few minutes, the 6-year-old has both the confidence and competence to be relatively independent. By the time a child leaves the preschool years, that child can be trusted to do many things alone and is proud of the ability to do so. The 6-year-old child also shows affection toward family members without the dependency or exaggerated self-assertion of the 2-year-old. Let's take a look at the ways in which parent–child relationships are altered in relation to children's transformation from toddlers to preschoolers and the ways in which parents support the developmental needs of their active, curious young children.

Early Attachment and Parent–Preschooler Relationships

We learned in Chapter 5 that infants and toddlers who are securely attached to their parents have parents who are consistently responsive to them. We also learned that secure attachment during those first few years is associated with a number of other positive developmental outcomes. Secure attachment is not only central to the well-being of infants and toddlers, it is also important for the optimum development of preschoolers. The attachment preschoolers have with their parents has a profound impact on their social–emotional development. It has been demonstrated through longitudinal studies that preschoolers who were securely attached as babies show more elaborate make-believe play and greater enthusiasm, flexibility, and persistence in problem solving. Attachment security during preschool also has been shown to be a reliable predictor of early conscience development (Laible & Thompson,

2000) and of the development of a positive view of the self. Such children have been found to be high in self-esteem, socially competent, cooperative, popular, and empathic. In contrast, preschoolers with avoidant attachment have been viewed as isolated and disconnected, and preschoolers with resistant attachment have been described as disruptive and difficult (Bar-Haim, Sutton, & Fox, 2000).

Although secure attachment during infancy is generally related to positive development during preschool, continuity of responsive caregiving determines whether securely attached infants continue to be securely attached during preschool (Bar-Haim et al., 2000; Landry, Smith, & Swank, 2001). When parents respond sensitively to their infants and continue to respond sensitively to their young children, more favorable social–emotional development is likely to occur. In contrast, at any point of children's development when parents react insensitively over a prolonged period of time, increased risk of maladjustment can be predicted (Landry et al., 2001). Securely attached preschoolers not only have parents who have continued to be responsive to their needs, but they also have parents who have adjusted their responsiveness to the developmental needs of their preschoolers. Parents of securely attached preschoolers are significantly more warm and accepting as well as less controlling of their young children in comparison to parents of insecurely attached preschoolers (Barnett, Kidwell, & Leung, 1998). Whether parents are sufficiently warm and accepting to their preschoolers is often tied to the circumstances of their lives. For example, Nair and Murray (2005) found that children of divorced parents have lower security scores in comparison to children in intact families. These researchers then explored the circumstances that contribute to differences in attachment security among preschoolers of divorced or married parents. They found that mothers from divorced families are younger, have lower income levels, and less education in comparison to married mothers. They also noted that divorced mothers reported higher levels of stress and depression, mentioned conflict with their spouses, and expressed a need for social support.

What This Means for Professionals. Anyone who reviews the research related to the behaviors of securely attached infants who become securely attached preschoolers is struck by the importance of parental responsiveness to the feelings and needs of children. It might be reassuring for parents to know that when they consistently respond to their children's questions, laugh with them, play with them, show affection for them, and comfort them, they are sustaining their children's attachment. If parents are aware of the many benefits of parental responsiveness, they might be inclined to relax more with their children and to participate more in playful activities with them. For professionals working with parents, they should be aware that circumstances that create hardships for parents might affect their responsiveness to their preschoolers and in turn compromise their preschoolers' sense of security. In these circumstances, social support is likely to alleviate some of the concerns of these parents and enhance the security of their preschoolers.

Promoting the Young Child's Sense of Initiative

According to Erik Erikson (1963), a crucial aspect of self during the preschool years comes from the achievement of a **sense of initiative**, which is primarily defined by the skills that demonstrate independence. Young children jump at almost any opportunity to show that "I can do it." Their sense of initiative is stimulated by their drive to discover their personal abilities as reflected by their seemingly endless energy and curiosity about the environment. Preschoolers are more likely to develop a sense of initiative when parents and other caregivers support their adventurous nature by encouraging their curiosity and allowing them to be active. On the contrary, if parents and other caregivers react to young children's exuberance and curiosity by inhibiting their activities and emphasizing that many of their normal behaviors are inappropriate, they contribute to preschoolers' **sense of guilt**. Essentially, the young child feels positive about behaviors that are supported by parents and other adults and guilty about behaviors that those significant others label as wrong or bad. Thus, the ways in which parents respond to the enthusiasm and curiosity of their preschool children sets them either on a road whereby they discover and feel good about their personal abilities or on a path whereby they begin to believe that it is wrong to want to discover their physical and social environments.

What This Means for Professionals. For young children, the world cannot be adequately understood and appreciated simply through observation. They must experience it by taking the initiative in becoming physically and psychologically involved in it. How young children discover the many things they need to know is by doing things and asking questions with the intent of gathering as much information as they can about the world in which they live. To find out the properties of sand, for example, children must be able to put their hands in it, sift it, make piles out of it, or mix water with it to make a sand castle or fort. *To discover* usually means *to enjoy* as seen in children's delight at discovering the properties of water, by jumping in it, splashing in it, and running through a water sprinkler. To be consistently engaged in learning, children need to have parents and caregivers who are patient with them and will provide them with opportunities for experimenting and trying out their new skills.

Parental Contributions to Preschoolers' Self-Esteem

When parents support the behaviors of their preschooler that reflect a sense of initiative, they also support their children's development of self-esteem. During these early years, children make judgments about themselves based on how well parents and others seem to like them (social acceptance). Their self-evaluations are linked as well to how good they are at accomplishing the tasks they attempt to master (competence). They have difficulty, however, in discriminating their competence at different activities, and when asked how well they can perform some activity they typically overestimate their ability and underestimate task difficulty. Preschoolers' overranking of their abilities reflects a high self-esteem, a quality that is highly adaptive at that age because it encourages them to persist at tasks during a period in which many new skills must be mastered (Harter, 1999). Preschoolers' tendency to evaluate themselves highly does not mean they are unaware of the judgments of others. Throughout the early years, children become increasingly conscious of what others think, and they begin to evaluate their own behaviors using those standards. Although most young children have high self-esteem, by age 4 some children give up when faced with challenges, concluding that they will not be able to accomplish the task or having been discouraged after failure. When nonpersisting preschoolers are asked why they have given up, they frequently report that their parents would be mad at them or punish them for making mistakes. Children as young as 2 or 3 years of age respond with disappointment or guilt when they fail at a task, such as not being able to tie their shoes, or when they have an accident, perhaps spilling their juice (Butler, 1998).

What This Means for Professionals. When parents understand that young children routinely overestimate their abilities and tend to feel disappointed and guilty when they fail at a task or cause an accident, they are more likely to understand their role in promoting their preschoolers' self-concept. Although preschoolers are highly interested in taking initiative in demonstrating what they can do, they need parental backup and encouragement. Parental backup consists of allowing the child to attempt a new skill while assisting the child to be successful in mastering that skill. Preschoolers need parents to provide assistance without taking over and to increasingly withdraw assistance as the preschooler becomes more adept. By and large, parents of preschoolers should back up when needed and back off when no longer needed. In addition to assisting their young children to meet their goals, it is essential that parents consistently encourage them in the process of accomplishing what they attempt to master. Parents encourage their children when they attend to children's feelings about their accomplishments and emphasize the progress children are making as they are engaged in an activity. Finally, parents promote their young children's self-esteem when they send a clear message to them that they are valued. Outlined in Figure 6.1 are several suggested ways in which a parent might help a child feel valuable, thereby boosting the child's self-esteem.

Talking to Young Children About Their Emotions

Whether their preschoolers are experiencing pride, guilt, or a variety of other emotions, it is helpful if their parents assist them in recognizing the emotions they are experiencing. Many parents begin actively capitalizing on their young children's rapidly developing verbal abilities by engaging them in conversations about emotions. Furthermore, a growing body of literature suggests that parent–child conversations about emotions promote young children's social and emotional development (Kuersten-Hogan & McHale, 2000). Whereas discussions regarding emotions generally have a positive impact on young children's social and emotional development, exposing children to harsh or distressed parental emotions increases the intensity of preschoolers' negative emotions and in turn contributes to their lowered social competence (Fabes, Leonard, & Kupanoff, 2001). Thus, preschoolers' negative emotions often reflect attempts to cope with harsh and distressed parenting and their lower levels of social competence reflects their ongoing attempts to cope with negative parental emotions.

1. Build a positive relationship
Parents should send clear messages to their children that they want to be with them by (a) arranging times to be fully available, (b) listening without being judgmental, and (c) expressing some of your own thoughts and feelings because mutual sharing helps children feel valued.

2. Nurture success
Parents should (a) be reasonable in expectations, (b) provide assistance to their young children when they are attempting to do things that they cannot do alone, (c) accentuate the positive in their children's work or behavior by using the language of encouragement, and (d) display their young children's artwork and other symbols of success in highly visible areas to promote their children's sense of pride in their accomplishments.

3. Foster the freedom to choose
Parents should provide children with a sense of responsibility and control over their own lives by giving them choices and manageable responsibilities, including involving them in the choice of when and in what order a task will be done.

4. Acknowledge emotions
Parents should accept their children's strong feelings and suggest constructive ways to handle them. Parents also should offer sympathy and support to their young children when their negative emotions reflect an affront to their self-esteem.

5. Prevent damage to the child's developing self-esteem
Parents should adopt a warm, rational approach to childrearing.

FIGURE 6.1 Recommended Ways to Foster Children's Self-Esteem

Source: Adapted from *The Construction of the Self: A Developmental Perspective,* by S. Harter, 1999, New York: Guilford Press.

Promoting Preschoolers' Self-Reliance

When parents assist their preschool children in their goal of mastering a variety of activities, they (a) help them learn responsible ways to behave, (b) promote their development of a positive self-image, and (c) contribute to their self-reliance. **Self-reliance** in young children refers to the ability to behave in ways that are considered by parents and other caregivers to be acceptable. Parents might encourage young children's self-reliance in a number of ways. Mauro and Harris (2000) studied the influence of parents on their young children's self-control and self-regulatory behavior by comparing parents' childrearing patterns to their children's ability to delay gratification. They found that young children whose parents use an authoritative parenting approach are better able to delay gratification than are children of permissive parents.

What This Means for Professionals. Parents should expect their young children to become increasingly more self-reliant and should not continually do things for them that they can do for themselves. On the other hand, when encouraging children to perform self-help and simple household responsibilities, parents need to keep in mind that young children will (a) take longer to perform these tasks, (b) need assistance along the way, and (c) require parental patience with their less-than-perfect performance. For example, in picking up toys after play, preschool children cannot be expected to clean up afterward efficiently, quickly, or completely. A positive way to promote the picking up of toys is to help the child with the job while showing the child how to do certain things and continually making favorable comments regarding the child's performance. These behaviors of parents serve as reinforcement and encouragement to young children, motivate them to try to do a good job, and help them feel proud of the level of performance they are currently capable of demonstrating.

Helping Young Children Discover Their Personal Boundaries

Children's consistent expression of their sense of initiative through active discovery contributes to their learning about **personal boundaries**—what they might or might not do, and what they can and cannot accomplish. Children's personal boundaries are revealed as they (a) make errors in judgment, (b) fail to accomplish goals, and (c) have conflicts with parents and other caregivers when boundaries and limits are not adhered to. In discovering their limitations during these early years, it is beneficial for children to learn that errors sometimes occur and that it is human nature to make mistakes. Being able to accept their nature as imperfect and feeling comfortable about it establishes young children's realistic notions of their abilities and contributes to their feelings of self-acceptance. Furthermore, the self-acceptance gained during the preschool stage affects future learning experiences and supports the development of a healthy self-esteem (Bigner, 1998).

What This Means for Professionals. Although it is important for parents to encourage their preschoolers' freedom to explore, thereby promoting their curiosity and sense of initiative, it is essential that parents closely monitor their youngsters' activities and establish reasonable parameters and rules of behavior. By establishing boundaries and regulations for young children, and at times redirecting their behavior, parents help them to understand which behaviors are safe and/or acceptable. The ways in which parents respond to their young children's mistakes are important as well. Because accidents and mishaps are a natural side effect of preschoolers' adventurous behavior, parents should expect (and be patient with) such things as spilled milk, the accidental toppling of objects, and other blunders that are a natural part of an active preschooler's day.

Thinking Critically

In the preceding discussion, we considered the ways in which the young child's sense of self is shaped by the parent's responses to the child. Drawing on Family Systems Theory (see Chapter 1), in what ways do you think the parent's sense of self is shaped by the enthusiasm, affection, and curiosity of the preschooler?

PROMOTING PRESCHOOLERS' PHYSICAL DEVELOPMENT

During the years that preschoolers are taking the initiative in accomplishing a variety of goals, developing their sense of self, and learning about personal boundaries, they are experiencing significant physical changes as well. The most obvious physical changes during these early years are in children's size and shape, as chubby toddlers are transformed into slimmer and taller preschoolers. Less obvious, but more crucial, developmental changes occur in the preschool child's brain and central nervous system. Together, the growth and development of the body and the brain provide young children with the ability to explore and master their worlds primarily through play that is undertaken with joy and exuberance. Parents are better prepared to promote their preschoolers' physical development if they are aware of the (a) nutritional needs of their young children, (b) brain development that occurs during these early years, and (c) preschool child's development of gross and fine motor skills.

Meeting the Nutritional Needs of Preschoolers

Providing adequate nutrition to preschool children plays a central role in promoting their physical development. Although physical growth slows during the preschool years resulting in young children requiring fewer calories than toddlers, it is important that they have a nutritious diet. When family food is limited (primarily due to poverty), young children often suffer from malnutrition which has a significant impact on their physical, emotional, and cognitive development. (Nelson, 2000; Tanner & Finn-Stevenson, 2002). Whereas most children in industrialized societies consume enough calories for energy, they do not always obtain adequate vitamins

Providing balanced nutritional meals and limiting sweets promotes young children's healthy physical development.

and minerals. The most common nutritional problem in the preschool years is an insufficient intake of iron, zinc, and calcium. Foods containing these nutrients often get crowded out by foods such as sweetened cereals, soda pop, and fruit juice. These foods are a poor substitute for a balanced diet, especially for young children who have smaller appetites. Thus, the diets of many American children often result in **iron-deficiency anemia**, a symptom of which is chronic fatigue. Anemia is three times more common in low-income families than in other families, yet parents of every social class tend to give their children candy, sugary drinks, sweetened cereals, and other sweets. Children who eat these foods are not only more likely to have a vitamin deficiency due to less consumption of nutritional foods but are more vulnerable to early tooth decay, one of the most common health problems of early childhood in the United States (Lewit & Kerrebrock, 1998).

Ways in Which Parents Influence Their Young Children's Dietary Practices. Although many young children in the United States and Canada do not have nutritious diets, there are many steps parents might take to improve their preschoolers' diets. According to Nicklas, Baranowski, Baranowski, and Cullen (2001), parents influence their young children's eating habits in at least five ways: (a) controlling availability and accessibility of foods, (b) meal structure, (c) food modeling, (d) food socialization practices, and (e) food-related parenting style. Regarding food availability and accessibility, parents control most of the foods entering their home as well as the methods of food preparation. They also control where the family goes out to eat. Consequently, children choose to eat foods that they are served most often, and prefer what is available and acceptable in the parental household. In their examination of the influence of meal structure on children's nutritional habits, Nicklas et al. (2001) reported that in those families where breakfast, lunch, and dinner are offered, the nutritional needs of young children were more likely to be met. Of these three meals, the eating of breakfast was noted to be especially significant because the children who consume breakfast regularly have more adequate nutrition than do young children who do not eat breakfast. In considering the impact of parental food modeling (where behaviors are learned by watching others), it was noted that children's acceptance of food follows the example of parents and siblings. For example, children put food in their mouths following an example of their mothers more readily than watching a stranger eating food. The way in which food socialization practices influence young children's food acceptance involves parents sharing nutritional information with their children through explanations, such as "which foods are good for us." These types of exchanges tend to foster the child's interest in food as well as increase food acceptance. Finally, Nicklas et al. (2001) found that the authoritative parenting style has a more positive impact on young children's nutritional food acceptance in comparison to authoritarian or permissive parenting styles. Authoritative parents influence their preschool children's food acceptance by using "questions, negotiations, and reasoning" in an attempt to shape or guide a child's behavior, thereby facilitating the development of the child's dietary self-control. Authoritative parents also provide small portions when introducing a new food.

What This Means for Professionals. Preschoolers' development of food preferences, as demonstrated by their refusal to eat certain foods, challenges parents to find creative approaches for assuring that their preschoolers receive adequate nutrition. The best way to resolve this issue is to search for solutions that balance the parent's goal of providing nutritional food with the preschooler's inability to tolerate certain tastes. When parents become irritated with their preschool children because of their youngsters' refusal of certain dishes or when they attempt to force them to eat foods that they dislike, the dilemma is not resolved in a way that takes into account the child's preferences. Based on the review of research that focused on factors impacting preschoolers' food choices by Nicklas and colleagues, we see that parents influence their young children's food preferences in a variety of ways.

An Example of Nutritional Issues in Poor Families in Nigeria. The previous discussion, which focused on the importance of food acceptance in terms of children's health, implied an adequate availability of food. Issues related to feeding children in many poor communities throughout the world are far more serious. For example, among poor families in Nigeria, feeding the family, including the children, is a major responsibility all mothers have, which impacts the well-being and survival of households. In these families, food security is not taken for granted and the poorer the household, the less likely it is that food security can be taken for granted. In these households, children learn early that their parents are caught up in economic conditions over which they have little control and that struggling for physical maintenance is a way of life. In these circumstances, obtaining enough food for the family is ranked as the second most difficult aspect of taking care of families by women (Pearce, 2000).

Understanding the Brain Development of Young Children

One of the reasons that adequate nutrition is so important during the early years is due to early brain development. As a result of the brain growth and development that occurs during the preschool years, young children react more quickly to stimuli and become better at controlling their emotions. For example, compared to a toddler, a 5-year-old child more quickly notices that another child is playing with a favorite toy but is less likely to object by throwing a tantrum. Instead, the preschooler is able to come up with a number of tactics for retrieving the desired toy, such as explaining ownership, offering another toy, or even offering a trade, which 2-year-olds almost never do (Berger, 2001). The brain development that occurs during the preschool stage of development makes it easier for young children to control their emotions and to come up with a variety of tactics for getting their needs met in a socially acceptable way. Although 3-year olds jump from task to task and have difficulty sitting still for long and are naturally impulsive, advances in prefrontal cortex development at about 3 or 4 make control of impulses more likely and formal education more possible (Posner & Rothbart, 2000). Whether or not preschoolers develop these abilities, however, depends not only on their physical development but also on the guidance they receive from parents and other caregivers. Unlike toddlers, preschoolers are amenable to parental suggestions regarding ways in which to handle conflicts. Young children who have parents who gently explain to them the options available for resolving conflict, such as sharing, trading, or taking turns, incorporate these skills more readily into their behavioral repertoire than do preschoolers who are not provided this kind of guidance (Merzenich, 2001). The emotional climate of the household also impacts the young children's development of problem-solving skills. When the parents and other family members get along and have a variety of strategies for dealing with stress, young children are better able to learn ways of resolving conflict. On the other hand, young children whose family life is highly stressful and whose parents do not assist them in learning to resolve conflict, have more difficulty in developing impulse control and consequently more problems interacting with other children (DeBellis, 2001).

The Promotion of Fine and Gross Motor Skills

There are a variety of ways in which parents might promote the developing motor skills of their preschool children. Keeping in mind that **gross motor skill** development requires the use of large muscles in the legs or arms as well as general strength and stamina, parents should insure that their young children have ample experiences in running, jumping, skipping, hopping, throwing, catching, climbing up, jumping

Charles Hanger.

The active, spontaneous play of these young children provides the optimum type of movement for the development of their gross motor skills.

down, tumbling, and balancing. All these activities are examples of gross motor skill abilities that develop during the early years. As preschoolers make notable progress in the development of their gross motor skills, parents might provide different materials and varying environmental challenges. For example, preschoolers quickly develop the ability to adapt their movements to meet varying environmental challenges, such as catching balls of different sizes and running up and down hills. Besides providing opportunities for movement and objects that facilitate the advancement of their children's gross motor skills, it is important for parents to consider the social conditions under which preschoolers exercise their developing gross motor skills. Running and playing with other children and adults is not only highly enjoyable for young children, it also assists young children in learning to coordinate the movements of their own bodies with the movements of other people. Being able to change directions while running in anticipation of another child's movement in a game of *tag* reflects the young child's development of **social coordination of movement**. Reaction time is another important component of developing gross motor skills. For developing reaction time, children must have experience in which they see or hear a stimulus and then quickly judge how to react. Traditional American games such as *musical chairs* or *red light, green light* require these kinds of quick motor reactions. In the game of *musical chairs*, for example, children learn to sit quickly after they notice that the music has stopped. They must make a quick decision regarding where they will sit. Finally, play that incorporates the motor dimensions of coordination and speed of movement is associated with the development of cognitive abilities of preschoolers (Planinsec, 2002).

Promoting Gross Motor Skills. There are a variety of ways in which parents might promote the development of their preschoolers' gross motor skills. First, parents should be alert to cues from their young children regarding their motivation to run, jump, skip, throw, kick, roll, tumble, and so forth. Second, parents need to be certain that preschoolers are provided sufficient space and appropriate structures on which to practice these skills. Third, it is essential for parents to take the necessary precautions for keeping their children safe from harm without holding them back in motor skill development. Because young children are not logical thinkers, it is imperative for parents to provide close supervision of their activities. And because preschoolers are highly motivated to climb up on things, parents need to check the stability of the structures their preschoolers attempt to climb, redirecting them when necessary. Finally, providing their preschool children with opportunities to play with other children supports the development of gross motor skills, social coordination of movement, and reaction time.

Promoting Fine Motor Skills. In addition to supporting their preschool children's development of gross motor skills, parents also need to attend to their young children's **fine motor skill** development, which involves the ability to coordinate smaller muscles in the arms, hands, and fingers. Parents promote these abilities when they provide opportunities, materials, and assistance for preschoolers' beginning attempts at writing, drawing, and other creative activities such as using scissors to cut out different shapes and using clay to represent objects in the environment. Parents might also keep in mind that greater dexterity in the use of fine motor skills during the preschool years allows young children to perform a variety of self-help skills. Thus, parents might persuade their young children to try an array of self-help activities that take advantage of the ability of young children to use their fine motor skills, such as dressing themselves and picking up their toys (Trawick-Smith, 2000).

What This Means for Professionals. The foregoing discussion highlights the importance of providing young children with a variety of objects designed to help them gain fine motor dexterity. Although children need to be given the opportunity to manipulate a diverse number of objects, certain objects have greater significance depending on the culture in which the child is reared. In most cultures, proficiency in using writing and drawing tools is highly desirable. When choosing pencils and crayons for preschoolers, though, parents should keep in mind that fat pencils and fat crayons are best suited for the short, fat fingers of very young children. Moreover, parents should be aware that preschoolers are capable of developing dexterity in the use of a variety of tools. Parents, therefore, might consider the goals they have for their children in choosing the tools they provide for them. For example, parents who wish to see artistic ability in their preschoolers must provide items such as crayons, pencils, paper, fingerpaints, and modeling clay.

Thinking Critically

Drawing on Bronfenbrenner's Ecological Model (see Figure 1.3, Chapter 1), how would you explain the role of cultural context in the development of young children's fine and gross motor skills? For example, how might differences in the child, the family, the community, the culture, and time, impact the development of those skills?

THE DEVELOPMENT OF PERSONAL AND FAMILY LIFE SKILLS

In addition to facilitating play and social interactions, advances in motor skills allow preschoolers to be more involved in self-care and to take on simple household responsibilities. As early as age 3, with some help from parents, young children can perform self-help tasks such as dressing themselves, picking up their toys, bathing, brushing their teeth, and eating with utensils. Even though assistance is needed in tying shoes, buttoning small buttons, or coordinating a fork and table knife at age 3, most children master these skills by age 5. Besides being able to take on increasing self-care responsibilities, preschoolers gain motor skill development through participation in household responsibilities (Berger, 2001).

What This Means for Professionals. Even though it is helpful for young children to become responsible for self-care tasks and be given household responsibilities, parents should take care that these responsibilities match the developmental capabilities of their preschool children. Parents need to be mindful as well of the requirement to guide, instruct, and support their youngsters' development of personal and family life skills. Showing youngsters how to brush their teeth, wash behind their ears, comb their hair, tie their shoes, and button their shirts are just a few of the ways that parents are consistently involved in promoting their children's self-care activities. Ongoing parental guidance as youngsters are learning family life skills include giving them responsibilities such as helping to straighten their rooms, putting dishes on the table at mealtimes, and helping with meal preparation. Examples of ways in which young children might assist with meal preparation include activities such as spreading mayonnaise on a slice of bread and placing slices of meat and/or cheese between slices of bread, and helping stir up cookie dough for making cookies. Children benefit, too, from being able to assist in feeding family pets, perhaps pouring water in the pet's water dish and putting pet food in the feeding dish.

The Household Responsibilities of Children in Traditional Cultures

In nonindustrialized societies, young children participate more extensively in household work than do young children in industrialized societies. For example, young children in India, Okinawa, the Philippines, Mexico, and Kenya carry out a range of jobs that most Canadian, European, and American children would not be expected to perform. These household responsibilities include collecting firewood, fetching water, herding and tending livestock, grinding grain, and harvesting vegetables. Children in nonindustrialized societies perform universal household tasks as well, such as dressing or preparing food at an earlier age than would be expected in families in industrialized societies. Finally, in almost all cultures, young girls are more often assigned child care duties than are young boys. The following vignette exemplifies the type of child care responsibilities that might be given to a young female living in a traditional culture:

> A 5-year-old girl in a small village in Kenya is up early. She has been assigned as the child nurse to her infant brother. Her mother and father have already gone to work in the garden, and she is left in full charge of her young sibling. When he awakes and cries, she picks him up and holds him close. As he calms down, she holds him on one arm and reaches with the other for a bottle to feed him. She must grip him tightly as she does this; he is 8 months old and very big for his age. After feeding him, she places him into a sling. Her brother wiggles and kicks—he does not seem eager to be confined. She then straps the sling to her back. She stands up, maintaining her balance, then walks off to play with friends in another part of the village (Trawick-Smith, 2000, pp. 217–218).

PROMOTING YOUNG CHILDREN'S COGNITIVE DEVELOPMENT

Although the years between 2 and 6 are referred to as the preschool years in the United States, Leach (1997) points out that the term *preschool* is a mundane name for a magical time. Leach argues that the term implies that these early years represent a "waiting time"—before school or even before preparation for school. The reality of this early developmental stage is that young children have a developmental agenda of their own. Furthermore, recent research has led to an appreciation of the impressive cognitive abilities that manifest themselves during these early years, including mathematics, language, and social understanding. For parents, the cognitive development of their young children often fascinates and sometimes confuses them. On the one hand, parents everywhere are captivated and delighted by the magical thinking of young children who wonder where the sun sleeps or who chatter away with invisible playmates. On the other hand, parents are frequently surprised by their young children's failure to comprehend metaphors and other ways in which adults and older children express themselves. We will now examine the role of parents in promoting the cognitive development of their young children. A discussion of the role of parents in the promotion of young children's language development is included in this section as well.

Insights from Piaget

According to Piaget, a striking difference between infant and preschooler cognition is the ability to use **symbolic thinking**, which involves the use of words, gestures, pictures, or actions to represent ideas, things, or behaviors. Similar to motor skill development, the ability to symbolize occurs in gradual steps and is dependent on interactions with other persons and objects in the environment. As monumental as symbolic thought might be, Piaget referred to the cognitive development between ages 2 and 6 as **preoperational thought.** Due to the constraints of preoperational thought, preschoolers' first symbolic concepts are not as complete or as logical as are those of older children and adults; thus they are referred to as **preconcepts**. An illustration of a preconcept used by preschoolers is **overgeneralization**. Young children know, for example, that whoever walks on two legs, is tall (according to the standards of young children), and speaks in a deep voice belongs to a particular class of persons (Piaget & Inhelder, 1969). The English word they learn for this class of persons is usually *Daddy*; the Hindu term is *Bapu*, and the Xhosa (South African) word is *Tata*. So when young children use the terms *Daddy, Papa, Bapu, Tata,* or other linguistic variations to refer to all men, they are demonstrating the ability to use preconcepts. The same classification ability is demonstrated when English-speaking preschoolers call dogs, cows, and horses, *doggies*. Besides calling all men by the term their culture uses for *father* and using one term to distinguish all large, four-legged animals, young children have difficulty in distinguishing specific members of a species from each other. This inability is evident in a young child who has seen a kitten down the street thinking another kitten seen in another place is the same one (Elkind, 1976).

Preschoolers' Egocentrism. It is the nature of young children to be egocentric in their thinking. To say that preschoolers' thinking is **egocentric** simply means that young children have an excessive reliance on their own point of view, coupled with a corresponding inability to be objective. By and large, young children tend to focus on one feature or perspective at a time. Their tendency to focus on one aspect of a situation to the exclusion of all others is called **centration**. Preschooler egocentrism shows up in young children's inability to share their toys, a fact that parents often fail to understand. Because parents frequently do not comprehend the limitations of young children's logic, they tend to scold them when they refuse to share their toys. The inability to consider two perspectives at once, however, means that very young children are unable to comprehend the concept of sharing. According to Piaget, the reluctance to share does not mean that young children are necessarily selfish. On the contrary, they frequently attempt to comfort others in distress. Their attempts to comfort another child or an adult, however, are likely to come in a distinctly egocentric form such as offering a toy or lollipop. These examples reflect the preschooler's lack of understanding about what might soothe another person as well their egocentric view that what is important to them is also valuable to others. The inability of preschoolers to consider two perspectives simultaneously can also be seen in their failure to **conserve** matter and volume. The inability to understand that the quantity of matter (such as clay) does not change when the shape changes, or that the volume of water remains the same if it is poured from a short squat glass to a tall narrow glass, is reflected in preschoolers' judgment (Piaget & Inhelder, 1969). Where that lack of understanding is likely to show up is if young children are given drinks in different-size containers. The young child is likely to complain that another child has more juice if the other child's glass is taller, even if the amount of juice is the same in both glasses.

What This Means for Professionals. Rather than expressing impatience with preschoolers when they do not share, parents might take their young children's perspective in the matter. Parents can be certain that each child has an identical toy or when noticing that two children are insisting on having the same toy might distract one of the children by offering that child an equally attractive toy. Because preschoolers lack the ability to conserve matter and liquid, parents need to be patient with them when they complain that they have less lemonade than the other children whose glasses are taller (even though they are narrower). Instead of providing a logical explanation to the prelogical preschooler regarding how the width of one glass compensates for the height of the other glass, it is better to take care that glasses chosen for their liquid refreshments are all the same height and width.

Insights from Vygotsky

Vygotsky agreed with Piaget that preschoolers are active learners (Brandstadter, 1998), but Vygotsky emphasized another point: Children do not strive alone; their efforts to understand a world that fascinates and sometimes confuses them are imbedded in a social context. Preschoolers notice things that happen and ask "*Why?*" with the assumption that others know why—and they expect answers. Meanwhile, parents, older siblings, grandparents, preschool teachers, and many others do more than answer: They guide a young child's cognitive development by (a) presenting challenges for new learning, (b) offering assistance with difficult tasks, (c) providing instruction, and (d) encouraging the preschooler's interest and motivation. Accordingly, children learn much of what they need to know through

guided participation in social experiences and in explorations of their world (Rogoff, Paradise, Arauz, Correa-Chavez, & Angelitto, 2003).

The parents' cognitive support is important particularly in enhancing young children's self-regulatory behaviors related to cognitive awareness and task management. Findings of Neitzel & Stright (2003) showed that mothers who provide more **metacognitive information** during scaffolded interactions had children who more frequently talked about their thinking and monitored progress on their cognitive tasks. Other aspects of scaffoldng frequently include regulating task complexity by giving instructions in small steps with frequent review. It seems that when parents provide instruction in small steps with frequent reviews, it reduces the cognitive load of a task and allows the child to receive maximum benefit from information contained in the parent's instructions. Parental emotional support also contributes significantly to predicting young children's help seeking in the preschool classroom.

Thinking Critically

Drawing on your comprehension of the role of parents in promoting young children's cognitive development, from the perspective of Vygotsky, how would you recommend that parents help their children to learn to pick up their toys and put them in their toy boxes?

Jo Hall/Merrill.

The parents in this picture understand that children are able to master tasks more quickly (and with less frustration) when assisted by adults.

An Indigenous Perspective Regarding Young Children's Developing Competency

In the previous discussions, we examined the views of Piaget and Vygotsky regarding ways in which parents can understand and support their young children's cognitive development. Another perspective of developing competency in preschool children may be observed in the ways in which young children in indigenous cultures everywhere learn by observing and listening in on activities of adults and other children. The source of learning and cognitive development in these cultures is through keen observation and listening, in anticipation of participation. This type of learning seems to be especially valued and emphasized in communities where children have access to learning from informal community involvement. In these communities, young children observe and listen with intent concentration and initiative, and their future collaborative participation is expected when they are ready. This tradition, which is referred to as **intent participation**, is prominent in many indigenous American communities (Rogoff et al., 2003).

Intent participation is a powerful form of fostering learning and contributes to notable learning such as that accomplished by young children learning their first language. Examples of this type of learning by young children has been observed in a number of different cultural communities. For example, young rural Senegalese children observe other people more than twice as often as do middle-class European American children. Navajo students quietly observe teachers more than twice as often as do Caucasian students in the same classroom and Mexican-heritage children are more likely to observe without requesting further information, compared with both U.S. Mexican-heritage and European-heritage children. Keen observation is often encouraged and taught in Suzuki instruction in Japan and Gikuyu parents take care to teach children to be good observers. An example of the indigenous parent's emphasisis on intent observation is seen when Polynesian children ask for instruction and are told to watch a skillful adult in action. In many indigenous communities, young children's observation skills are emphasized and honed as they attend closely to ongoing events in order to learn the practices of their community (Rogoff et al., 2003).

The Role of Parents in Promoting Language Development

From infancy to early childhood, one undeniable change takes place—children learn to talk. In cultures around the world, young children's rapid language development represents a language explosion, with words and sentences bursting forth. By age 6, the average child has a vocabulary of over 10,000 words because during these early years children learn words at the rapid rate of 10 to 20 new words per day through a process called **fast mapping** (Gray, 2006). Furthermore, even though different languages have different subject, verb, and object placement, young children's word placement matches the grammatical structure of their native language from the time they first string two words together. Moreover, young children demonstrate an understanding of verb tense in their language (Allen & Crago, 1996).

An example of preschoolers' knowledge of verb tense is demonstrated in the following example. The young child who says "I played with Sally today" comprehends that *ed* is added to a verb to represent past tense. When that same child says "Sally and I goed to the park," the child is still demonstrating a basic understanding of past tense. In the second example, the child uses **overregularization**, whereby a standard rule of past tense is applied to the English language, which has many exceptions to the standard rules. The remarkable advances in language development during the preschool years are further exemplified in young children's social speech. Preschool children are extraordinarily adept at producing socially adaptive behavior in their verbal communication. For example, 4-year-old children speak differently to 2-year-olds when they see themselves in a teaching role than when they are attempting to engage a younger child in informal play. Additionally, young children's speech reflects the social skills of turn taking and topic maintenance (Woodward & Markman, 1998).

What This Means for Professionals. There is no question that the preschool stage of development is an impressive time of language development. The extraordinary growth of vocabulary that occurs during the preschool years is matched by an impressive understanding of basic grammar and socially adaptive language. There are, nevertheless, variations in language development and these variations can be traced to parent–child interactions. First of all, preschoolers need to hear new words in order to learn them. It is, hence, beneficial for young children when their parents continually engage them in verbal dialogues and respond to their questions and other verbal comments. Young children's language development (especially vocabulary expansion) is further promoted when adults label new things for them. For instance, a parent might point to some animals the child sees at a distance and say, "See the deer are running across the field." In less than a minute, the words *deer* and *field* enter the child's vocabulary.

Finally, whereas the language development that occurs during the preschool stage is impressive, young children's pronunciation takes a little longer to perfect. It is important that parents do not attempt to correct their young children's pronunciation because that approach actually hampers their preschoolers' language development. Instead of calling attention to their youngsters' mispronunciation, parents should respond to their preschoolers' speech as if they had pronounced the words correctly. In their responses to their young children's mispronunciations, however, it is important for parents to repeat back the words correctly, thereby modeling the correct pronunciation. For example, the child might say, "Mommy, Daddy said we are going on a twip!" In response, Mommy could say "Oh yes! We are going to go on a trip!"

How Young Children Understand Speech. Even though young children's speech reflects their social understanding of turn taking, topic maintenance, and social adaptation, they are somewhat limited in comprehending the speech of others. First, the preoperational thought of young children prevents them from understanding the concept of reversibility, which shows up in their failure to accurately comprehend

reverse-order sentences (Woodward & Markman, 1998). An example of this misunderstanding can be detected in the statement whereby the parent says to the child, "You can have a cookie after you wash your hands." Because young children understand the sequence of action in the order that it is presented, the child believes the parent is actually saying, "You can have a cookie, then you should wash your hands." Not only does the child think that cookie eating precedes hand washing in this instance, the child is less likely to have paid attention to the second half of the sentence. The failure to attend to the second stated action in the sentence is due to preschoolers' egocentric tendency to focus on one thing at a time.

Still another limitation of children's linguistic understanding stems from their inability to comprehend metaphors—that one word or phrase can mean different things when used in different contexts. Their inability to grasp metaphors means that young children are quite literal in their understanding and use of speech. As a case in point, if a father tells a preschool child on the phone that he will be home in a little while but that he is "tied up right now," the child believes the father is literally tied up. The concerned child might turn to the mother and ask, "How is Daddy going to get untied." The child's lack of understanding that words might mean different things in different contexts means their language understanding is very context bound. An illustration of this language limitation is apparent in the situation where a parent has taken the child into the deep end of the swimming pool and the child learns from that experience that *deep* means over one's head. When that same parent says to the young child the following week that it is okay to step in puddles after a rain while wearing rain boots, but not to step into deep puddles, the child will feel free to step into any puddle that is not over the child's head. Still another restriction of young children is their lack of ability to understand complex, multiaction sentences (Woodward & Markman, 1998). For instance, a young child would have trouble making sense of the following request: "Tommy, pick up your toys, go wash your hands, and put on your jacket." The parent who uses a sentence such as that expects the child to attend to several different requests, which is very difficult for the egocentric young child.

What This Means for Professionals. First, parents should be certain that they speak clearly, and face-to-face, with their young children so that their children have the opportunity to watch the formation of their words and clearly hear how sentences are formed and words are pronounced. Second, it is better to use short, concrete sentences, state one request or idea at a time, and give the child an opportunity to think about and process each request separately. Third, it is important for parents not to use metaphors when talking to their preschool children, who rely on literal comprehension. Fourth, parents need to understand that even though a child has learned the meaning of a word, the child might not understand the usage of that word in a different context. Therefore, parents should be very patient with their young children and not assume that they are misbehaving when they have not followed through with instructions. It is possible that the child has not clearly understood the meaning of words used in a context that does not match the one in which the words were learned. Finally, some parents need to be reminded of the importance of slowing

When parents speak face to face with their young children, those children are able to see how words are formed.

down their pace when speaking to their young children, thus providing sufficient pauses to encourage parent–preschooler dialogue.

Thinking Critically

Drawing on the previous discussion that focused on how young children understand adult speech, describe how you might instruct preschoolers to come to dinner after they have put away their toys and washed their hands.

CHALLENGES AND CONCERNS OF PARENTS OF YOUNG CHILDREN

There are a number of areas in which young children sometimes experience problems and parents typically require additional information in order to help their children with those difficulties. Those problems not specifically related to the preschool children's developmental stage are presented in Chapters 9 and 10. The two most common areas of concern for parents of preschool children are sleeping problems (including bed-wetting) and sibling conflict.

Sleeping Problems

Childhood sleep disturbance negatively impacts children as well as their parents. For parents, their young children's sleep problems are associated with parental fatigue, stress, depressed mood, marital tension, and negative parent–child interactions. For children, disrupted sleep schedules contribute to less positive and more negative behaviors in preschool. It has been suggested that fatigue from disrupted sleep interferes with the young child's attention focus and performance and also produces a stress response to environmental triggers culminating in over-arousal and a greater likelihood of negative emotionality (Bates, Viken, Alexander, Beyers, & Stockton, 2002). Four sleep-related problems (bed-wetting, difficulty going to bed, waking up at night, and sleeping with parents) are at the top of parents' list of preschool children's behavior problems. Fortunately, most sleep problems are amenable to treatment, and much of the negative impact on family functioning is alleviated with successful intervention (Kuhn, Mayfield, & Kuhn, 1999). The importance of successful intervention for sleeping problems that arise during the preschool years is that early sleep problems might forecast later behavior and/or emotional problems. For instance, Gregory and O'Connor (2002) found that sleep problems at age 4 predicted behavioral–emotional problems in midadolescence.

The first step in alleviating childhood sleep disturbances is to determine if there are coexisting child behavior problems. Young children who are noncompliant, defiant, or aggressive, might respond paradoxically to sleepiness by exhibiting overactive behavior, irritability, or decreased attention span. In these situations, the combination of the child's sleep problem and a frustrated parent might lead to a family crisis. In some cases, treating the child's behavior problem might result in a resolution of the sleep problem. In other situations, treatment of the youngster's sleep disturbance alleviates the child's behavior problem. In situations where the child's sleep disturbance contributes to or reflects behavior problems, a comprehensive assessment of pediatric sleep disturbances within an outpatient clinic might be necessary before a plan of intervention can be developed. In the majority of families, however, parents and their children benefit greatly when parents learn ways to assist their children with their sleep problems (Kuhn et al., 1999).

Sleep Disturbance Related to Bed-Wetting

Among preschoolers, a common problem associated with sleeping is **enuresis**, defined as repeated voiding of urine during the day or at night into bed or clothes, with a frequency criteria of at least twice per week for at least 3 months (American Psychiatric Association, 1994). Although bed-wetting is sometimes related to psychological reasons such as family stress and behavioral disturbance in the child, two biological reasons are primarily associated with enuresis. First of all, the maturation of the nervous system (which helps children achieve bladder control) occurs at different rates among young children. Because the maturation of the nervous system occurs somewhat later for boys as compared to girls, bed-wetting is more common for boys than for girls. Finally, some children sleep more soundly than do others, and the combination of a very sound sleep pattern combined with less mature bladder control frequently contributes to bed-wetting. Although medical intervention is available for treatment of enuresis, the bell-and-pad method of conditioning is the only major treatment that has enduring benefit after being withdrawn. Although that method is the most cost-effective (based on a 10-year review of various treatments), it appears to be underused. In addition to the bell and pad, other psychological approaches are commonly used. These include retention-control training, evening fluid restriction, nightime toileting, and rewards (Mikkelsen, 2001).

What This Means for Professionals. Because bed-wetting is not under young children's control, it is important that parents not overreact to wet sheets or hold children responsible for incidents of bed-wetting. It is recommended instead that parents adopt a detached attitude toward bed-wetting, providing encouragement to their children in their attempts to control their bed-wetting yet remaining unconcerned about the outcome. Although a number of techniques are recommended for dealing with bed-wetting, parents need to keep in mind that patience and bed pads will go a long way in getting both preschoolers and their parents past the bed-wetting problem. The most important recommendation in dealing with bed-wetting is that children not be made to feel ashamed or guilty for behavior that is not under their control.

Helping Young Children Get a Good Night's Sleep. Helping young children to get a sufficient amount of sleep is an important priority because loss of sleep not only has a detrimental impact on their health but also interferes with preschoolers' ability to interact with others. Most of the problems related to the sleep patterns of young children are night waking, failing to settle at night, and calling persistently for parental attention.

Many American parents respond to young children's problems with going to sleep by forcing them to go to bed at a time the parents designate and failing to respond to their cries or pleas to get back up. Although this has become a popular method for dealing with young children's sleep problems, there are far more sensitive and more beneficial ways for dealing with young children's sleep problems. Based on the strong evidence that parental responsiveness is the best predictor of children's attachment, ignoring a child's pleas and cries is not a recommended approach. Although sleep disturbances are common in the United States, they are less common in other cultures, which shows that sleep disturbances of young children might be culturally determined. It is suggested that sleep disturbances of American preschoolers might be related to the ways in which their parents deal with bedtime. Many Asian families, for instance, expect their young children to sleep in their siblings' or parents' bed and do not report any sleep disturbances

(Brophy, 2000). Although cosleeping with young children is not an acceptable practice for most Americans, due to their emphasis on independence and individuality, abrupt separation from parents without sufficient preparation for bedtime is not recommended. One of the ways that many parents assist their young children in making the transition to beditme is through the reading of bedtime stories. This activity helps young children settle down and allows them to experience focused parental attention, which provides the emotional support they need for making the transition of going to bed. Parents' reading of bedtime stories also provides young children with face-to-face reciprocity, which has been found to promote young children's self-regulatory behavior (Feldman et al., 1999). Another way in which parents assist their young children's regulation of sleep patterns is when they establish a regular bedtime for them, especially if they align that bedtime with the children's normal onset of sleep (Ansbaugh & Peck, 1998). In addtion to establishing a regular bedtime, and reading stories to assist in the transition to bedime, it is important for parents to monitor how much time their children are sleeping during the day. Whereas many young children benefit from an afternoon nap, those who sleep for more than a couple of hours during the day are likely to experience difficulty getting to sleep and/or sleeping through the night. In these cases, it is recommended this parents alleviate that problem by waking a preschooler earlier from a long daytime nap.

Although children settle down more easily when parents read to them, after parents leave their rooms, preschoolers sometimes imagine that monsters are under their beds or in their closets. These nighttime fears are related to young children's anxiety about being separated from other family members as well as children's active imaginations that cause them to interpret shadows and noises as monsters lurking in the dark. In response to their young children's worries about monsters, parents often attempt to alleviate children's feelings of anxiety by providing them with logical explanations of how there are no monsters and that they should not be afraid. One problem with such a response is that young children are not very logical in their thinking (Piaget & Inhelder, 1969); therefore, reasonable explanations from their parents do little to alleviate the fear of monsters. Another difficulty with that rejoinder is that telling children that they should not be afraid minimizes children's feelings and does not provide them with the comfort they seek. As a reminder, parents of securely attached preschoolers are significantly more warm and accepting as well as less controlling of their young children in comparison to parents of insecurely attached preschoolers (Barnett et al., 1998).

What This Means for Professionals. It is recommended that parents show their young children that they care about their concerns. Children need to have their parents reassure them that they can and will protect them and keep them safe. Accordingly, calm and loving reassurance from parents is the best approach for dealing with those troublesome monsters. A night-light in the child's bedroom is another way to alleviate nighttime fears as children can notice familiar surroundings before dozing off. Finally, attachment objects such as stuffed animals tend to ease children's feelings of separation and make bedtime more calming.

Thinking Critically

Research findings have consistently demonstrated that sensitive, responsive caregiving predicts preschooler attachment, which contributes to a number of positive outcomes for young children. Do you think these findings mean that parents should respond sensitively to their young children throughout the day then ignore their pleas at bedtime? If not, what can American parents learn from Asian parents about handling bedtime?

Sibling Conflict

Although problems with siblings certainly exist, the impact of siblings on the social development of children is more positive than negative. Children learn many social skills from brothers and sisters, and sibling influence is especially valuable in many cultures throughout the world in which older siblings act as caregivers of younger siblings. Also, having older siblings is positively related to young children's cognitive development, especially the development of **theory of mind**. Theory of mind refers to an understanding of human mental processes such as trying to understand a playmate's anger or determining when a sibling will be generous. In addition to age and language ability, having at least one older brother or sister has a significant impact on children's cognitive development. It has been estimated that regarding theory of mind development, two older siblings are equivalent to approximately 1 year of chronological age. Furthermore, children learn valuable lessons when they adjust to the arrival of a new sibling (Volling, McElwain, & Miller, 2002). Where there are siblings in a family, however, there are inevitable spats and conflicts. Although parents may fail to appreciate it at the time, these interactions usually have a positive influence on children's developing ability to resolve conflict. Furthermore, unilateral oppositions of young children are likely to be imbedded in the midst of positive interchanges, and after their mild spats young children are likely to remain near one another and to continue their positive interaction (Vandell & Bailey, 1995).

How parents respond to young children's conflicts with their siblings makes a difference in how children resolve these conflicts, how they feel about themselves in relation to their siblings, and whether or not they will benefit from sibling rivalry and conflict. Vandell and Bailey (1995) summarized the following parental influences on siblings' ability to resolve conflict. First, punitive parenting approaches are associated with high levels of sibling conflict. Second, conflicts are minimized when children's emotional needs are met by their parents and there is no favored child in the family. Third, when parents act as mediators of siblings' conflicts by referring to moral principles as well as to children's feelings, young children engage in relatively mature forms of conflict, using justification for their actions and moral reasoning themselves. Fourth, parents need to be sensitive in their interventions, keeping in mind that parental interruption of constructive sibling conflicts might deprive young children of the opportunity to develop necessary social problem-solving skills. Finally, although sibling rivalry is inevitable and often has a positive impact on children's development, high levels of sibling jealousy often signal problems in family relationships. For example, according to Volling et al. (2002), young children display more sibling jealously when they have less secure attachment to their mothers, and when their parents have more negative than positive marital relationships. In explaining the relationship between negative marital relationships and higher levels of jealousy among preschool children, Volling and colleagues suggested that more positive marital relationships help preschool children to regulate their behavior. Another factor, identified as helpful in managing sibling jealousy, was when preschool children have a better understanding of others' emotions. Preschoolers are cognitively capable of understanding others' emotions if parents assist them in this process. The parenting strategy of induction, which was explained in Chapter 3, is an excellent choice for helping young children to develop empathy for others. The combination of greater social understanding and empathy training helps preschoolers understand, for example, why parents direct more attention to a younger sibling (e.g., *He's my baby brother and Mommy and Daddy have to rock him and carry him because he cries a lot*).

What This Means for Professionals. Even though siblings should be encouraged to work out their differences without parents taking sides or taking over, it is beneficial for parents to provide guidelines for conflict resolution that maximize the chances that cooperation will occur. For example, two young children might be arguing over which one of them should be able to play with a particular toy. Instead of telling the children how to resolve the spat, parents might express a belief in the children's ability to resolve the problem on their own. After showing confidence in their children's capability to settle the matter themselves, the parents might provide a couple simple guidelines regarding how to negotiate their differences. They might tell their children, for instance, that they should make a decision only after talking over the problem with each other. They might also tell their children that they should try to reach a compromise that makes both of them happy. When children work out their problems and come up with equitable solutions, it is important that parents show approval of their children's problem-solving efforts. When parents congratulate their young children for resolving their conflicts, they encourage them to engage in problem solving in the future. Furthermore, as parents continually express a belief in their young children's capacity to resolve conflict, children become increasingly more capable of conflict negotiation.

SUMMARY

- During the years between ages 3 and 6, young children in cultures throughout the world make tremendous advancements in the social–emotional, physical, and cognitive domains of development. They toddle into the preschool stage with the fundamental skills of reaching, grabbing, and discovering the properties

of things through direct contact with those objects, and they leave by running, skipping, tumbling, jumping, and romping.
- By the end of the preschool years, young children have gained the ability and skills necessary to begin to use the tools of their culture. As they gain a greater understanding of their environment and become skilled in the use of a variety of tools, young children start to form impressions about their competence and self-image.
- Behind all of the remarkable achievements of children during these early years are parents who play a key role in supporting their children's goals to realize their developmental potential. The materials and objects that parents make available to their youngsters, and the freedom they grant them to move about within a safe environment, promote their preschoolers' development. Parents further support their young children's development by the ways in which they speak to and listen to them.
- Finally, when parents are confronted with problems related to getting their children to go to bed, bed-wetting, and sibling conflict, they need to be understanding and supportive of their children's feelings and to seek out information and guidance to match their care to their children's specific needs.

KEY TERMS

- centration
- conserve
- egocentric thought
- enuresis
- fast mapping
- fine motor skill
- gross motor skill
- guided participation
- intent participation
- iron-deficiency anemia
- metacognitive information
- overgeneralization
- overregularization
- personal boundaries
- preconcept
- preoperational thought
- reverse-order sentences
- sense of guilt
- sense of initiative
- self-reliance
- social coordination of movement
- symbolic thinking
- theory of mind

USEFUL WEB SITES

The Department of Health and Human Services has an excellent website for preschoolers' parents

http://www.cdc.gov/ncbddd/child/preschoolers.htm.

This site provides information on developmental milestones, positive parenting, and child safety. It also provides links to a number of valuable resources. English or Spanish options are available.

KeepKidsHealthy.com is a pediatrician's guide to keeping children healthy and safe. The link focusing on preschoolers is

http://www.keepkidshealthy.com/preschool/preschool.html

This site provides links to a health library, parenting experts, parenting tips, safety tips, and first aid. It also provides links to a number of relevant online resources.

North Dakota State University Extension Service also offers valuable information to parents of preschoolers

http://www.ext.nodak.edu/estnews/pipeline/p-parent.htm

This site provides an online newsletter that helps parents better understand their preschool children. It has suggestions for ways in which parents might assist their preschoolers in reaching their physical, emotional, and cognitive potential. It also offers advice for parents who want to build their children's self-esteem, and help their children develop creativity.

HENRY
18

Parents and Their School-Age Children

Objectives

After completing this chapter, you should be able to

- Identify several ways in which parents might promote the development of their school-age children's sense of initiative, through the development of their skills and competencies
- Describe the concept of coregulation and explain how this plays out in the relationship between parents and their school-age children.
- Describe the ways in which parents' socialization patterns influence the social relationships of their school-age children.
- Explain the advantages for school-age children when their parents get them involved in organized adult-supervised leisure activities.
- Demonstrate an understanding of the home environments of childhood victims and bullies, including the parenting behaviors associated with these behaviors.
- Identify the ways in which parents might promote the physical development of their school-age children, including providing movement activities and good nutrition.
- Explain the role of parents in school-age children's overweight problems, and also identify ways in which parents might insure that their children maintain a healthy weight.
- Show an understanding of the role of parents in promoting their school-age children's school achievement.

If parents were asked to pick the easiest years of childrearing, they would probably choose the years from 7 to 11 when children (a) master dozens of new skills, (b) are able to learn quickly and think logically, and (c) live in a social world wherein most children think their parents are helpful, their teachers are fair, and their friends are loyal. As you will see in the forthcoming discussions, the interactions school-age children have with their parents are impacted by their parents' childrearing beliefs, the socioeconomic level of their families, and the cultures in which they live. You will also discover that, in families everywhere, parents are important influences on every aspect of school-age children's social–emotional, physical, and cognitive development.

PROMOTING SCHOOL-AGE CHILDREN'S SOCIAL–EMOTIONAL DEVELOPMENT

Around the age of 7, children move from the closely supervised and limited world of the younger child and begin to explore the wider world of neighborhood and school. In these broadening ventures, school-age children experience greater vulnerability, increasing competence, ongoing friendships, troubling rivalries, and deeper social understanding. Although not as closely supervised by parents and other adults as they were during the preschool years, school-age children's social and emotional lives continue to be shaped by family interaction patterns. Elementary school children's social–emotional development is influenced as well by the degree to which their parents provide organized activities for them and monitor their informal leisure activities. We will now examine the interplay between school-age children's expanding freedom and parents' guiding forces and the impact of these interactions on children's social and emotional development.

Parental Influences on the Acquisition of Skills and Competencies

Based on their level of success in mastering the skills valued by their parents and other significant adults, school-age children judge themselves as competent or incompetent, productive or failing (Erikson, 1982). Children are assisted in their

According to Erikson, parents and other significant adults in school-age children's lives play an important role in helping them develop a sense of industry.

Anthony Magnacca/Merrill.

quest for competence when their parents (a) encourage them to try out new things, (b) provide the materials and instruction needed to learn new skills, (c) pay attention to the progress their children are making in developing competence in a particular area, and (d) provide direct help when needed. Two of the most meaningful activities for the development of skills and competencies during the school-age years are sports and hobbies. The discipline, self-direction, and sense of competence that come from working on a hobby or playing sports contribute to school-age children's developmental need for a **sense of industry.** Furthermore, investing the necessary time to become knowledgeable about or skillful in these types of activities help define for children the ways in which they are unique, thereby contributing to their later identity development (McHale, Crouter, & Tucker, 2001). The development of skills and capabilities also contribute to children's development of a strong sense of self-worth. It has been shown that children who feel confident in at least one area of their lives are likely to have a higher self-esteem in comparison to those children who lack confidence in their abilities across several areas of their lives. Furthermore, high self-esteem helps children to view the rest of their lives from a more positive perspective. They are able to believe, for example, that even when their efforts are not successful in certain academic, athletic, or social situations, they are still worthwhile individuals (Colarossi & Eccles, 2000; Harter, 1998).

Thinking Critically

Go back in your mind to middle childhood and consider some activity (such as sports, dance, or art) that you began to feel you were "good at." What were the feelings of pride about being competent at that particular thing? What do you remember about the ways in which your parents or other caring adults supported your development of competence in that area?

Parent–Child Coregulation of Behavior. Another way in which parents contribute to their school-age children's social development is through sharing social power with them. Children are prepared for a greater sharing of social power during middle childhood due to their advances in cognitive development. Thus, **parent–child coregulation** becomes a predominant aspect of appropriate child socialization during this developmental stage (Masten & Coatsworth, 1998). The advantage of parent–child coregulation is that is has been associated with fewer behavior problems in school-age children (Deater-Deckard & Petrill, 2004). An example of coregulation is demonstrated in the following exchange: Charlie: "Mom, can I invite Tommy and Mike over for dinner? Mom: "Sure, that will be great. We're having spaghetti; I remember that those two seem to like my spaghetti. If Tommy and Mike come for dinner, will you please be sure that they pick up their dishes, rinse them off, and put them in the dishwasher after we have finished eating?" Charlie: "Okay, Mom."

What This Means for Professionals. It is important that parents make adjustments in their child socialization patterns to accommodate their children's need to develop the skills of coregulation during the school-age years. Whereas it is desirable for parents to support parent–child coregulation in many daily activities, the entire parent–child relationship is not coregulated. It is essential that parents of school-age children continue to structure their school-age children's daily activities, monitor their whereabouts, require certain levels of responsible behavior, and step in to exercise more control when necessary. It is possible, however, for parents to provide guidelines for their children's behavior without taking away their children's developing ability to work with parents in the coregulation of their behavior.

Parental Influences on Children's Social Relationships

During middle childhood, peer relationships become increasingly important. It has been found that children who are liked and accepted by their peers have more positive social traits, better social problem-solving skills, more constructive social behavior, and better friendship relations in comparison to less popular children. On the other hand, rejected children are more aggressive, more withdrawn, and less socially skilled than are children who are liked and accepted by their peers (Khaleque & Rohner, 2002). As will be demonstrated in the upcoming discussion, parents play a key role in their children's development of the social skills necessary for making and sustaining friendships. Unfortunately, some parents influence their children's development of negative behaviors that contribute to their rejection by other children.

Childrearing Patterns and Children's Social Relationships. The types of relationships children form with their peers have been consistently linked with their parents' childrearing patterns. Findings from Baumrind's (1991b) research show that school-age children of authoritative parents have more positive relationships with their peers than do children whose parents are authoritarian, permissive, indulgent, or uninvolved. The encouragement of children's participation in decision making by authoritative parents appears to provide them the experience needed to engage in thoughtful and responsible behaviors when interacting with their peers. According to Hart, Newell, and Olsen (2003), the behavioral control exercised by authoritative parents promotes their children's ability to use self-regulation in social situations. The authoritative parenting style also has been related to children's behaviors that reflect empathy and altruism (Aunola, Stattin, & Nurmi, 2000) and more positive social functioning with family members and peers (Zhou, Eisenberg, & Losoya, 2002).

In comparison to children whose parents are authoritative, children whose parents are authoritarian tend to be less socially adept (Aunola et al., 2000) and more at risk for behavior problems. The social problems of children whose parents are authoritarian have been attributed to their parents' overly strict and often harsh use of discipline. Authoritarian parents frequently rely on physical punishment in disciplining their children and the use of physical discipline is often supported by cultural beliefs. The findings of Lansford, et al. (2005), however, showed that physical discipline has a negative impact on children's development even in cultures where this approach to discipline is endorsed. In their interviews of parents and school-age children in China, India, Italy, Korea, the Philipines, and Thailand, Lansford and colleagues discovered that the higher use of physical punishment is consistently associated with more aggression and anxiety in children.

Children of permissive parents also have more difficulties in peer relationships than do children of authoritative parents due to their behaviors that are typically immature. They often lack impulse control, and show less social responsibility in comparison to children whose parents are not permissive (Baumrind, 1991b). Other school-age children who tend to suffer socially are those whose parents are uninvolved (Steinberg, 1996). Because children of uninvolved parents receive low levels of affection and often endure high levels of criticism and hostility from their parents, they are likely to experience problems in developing and sustaining friendships with other children. As early as preschool, these children tend to be noncompliant and their noncompliant behavior is associated with peer rejection during the school-age years (Jacob, 1997).

The Impact of the Neighborhood on Parenting Styles. Parents influence their school-age children's peer relationships by the parenting styles they adopt, but the communities in which they live impact parents' childrearing patterns. When families live in communities with a low incidence of crime and parents enjoy social support, there are fewer parenting challenges and the outcomes for children are generally better. In contrast, as neighborhood conditions worsen, parental emotional support is weakened. Furthermore, as surrounding environments become poorer and more dangerous, parents tend to rely more on physical discipline. Overall, the positive influence of social support on parents is strained and lessened in poorer, high-crime neighborhoods (Ceballo & McLoyd, 2002).

Thinking Critically

Why do you suppose that parenting challenges escalate when neighborhood conditions worsen?

Parental Structuring of Children's Leisure Time

There are many advantages for school-age children whose parents get them involved in organized adult-supervised leisure activities. One of the primary benefits is that these activities provide opportunities for children to make and sustain positive peer relationships. Adult-supervised activities also reflect parental involvement and monitoring, both of which are linked to more positive peer relations and fewer behavior problems among children (Kilgore, Snyder, & Lentz, 2000). For children in the United States, these activities typically fall into the following categories: sports (e.g., soccer, football, and baseball), music, band, dance lessons, drama, crafts, Scouts, church synagogue activities, and recreational camps. All these activities assist children in achieving peer group status while broadening their scope of learning. Furthermore, being involved in positive peer group organizations extends children's peer group interactions beyond the classroom, and provides them with opportunities to interact with other children who share their interests (Elkind, 2003).

Another advantage for children whose parents get them involved in organized activities is that these activities often provide opportunities for children to learn about cultural practices other than their own and develop friendships with children from a variety of cultural backgrounds. For example, Canadian children who identified with the cultures of India, Pakistan, and Bangladesh reported that leisure activities allowed them to enter and exit from different cultural communities with relative ease. According to these children, structured recreational activities allowed them to learn about diverse cultural practices and to develop friendships with children from a variety of cultural backgrounds (Tirone & Pedlar, 2005).

The Overbooked Child. Whereas being involved in organized activities has many benefits for children, parents should be careful not to overbook their children's time. When their leisure time is allocated to a multitude of activities, children have less time for unstructured play, and less time for meaningful family activities (Fishman, 1999). Elkind (2003) expressed concern regarding the overscheduling of children's lives and emphasized the need for children to have a balanced childhood in which they go to school, do a little homework, and play fort or other childhood games after school. To illustrate the difficulties faced by children whose lives are highly organized, Elkind tells the story of 9-year-old Kevin who was anxious, having trouble sleeping, and complaining that he was tired all the time. When Kevin's mother was asked about her son's schedule, it was discovered that she had enrolled him in "a dizzying number of extracurricular activities." In addition to school, Kevin had piano lessons twice a week and was involved in three team sports, church activities, and Scouts. In separate discussions with Kevin and his mother, Elkind discovered that Kevin was on the brink of depression and not having a happy childhood, as suggested by comments that he missed playing with his friends in the neighborhood. Kevin said that he missed the following activities that he used to do with friends: riding bikes, having water balloon fights, and building forts out of cardboard boxes.

Elkind's concerns regarding the overscheduling of children's time are echoed by Rosenfield and Wise (2000), who suggested that parents of school-age children avoid the "hyperparenting trap" of overscheduling their children. Rosenfield and Wise conjectured that parents who over-schedule their children's lives seem to feel remiss that they are not being good parents if their children are not in all kinds of activities. They also pointed out that children whose lives are overscheduled are under pressure to demonstrate success in many areas. Elkind stressed that children who are pressured to achieve to the extent that they are involved in too many activities miss out on time to (a) play in a natural and creative way, (b) participate in family relationships, and (c) pursue self-awareness. According to Rosenfield and Wise, time for unstructured play allows children to follow their interests, express their personalities, and learn ways in which to structure their own time. Unfortunately, children who are running from one activity to the next have little time for these family experiences and also have less time to pursue personal interests.

What This Means for Professionals. First, it is important to remember that extracurricular activities per se are not the problem. Children who participate in such activities reap valuable rewards. Involvement in sports, for example, has been shown to be related to elevated self-confidence, higher levels of academic performance, more involvement with school, fewer behavior problems, less likelihood of taking drugs, and decreased probability of engaging in risky behavior (Elkind, 2003). Even though the provision of out-of-home organized activities is potentially advantageous to their children, parents need to avoid the "more is better" trap or the "my child is busier than your child" syndrome.

Guidelines for Choosing Children's Out-of-Home Activities. Hamner and Turner (2001) provided several excellent guidelines for assisting parents in choosing out-of-home activities for their school-age children. They suggested that parents select activities for their children judiciously, being careful not to overcommit children's time. They also recommended that parents help their children select activities in which they can be successful by (a) examining alternatives carefully, and (b) considering the time commitment and competitive aspects of these activities. In addition to parental involvement in the selection of activities for their children, Hamner and Turner recommended that parents provide encouragement and guidance as children choose their own activities.

The Parent's Role in Children's Informal Leisure Activities. Besides supporting their children's involvement in organized out-of-home group activities, it is important that parents encourage home-based leisurely group activities that encourage their children's friendships, such as skating parties and hiking trips. When promoting informal leisure activities for their children and their children's friends, parents need to carefully monitor and supervise these activities because higher rates of problem behaviors such as delinquency and the use of drugs and alcohol are associated with the lack of parental monitoring of their children's leisure activities (Kilgore, Snyder, & Lentz, 2000). Furthermove, it is important to keep in mind that low socioeconomic children might require more parental monitoring because they are less likely to be involved in adult-supervised organized activities. For example, Zeijl, Poel, and Bois-Reymond (2001) found that children of highsocioeconomic status received considerably more opportunities for organized, adult-supervised activities in comparison to children from lower socioeconomic families. Socioeconomic differences in children's involvement in adult-supervised activities also were reported by Lareau (2002), who found that middle-class parents arrange out-of-school activities to cultivate their children's talents and working-class and poor parents leave the arrangement of leisure activities to the children themselves.

Thinking Critically

Consider the leisure-time activities of your school-age siblings or other school-age children that you know. Based on the previous discussion, see if you can identify the various ways in which their parents or guardians are involved in supporting these activities. Or, think back to when you were a school-age child and identify the ways in which your parents encouraged your leisure time activities.

Childhood Victims and Bullies and Their Parents

We will now address a serious problem seen in school-age children's peer relations—the presence of bullies and victims in the neighborhood and school. **Bullying** was once considered to be a normal part of school-age children's play, an unpleasant experience, certainly, but of little long-range consequence. After having recently looked at the situation more closely, though, researchers now realize that bullying is a considerable problem for school-age children, harming both the bullies and the victims. Childhood bullying is defined as repeated aggression in which one or more children harm or disturb another child physically, verbally, or psychologically (Wolke, Wood, & Stanford, 2001). When children physically bully other children, they hit, kick, push, and/or take personal belongings; when they verbally bully other children, they use name calling and threatening; and when they psychologically bully other children, they exclude them or gossip about them (Nansel et al., 2001).

The Impact of Bullying and Victimization on Children's Well-Being. Although bullying sometimes allows children to achieve their immediate goal, it is a risk factor for future maladaptive behaviors. For example, Nansel, Craig, Overpeck, Saluja, and Ruan (2004) found that school-age bullies are at greater risk for becoming involved in delinquency, crime, and alcohol abuse during their teenage years. Both immediate and long-term negative consequences also have been documented for victims. When children consistently confront the humiliating experiences of bullying, such as having to hand over their lunch money or being beaten up while others watch, the effects are detrimental at the time and persist over time (Berger, 2005). The damaging effects for child victims are anxiety, depression, underachievement, low self-esteem, and loneliness (Kochenderfer-Ladd & Wardrop, 2001; Schwartz, 2000). Victimized children also tend to be more withdrawn, cautious, quiet, and insecure, as well as less outgoing (Schwartz, 2000). Moreover, child victims are lonelier and less happy at school and have fewer good friends than other children (Nansel et al., 2001; 2004). One possible reason that bullied children tend to feel lonely is because other children are likely to avoid them for fear of being bullied themselves or losing social status among their peers. A common way in which victims respond to bullying is through avoidance behavior (such as not going to school or refusing to go to certain places) (Nansel et al., 2001).

The Parents of Childhood Bullies and Victims. Even though the behaviors of childhood bullies take place in peer groups outside the family, important differences have been found between the families of children who are bullies or victims, and the families of children who are neither bullies or victims (Stevens, Bourdeaudhuij, & Oost, 2002). In comparison to other families, interparental violence is more common in the families of children who become bullies or victims (Baldry, 2003). Besides this common experience, there are different family dynamics that contribute to children's assuming the roles of bullies or victims in their peer groups. Evidence suggests that bullies come from homes in which parents favor physical discipline, are frequently hostile and rejecting, have poor problem-solving skills, are accepting of aggressive childhood behavior, and/or teach their children to retaliate at the least provocation (Demaray & Malecki, 2003).

In contrast to parental behaviors that contribute to bullying, parenting influences on the likelihood that children will be the victims of bullies have been found to be gender related. Maternal overprotection has been associated with the victimization of boys and poor identification with mothers has been linked to the victimization of girls. In explaining the relations between maternal overprotection and the victimization of boys, it has been suggested that overprotective parenting likely interferes with the development of behaviors such as independence and assertion that are valued by male peers, and needed by boys to defend their position in the dominance hierarchy common to school-age peer groups. Being seen as independent and assertive also likely contributes to school-age boys' sense of self-confidence and adequacy in their peer groups. For girls, the link between victimization and low maternal identification is related to perceptions of the mother as hostile and rejecting. Low maternal identification might threaten girls' need for affiliation and their development of the social skills needed to relate closely and effectively with others. The parenting behavior most predictive of girls' victimization is perceived threat of rejection, which is experienced when girls' mothers threaten to abandon them, send them away, or stop loving them when they misbehave (Finnegan, Hodges, & Perry, 1998).

What This Means for Professionals. The previous discussion points to ways in which parents might alter their parental behaviors to prevent their children from assuming the roles of bully or victim. For professionals working with these parents, the prevention strategy developed by Hanish and Tolan (2001) might be a useful intervention plan. This five-step strategy, designed to prevent childhood bullying and victimization, recommends that parents (a) monitor their children's activities and whereabouts; (b) develop and use rules and consequences; (c) reframe behaviors in positive, instead of negative, ways; (d) focus on their children's positive behaviors; and (5) develop and use effective listening skills.

Thinking Critically

What have you learned from the previous discussion that you might, as a professional, recommend to parents to prevent their children from acting as bullies? For parents whose children are being victimized by other children, what steps would you recommend that these parents take?

PROMOTING THE PHYSICAL DEVELOPMENT OF SCHOOL-AGE CHILDREN

Now that we have considered the influence of parents on school-age children's social–emotional development, we will turn our attention to the ways in which parents contribute to the physical growth and development of their school-age children. As will become apparent in the upcoming discussion, parents play a crucial role in keeping their children healthy and safe while promoting their children's involvement in activities necessary for optimal physical development.

The Importance of Meeting School-Age Children's Nutritional Needs

Whereas middle childhood is generally a time when children are the healthiest, and growth is slower than during the preschool years, adequate nutrition remains an important issue. Both the quantity and quality of the food school-age children eat affects their ongoing growth, height, weight, motor skill development, and cognitive ability. Whether school-age children receive sufficient nutrition, though, is related to where they live, whether or not they live in poverty, and which types of food are served in the home.

The Impact of Nutrition and Malnutrition on Children's Physical Development. For school-age children whose parents provide adequate nutrition, their growth and physical development give them the strength and agility to participate in many playful adventures, such as running, jumping, throwing, catching, climbing, swimming, and tumbling. All these activities are important for school-age children because they promote the development of their motor skills. Unfortunately, children whose parents do not provide adequate nutrition for them are less active than is desired. It has been demonstrated that malnourished children engage less in physical activity due to a lack of available energy (Parizkova, 1998). Not only does the nutrition parents provide for their children support their physical activity, it also promotes their physical growth.

In more affluent countries, such as the United States, most parents are able to see to it that their school-age children get sufficient nutritious food to grow as tall as their genes permit (Troiano, Briefel, Carroll, & Bialostosky, 2000). In countries where food is often in short supply, however, children of poor parents frequently suffer from malnutrition, which negatively impacts their physical development in a variety of ways, one of which is stunted growth. For example, trained health workers in rural Pakistan conducted height and weight measurements of children in 32 primary schools and compared these measurements to their parents' occupations. Their findings revealed that children with stunted growth came from poorer families where their fathers were farm workers, shopkeepers, or government employees. Children whose growth was not stunted were the children of the landlords (Khuwaja, Selwyn, & Shah, 2005). Although the stunting of their children's growth is a serious concern for parents in developing countries, being unable to properly feed their children contributes to many other worries as well. In impoverished countries, malnutrition permeates all aspects of children's health, growth, and development. For instance, more than 50% of the deaths of children in developing countries can be attributed to malnutrition, which is most often in combination with serious infection (Neumann, Gewa, & Bwibo, 2004).

The Link Between Nutrition and Cognitive Development. Parents' ability to provide adequate nutrition for their children not only impacts their children's physical growth and ability to participate in physical activities, it also affects their cognitive development. Taras (2005) found that American children with iron deficiencies sufficient to cause anemia are at a disadvantage academically, and concluded that food insufficiency is a critical problem affecting these children's ability to learn. Looking outside the United States, Tarleton et al. (2006) examined the cognitive functioning of Bangladeshi children between the ages of 6 and 9, and found that malnutrition of school-age children in that country is associated with a lower level of cognitive functioning. Similar findings have been reported by Sungthong, Mosuwan, and Chongsuvivatwong (2002), who studied the impact of malnutrition on school children in southern Thailand, and found that children with iron-deficiency anemia had the poorest cognitive functioning and also below-average math/language achievement.

Problems That Poor Parents in the United States Face in Feeding Their Children. Although there are programs in the United States to help poor parents to provide adequate nutrition for their children, Taras (2005) has pointed out that children's malnutrition in the United States needs to be better understood. For example, it was discovered that school breakfast programs improve attendance rates and decrease tardiness but do not improve cognitive development and academic performance except for severely undernourished children. Another dilemma facing low-income American parents' attempts to provide adequate nutrition for their children was highlighted by Bhattacharya, DeLeire, and Haider (2003), who found that both poor and rich families increase their fuel expenditures in response to unusually cold weather. They discovered, however, that poor families reduce their food expenditures by approximately the same amount as their increase in fuel expenditures. Thus, poor parents spend less on food and they and their children eat less food during cold-weather budgetary shocks. The conclusions of Bhattacharya and colleagues were that existing social programs fail to cushion these cold-weather shocks.

Liz Moore/Merrill.

Physical activity is an excellent way to prevent childhood overweight problems. For children who are already overweight, physical activity is helpful for getting their weight into the normal range.

Nutrition and the Growing Problem of Children Being Overweight

Whereas many children throughout the world suffer from malnutrition due to their parents being unable to provide sufficient nutrition, many school children in the United States are consuming too many calories in comparison to their physical activity. The result is that a greater proportion of American children are overweight today than ever before. This situation has sounded a public health alarm because children who are overweight are more susceptible to a variety of diseases, especially orthopedic and respiratory problems, as well as Type II Diabetes. Moreover, children who are overweight are less able to participate in physical activities, are often shunned by their peers, and are much more likely to end up obese when they are adults. Several social factors have been identified as contributors to children's overweight problems. These inlcude (a) their eating habits as well as the types of food and drinks they consume, (b) their level of physical exercise, (c) the amount of time they spend watching television, and (d) their parents' attitudes about food (Dietz, 1999).

Do Children Who Are Overweight Eat Too Much? A common belief regarding adults and children who are overweight is that these individuals eat too much. Based on this belief, reducing food intake by dieting is a popular approach to losing weight for adults. Even for adults, reducing calories without increasing exercise is likely to be a temporary solution to weight control. This approach to helping children who are overweight reach an appropriate height–weight ratio is not recommended due to the growing child's need for adequate nutrition. Furthermore, the evidence from studies of children's eating habits does not support the belief that children who are overweight eat more than do children who are not overweight. Troiano et al. (2000) compared the diets of children who were overweight to those who were not overweight and found no significant differences between the two groups in overall food intake. A difference was found between these two groups, though, in the consumption of nonnutritive sources of energy. For children who were overweight, a higher percentage of their energy source was derived from nonnutritious sources, especially the consumption of soft drinks. In a similar study of a large sample of school-age children, Cullen, Ash and, Warneke (2002) found that more than half of the total beverages consumed by fourth- to sixth-grade students were sweetened beverages. Furthermore, children who drank the most sweetened beverages consumed more calories in comparison to children who did not drink sweetened beverages. High-fat vegetable consumption (such as french fries) was also greater for those with the highest soft drink consumption. Furthermore, fruit consumption was much lower for children with the highest soft drink consumption. The conclusions from both of these studies were that excessive drinking of sweetened beverages is linked to the poor nutrition of children as well as to childhood overweight problems.

The Role of Physical Inactivity. Providing healthy food for their children and limiting their intake of sweetened beverages are important goals for parents who wish to prevent their children from having problems related to being overweight. An equally important goal for parents who wish to help their children maintain a healthy weight is to insure that they are participating in physical exercise. In demonstrating the link between childhood obesity and low levels of physical activity, Steinbeck (2001) emphasized that excess fat is the result of an imbalance of energy intake (food) and energy output (physical activity). Steinbeck points to evidence that physical activity for the entire population of the United States is declining, and that declining physical activity is a major factor in the increasing prevalence of obesity problems among American children. One of the factors Steinbeck associated with declining physical activities among children is that many childhood leisure activities, including television viewing, contribute to children's lives becoming less active and more sedentary. Furthermore, the time that children might spend being engaged in physical activities is sometimes limited by safety concerns, lack of suitable environments, and a shortage of time spent with family. For school-age children who are overweight, Steinbeck recommends that parents increase their children's physical exercise to allow them to grow into their weight. Steinbeck emphasized that the parental goal of promoting children's involvement in physical activities must include considerations of space, access, and appropriate types of play for school-age children. Another emphasis of Steinbeck is the need for parents to understand that children model their behaviors on parental behaviors. Accordingly, the family activity model, which emphasizes physical activities for the entire family, is a useful approach to helping children maintain a healthy weight.

The Role of Television Viewing. Closely associated with school-age children's declining participation in physical activity is the upsurge in the time they spend watching television, which is a prime contributor to the rise in childhood obesity. There are three ways in which researchers have linked television viewing and childhood weight problems. First, the more time children spend participating in sedentary leisure activities, such as watching television, the less time they are engaged in physical activities. Second, watching television lowers children's rates of metabolism (Steinbeck, 2001). Third, the more time children spend watching television the higher their intake of high sugar and junk foods. The image of a child sitting in front of the television snacking on salty munchies and drinking a sweetened beverage easily comes to mind (Gable & Lutz, 2000). Unfortunately, television viewing is the most common free-time activity of school-age children and they spend more time watching television in the winter months than at other times of the year, suggesting that children habitually watch television because they have nothing better to do (McHale et al., 2001).

The Impact of Parental Attitudes About Food. Concerns about the excessive weight of many American children have centered on the elimination of gym classes in schools, the high rates of consumption of sweetened beverages, and the watching of too much television. While all these factors are important, less notice has been given to the role that parents' attitudes about food play in their children's weight problems. In Steinbeck's (2001) study to determine the causes of childhood obesity, the family's food beliefs and eating patterns were identified as one of the factors that contribute to childhood weight problems. In a similar study, Variyam (2001) studied a group of parents whose children were overweight and found that parents' unwillingness to change was a primary contributor to their children being overweight. Variyam also reported that these parent's own overweight status, and more importantly, how they viewed their overweight status, affected their children's weight condition. They discovered that parents who were overweight tended to have children who were overweight and also were inclined to underestimate their own overweight status. Finally, nutrition labeling on processed foods has been in effect since mid-1994 and consumer surveys indicate that reading food labeling influences food choice. Nonetheless, a substantial proportion of parents in Variyam's study reported that they rarely or never read nutrition labels. This group of parents, who did not use labels to guide their food choices, had more children who were overweight than did parents who regularly used nutrition labels to guide food choices.

What This Means for Professionals. To prevent their children from becoming overweight and to respond to the needs of their children who are already overweight, there are several things that parents might do. First, parents need to understand that too much time spent watching television puts their school-age children at risk for becoming overweight. To offset this risk, parents might monitor the amount of time spent watching television. Second, parents need to encourage their children's involvement in physical activities, and a number of recommendations for increasing children's physical activities have been previously suggested. Third, it is helpful if parents select food for their children that is nutritious and limit their children's consumption of nonnutritive beverages. Finally, it is important for parents to examine their own attitides about food, and their willingness to assist their children in maintaining a healthy weight.

Thinking Critically

How do you feel about the finding that more American children are becoming overweight while children in many other countries often lack sufficient nutrition to reach their maximum growth? In what ways are the malnourishment of some children and overweight of others related to these children's involvement in physical exercise?

Promoting Motor Skills

Not only is the engagement of school-age children in physical activities important for maintaining their weight, it is also necessary for promoting their motor skill development. During middle childhood, children are typically engaged in numerous physical activities, like learning to ride bikes, in-line skating, swimming, climbing trees, jumping rope, and participating in a variety of organized sports (e.g., soccer, baseball, football, hockey). In an earlier discussion on the ways parents might promote their children's social development, we learned that organized activities assist

Courtesy of USDA Natural Resources Conservation.

Many school-age children within and outside the United States develop gross motor skills as they learn to ride horses, herd cattle, and participate in a number of physical activities associated with rural life.

children in making and sustaining friendships. Activities that require a great deal of movement also support the development of children's motor skills. In the selection of organized sports, however, parents should remember that the skills necessary for playing many games (such as baseball, football, or soccer) take time for school-age children to master because they do not have the strength, endurance, and hand and eye coordination that adolescents have. Thus, although many benefits are derived from sports participation, it is important for parents to be patient with school-age children's performance and to understand that the development of skills in sports take time, practice, and patience. Finally, the extent to which parents, themselves, are engaged in outdoor activities impact the degree to which their children participate in physical activities. Interactive play within the family provides numerous benefits for school-age children. Many of the movement games that children play with their friends are fun to play with family members as well. Also, the informal games that children play with parents and friends are less competitive than organized sports and are also a better match for the motor skills of school-age children. Furthermore, parents have the opportunity to plan family activities that maximize the possibility of movement, such as touch football, hiking, swimming, and treasure hunts. Children growing up in families that take part in outdoor activities such as these have many opportunities to be physically active while spending valuable time with family members.

The Role of Parents in Injury Prevention

Parents everywhere want their children to be able to enjoy playful activities but want them to remain safe while doing so. Keeping school-age children safe is a challenge, though, because children at this age both enjoy and need to participate in many physical activities that require speed, a great deal of movement, and many other factors that potentially place them at risk for incurring injury. Although children will undoubtedly suffer minor injuries that are virtually impossible to prevent and still remain actively involved in play, it is necessary that parents ensure children's safety as they engage in these activities.

How Parents Might Prevent Childhood Injuries. With the goals of preventing serious injury to children and demonstrating that child safety is an attainable goal, Timpka and Lindqvist (2001) showed that coordinated efforts by parents, children, and a concerned community can reduce serious injury and possible deaths of children. They emphasized that to improve children's safety in their communities, all parents should have information about risk factors for child injuries. Then, both structural and educational measures need to be put into place with the goal of improving child safety. For instance, parents need to insure that their children have driveway visibility along the routes where they walk or bike. To determine if such obstructions exist, it is helpful if parents walk or bike those routes, along with their children, while pointing out such hazards. For this exercise, parents should note that obstructions that do not interfere with their own visibility might, nevertheless, limit the visibility of their children, due to adult and child height differences. If parents identify shrubberies that obstruct their children's views, they might ask the owners of the property to cut the shrubberies back, instruct their children to take careful precautions at that driveway, or to take an

Phyllis Heath.

While it is important for parents to promote their school-age children's involvement in physical activities, safety precautions should be taken to prevent serious accidents.

alternate route. School-age children benefit as well when parents provide them with safe cycling information, including the requirement to wear a bike helmet. Finally, parents should let children know they are concerned about their safety and outline for them the safety precautions they should take when engaging in various activities.

Thinking Critically

Consider an accident that you or another child experienced during the school-age years that involved play activities. Based on the previous discussion, how might parents prevent an accident like that from occurring?

Keeping Children Safe in Unsafe Communities. Although parents everywhere are concerned about their children's safety, keeping children safe in **unsafe communities** requires heightened parental vigilance. Unfortunately, in many communities in the United States, families are living in neighborhoods plagued by violence, crime, and drug activity (U.S. Department of Health and Human Services, 2000). In these neighborhoods, parents and children are directly and indirectly exposed to robberies, physical assaults, and murders (Veenema, 2001). Thus, a high priority for parents in these communities is keeping their children safe. The steps taken by parents in dangerous neighborhoods to insure the safety of their children revolve around three major themes: (a) monitoring their children's whereabouts, (b) educating their children regarding safety, and (c) improving community life. In interviews by Jarret, Jefferson, and Roach (2000), mothers in a high-risk community cited the following ways in which they cope with community violence: keeping their children physically close, providing constant supervision, teaching them practical household safety skills (such as not sitting by windows), and restricting neighborhood activities (for example, the use of community playgrounds). Some of these mothers also had spoken to neighborhood drug dealers, telling them to take their business elsewhere. In interviews of fathers in a high-risk community, Letieca and Koblinsky (2004) noted that they also emphasized the need to be vigilant in monitoring their children's whereabouts. These fathers stressed that they watched their children everywhere, in the home, on the front steps, in the yard, and in the public parks. Several of them also stressed that they never allowed their children to play outside after dark. Furthermore, many expressed a need to know where their children were at all times in case of violent incidents that might occur so that they could quickly get their children out of harm's way.

Thinking Critically

Many parents choose the neighborhoods in which they will live with their children based on whether or not those neighborhoods are safe places for children, whether there are neighborhood parks, what the schools are like, and so on. Yet many other parents are bringing up their children in unsafe neighborhoods. What societal factors, do you suppose, are associated with parents rearing their children in unsafe neighborhoods?

PROMOTING SCHOOL-AGE CHILDREN'S COGNITIVE DEVELOPMENT

So far, we have discussed the important responsibility of parents in helping their children make and sustain friendships, and learn to be competent in various skills. We also learned that parents everywhere have challenges related to providing appropriate levels of nutrition for their children and keeping their children safe while they are engaged in play activities. Now that we have examined the ways in which parents impact the social–emotional and physical development of their school-age children, we will turn our attention to the role of parents in promoting the cognitive development of their school-age children. In the upcoming discussions, you will discover that the views of Piaget and Vygotsky are useful for helping parents to maximize their school-age children's cognitive potential. We will also focus on the significant role that parents play in promoting their children's academic achievement.

Promoting Logical Reasoning

According to Piaget, in comparison to preschoolers, who make judgments based on intuitive thinking and are easily fooled by appearances, school-age children are logical thinkers. The logical thinking of school-age children emerges as egocentrism decreases, allowing children to decenter their attention. As children develop the ability to decenter their attention, they are able to take into account multiple aspects of a situation, which greatly enhances their problem-solving ability. One advantage of school-age children's ability to decenter their attention is that they are able to focus on present, past, and future events. They are, therefore, capable of planning ahead and considering how current efforts relate to future accomplishments (Piaget & Inhelder, 1969). An aspect of logical reasoning that develops during middle childhood is the ability to classify, which helps school-age children to put objects in more sophisticated categories than they were able to do during the preschool years.

What This Means for Professionals. The logical thinking abilities of school-age children means that parents can feel freer to use more complex speech with them because, unlike younger children, school-age children are able to understand metaphors, realize that some words have multiple meanings, and comprehend reverse-order sentences. Capitalizing on their children's developing ability to decenter their concentration, parents can point out to their children the ways in which their behaviors affect others, thereby promoting their development of empathy. For example, parents could say to their first-graders that when they share with other children, those other children are pleased and more likely to share with them. Parents might assist their school-age children in the development of their ability to classify by supporting their interests in collections of various objects and by making recommendations for categorization, ordering, and collecting that their children might not have considered. Parents can capitalize on their children's ability to consider past, present, and future events by providing them with calendars and watches. By encouraging school-age children to use their watches to monitor events in their daily lives and assisting them in the use of their calendars to keep up with and plan for future events, parents offer their children the experiences they require for continued development of their ability to decenter their attention.

Thinking Critically

Try to recall the ways that you as a school-age child expressed your ability to classify by collecting certain objects. What were the ways in which your parents, or other significant adults in your life, supported your interest in having a collection?

The Parental Use of Guided Participation

You might recall from an earlier chapter that Lev Vygotsky theorized that parents and other adults shape children's cognitive development through the process of guided participation. According to Kermani and Brenner (2000), through the process of guided participation, parents lead their children toward greater understanding of the task at hand while assisting them in the development of their own comprehension of the task. The following example demonstrates the ways in which a parent might use guided participation to support the cognitive development of their school-age children.

Suppose a child attempts to solve a jigsaw puzzle, gets discouraged, and stops trying. Although it appears at first glance as if the task is beyond the child's ability to accomplish, that is not necessarily the case. The child might be successful in putting the puzzle together if the parent provides guided participation to facilitate the child's learning experience. Guided participation might include: (a) remarks designed to motivate the child to solve the problem, "Oh, I think you can do it; let me help you"; (b) assisting the child in focusing attention on the important steps, "First, we have to study the picture, then try to match the puzzle pieces to the picture"; (c) providing instruction, "Sometimes we need to rotate the pieces to get them to fit into a certain space"; and (d) encouraging the child's interest and motivation, "See, you're making progress. I thought you could do it."

The Role of Parents in Children's School Achievement

As you will learn in the upcoming discussion, school-age children's achievement has been related to their parents' childrearing patterns, expectations of academic success, ages when they were born, cultural values, and whether or not they are recent immigrants.

The Impact of Childrearing Patterns and Parental Attributions. Both childrearing patterns as well as parental attributions regarding their children's abilities have been linked to the achievement levels of school-age children. The authoritative parenting pattern has been consistently associated with higher levels of achievement for children, whereas the authoritarian, permissive, and uninvolved parenting patterns have been linked to low levels of achievement. Authoritative parenting enhances children's achievement behavior in a number of ways. For example, positive parental beliefs and attributions emphasizing children's abilities support children's positive self-perceptions. Moreover, a tendency of authoritative parents to provide optimal challenges for their children encourages their children's independent and active problem solving. Other ways that authoritative parents promote their children's achievement is by recognizing their individual interests and unique personalities (e.g., Garg, Levin, & Kauppi, 2005; Jones et al., 2000). Across all parenting styles, parents who think their children are capable of achievement are more likely to have children who are academically successful. In particular, children have higher levels of achievement when their parents attribute academic success to ability and lack of academic success to lack of effort. In contrast, children have lower levels of achievement when their parents hold the view that their children have low academic ability (Bempechat, Graham, & Jimenez, 1999).

The Impact of Poverty on Children's Academic Achievement. School-age children's level of achievement is also affected by whether or not they and their parents live in poverty. The research shows that when parents are unable to provide sufficient income to raise the family out of poverty, their children have lower achievement scores. On the other hand, there is evidence that when the family's income level improves, children's achievement levels advance as well. For example, Hofferth, Smith, and McLoyd (2000) compared the achievement scores of children whose mothers were on welfare to those whose mothers had previously been on welfare. Their results showed that children whose mothers were able to leave and remain off welfare scored consistently higher on achievement in comparison to children whose mothers were still on welfare. Similar results have been found for low-income working families. Huston, Duncan, and McLoyd (2005) assessed the effectiveness of an employment-based anti-poverty program, which had strong work supports for adults living in poverty. This program, called New Hope, was designed to raise total income above the poverty threshold by providing two important work supports: extensive child-care assistance and health care subsidies. To be eligible for participation in the program, parents were required to be employed fulltime (30 or more hours a week). The project provided access to community service jobs for parents who were unable to find market-based employment. New Hope was not tied to the welfare system but available instead to all adults with low incomes. Thus, the goal was not simply to move parents from welfare to work but to reduce family poverty. Two years after families entered the program, parental employment and income increased and there was increased participation by children in structured out-of-school activities. The impact on school-age children was substantially better academic performance, higher levels of positive social behavior, and lower levels of problem behavior in school.

The Influence of Parental Age on Children's Academic Success. Another factor that influences children's school achievement is parental age. School-age children who were born when their parents were adolescents have lower levels of academic achievement in comparison to those born when their parents were older. For example, Levine, Pollack, and Comfort (2001) found that early motherhood is related to school-age children's low test scores and grade repetition. These researchers concluded that the low achievement of these children is almost entirely explained by the prebirth individual and family background factors of the teen mothers themselves. They speculated that young mothers' lack of maturity, fewer life experiences, and lower levels of social support contribute to less effective parenting skills. They suggested that when young mothers lack effective parenting skills, they are less able to appropriately shape the activities and behaviors of their children that lead to academic achievement.

Cultural Influences on Children's School Achievement. Parental goals are imbedded in cultural norms, and when parental goals are reflected in their children's school environment, it is easier for these children to achieve. On the other hand, mainstream cultural norms frequently create challenges for minority children and their parents. The problem for these children is that academic success is often contingent on the acceptance of mainstream cultural values that are at times different from the values they learn at home and in their communities. This reality creates a dynamic in which many ethnic minority children are consistently penalized for not expressing the values and behaviors promoted by the mainstream majority culture (Boykin & Allen, 2000). Over time, this situation contributes to children questioning their place in school. The resulting disconnect contributes to the development of negative views of academic success.

There is mounting evidence, however, that when the basics of children's culture are included in learning tasks and contexts, children improve in performance, engagement, and motivation (Bailey & Boykin, 2001; Boykin & Cunningham, 2001). Thus, the achievement expectations of ethnic minority parents need to be matched by culturally relevant school environments that support the cultural values of all children. For instance, Sankofa, Hurley, Allen, and Boykin (2005) demonstrated that when African American children are placed in learning environments that allow for the expression of **communalism,** their achievement levels improve. Communalism is a common value in traditional families and communities that emphasizes group (family and community) cooperation and the success of the group rather than the success of the individual.

Parents and Children Who Have Recently Immigrated. The ways in which parental expectations, culture, and children's school achievement are interrelated is also exemplified in studies of parents and children who are recent immigrants. Although these parents typically have high hopes for their children's school achievement, they face challenges in assisting their children to achieve academic success. An example of this problem is seen with Korean American families, whose high levels of parent–child communication and home supervision are cultural norms that have a substantial impact on children's educational achievement. The difficulty for parents who are recent immigrants is that they often are not sufficiently proficient in English to promote their children's school achievement. For instance, Kim (2002) found that Korean American parents who have a higher level of English proficiency tend to have higher levels of parental involvement, resulting in their children's educational success. In a similar study, Bhattacharya (2000) studied South Asian school children who had immigrated to the United States with their parents and had below-average grades. In this study, parents' low level of proficiency in English was found to be a critical factor in low school achievement.

Thinking Critically

Based on the previous discussion, what recommendations would you make to parents who want to help their children achieve in school? Also, what steps might be taken by communities to support all parents in their efforts to raise their children's achievement levels?

SUMMARY

- In this chapter, we learned that there is a link between parental childrearing patterns and children's abilities to make and sustain friendships.
- We also examined the parenting patterns and aspects of the parental relationship that contribute to childhood bullying and victimization.

- Next, we considered the role of parents in providing adequate nutrition for their children. The discussion included a focus on the negative impact of undernutrition on children's development. We also focused on the problem of children being overweight.
- The benefits of physical activity for school-age children were addressed as well, and suggestions were provided that parents might use to support their children's activity levels while keeping them safe.
- Finally, we examined the role of parents in supporting their children's cognitive development. An important focus of that discussion was the role of parents in children's academic achievement.

KEY TERMS

- bullying
- communalism
- parent–child coregulation
- sense of industry
- unsafe communities

USEFUL WEB SITES

Parent Resources/USA Government is an excellent site for parents of school-age children.

http://usa.gov/topics/parents_young.shtml

This site has links for parents of children at different ages. Some of the topics at this site are: ways to provide good nutrition, activities for parents and children, back-to-school tips, bicycle safety, homework help, and tips on selecting summer camps.

Children First—The website of the National PTA

http://www.pta.org/

PTA publications and programs, including selected articles, links to web pages of state and local PTAs, and links to organizations of interest to parents of school-age children are highlighted on this site.

Children's Literature Web Guide

http://www.ucalgary/.ca/~dkbrown/

Explore here to learn more about selecting children's books, and the "Resources for Parents" section is especially good. The goal of this site is to gather together and categorize books for children.

Kids' Money

http://www.kidsmoney.org

Here you will find a survey on family allowance practices; articles focused on teaching kids to be thrifty, money management, and investing; a parent's book list; and a discussion group on children's money.

Parent–Adolescent Interactions

Objectives

After completing this chapter, you should be able to

- Explain the ways in which various parenting styles impact the development and well-being of adolescents.
- Demonstrate an understanding of the benefit for adolescents when they and their parents spend quality time together.
- Identify the ways in which parent–adolescent attachment plays out in the lives of adolescents and the benefits of that attachment relationship for adolescents' well-being.
- Describe the link between parent–adolescent relationships and the adolescent's conceptions of the self, including the adolescent's concept of identity and self-esteem.
- Identify the sources of parent–adolescent conflict, the ways in which parent–adolescent conflict changes over time, and with which parent the adolescent is more likely to have conflict.
- Describe the changes in the family system when children reach adolescence, and when emerging adults leave home, as well as the circumstances related to some young adults returning home to their parents after residing elsewhere.
- Demonstrate an understanding of the role that parents play in the problems adolescents sometimes face, such as being overweight or underweight, depression, substance abuse, and crime and delinquency.

"My parents and I got along okay during my adolescence. When I was about 12-years-old, my dad sat down with me and told me that I would be going through a lot of changes over the next few years and there would be times that we might not see things eye to eye. He told me not to worry about it, that we would talk things over but mostly we were going to have a good time with it."

—Unpublished quotation from a 20-year-old male

Adolescence is a stage of major developmental changes, which calls for a number of alterations in the parent–child relationship. In this chapter, we will explore the ways in which the developmental changes of adolescents affect their relationships with their parents and how their relationships with their parents impact adolescents' development. First, we will consider the various parenting styles, as they relate to adolescent development. We then will focus attention on two important aspects of adolescent development: (a) adolescents' attachments to their parents, and (b) the role of parents in supporting adolescents' self-esteem and quest for identity. Next, drawing from Family Systems Theory, we will examine the disequilibrium that occurs in the family system as parents and other family members adapt to the developmental changes of adolescents. After that, we will consider the challenges encountered in parent–adolescent relationships, including parent–adolescent conflict, and the role of parents in the prevention of adolescent depression, and parental influences on adolescent risk behaviors.

PARENTING STYLES AND ADOLESCENT DEVELOPMENT

In general, the most favorable outcomes for adolescents, by American standards, are linked with authoritative parenting. For adolescents living in non-Western countries and ethnic minority families, traditional parenting has been associated with positive outcomes. In contrast to the many positive effects of authoritative or traditional parenting, authoritarian, permissive, indulgent, and uninvolved parenting styles negatively impact adolescent development. Adolescents are also negatively impacted when parents have inconsistent parenting styles.

The Impact of Authoritative Parenting on the Lives of Adolescents

Adolescents whose parents are authoritative have higher psychosocial maturity (Mantzipoulos et al., 1998), as well as higher levels of reasoning ability, empathy, and altruism (Aunola et al., 2000). They also have higher school achievement and better relationships with family and peers (Garg et al., 2005; Steinberg, 2000). Another advantage for adolescents whose parents are authoritative is that they are more optimistic and have better self-regulation than adolescents whose parents are not authoritative (Jackson, Pancer, Pratt, & Hunsberger, 2000; Purdie, Carroll, & Roche, 2004). There are a variety of reasons why adolescent children of authoritative parents have positive outcomes. First, adolescents are at a juncture in their lives when they are developmentally more capable of exercising more autonomy and self-regulation than they were when they were younger (Steinberg, 2000; Zimmer-Gembeck & Collins, 2003). At the same time, they have less experience than adults in understanding and dealing with their own impulses and abilities. Thus, they require experiences that allow for greater autonomy, but do not deal well with excessive independence. Authoritative parents, whose level of control is neither permissive nor strict, achieve a balance between providing their adolescent children an appropriate level of freedom while, simultaneously, requiring them to behave in a responsible manner. Besides using an optimum level of control, authoritative parents are responsive to the needs of their adolescent children. Because their parents express love and concern for their well-being, adolescents with authoritative parents are better able to believe in their own worth. Responsive parenting also contributes to adolescents' identifying with their parents and embracing parental values, which leads them to behave in ways in which their parents would approve (Arnett, 2007).

The Traditional Parenting Pattern and Its Impact on Adolescents

As pointed out in Chapter 2, parents in non-Western cultures as well as many parents in ethnic minority cultures within the United States have a style of parenting that has been designated by Baumrind (1987) as traditional. In traditional cultures, the *role of parent* carries greater inherent authority and parents are not expected to provide reasons why they should be obeyed (Lieber, Nihira, & Mink, 2004). Lest this parenting style be mistaken for the authoritarian parenting style, it is important to remember that, unlike autoritarian parents, traditional parents combine high parental control with high parental responsiveness. Furthermore, because parents and adolescents in many tradtional cultures spend their days together, working side by side, and share responsibilities for caring for younger children, they develop a sense of interdependence and shared obligations (Lim & Lim, 2004). Examples of the high levels of closeness between adolescents and their parents in traditional families are exemplified by the concept of **familism** in the Latino culture and the concept of amae in the Japanese culture. *Familismo* represents a primary Latino cultural belief, which emphasizes the love, closeness, and mutual obligations of family life. The term *amae* was described in an earlier chapter as a Japanase cultural value that emphasizes the closeness of mothers and children (Hsai & Scanzoni, 1996).

Because stricter parenting is balanced by greater closeness, the traditional parenting pattern generally contributes to positive outcomes for adolescents (Chao, 2001). One of the advantages for adolescents in traditional families is that the child-rearing efforts of their parents are typically buffered by the support of members of their extended families. The greater involvement of extended family members in traditional families, especially grandparents, provide adolescents in these families with opportunities for guidance and closeness from parents as well as other adult family members (Fuligni et al., 1999). An example of the positive impact of traditional parents on adolescent development is seen in Latino families, wherein adolescents generally accept the authority of their parents and also express a strong sense of attachment to their families (Harwood et al., 2002). Similarly, the traditional parenting styles of Asian-American parents are related to high rates of achievement and fewer problems for Asian American adolescents (Tseng, 2004).

What This Means for Professionals. In light of the overwhelming evidence that authoritative and traditional parenting patterns are associated with positive outcomes for adolescents, it is important to consider what these two parenting patterns have in

High levels of parental responsiveness in traditional cultures contributes to close parent-adolescent relationships.

common. Whereas the goal of the authoritative parenting style is the promotion of *in*dependence and the goal of the traditional parenting style is the promotion of *inter*dependence, both of these parenting patterns combine high parental expectations with high parental support. In the case of the traditional parenting style, the support provided by the parent is further augmented by support from extended family members. Whether parents value independence or interdependence for their adolescent children, the message is clear—adolescents fare better in homes where their parents and/or other caregivers are involved in their daily lives, provide clear guidelines for their behavior, and support them in their attempts to live up to parental and societal expectations.

Thinking Critically

Perhaps you had not considered that adolescents in different cultures who have positive outcomes have parents who emphasize the combination of parental support and control. How do you think this information might help you in working with adolescents and parents in varying cultures?

Adolescents and Authoritarian Parents

In contrast to the authoritative and traditional parenting styles, the authoritarian parenting style has been consistently associated with adverse consequences for adolescents. Authoritarian parents are those parents whom adolescents describe as strict and not very or only somewhat supportive (Caputo, 2004). In comparison to adolescents with authoritative or traditional parents, adolescents whose parents are authoritarian are less self-assured, less creative, and less socially skilled. In addition, they tend to have lower achievement and be more dependent, and are also more likely to conform to peers (Aunola et al., 2000; Mantzipoulos & Oh-Hwang, 1998). Moreover, adolescents with authoritarian parents are more at risk for behavior problems such as substance abuse, crime, and delinquency (Baumrind, 1991a).

The higher vulnerability of children from authoritarian families might be explained by the fact that authoritarian parents restrict their children's interactions and short circuit interpersonal family conflicts by imposing rules intended to prevent conflict from occurring. In this family environment, adolescents are deprived of opportunities to practice the skills of compromise and conflict resolution in relationships. Furthermore, the harsh strictness of authoritarian parents puts them in a position of not having as much influence on their children's decision-making in comparison to children's peers (Allès-Jardel et al., 2002). For example, Bednar and Fisher (2003) found that adolescents with authoritarian parents consult peers more often than parents when making moral and informational decisions. According to Caputo (2004), the key issue in regard to authoritarian parents is likely to be their relatively nonsupportive demeanor rather than their strictness toward their adolescent children because traditional and authoritative parents are also strict, but they buffer their strictness with supportiveness. The findings that adolescents fare better when parents combine authority with support suggest that authoritarian parents might be encouraged to increase their support for their adolescent children. According to Wright and Fitzpatrick (2004), efforts to persuade authoritarian parents to be more supportive of their children would benefit adolescents in regard to delinquency, health, mental health, and academic achievement.

Adolescents and Permissive Parents

Negative outcomes for adolescents have also been consistently linked with permissive parenting. Adolescents, whose parents are permissive, lack sufficient direction and guidance to help them to make mature decisions at a time in their lives that mature decision-making is a crucial aspect of development. The reluctance of permissive parents to provide adequate guidance and sufficient monitoring contributes to a number of adverse consequences. Adolescents whose parents are permissive are likely to be immature and irresponsible and inclined to conform to their peers. They also have lower levels of academic achievement (Aunola et al., 2000); a tendency to be dependent, passive, and conforming; and are less self-assured, creative, and socially skilled than other adolescents (Jones, et al., 2000). Moreover, they tend to lack impulse control and to be more immature, and less self-reliant, socially responsible, and independent in comparison to children of authoritative parents (Baumrind, 1991b). An example of the link between permissive parenting and adolescents' lower impulse control and less mature behavior was illustrated by Paschall el al. (2003). These researchers studied African-American male adolescents and found that their mothers' perceived control of their sons' behavior was a deterrent of delinquent behavior. Their findings emphasize that adolescents need the guidance of involved parents when confronting decisions regarding whether or not to engage in delinquent behavior. Unfortunately, when adolescents do not perceive that they can rely on their parents for guidance, they often look for direction from their peers. For example, Bednar and Fisher (2003) found that adolescents with permissive parents were more likely to consult peers than parents in making moral choices.

Adolescents and Indulgent Parents

Adverse consequences for adolescents have also been attributed to having indulgent parents. Adolescents with indulgent parents tend to be irresponsible and immature and conform more to their peers in comparison to adolescents whose parents are not indulgent. They are also less self-reliant, socially responsible, and independent, and more inclined to have lower academic achievement (Baumrind, 1991a, 1991b; Steinberg, 1996; 2000). These adolescents are also at risk for being involved in behaviors such as crime and delinquency. Although their parents have provided them with responsive care, they have not required the kind of responsibility that is associated with healthy development. One of the most negative characteristics of adolescents whose parents are indulgent is a tendency to be manipulative toward others, particularly toward their own parents (Steinberg, 2000). It seems that being indulged by parents leaves adolescents with a sense of entitlement that plays out in their families as well as in their relationships outside of the family.

Adolescents and Indifferent Parents

Adolescents from all ethnic groups in all societies benefit if they think they are loved and appreciated and suffer if they feel rejected and unwanted (Khaleque & Rohner, 2002). Unfortunately, the indifferent parent's lack of affection and/or high levels of criticism and hostility contribute to the development of adolescent aggressiveness and impulsivity. Adolescents, whose parents are disengaged, are usually impulsive. Because they tend to be impulsive, they frequently have problem behaviors, such as delinquency, early sexual involvement, and drug use. The problem behaviors seen in

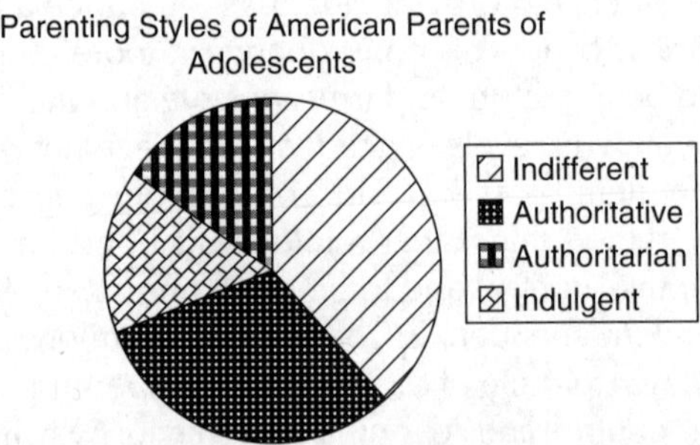

FIGURE 8.1

Source: "Patterns of Competence and Adjustment Among Adolescents from Authoritative, Authoritarian, Indulgent, and Neglectful Families," by S. D. Lamborn, N. S. Mounts, L. Steinberg, & S. M. Dornbusch, 1991, *Child Development, 62*, pp. 1049–1065.

adolescents whose parents are indifferent also have been linked to their parents' lack of monitoring of their activities (Wright & Fitzpatrick, 2004). Furthermore, because they have little parental support, adolescents with indifferent parents frequently experience poor academic performance (Gorman-Smith, Tolan, Henry, & Florsheim, 2000), and complete fewer years of education (Caputo, 2004).

The Issue of Parental Inconsistency

In examining the effects of parenting styles on adolescents, most researchers have either studied one parent or combined ratings of the two parents into one. This approach, however, does not address the issue of parental inconsistency. When adolescents are confronted with differing expectations from their parents, they are placed in a difficult position. They must make the tough decision of going against the wishes of one of their parents or rejecting the requests of both parents. Consequently, they experience a variety of negative outcomes, including lower school performance, delinquency, depression (Juang & Silbereisen, 1999), and externalizing behaviors (Lindahl & Malik, 1999). The finding that inconsistency between parents detrimentally impacts their adolescent children's development does not mean that parents must always agree with the other's views regarding ways to socialize their adolescent children. When parents have disagreements related to child socialization, it is important for them to discuss their points of disagreement. By talking over their dissimilar points of view, they are better prepared to negotiate their differences, rather than presenting their adolescents with conflicting expectations.

QUALITY TIME AND PARENT–ADOLESCENT ENGAGEMENT

The previous discussions emphasize that adolescents have higher achievement levels, better friendship relations, and lower levels of delinquency when their parents combine parental support with parental control. Both the authoritative and traditional parenting styles include a combination of these two dimensions and adolescents whose parents are authoritative or traditional fare much better than adolescents whose parents are authoritarian, permissive, or uninvolved. In addition to receiving sufficient parental control and support, adolescents are also more likely to thrive when they and their parents spend quality time together. For instance, Wright and Fitzpatrick (2004) found that spending more quality time with parents and family reduces adolescent substance abuse. From the perspective of these researchers, more quality time spent with their adolescents affords parents a greater opportunity to model the appropriate use of substances. In addition, the more quality time adolescents spend with their parents and families, the less time they are likely to spend with peers who might be more prone to substance abuse. Further support for parents spending quality time with their adolescents is provided by Aunola, Stattin, and Nurmi (2000) who found that parent–adolescent relations characterized by lower levels of engagement leads to adolescents' maladpative achievement strategies.

Listed in Figure 8.2 are 25 recommendations of ways in which parents and adolescents might spend quality time together. This list is based on suggestions from a classroom of college students who said these were the activities they enjoyed doing with their parents during adolescence.

1. Go to local sports activities together.
2. Go to the activities in which adolescents are involved, such as sports events, dance, and band/choir concerts.
3. Go shopping together for clothes, shoes, special equipment, groceries, presents for other family members' birthdays, mother's day, father's day, and holiday celebrations.
4. Be active together, such as walking, hiking, biking, fishing, swimming, boating, tubing, golfing, tennis, bowling, and playing touch football, tag, or other activities in the yard.
5. Cook together, either in the kitchen or on the grill, especially fun foods such as making cookies or cakes, and/or make homemade pizza together.
6. Eat family meals together at home, in restaurants, and/or on family picnics.
7. Take adolescents and their friends out for pizza, hot dogs, and so on.
8. Make homemade ice cream, and/or ice cream sundaes, ice cream floats, milk shakes, and/or snow cones.
9. Travel together, which might include staying at hotels, going on a family cruise, or going camping, complete with bonfires and roasting marshmallows.
10. Explore new places together, such as museums, caves, and so on.
11. Volunteer together to benefit others, such as cleaning up hiking trails, doing yard work for grandparents or other older persons, or helping raise money for a worthy cause.
12. Have a designated movie night, where parents and adolescents either go to a movie together or choose a movie to watch at home.
13. Play board games together.
14. Read the same book, then discuss it.
15. Spend the day at an amusement park.
16. Work on a project together, such as building something, or painting the adolescent's room.
17. Visit relatives together.
18. Go to a play together.
19. Help with homework.
20. Arrange and carry out a scavenger hunt.

Continued

21. Celebrate together—birthdays, achievements, and other events, together with cake, song, and balloons.
22. Play video games together and/or make your own home movie.
23. Get haircuts together and, for girls, get manicures and pedicures together.
24. Go to a professional sports event, such as a baseball game, football game, or the races.
25. Go to the zoo.

FIGURE 8.2 25 Ways for Parents and Adolescents to Spend Quality Time Together

DEVELOPMENTAL CHANGES AND PARENT–ADOLESCENT RELATIONSHIPS

We will now consider the ways in which the developmental changes of adolescents alter the parent–child relationship and the contributions parents make to adolescent development. We will examine the positive impact of parent–adolescent attachment, and the link between adolescents' relationships with their parents and their conceptions of self. We will also discuss the changes that occur in the family system when children reach adolescence and when adolescents are launched into early adulthood.

Adolescents' Attachment to Their Parents

As the adolescent is transforming from child to adult, parents remain a source of love, support, protection, and comfort, and are among the people to whom adolescents are most closely attached (Allen & Land, 1999). Furthermore, adolescents consistently

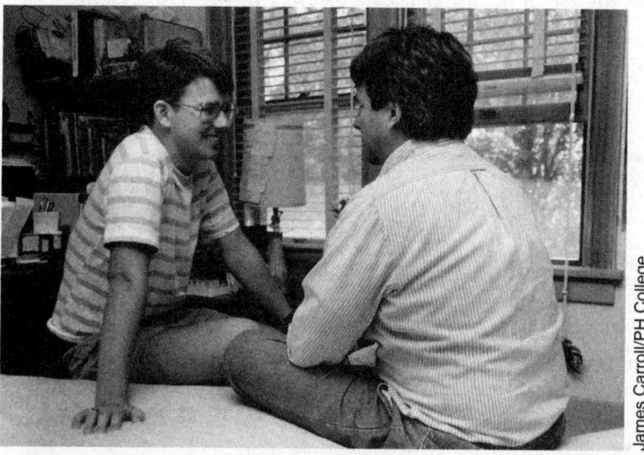

James Carroll/PH College.

Informal discussions between adolescents and their parents help to prevent many problems and contribute to better resolution of differences that occur.

report that their parents are the most important people in their lives, and most of them maintain emotional closeness to their parents throughout adolescence. The degree to which emotional closeness exists between parents and adolescents is related to whether or not adolescents perceive their parents as accepting of them. When parental acceptance is present, it promotes both secure attachment and positive outcomes (Engels, Finkenauer, & Meeus, 2001; Richaud de Minzi, 2006). The positive consequences of parental attachment for adolescents are fewer negative expectations, higher self-esteem, and more positive social relations (Allen & Land, 1999).

The way that parental attachment contributes positively to adolescents' social relations is that supportive parents provide adolescents with the confidence to explore social relationships outside the family. According to Freeman and Brown (2001), securely attached young people learn from their interactions with their parents how to initiate and maintain satisfying and warm friendships, thereby contributing to their competence in friendships and romantic relationships. In addition to having more constructive social relations, adolescents who report close, supportive relationships with their parents are more autonomous as well as more self-reliant (Chirkov & Ryan, 2001). In contrast to the positive outcomes associated with parental security, lack of parental security during adolescence is associated with adverse outcomes, including depressive symptoms, low levels of self-esteem and negative social relations (Allen & Land, 1999). Furthermore, adolescents who are not securely attached to their parents are also more likely to use illegal substances than are those who are securely attached (Mosher, Rotolo, & Phillips, 2004). Finally, adolescents with lower levels of attachment to their parents are more fearful of criminal victimization in comparison to adolescents with parental security (Wallace & May, 2005).

What This Means for Professionals. The research that has related positive adolescent outcomes to parent–adolescent attachment highlights the importance of close relationships between adolescents and their parents. It particularly emphasizes that parents need to be responsive to their adolescents' feelings because responsiveness is the single best predictor of the development or maintenance of attachment. Thus, parents preserve parent–adolescent attachment when they attend to their adolescent children's basic needs, support their goals of becoming increasingly more autonomous, and respond to their need to feel that their parents love and understand them.

Thinking Critically

Consider an example of an interaction between you and your parent/s when you were an adolescent that demonstrates the concept of parent–adolescent attachment. See if you can identify the elements of parental responsiveness in your example.

Parental Influences on Adolescents' Conceptions of Self

Advances in cognitive abilities during adolescence result in the tendency of adolescents to engage in self-reflection. The newly acquired ability to use abstract thinking leads to adolescents asking questions about themselves such as "Who am I?" "What am I good at?" "How do others see me?" "Do I matter to significant others?," and "What is my future life likely to be like?" These questions represent adolescents' quest for identity and the answers to these questions impact adolescents' self-esteem as well as their identity achievement. In the upcoming discussions, we will see that parents are important contributors to adolescents' conceptions of self.

The Ways in Which Parents Impact the Self-Esteem of Their Adolescent Children. Self-esteem has been identified as an indicator of psychosocial well-being (Ruff & Keyes, 1995). In attempts to understand environmental factors that might account for variations in adolescent self-esteem, researchers have discovered that the quality of the parent–adolescent relationship is particularly important. These findings have demonstrated that, for both adolescent boys and girls, perceived rejection by parents is a risk factor for low self-esteem as well as for problematic behaviors. Although adolescents whose parents are rejecting tend to have low self-esteem, adolescents whose parents provide love and encouragement usually have high levels of self-esteem (Harter, 1999; Steinhausen & Metzke, 2001). The value of the nurturing aspect of parenting for promoting adolescent self-esteem is further supported by numerous findings that higher self-esteem levels of adolescents are linked to the authoritative parenting pattern (Baumrind, 1991a, 1991b; Steinberg, 2000). Authoritative parents are consistently supportive of their children. The way in which parental support enhances adolescents' levels of self-esteem is explained by the research of Marshall (2001) who found that **perceived mattering** to parents is associated with adolescent well-being. According to Marshall, one's sense of mattering consists of *the psychological tendency to evaluate the self as significant to specific other people* (p. 474).

What This Means for Professionals. Probably the most important goal of parenting is to promote a child's self-esteem. We know that adolescents' self-esteem and positive development are impacted by the love and encouragement they receive from their parents. Based on these findings, the direction is clear—parents should find ways to send a clear message to their adolescents that they love them and that they believe in them. Noticing the things that adolescents care about, spending quality time with them, asking them how they feel about things, and including them in important family decisions can go a long way toward building adolescents' self-esteem.

The Role of Parents in the Adolescent Quest for Identity. Adolescents' greater cognitive capacity for self-reflective thought influences their self-esteem as well as their quest for identity. As described in Chapter 2, each stage of life has a central psychosocial issue to be resolved. According to Erikson (1968, 1982), the issue to be resolved during adolescence is **identity achievement**. Identity achievement consists of being able to establish a clear and definite sense of who one is and where one fits into one's particular culture. In an earlier study, Marcia (1966) found that family interactions have a strong impact on the identity formation of adolescents. The influences of family environment, child-rearing practices, parental attachment, and parenting style on identity development have also been documented in recent research.

Parental attachment and identity exploration. The link between adolescent identity and secure attachment to parents has been supported by Meeus, Oosterwegel, and Vollebergh (2002), who showed that an aspect of attachment, namely communication, fosters the exploration of identity by encouraging the exploration of identity alternatives. They found that bidirectionality (for example, the parent being concerned and asking about adolescent problems and the parent telling the adolescent about parental problems) is one aspect of communication that promotes adolescent identity. The other feature of communication that these researchers identified as important for adolescent identity is the extent to which parental communication is focused on helping adolescents to understand themselves better.

Parenting styles and identity exploration. Identity achievement and identity moratorium are generally considered to be the most positive ways in which to resolve the identity crisis. Adolescent identity achievers, or adolescents who enter into a moratorium phase before taking on adult roles, tend to have authoritative parents who encourage independence and rarely use controlling and regulating behavior (Marcia, 1994). Research findings show that adolescents are better able to explore identity issues in families where disagreements with parents are permitted. Furthermore, differentiation from parents, an essential aspect of identity formation, is encouraged when parents allow their adolescents to develop their own opinions (Holmbeck, Paikoff, & Brooks-Gunn, 1995). For adolescents with **identity diffusion**, it is easy to see that a lack of goals or clear direction prevent them from making progress toward their future lives. These adolescents tend to have parents who fail to assist them in exploring identity issues. For **identity foreclosure**, however, there are negative or positive ways in which adolescents reach identity resolution. Young adolescents who leave school early and/or become teenage parents represent negative aspects of identity foreclosure and, for these adolescents, parental support is generally lacking. An interesting finding by O'Connor (1995), however, suggest that some adolescents might choose identity foreclosure as a result of parental support. For example, Matos, Barbosa, Almeida, and Costa (1999) reported that adolescents who describe their relationship with their parents as warm and close typically adopt their values and belief system without much exploring. The findings of Matos and colleagues might help explain why we see many young persons go into careers that are similar to those of their parents.

The identity quest of adolescents in ethnic minority cultures. Adolescents who are members of ethnic minority groups within a society, such as the United States, experience more than one culture when growing up and face the challenge of incorporating these diverse influences into their identity (Phinney, Romero, & Nava, 2001; Tse, 1999).

In the process of choosing an identity that incorporates positive aspects of both cultures, ethnic minority youths tend to experience a cultural conflict in values. An example of a cultural conflict that might impact an adolescent's **quest for identity** is seen in the area of romantic love, which includes dating and sex. A vital aspect of identity development in the American majority culture includes experimenting with various possibilities in love by dating different people. By participating in dating, adolescents develop intimate relationships with others and gain sexual experience with them. The practice of dating conflicts sharply, though, with the values of certain American minority groups. For Asian American adolescents, for example, dating is frowned upon and premarital sexual experimentation is considered disreputable—especially for females (Wong, 1997).

Due to the confusion and challenges associated with their identity quest, ethnic minority youths need parents who will support them through this process. One of the ways in whch ethnic minority parents assist their adolescents in their quest for identity is by helping them to have pride in their ethnic minority membership. As emphasized in Chapter 2, an important component of child socialization in ethnic minority families is racial socialization, which acts as a buffer against negative racial messages in the environment. You might recall that racial socialization includes providing a home that is rich in racial culture and socializing children to be proud of their racial heritage (O'Brien et al., 2002). To prevent **ethnic identity foreclosure** whereby adolescents identify either with their ethnic group or with the majority culture without sufficient exploration of the values of the other culture, parents in ethnic minority families make a valuable contribution to their adolescent children's identity quest when they assist them in seeking a **bicultural identity**. Parents who promote their adolescent children's bicultural identity (a) preserve ethnic traditions so that their children have pride in their ethnic heritage and (b) simultaneously provide support for their children's membership in the mainstream culture. To determine the value of assisting ethnic minority adolescents in their quest to achieve a bicultural identity, Tse (1999) analyzed autobiographical accounts of Asian American adolescents. The findings of these reports revealed that after a period of searching and finding out that they were not fully comfortable with either the mainstream culture or their ethnic culture, adolescents of Asian descent were able to view an Asian American identity as positive and self-validating.

What This Means for Professionals. It is important for parents in varied cultures within the United States to be sensitive to, and supportive of, the unique identity challenges faced by their adolescent children. Conflicts between the values of ethnic minority groups and those of the majority culture, however, make this parental responsibility especially problematic. The challenge for parents in ethnic minority cultures in the United States is to be certain that their adolescent children respect the values of their ethnic group as well as those of the majority culture of which they also are members. By providing them with information designed to promote their ethnic identity, while emphasizing the opportunities that are available in American society, parents in ethnic minority groups help their adolescent children to develop a bicultural identity.

Thinking Critically

How important do you think it is for minority youths to have a bicultural identity? What steps would you recommend that ethnic minority parents take in order to assist their adolescent children in the development of a bicultural identity?

The identity quest of gay and lesbian adolescents in the United States. Similar to other adolescents, gay and lesbian adolescents face normative developmental challenges associated with renegotiating relationships with their parents. Like other youths, gay and lesbian adolescents undergo the process of separation–individuation from their parents in order to establish an autonomous adult identity. Concurrently, they face unique challenges associated with **sexual orientation identity** development. According to Floyd, Stein, and Harter (1999), sexual orientation identity formation for gay and lesbian youths involves personal acknowledgment of sexual orientation as well as public presentation and public recognition. In the consolidation of their sexual orientation, gay and lesbian adolescents become more comfortable and open about their sexual orientation. Because the identity quest of adolescents who are gay or lesbian is a complex process, parental acceptance is especially important. It has been found that gay and lesbian adolescents feel most comfortable with their sexual orientation when their parents accept their homosexuality.

Unfortunately, the reactions of parents to the disclosure of homosexuality are often unpredictable, making the decision to come out during adolescence an especially difficult one (Flowers & Buston, 2001). Thus, many gay and lesbian adolescents fear that their parents might reject them should they reveal their sexual orientation. In their study that examined gay men's retrospective accounts of their gay identity formation during adolescence, Flowers and Buston (2001) identified a number of concerns of gay adolescents. The comments of these men in recalling their adolescent years reflected fears related to being perceived as being different: "I was terrified of being different." Comments also showed that these men felt their identity quest was "defined by differences" during a stage of development in which acceptance by others contributes to positive social–emotional development. Their concerns regarding lack of acceptance by parents and peers were demonstrated in comments that reflected feelings of "alienation and isolation." The need to achieve an identity that incorporated their sexual orientation was evident in comments related to wanting to be open about their sexuality but being plagued by "fears of telling others." Finally, their comments reflected a need to achieve an identity that included acknowledgment of their sexual identity to achieve "wholeness and integrity."

Whereas adolescents who are gay or lesbian tend to have a number of concerns about discussing their sexual orientation, it has been shown that adolescents from highly supportive families tend to come out at a younger age. In their study of parents and their gay and lesbian adolescent children, Floyd et al. (1999) found that when adolescents perceive that their parents have relatively accepting attitudes regarding sexual orientation, they have greater consolidation of sexual orientation identity. Acceptance by parents helps to bolster and reinforce gay and lesbian adolescents' progress in that aspect of their identity development. Conversely, family environments that are low in support hamper the gay or lesbian adolescent in the coming out process. Parental lack of acceptance of their adolescent children's sexual orientation contributes to some adolescents feeling that they must hide their sexual orientation from their parents to maintain parent–child harmony. In families with a gay or lesbian adolescent member, lack of acceptance of the youth's sexual orientation leads to significant stress in the parent–child relationship. Whether parental disapproval contributes to gay or lesbian adolescents concealing their sexual orientation to get along with their parents or contributes to strained parent–child relationships, the lack of parental support interrupts the separation–individuation process of identity formation.

What This Means for Professionals. Parental acceptance is one of the most important components of effective child socialization patterns. Parental acceptance and support predicts parent–adolescent attachment and is a critical component of both authoritative and traditional parenting styles. Furthermore, having parents who are warm and supportive predicts positive outcomes for all adolescents, not just adolescents who have the same sexual orientation as their parents. Parental warmth and acceptance are especially critical to the adjustment of gay and lesbian youths, who must confront negative attitudes regarding their sexual orientation from peers and the general public. As they work through the challenges related to being gay or lesbian in a primarily heterosexual society, having parents who demonstrate that they love and respect them (regardless of their sexual orientation) is very beneficial. As noted by Heights and Beaty (1999), strong parental support is important in reducing the personal and social conflicts that plague many homosexual adolescents during the important period of identity formation.

Laima Druskis/PH College.

Parent–adolescent conflict is a normal part of parent–adolescent relationships and usually occurs within the context of a close parent–adolescent relationship.

PARENT–ADOLESCENT CONFLICT

Adolescence is a challenging time for adolescents as well as for their parents. The degree of parent–adolescent conflict that has been attributed to that stage, though, has been largely exaggerated. Early Western theorists such as G. Stanley Hall (1904) and Anna Freud (1946) made it seem as if parent–adolescent conflict is universal and inevitable and that all adolescents and their parents experience intense conflict over many years due to adolescent rebellion. The earlier conceptions of adolescence as a time of storm and stress, due to high levels of conflict between adolescents and their parents, have generally been denounced because numerous studies in the past several decades have indicated otherwise. Two studies during the 1960s were instrumental in dispelling the stereotype of "adolescence as a time of storm and stress." Both of these studies showed that although parents and adolescents often disagree, their arguments are mostly over minor issues, such as curfew and cannot be characterized as highly conflicted. Furthermore, these researchers discovered that the majority of adolescents like, trust, and admire their parents (Douvan & Adelson, 1966; Offer, 1969).

Before we get carried away by a glowing image of family harmony during adolescence, it is important to acknowledge that conflicts between parents and adolescents are higher during adolescence than during childhood. Contemporary research has shown that parent–adolescent conflict is at its highest during early adolescence and that it declines significantly from early to late adolescence. By middle adolescence, conflict with parents becomes less frequent but more forceful, followed by a substantial diminishing of conflict by late adolescence (Laursen, Coy, & Collins, 1998). The conflict that occurs between youth and their parents during the adolescent years is best described as a "series of minor disputes" rather than a period of storm and stress (Steinberg, 2000). Furthermore, adolescents and their parents tend to agree on the most important aspects of their lives. The findings that parent–adolescent conflict increases during adolescence do not contradict research findings that emphasize parent–adolescent closeness and mutual respect. Conflict and closeness in relationships are not mutually exclusive. Family conflict resolution has been linked to aspects of psychosocial development, including identity formation and the development of social cognitive skills. Furthermore, effectively managed parent–adolescent conflict fosters the interpersonal adaptations necessitated by the physical, social, and cognitive changes of adolescents (Smetana, Abernathy, & Harris, 2000).

Sources of Parent–Adolescent Conflict

So far, we have not considered why conflict with parents rises when children become adolescents or why conflict with parents during early adolescence is especially high. Biological, cognitive, and psychological changes of adolescents can be pointed to as part of the explanation for parent–adolescent conflict and further understanding is possible if we consider the role of cultural norms. Biologically, the increased size and strength of adolescents make it more difficult for parents to impose their authority on them than it was when they were younger. Cognitively, adolescents' increased capacity for abstract thinking makes them more capable of presenting an argument in the face of parental directives. Parents, therefore, face more difficulty in quickly prevailing when engaged in verbal conflicts with their adolescents in comparison with verbal conflicts when their children are younger. A primary source of parent–adolescent conflict is the mismatch between parent and adolescent expectations of autonomy for the adolescent (Smetana et al., 2000). Although both parents and adolescents in Western societies generally agree on the ultimate goal of adolescent independence, there are often conflicts related to the pace of that independence. Another source of parent–adolescent conflict is adolescent sexual maturity, where parental concerns regarding their adolescents' sexual behaviors might provoke conflict (Arnett, 2004).

Thinking Critically

Do you recall the arguments you had with your parent/s during adolescence? Do you remember what the arguments were about? Can you identify a link between those arguments and your goal to become more independent?

Conflict Arising from Indirect Communication

As clarified earlier, most parent–adolescent conflict is over relatively minor issues. Arnett (2004) suggests that some of these arguments might stem from parental expressions of disapproval that are substitutes for unexpressed parental concerns regarding their adolescents. For example, parents tend to have limited communication with their adolescents about sexual matters. Given the risks associated with sexual activity during adolescence, such as sexually transmitted diseases and pregnancy, it is unlikely that the typical parent is unconcerned with these issues. Statements such as "You can't go out of the house wearing that dress" might mean "You look too sexually provocative in that dress, and I'm worried about what others will think of you." Arnett speculated that sexual matters are not the only issues that tend to be argued over in this indirect manner. A comment by a parent, such as "I don't want you hanging out with those two boys," might reflect the following parental concern: "I've seen those boys smoking and have overheard them using some tough language. I'm afraid that they might be using drugs and will influence you to do the same." Although American parents might have legitimate concerns for the safety and welfare of their adolescent children, they must balance these concerns with the cultural emphasis on promoting the independence of their adolescents. This mismatch of parental concern and cultural beliefs regarding the parental role in relation to adolescents, undoubtedly, fosters the indirect style of communication described here.

What This Means for Professionals. Although concern about their adolescent children's sexual behavior and affiliation with peers who are exhibiting risky behaviors is natural, indirect communication about such concerns is not the best approach for parents to take. Not only does indirect communication frequently insult the adolescent, it is typically confusing and often leads to parent–adolescent conflict. When the parent says, "The movie is over by 9:00, and I want you home by 9:30," the adolescent does not realize what is going on in the mind of the parent and the directive sounds arbitrary and authoritarian. If parents are concerned about their adolescent children making responsible choices, it is better if they sit down with them and let them know that they care about them and want to be sure that they will be careful in making decisions.

The Role of Culture in Parent–Adolescent Conflict

Despite the fact that the same biological and cognitive changes occur in adolescents throughout the world, parent–adolescent conflict is not universal (Arnett, 1999). Actually, it is rare for parents and adolescents in traditional cultures to engage in the kind of frequent bickering that is typical of parent–adolescent relationships in the American majority culture (Rothbaum, Pott, & Azuma, 2000). One reason for low parent–adolescent conflict in traditional cultures is due to the economic interdependence of parents and adolescents in these cultures. Although parent–adolescent economic interdependence partly explains the low conflict in traditional cultures, it does not explain the low conflict seen between parents and adolescents in highly industrialized traditional cultures, such as Japan (Zhou, 1997). Findings of low parent–adolescent conflict in developing traditional cultures as well as in highly industrialized traditional cultures suggest that cultural beliefs regarding parental authority are more important than economics (Arnett, 2007).

CHANGES IN THE FAMILY SYSTEM WHEN CHILDREN REACH ADOLESCENCE

When children become adolescents, they undergo developmental changes that contribute to alterations in their behaviors. Their behavioral changes impact the behaviors of other family members, which results in family disequilibrium. The time of greatest disequilibrium in the family system occurs during early adolescence (ages 10 to 14) when puberty and sexual maturity occur, the cognitive capability of **abstract thought** is achieved, and the psychological quest for a unique identity begins. The hallmark of the ability to engage in abstract thinking is that adolescent thought is no longer tied to a concrete reality. Adolescents begin to consider life's problems and challenges in terms of possibilities (Piaget & Inhelder, 1958). The ability to consider many possible alternatives to the established order of things coincides with their quest to discover who they are and what future goals they will choose for themselves. A normal and natural aspect of this process is the questioning of parental

This mother and daughter are in the process of altering their roles to suit the mother's transition into middle-age and the daughter's into adolescence.

authority and challenging previously established rules and boundaries. It is, therefore, necessary for parents to make adjustments in their guidance style that allow for the exploration of possible exceptions to the usual rules while encouraging their adolescent children's quest to understand who they are. As previously noted, although parent–adolescent relationships are more conflicted during early adolescence, they are less conflicted during late adolescence when a balance toward greater equilibrium in the family system has been achieved (Smetana et al., 2000).

Thinking Critically

Consider an example of disequilibrium that occurred in your family during your adolescent years. How did you, your parents, and other family members adapt to that imbalance?

What This Means for Professionals. Although family stability contributes to a sense of shared history and a certain degree of predictability, families are dynamic systems characterized by stability and change. The changes that occur in the family system when children reach adolescence challenge members to adapt to these changes, and to redefine their roles in relation to each other. It is important for parents to consider the growth-producing aspects of the disequilibrium that occurs in the family system when their children reach adolescence. When parents enfranchise their adolescent children into increasingly more responsible roles, parents and adolescents both benefit as the family system integrates the development of these new family roles into a family system marked by vitality and growth.

The Launching of Young Adults

As children enter adolescence, there is greater disequilibrium; and throughout adolescence, a state of stability is gradually regained as both parents and adolescents adjust to each other's developmental changes. Then, as adolescents make the next major transition, from adolescence to emerging adulthood, disequilibrium again manifests itself in the parent–child relationship. The challenge, at this point, is a test of both the parent's and adolescent's ability to adapt to greater independence from each other. Whereas the launching of young adults is a normative event, there is considerable diversity in patterns of leaving home. Moreover, when young adults leave home, their relationships with their parents are impacted in either a positive or a negative direction, depending on the timing of and reason for the move and how they and their parents handle this important transition. There is a tremendous difference between the young adolescent who runs away from an abusive or neglectful home and a young adult who goes off to college or takes on another adult role with the full involvement and support of parents.

Most American adolescents leave home between the ages of 18 or 19, which is several years earlier than in most other countries. Continuing to live with parents after reaching adulthood is especially common in southern European countries. For example, in Italy, 65% of men and 44% of women in their mid-twenties still live with their parents (Cherlin, Scabini, & Rossi, 1997). Even though most Americans leave home around the ages of 18 or 19, many others remain in their parents' home for several more years. The pattern of delayed leaving home in the United States appears to be closely related to socioeconomic changes—in particular, to the escalating numbers of unemployed young adults (Bynner, 2000). In an attempt to understand the reasons why some young people leave home early whereas others continue to reside with their parents into young adulthood, Cooney and Mortimer (1999) found that family structure has the strongest effect on the timing of leaving home. Male adolescents living with a single parent are five times more likely, and female adolescents twice as likely, to leave home early than are adolescents living at home with both parents. Even when young adults leave home at the typical ages of 18 or 19, they do not always continue to reside separately from their parents. Between 40% and 50% of young adults in the United States move out of their parents' home, then come back, and subsequently move out again during their late teens and twenties. The phenomena of young adults going back to live with parents, after having previously resided away from home, is frequently referred to as *incompletely launched young adults*. Even though the popular movie, *Failure to Launch,* focused on a young man who had a well-paying career, young adults in the United States who tend to return to the nest typically come from working class backgrounds and are usually unemployed young males.

Thinking Critically

What are some examples of disequilibrium that required adjustment by you and your parents when you left home? What do you think the challenges might be for young adults who move back home with their parents?

PROBLEMS THAT ADOLESCENTS SOMETIMES FACE

Although the typical adolescent does not experience internalizing problems such as depression or eating disorders or become involved with risky behaviors such as drug usage, crime, or delinquency, there is a sizable number of adolescents for whom these problems occur. By understanding the role that parents play in the development of these problems, it is possible to provide recommendations regarding the ways in which parents might prevent such problems from occurring.

The Role of Parents in Adolescent Depression

As previously discussed, early adolescence is a stage of transition from childhood into the increasingly complex time of adolescence wherein significant developmental changes are occurring. The newly developed capacities for abstract reasoning allow adolescents to see beneath the surface of things and envision hidden threats to their welfare. Even in response to the same events, adolescents report more negative moods than do preadolescents or adults. The self-reflective capacity for picking up on real or imagined intimidation comes at a time when a number of other changes in their lives potentially increase the stress level for adolescents (Petersen, Leffert, Graham, Alwin, & Ding, 1997). Although studies have documented increases in depressed affect during adolescence, the findings of Heath and Camarena (2002) demonstrate that (a) most adolescents do not show increases in depressed mood during early adolescence and that (b) depressed mood is typically followed by a decrease in depression symptoms. Although the typical adolescent does not experience depression, a smaller proportion have persistent symptoms of depression and are more at risk for problematic behaviors than other adolescents. Researchers studying adolescent depressed affect have shown that the experience of depressed mood is related to other serious consequences for adolescents, such as emotional and disruptive behavior, truancy, drug abuse, pregnancy, suicide attempts (DiFilippo & Overholser, 2000; Heath & Camarena, 2002), and eating disorders (Johnson, Cohen, & Kotler, 2002).

Research findings showing that adolescent depressed affect is not a typical experience, and that it is most often short lived, suggest that the adolescent's social environment plays a role in the occurrence or nonoccurrence of depression symptoms. Adolescents are less likely to experience depression when they have secure

Although adolescents report more negative moods than do preadolescents or adults, adolescents who have close relationships with parents are less likely to experience depression.

Skjold/PH College.

attachments to their parents (Liu, 2006), when parents themselves are not depressed (Sarigiani, Heath, & Camarena, 2003), and when they are not going through a transition related to their parents' divorce or remarriage. Even though all of these factors are related to adolescent depression, dealing with a family in transtion seems to be particularly difficult for adolescents. Barrett and Turner (2005) found lower levels of depressive symptoms among adolescents from mother–father families compared to all other family forms. The link between adolescent depression and family transitions was also reported by Brown (2006), who found that while adolescents are undergoing a family transition, they typically report lower well-being in comparison to adolescents in stable, two-biological-parent families.

What This Means for Professionals. Because adolescents who are securely attached to parents are less likely to experience depression, behaviors that promote adolescent attachment should be given high priority. Studies of attachment have demonstrated that responsiveness to feelings is the best preditor of attachment. Thus, it is helpful when parents respond to their adolescents' cares and concerns. If parents are experiencing depression themselves, they might need to seek assistance to reduce their own levels of depression because parental depression tends to prevent parents from being sufficiently responsive to their adolescents. Also, because the research shows that adolescents are at greater risk for experiencing depression during the marital disruptions of their parents (Cuffe, McKeown, & Addy, 2005), steps might be taken to support adolescents whose parents are divorcing. For example, efforts might be made to strengthen the adolescent's coping skills. Finally, parents need to be aware of signs of adolescent depression that might suggest the need for professional intervention (Dori & Overholser, 1999).

Thinking Critically

If you, as a professional, were talking to parents about their adolescent child's depressed mood, what recommendations would you give those parents?

The Role of Parents in Adolescent Problems of Being Overweight

Over the past 2 decades, the occurrence of obesity has tripled in adolescents (Bassett & Perl, 2004). Approximately 22% of U.S. adolescents are overweight (U.S. Department of Health and Human Services, 2001) and a considerable number of American youth have eating disorders such as anorexia nervosa or bulimia. Adolescents with weight problems tend to have other health problems and are at risk for negative psychological outcomes, such as social stigmatization and low self-esteem (Tanofsky-Kraff et al. (2005).

Overweight amongst adolescents is a multifaceted health problem related to a number of influences including level of physical activity (Gordon-Larsen, McMurray, & Popkin, 1999), eating habits, and participation in sedentary activities such as watching television (Crespo et al., 2001). Researchers have also documented the interplay between family factors and adolescent overweight. For example, overweight adolescents are likely to have overweight parents (Whitaker, Wright, Pepe, Seidel, & Dietz, 1997), and the famlies of overweight adolescents tend to be at the low socioeconomic level (Goodman, 1999). Furthermore, the prevalence of overweight is higher among adolescents who lack health insurance or have public insurance (Haas, Lee, & Kaplan, 2003). The findings that socioeconomic factors contribute to adolescent overweight suggest that the presumed link between adolescent weight problems and personal choice should be re-evaluated. As noted by Goodman, Slap, and Huang (2003), choice is assumed to belong to the individual, which contributes to the belief that risk is also a property of the individual. Yet, current research findings suggest that the behavioral choices of adolescents are constrained by socioeconomic factors that likely affect the availability of more expensive but less fatty foods. For example, Neumark-Sztainer, Story, and Hannan (2002) found that fruit and vegetable intake is highest among adolescents in more affluent families and lowest among adolescents in low income families. They also found that the percentage of adolescents getting more of their energy from saturated fat is highest among adolescents from famlies with the lowest income levels. Finally, the finding that overweight adolescents are less likely to have health coverage points to the difficulty that low-income parents might encounter in attempts to consult a physician regarding ways to help their adolescents maintain a healthy weight. Although low-income parents face more challenges than do other families in overweight prevention, parental involvement is critical to attaining favorable results in overweight prevention. Parents are typically responsible for determining

The maintenance of a nutritious diet is important for promoting adolescent growth and development.

Michal Heron/PH College.

food offerings both in and away from home, and also influence family exercise and recreation. Furthermore, it has been shown that weight loss programs are more likely to succeed when at least one parent is involved (Stice, Shaw, & Marti, 2006).

Parents and Their Adolescent Children Who Are Underweight

American adolescent girls are presented with a cultural norm that portrays the ideal female body as slim at a time when their bodies are biologically tending to become less slim and more rounded. In response to this dilemma, many adolescent females become distressed at the biological changes taking place in their bodies and attempt to resist these changes. Many of them develop extreme weight-loss behaviors such as fasting, "crash dieting," and skipping meals (Rosenblum & Lewis, 1999). When weight loss behaviors become extreme, adolescents develop one of two eating disorders, **anorexia nervosa** (intentional starvation) or **bulimia nervosa** (binge eating and purging). Although anorexia is more common than bulimia, about half of all anorexics are also bulimic, which means they tend to avoid food except for episodes of binging and purging. The family factors associated with adolescent anorexia, or bulimia, suggest that these girls have parents who are highly controlling (Shisslak & Crago, 2001). Whereas anorexic girls are outwardly well behaved, it has been suggested that their eating disorders represent efforts to assert control of their lives in the face of overly controlling parents (Arnett, 2007). Researchers also have shown a link between parental eating patterns and adolescent eating disorders. For instance, many adolescent girls with excessive weight-loss behaviors have mothers who model weight-loss behaviors (Benedikt, Wertheim, & Love, 1998). Another contributor to weight loss behaviors that occur during adolescence is adolescent depression (Johnson et al., 2002) and self-hatred (Berghold & Lock, 2002).

What This Means for Professionals. Families differ in the frequency of when they eat together but family meal frequency might hold a key for addressing eating disorders in adolescents. For example, Fulkerson, Strauss, Neumark-Sztainer, Story, and Boutelle (2007) confirmed earlier studies that adolescents whose families provide meal frequency, as well as a positive mealtime atmosphere, are more likely to have healthy eating patterns and less likely to have eating disorders. Furthermore, because adolescent eating problems primarily affect adolescent girls, mothers might be mindful of their own concerns with slimness and the dieting behaviors they are modeling for their adolescent daughters. Also, parents should be aware of the cultural ideals that adolescent girls in the United States must confront and be certain that their adolescent daughters are able to put these idealized images of female slimness into perspective. Moreover, it is important for parents to understand that being overly controlling is not beneficial for children and particularly detrimental to adolescents who need to become increasingly more self-reliant.

The Role of Parents in Adolescent Substance Abuse

A variety of family factors have been linked to drug usage among adolescents. One of the strongest familial factors associated with adolescent drug use is living apart from parents. Drug usage is significantly higher among highly vulnerable adolescents who live with relatives other than parents or who are in foster care. It seems that the positive influences of parental communication, supervision, and support serve as protective factors that lessen the risk for substance abuse. Although adolescents who do not live with their parents are more susceptible to drug usage, those who develop meaningful relationships with other caring adults (e.g., grandparents, neighbors, or teachers) are less likely to initiate drug use than at-risk youths without such support (Delva, Wallace, & O'Malley, 2005).

Obviously, not all adolescents who live with parents are drug-free; in reality, the behaviors of many co-residential parents contribute to their adolescent children's drug usage. Adolescents are more likely to use substances when one or more members of the family use substances or when parents have a lenient attitude toward substance abuse (Bogenschneider, Wu, Raffaelli, & Tsay, 1998). For example, Hartman, Lessem, Hopfer, Crowley, and Stallings (2006) confirmed previous findings of the familial nature of alcohol abuse and dependence. They found that both adolescent alcohol abuse and alcohol dependence are related to parental alcohol usage. Thus, adolescents need parents who are both physically and emotionally present and also do not present a model of drug abuse or dependency. Additionally, there are a number of things that parents might do to lessen the likelihood that their adolescent children will use drugs. Parental characteristics that have been shown to prevent adolescent drug abuse are authoritative parenting (Baumrind, 1996), parental monitoring (Barnes, Welte, & Hoffman, 2005) parental religiosity, and spending more quality time with adolescents (Barrett & Turner, 2005). Spending quality time with their adolescent children not only affords parents a greater opportunity to model appropriate use of substances, it also provides the emotional support adolescents need to make more responsible choices (Caputo, 2004). Another way in which close parent–adolescent relations serve as protective factors against substance abuse is that a close parent–adolescent relationship is linked to lower orientation to peers, which is in turn related to lower substance use (Bogenschneider et al., 1998).

Thinking Critically

As a professional, what recommendations would you provide to parents to help them prevent drug usage by their adolescent children?

The Role of Parents in Adolescent Crime and Delinquency

When one examines the lives of adolescents who become involved in crime and delinquency, a clear pattern emerges that is suggestive of problems in the parent–adolescent relationship. Although there are a number of other contributing factors, insufficient parent monitoring and certain parent socialization patterns have been consistently linked to adolescent crime and delinquency. Adolescents are considerably more likely to engage in delinquent acts when parental monitoring is lacking (Jacobson & Crockett, 2000). Adolescents are also more inclined toward delinquent behavior when their parents are authoritative, permissive (Baumrind, 1991a), indulgent (Steinberg, 2000), or indifferent (Jacob, 1997). Adolescents who run away from home are also more likely to become involved in crime and delinquency (Baker, McKay, Lynn, Hans Schlange, & Auville, 2003). Adolescents who run away from home deserve special attention because the experience of running away amplifies not only their risk for delinquency, but also exposes them to the threat of victimization (Stephenson, 2001). Young people who run away are likely to steal food, to be involved in other thefts, to use drugs, and to attempt or complete suicide (Ennett, Bailey, & Federman,1999; Yoder, Hoyt, & Whitbeck, 1998).

In considering the ways in which parents contribute to adolescent high-risk behaviors, Karabanow (2002) used social control theory to explain that parental control serves as a deterrent of crime and delinqency, including runaway cases. Social control chiefly serves to dictate the norms of proper behavior through social support, encouragement, and relationship building. The goal of social control is to encourage social integration into society. Thus, parental direction and monitoring serve to maintain social relationships and the individual's attachment to conventional social norms. Further, attachment to an adult provides a stable source of support and helps prevent high-risk behaviors, including running away from home (Lapsley & Edgerton, 2002). It is important to emphasize that social control is based on support and encouragement, which maintains parent–adolescent closeness. In contrast to social control designed to build or maintain family relationships, coercive control does not promote family cohesion. In the face of coercive parental control, an adolescent might be more likely to become involved in crime or delinquency or to run away from home (Hagan & McCarthy, 1997).

Thinking Critically

Based on the previous discussions regarding the role of parents in adolescents' engagement in high-risk behaviors, what do you think are the three most important things that parents might do to prevent adolescent high-risk behaviors?

What This Means for Professionals. Research findings have demonstrated the importance of parental warmth and acceptance for helping adolescents to go in a positive direction with their lives and for preventing them from engaging in risky behaviors. Whether parents are considering ways to keep their adolescent children on a positive path or preventing them from engaging in risky behaviors, the message is clear—adolescents need parents who are involved with them and use child socialization styles marked by warmth and acceptance.

SUMMARY

This chapter explored the role that parents play in the lives of their adolescent children. A consistent theme has been the positive influence of authoritative and traditional parental styles that emphasize authority coupled with responsiveness. Attention has been drawn as well to research findings that demonstrate that these patterns of parenting are instrumental in promoting adolescents' higher self-esteem, higher achievement, and more positive relationships with others. The role that parent attachment and parent–adolescent conflict play in adolescent development has been discussed as well. We also examined the link between parent–adolescent relationships and adolescent depression and eating disorders. Finally, research evidence was presented showing the ways in which adolescent risk behaviors are related to parent–adolescent relationships. Based on the examination of adolescents and their parents in different cultures and various circumstances, one factor stands out—close, supportive interactions with parents are crucial to the positive development of adolescents.

KEY TERMS

- abstract thought
- anorexia nervosa
- bicultural identity
- bulimia nervosa
- ethnic identity foreclosure
- familism
- identity achievement
- identity diffusion
- identity foreclosure
- perceived mattering
- quest for identity
- sexual orientation identity

USEFUL WEB SITES

The Harvard School of Public Health has a top-ranked website at

http://www.hsph.harvard.edu/chc/parenting/raising.html

This site provides information from the Harvard Parenting Project targeted at parents, educators, policy makers, and the media. The "Raising Teens" section focuses on techniques for effective parenting of teenagers.

Another excellent site for helping parents of teenagers is the Tufts University Child and Family Web Guide at

http://www.cfw.tufts.edu

This site has links to a number of topics of interest to parents of adolescents, such as self-esteem, bullies, drugs and alcohol, eating disorders, mentoring, out-of-school time, and peer pressure

The Resource Center of the Department of Human Resources provides an excellent link for parents of adolescents at

http://www.abcdparenting.org

At this link is the ABCD Parenting Program which is designed to help parents understand and cope better with the challenges of early adolescence. It has separate links for parents and professionals and, in addition to other topics, includes material about communication, problem solving, decision making, and alcohol and other drug use.

The Relationships of Young Adults, Their Parents, and Their Children

Objectives

After completing this chapter, you should be able to

- Identify examples of the enduring bonds that adults usually have with their parents.
- Describe the economic interdependence that exists between adults and their parents and how this interdependence differs across cultures.
- Demonstrate an understanding of the diversity that exists in the living arrangements of adults and their parents.
- Describe the way in which adults' participation in parent–child relationships with their parents maintains their ongoing attachment to their parents, and the implications of that attachment for other intimate relationships.
- Explain the ways in which the experience of being a parent contributes to higher level reasoning.
- Identify the way in which Vygotsky's concept of scaffolding might be applied to the behaviors of parents toward their children.
- Explain the ways in which the roles of parenthood vary throughout the world, including the ways in which young adults align their parenthood roles with those of their own parents who become grandparents to their children.
- Describe how each family member's behavior affects the behavior of all other family members, including the changes that occur in parent–child relationships when members are added to the family system.

THE ENDURING BOND BETWEEN YOUNG ADULTS AND THEIR PARENTS

The consensus of the research is that young adults become independent without seriously harming the strong bonds they have with their parents. Young adults tend to seek peer-like relationships with their parents and many count their parents among their best friends. Furthermore, parents are of lasting importance for the psychological well-being of their grown children (Van Wel & Hub Abna, 2000). For example, the findings of Robinson (2000) showed a link between relationships with parents and other intimate relationships of young adults. Specifically, they found that a positive relationship with mothers and greater adaptability in the family system during adolescence were related to more positive intimate relationships in young adulthood. Further support for the link between parental relationships and other intimate relationships during young adulthood was provided by Dalton, Frick-Horbury, and Kitzmann (2006), who found that young adults who reported that they had experienced positive parenting as children had more positive relationships with others during adulthood. These young men and women said that they were responsive to others themselves, had relationships with others that were meaningful, and viewed themselves as capable of forming meaningful relationships. The importance of young adults' relationships with their parents is further supported by Wels, Bogt, and Raaijmakers (2002), who studied changes in the well-being of young adults and concluded that young adults maintain a positive and reasonably stable relationship with their parents over a long period of time. They also emphasized that parents are of lasting importance for the well-being of their adult children and that the parental bond ranks in importance alongside having a partner or best friend. On the other hand, negative behaviors of parents during childhood and adolescence are also played out during young adulthood. As a case in point, Ravaja & Keltikangas-Jarvinen (2001) found that maternal and paternal frequency of alcohol intake, getting drunk, and smoking were associated with novelty-seeking behaviors of young adult men and women.

The Economic Interdependence of Young Adults and Their Parents

In much of the world, such as in China, India, and Mexico, working to help support the family is expected of young adults. In China, for example, when children become young adults they have the **filial duty** to financially support their parents (Lee & Sung, 1998). Furthermore, it is in the context of poverty and dependence on family members for survival that we see the greatest emphasis on the older generation's economic dependence on the younger generation. In many industrialized societies (such as the United States and Canada), on the other hand, most young adults are not expected to contribute to the financial support of their parents. In societies in which it is not anticipated that young adults will contribute to the economic maintenance of their parents, financial aid is typically from the parent to the child. For example, the research of Kim and Schneider (2005) describes parental support of their young adult children's transition to college as "social capital in action." According to these authors, the goals of parents and their young adult children are aligned when parents provide the necessary resources and information that allow young adults to make informed choices about college. Even those young adults who do not go to college usually accept some form of financial assistance from their parents (Zarit & Eggebeen, 1995).

VARIATIONS IN THE LIVING ARRANGEMENTS OF YOUNG ADULTS AND THEIR PARENTS

In addition to considerable variation in economic interdependence between young adults and their parents, there is diversity in the living arrangements of the two generations. Young adults in traditional cultures typically continue to live with their parents but the roles of parents and children are somewhat shifted such that adult children are expected to begin contributing to the financial welfare of their parents (Lee & Sung, 1998). These living arrangements are quite different from those seen in Western societies, where most young adults move out of their parents' home sometime during young adulthood. For young people in the United States, this move typically occurs around the ages of 18 to 19, which is several years earlier than in most other Western countries (Goldscheider & Goldscheider, 1999). In contrast to the early exodus of young adults in the United States and Canada, young adults in European countries are more likely to continue to live at home even while attending college. For example, in Germany, the typical ages for leaving home are 23 for males and 21 for females, and these ages of departure from their parents' home are similar in most other European countries (Juang, Silbereisen, & Weisner, 1999). In Greece, Spain, and Italy, more than half of 30-year-olds still have not achieved the full autonomy associated with a job and a home of their own (Fernandez & Antonio, 1997). Young adults are also likely to live with their parents in Eastern countries. For example, in Japan at least 10 million single young adults are living at home with their parents (Masahiro, 2001).

Not only do young adults in the United States leave home several years younger than in many other cultures, one of the developmental challenges facing these young adults is to live independently of their parents. Research has shown that the living arrangements of young adults affect aspects of their personal development, especially their identity development. In a comparison of university students who continued to reside at home and those who resided away from their parents, Jordyn and Byrd (2003) found differences in personal adjustment. They found that young adults who do not reside with their parents confronted more difficult adjustment problems but also used more direct, problem-focused coping strategies in comparison to those who resided with their parents. They also found that young persons who lived apart from their families were more likely to have established an adult identity, whereas those who continued to reside with their parents were still in the process of developing an adult identity.

Thinking Critically

Were you able to identify with the findings that university students who live away from parents confront more difficult challenges but also learn to more effectively resolve problems? What are some examples of problems you encountered that you feel you have mastered as a young adult living independently from parents?

Factors Influencing the Timing of Young Adults Leaving Home. In the United States, the timing of departure from the family home is related to whether the young adults' biological parents are still married to each other, parental expectations of when their adult children should leave home, parental resources, and other economic dimensions such as housing costs, job opportunities, whether or not adult children have remained single, and, for women in particular, the extent of government-provided cash assistance to low-income parents and their children. The clearest change in parent–child relationships that affects whether young adults live with or apart from their parents is whether the parents of these young persons continue to be married to each other. Young adults leave home sooner from nontraditional families than from two-biological-parent households. Furthermore, the differences are particularly large when leaving home to attend college because this is one route that young adults in never-divorced families are significantly more likely to take in comparison to young adults in other families (Goldscheider, 1997).

Thinking Critically

Why do you suppose adult children of two-biological-parent households are more likely to live with their parents than are adult children from other households?

Adult Children Who Move Back Home to Live with Their Parents

In the past, most young adults in industrialized societies left home to go to college, to marry, and/or to set up separate households. Hence, the term "**empty nest**" came to describe the home from which these young adults were launched into independent living. Although this pattern of transition into adulthood continues to define most living arrangements of young adults in industrialized societies today, there have been recent changes in the patterns of intergenerational living in some countries. Increasing numbers of young adults are now living with their parents well into their 20s in the

United States, which has led to the empty nest being redefined as the "**full nest.**" The trend of twentysomethings returning home to live with their parents is becoming so commonplace that there is little stigma linked to "boomeranging." In reality, for many young adults, it might represent a contemporary rite of passage (Perina, 2003). To better understand this phenomenon, Cohen and Casper (2002) used data from the Current Population Surveys to provide an image of coresidential living arrangements of parents and their adult childrem who previoiusly resided elsewhere, then moved back in. These researchers reported that the highest proportion of adults returning to live with parents are in their late twenties, have no homes of their own, have lower incomes, and are more likely to be male. Their interpretation of these findings were that residential independence is generally preferred but socioeconomic reasons, including a lack of employment or low-paying jobs, contribute to adult children moving back in with their parents. Another perspective regarding why many young adults return to live with parents, after residing apart, is offered by Perina (2003) who suggested that stay-at-home adult children take on a different role than the role they had before they moved out. According to that view, the young adult who moves back home often acts as a sounding board, friend, or confidante to a mother or father. Furthermore, contemporary parents, many of whom are Baby Boomers, might set the stage for their adult children moving back home by promoting a peerlike rapport with them.

Living Arrangements in Full-Nest Families. Contemporary living arrangements between parents and their young adult children in industrialized societies are in sharp contrast to the economic interdependence between the generations that is seen in many traditional cultures. Whereas adult children in traditional cultures are expected to contribute to the economic well-being of their parents (Lee & Sung, 1998), most young adults living with parents in industrialized societies do not contribute to the financial resources of the parental household. In contrast, many adult children living with their parents are permitted to spend their wages on luxuries without paying rent or contributing to expenses related to running the household. An example of this pattern of coresidence among Japanese single adults and their parents was described by Masahiro (2001) who pointed out that the majority of young Japanese single adults who live with their parents have jobs and are able to enjoy affluent lifestyles while their fundamental needs are met by their parents. Furthermore, most of these young Japanese single men and women do very little housework. Instead, their mothers do the housework for their sons and daughters after they become adults.

Thinking Critically

Given the large numbers of adult children living at home with their parents, you probably know a family that includes at least one adult child member. Based on your observations, in what ways does that family fit the characteristics previously described?

PARENTHOOD AND THE SOCIAL–EMOTIONAL DEVELOPMENT OF YOUNG ADULTS

Whether living together or apart, individuals become less dependent on their parents during young adulthood in comparison to earlier years. Nevertheless, the parent–child relationships in which they continue to be involved are important influences of young adults' social and emotional development. Participation in parent–child relationships as adult children contributes to individuals' ongoing attachment to their parents (Wels, Linssen, & Abna, 2000) and the **achievement of intimacy** with others (Goldhaber, 2000; Robinson, 2000; Wels et al., 2000). For those young adults who become parents, participation in simultaneous relationships with their parents and their children is related to their development of a sense of generativity (Erikson, 1968; Goldhaber, 2000).

The Attachment of Young Adults to Their Parents

The central theme of attachment theory, which was explained in Chapter 2, relates to the implications of optimal and nonoptimal social attachments for psychological well-being (Ainsworth et al., 1978). A related perspective emphasizes a balance between **individuation** and **connectiveness** (Baumrind, 1991a). According to this view, attachment and individuation should be considered as dual and equally important pathways to development. Thus, a differentiated sense of self (individuation) can be achieved during young adulthood without severing emotional ties (connectiveness) with parents. Moreover, young persons benefit from relationships with their parents in which both their separateness and individuality are supported. Following these theoretical suggestions, researchers have demonstrated that relationships with parents that are marked by supportive forms of connectiveness and satisfying forms of separateness contribute to young adults' adaptive functioning. An example of the benefit of young adults' attachment to their parents was demonstrated by Leonardari

The parent–child attachment, which begins during infancy and continues throughout adulthood, is obvious in the scene depicted here.

PH College.

and Kiosseoglou (2000), who explored the links among attachment patterns, psychological separation from parents, and young adults' adaptive functioning. In their study of university students in Greece, they found a positive association between security of attachment and freedom from guilt, anxiety, and resentment toward parents. Additionally, students with secure attachment to their parents scored higher on self-esteem and lower on measures of anxiety and loneliness. Further evidence of the importance of young adults' attachment to their parents comes from the findings of Wels et al. (2000) who studied the relation between changes in the parental bond and in the psychological well-being of young adults. Their findings were that changes in the parental bond correspond to a parallel change in the psychological well-being of the young adults. They also found that this connection does not become weaker as young adults grow older. On the contrary, they showed that parents continue to have an important impact on the psychological functioning of their young adult children. Their findings suggested, however, that fluctuations in the quality of the parental bond have more repercussions for the emotional stability of young women than for young men.

Thinking Critically

How would you explain the parallel between young adults' attachments to their parents and their psychological well-being? How do you account for the finding that fluctuations in the young adult–parent bond having more repercussions for young women that for young men?

The Role of Parents in Promoting Young Adults' Achievement of Intimacy

It is easy to confuse the concepts of attachment and intimacy especially because both are related to parent–child closeness. The distinction is that attachment to parents is related to the individual's psychological well-being, such as to levels of self-esteem and to feelings of security versus feelings of loneliness or anxiety (Leonardari & Kiosseoglou, 2000). In contrast, successful resolution of the issue of intimacy enables the young adult to maintain committed, enduring intimate relationships (Erikson, 1968). The role of parents in promoting young adults' achievement of a sense of intimacy is that many of the patterns that young adults bring into their intimate relationships with significant others are developed in the relationships they have with their parents. As noted by Van Schaick and Stollberg (2001), the impact of parental involvement is a significant influence on all relationship dimensions in the lives of young adults. Although the parental influence on young adults' achievement of intimacy is similar for young men and young women, research suggests that there are gender differences in this influence. For example, Robinson (2000) demonstrated that a positive relationship with one's mother during adolescence was related to more positive intimate relationships in young adulthood.

Because parental involvement contributes to the quality of young adults' intimate relationships, it is not surprising that parental divorce might have a negative impact on the quality of these relationships. Recent studies, however, suggest that it is important to examine multiple factors when assessing the impact of divorce on young adults. For example, Richards and McCabe (2001) found that whereas high levels of interparental conflict is negatively associated with young adults' social adjustment and intimacy with parents, high intimacy with at least one parent is positively related to adjustment. Furthermore, even when parents have divorced, having close relationships with both mother and father was found to be the most important predictors of psychological adjustment. In addition to maintaining close relationships with parents, the findings of Shulman, Sharf, and Lumer (2001) showed that young adults who are able to achieve an integrative perception of divorce have more positive adjustment. They found that an integrative perception of parental divorce was related to young adults' higher levels of friendship, enjoyment, and intimacy, and to fewer problems in romantic relationships. An integrated perception of divorce consists of re-examining stressful events, and focusing not only on painful feelings but also on the future and its possibilities. Such an attitude contributes to the search for new perspectives and accepts change, without denying reality. Another factor that was linked with more positive romantic relationships was their mother's marital status. Maternal remarriage was associated with higher levels of friendship, enjoyment, intimacy, and passion, and fewer problems in their romantic relationships (Shulman et al., 2001).

Thinking Critically

Why do you suppose that the quality of young adults' relationships with their parents is linked with the quality of their friendships, and romantic relationship?

Parent–Child Relationships and the Achievement of a Sense of Generativity

We will now turn our attention to the ways in which the achievement of a **sense of generativity** derives from the parent–child relationships in which young adults participate with their children and with their parents. Included also in this discussion are the contributions that young adults make to their parent's ongoing generativity needs.

Parenthood and the Development of a Sense of Generativity. As noted by Goldhaber (2000), each of Erikson's stages builds upon those that precede it and each moves the individual more fully into the role of a mature, active participant in one's culture. Therefore, the achievement of a sense of intimacy, whereby individuals have been able to join their lives with others, better prepares them for the next step in which they consider the significance of their efforts for the next generation. As Erikson (1968, 1982) points out, even though generativity might take a variety of forms, its chief expression is found in "establishing and guiding the next generation. In their establishment of a sense of generativity, young adults develop the ability to care for others, which is a basic strength that reflects young adult maturity.

Generativity and Gender. In cultures throughout the world, maintaining a household and caring for children has been a primary source of generativity for women. Conversely, providing food and other goods for the family has been the main way in which men have been able to achieve a sense of generativity. Although in many cultures the socialization into distinct gender roles (emphasizing men's roles as family providers and women's roles as wives and mothers) continues to occur, this picture has shifted considerably during the past 50 years in most industrialized societies. The most current U.S. census data show that the majority of married women in the United States were working in paid employment outside the home, including those whose youngest child was in school (U.S. Bureau of the Census, 2000). The husbands of almost all of these women also were employed, and the majority of these husbands shared household responsibilities with their wives—sometimes providing a major portion of child care responsibilities. Despite the fact that in the United States both parents are likely to be working, not all couples work out an amicable dual-worker, dual-parent relationship. Nevertheless, it has been found that the happiest couples do not work either very long or very few hours. This balance allows both parents to contribute to the household finances as well as to the unpaid labor needed to maintain a household (Moen & Yu, 1999).

Thinking Critically

Why do you suppose that young people do not typically mention that they are engaged in rearing children when they are asked the question "What do you do?" Consider your answer in terms of gender and cultural norms.

Generativity and Culture. The drive to be generative is a powerful theme of adulthood and occurs in two major ways—through parenthood and through employment. The expression of this desire is variable, however, and is dependent on the diverse roles of individuals in various cultures. At the cultural level, there are differences in generativity goals related to individualism and collectivism. For a parent in an individualist culture, such as the majority culture of the United States, generativity needs might take any of the following forms: (a) being the best parents they can be, (b) achieving individual success in their occupational roles, or (c) seeking to be the best parents possible while being highly competitive in their occupational roles. In contrast to the drive for individual success in their work and family roles, young adults in collectivist cultures, such as ethnic minority cultures in the United States, are more likely to link generativity with communal living. These parents are able to attain a sense of generativity through being involved in cooperative efforts that maximize the likelihood of group success in the family as well as in the workplace (Goduka & Kunnie, 2003).

The emphasis on success in collectivist cultures is derived from being a good parent and/or a good worker and simultaneously earning the respect of their children, grandchildren, parents, coworkers, and individuals in their community. An example of cultural collectivism is found in Latino family life wherein *la familia*, or familism, is a core family value. We learned in Chapter 8 that familism is the constellation of beliefs that define the roles and expectations of family members in relation to the needs of the collective, as opposed to the needs of the individual. *La familia* refers to the cultural belief that families should live near their extended kin and have strong kinship ties, particularly in times of need (Fuligni et al., 1999). Whether one lives in an individualistic culture or a collectivist culture, at the individual level, the roles of parent and worker contribute to a sense that one's contributions to the family and/or the workplace are valuable. The evaluation of one's success in these roles contributes to a sense of generativity, which becomes integrated into the individual's sense of self (Erikson, 1982; Goldhaber, 2000).

What This Means for Professionals. For young adult parents in collectivist cultures, it is important to align their quest for generativity with the values of their extended families and communities. By recognizing the important roles of family and community members, young parents in these communities are able to access valuable support of their efforts to achieve a sense of generativity. For professionals working with parents in collectivist cultures, it is helpful when they recognize that the young adult's role as a parent is likely to be integrated with extended family and community roles. Therefore, the establishment of a relationship with these young parents must be based on a respect for the traditions of shared caregiving and other family and community supports that are an integral part of collectivist cultures. For example, in referring to a young adult's family, a teacher or other professional might keep in mind that a person who is living in a collectivist culture might consider parents, siblings, aunts, uncles, and cousins as family members in addition to children and a spouse or partner.

Generativity Is a Two-Way Street. The achievement of a sense of generativity is linked not only to childrearing but also to the quality of adults' relationships with their parents. Young adults' development of a sense of generativity, therefore, is related to caring for their children as well as being responsive to the needs of their parents. As noted by Erikson (1982), the young adult still relies on the support and guidance of parents, and the mature adult, in turn, "needs to be needed." Thus, the interdependence of parents and children is a lifelong process. Examples of this interdependence can be observed in the ways in which young adults involve their parents in the planning of and participation in their weddings, the births or adoptions of their children, family birthday parties,

Charles Hangar.

One of the ways that families maintain their cohesiveness is through their participation in family rituals that mark significant transitions in family members' lives.

and graduation celebrations. Recent evidence of the mutual effect of parents and their adult children on each other's psychological development was provided by Knoester (2003) who assessed the extent to which changes in the psychological well-being of young adults were related to changes in their parents' psychological well-being, and vice versa. Their research findings demonstrated that adult children and their parents continue to influence each other's well-being as both generations age.

Additionally, families develop many rituals for celebrating religious and other holidays in which young adults, their children, and their parents are all included. Furthermore, young adults and their parents regularly visit, have family meals together, share caregiver responsibilities, and participate in a number of other activities designed to maintain family cohesiveness across generations. Family rituals also reflect satisfaction with family relationships and provide roles for both older and younger family members. As noted by Fiese, Tomcho, and Douglas (2002), family rituals serve to highlight how culture, the family, and individual characteristics intersect to shape the whole family. Finally, rituals reflect the ways in which young adults and their parents support each other at times of family crises, such as illness or death (Murphy et al., 1998).

Thinking Critically

What examples of interdependence have you observed between young adults and their parents in the planning and carrying out of family celebrations and/or the mutual support demonstrated during family crises?

Generativity Issues of Cohabitating Young Adults and Their Parents. Although marriage and parenthood typically occur together, young adults in contemporary society often live together without being married. The cohabitation of young adults is related to less parental support or intergenerational exchange of support. Cohabiting young adults are significantly less likely than are married young adults to be in exchange relationships with their parents. Most notably, these young persons are much less likely than their married or single compatriots to be giving and receiving assistance with household tasks. They are also less likely than are married young adults to name their parents as persons they would turn to for emergency support. A possible explanation for low levels of intergenerational exchange between cohabiting adults and their parents is that cohabitation is not institutionalized. Because parents of cohabiting young adults face uncertainty regarding what their role as parents should be, they frequently back away. Similarly, adult children, who are confronting their own doubts regarding the permanency of their cohabiting relationship, may make few demands on parents. Furthermore, these young adults might be less likely to participate in the behaviors of married couples that create and strengthen the ties between them and parents, such as visiting on vacations, spending holidays together, or involving parents in family events and rituals. Consequently, the social distance is likely to generate barriers to flows of routine kinds of assistance (Eggebeen, 2005).

Challenges to the Development of Generativity: Unintentional Parenthood. Most adults choose to become parents, and the universal reason for choosing parenthood is the expectation of achieving a sense of generativity (Erikson, 1982; Goldhaber, 2000). Many parents, however, have children without weighing the costs or advantages of childrearing. For numerous young persons, the pregnancy is unintentional due to not having used birth control or as a result of the failure of birth control methods. Individuals who are most likely to have unwanted pregnancies are typically the most vulnerable because younger, poorer, and less educated adolescents and young adults are more likely to experience unplanned pregnancies (Monahan, 2001). Moreover, young adults who began their childbearing during adolescence are the most vulnerable in terms of their ability to care for and provide the basic necessities for their children. A further complication of unplanned early parenthood is that the experience of childbirth for these young parents is likely to be associated with the trauma of having a low-birth-weight baby and/or a premature birth (Cornell, 2001).

What This Means for Professionals. Based on the preceding discussion, young parents who have unplanned pregnancies are the least prepared for parenthood and have the fewest resources to help them to be successful in their roles as parents. In these situations, their parents are typically willing to provide financial support for them while also supporting and providing care for their grandchildren. In addition to requiring assistance from their parents, young adults who give birth to children who were not planned for generally benefit from the support of professionals who can help them to adapt to their roles of early parenthood and ensure that their children receive the care and attention needed for positive development.

The professional services needed by young parents in these situations include programs designed to help them remain in school so that they have more occupational opportunities. In addition to the advantages of education focused on career preparation, parent education courses help unprepared young parents adjust to their role of parent, help them to understand their children's normal development, and assist them in the development of skills designed to enhance parent–child interaction. Because their children are often designated as being at risk for developmental problems associated with low socioeconomic status, subsidized day care programs are available for them. Community organizations that ensure that their children will receive medical care and adequate nutrition are also beneficial for parents whose pregnancies were not planned.

THE INFLUENCE OF PARENT–CHILD RELATIONSHIPS ON YOUNG ADULTS' COGNITIVE DEVELOPMENT

Young adults' relationships with their parents not only affect their social-emotional development, they also impact their cognitive development. In the upcoming discussions, we will consider how the challenges of working out their relationships with their parents influence the ability of young adults to reason at higher cognitive levels. We will also examine the various ways in which the responsibilities of young parenthood provoke advanced problem-solving abilities.

Parenthood and Higher Level Reasoning: A Piagetian Perspective

As young adults thoughtfully consider the real-life dilemmas that are a necessary part of their relationships with their parents and their children, they increasingly align their thinking processes with their contextual awareness. For many problems in young adults' parent–child relationships, there are no single solutions, no predetermined right answers, and no absolute rules. The ups and downs in the lives of their parents and children often lead young adults to consider the world in novel, more complex, and less rigid ways. Fortunately, young adults are generally able to come up with appropriate solutions to their various challenges. Followers of Piaget believe that, in comparison to adolescents, young adults are better problem finders, which helps them to discern the problems that need their attention. According to these theorists, young adults are also capable of **dialectical reasoning**, which allows them to come up with more effective solutions to the problems they encounter (Arlin, 1975; Riegel, 1976).

Examples of Young Parents' Problem-Finding Ability. The problem-finding capability, seen in adulthood, emphasizes that the ability to provide solutions to problems can be applied only once these problems have been identified. For instance, to remedy a child's earache or stomach upset, the parent must first determine that a problem exists as well as what that problem is likely to be. Similarly, buying a child a new pair of shoes must be preceded by a realization that the shoes the child is currently wearing are getting too small or becoming too worn. Moreover, providing emotional support to a child who is feeling disappointed or depressed must be preceded by the ability of a parent to recognize that something seems to be bothering the child.

The Dialectical Reasoning of Young Parents. After problem finding, young parents typically are compelled to make logical decisions for which there are a number of possible solutions. Due to their ability to use dialectical reasoning, these parents are able to make decisions that involve the recognition and tolerance of ambiguities and contradictions in many life dilemmas. An example of dialectical thinking is seen in the situation in which young parents, in considering day care for their children, are confronted with the dilemma of whether to choose the child care program that is less expensive and closer to their home or the one that costs more and is farther away from their home. The easier solution to the problem is to choose the less expensive and more conveniently located child care setting. If the less costly and more opportunely situated day care facility has child care providers who use a form of discipline that is not consistent with the values of the parents, however, these parents might engage in dialectical reasoning to resolve the child care dilemma. An example of dialectical reasoning in this situation would take into account the expense and expediency as well as values regarding what these young parents consider to be the best environment for their children. Like the child care quandary, there are numerous other childrearing challenges in which the ability to use dialectical reasoning helps young parents to arrive at more satisfactory solutions.

Thinking Critically

What examples come to mind of issues that young parents face that demonstrate the concept of dialectical thinking? What example of young parenthood can you think of that demonstrates the concept of problem finding?

Experiences That Promote Young Parents' Higher-Level Reasoning. A variety of complex life circumstances associated with adulthood provide opportunities for young parents to develop their problem finding and dialectical thinking. While in the process of pursuing an advanced degree, for example, individuals are challenged to engage in the critical thinking process that is based on those aspects of reasoning. Moreover, it has been demonstrated that the critical thinking process engaged in within college classrooms impacts the parenting decisions of young adults. Researchers have found, for instance, that college-educated persons are more likely than those who are not college educated to have an authoritative child socialization pattern (Hoff-Ginsberg & Tardif, 1995). One of the primary features of the authoritative pattern of parenting is the willingness of parents to provide reasons for their actions and to engage their children in problem-solving activities (Baumrind, 1971, 1991a; Steinberg & Levine, 1997).

Real-life experiences that promote higher level reasoning processes occur both inside and outside formal educational settings. For young adults who do not go to college, they typically take responsibility for their own financial well-being while considering their future direction in life, such as gaining and keeping employment. While struggling with these real-life decisions, many of these young people enter into committed partnerships and/or become parents and begin to make multifaceted decisions—including ways in which to provide suitable housing for their families and how to feed and care for their infants and children. Because their real-life circumstances do not provide easy answers, these responsibilities are likely to promote young adults' ability to engage in problem finding and dialectical thinking.

Parenthood and Vygotsky's Concept of Scaffolding

Another theoretical approach to understanding the ways in which parent–child relationships contribute to young adults' cognitive development is provided by Lev Vygotsky. Vygotsky (1978) postulated that individuals are better able to demonstrate proficiency in various activities when supported by persons with specialized expertise. As noted in Chapter 1, Vygotsky emphasized that with the help of their parents or other more accomplished persons, individuals can often reason at a higher level than they can by themselves. We also learned earlier that, through activities, such as modeling, instruction, and direct support, more competent persons provide **scaffolding** for the skill development of less experienced individuals. Although discussions of the concept of scaffolding typically focus on the role that parents and teachers play in sustaining the learning experiences of young children, there are many occasions whereby the problem solving of young adults is scaffolded by interactions with their own parents and/or spouses or partners.

Parental Scaffolding of Young Adults' Academic Success. As noted earlier, college students typically receive financial assistance from their parents that enables them to pursue studies in preparation for careers. In addition to financial backing, young adults often benefit from consultation with their parents regarding important decisions they are making, such as the selection of a major and/or choice of a career. Furthermore, findings cited earlier showing a link between parental support and academic success suggest that young adults' academic success is scaffolded by the relationships they have had and continue to have with their parents (e.g., Fuligni et al., 1999).

Thinking Critically

What are the various ways that your parents or other parental figures in your life are currently involved in the scaffolding of your academic success and/or career preparation?

Behind the academic success of most young adults are parents who are emotionally and financially involved in helping their children achieve their dreams.

Leima Druskis/PH College.

Parental Scaffolding of Young Parents' Childrearing Efforts. The role that parents play in scaffolding the ongoing development of their young adult children is not limited to assistance provided to those who are pursuing academic degrees and making choices regarding future careers. Most young adults benefit as well from parental support when they become parents. Even when young adults have been financially independent for a period of time, their parents are likely to provide financial, practical, and emotional assistance to them after they become parents. Examples of intergenerational financial support range from the gifts or loans that parents provide their young adult children for buying their first house to the clothing and toys they buy for their grandchildren. Even though financial and practical support are excellent examples of ways in which the older generation of parents scaffolds the efforts of the younger generation of parents, perhaps the most important scaffolding role of older parents is that of emotional supporter. When young adults experience real-life problems, such as difficulties with the rearing of their children, illnesses, or life crises, they typically turn to the same individuals who were there for them at earlier developmental stages when they had skinned knees or wounded hearts (Zarit & Eggebeen, 1995).

Finally, the most common practical help that parents make available to their young adult children is related to assistance with child care. Even in the majority cultures of the United States and Canada, where grandparents, aunts, and uncles do not typically assume coparenting roles, they frequently provide some level of child care if they live in close proximity to their children and grandchildren. Furthermore, circumstances such as parental death, illness, or teenage parenthood often influence these relatives to step in and scaffold young parents' childrearing efforts. The majority of unmarried adolescent parents live with their parents who provide financial, practical, and emotional support, thereby extending the childrearing efforts of these young parents. The scaffolding provided by older parents to unmarried young parents is particularly important for these young parents who are the most vulnerable in terms of their ability to care for and provide the basic necessities for their children (Cornell, 2001).

What This Means for Professionals. The foregoing discussion emphasizes the important role of parents in providing continuing support for their children in a variety of areas. Being able to scaffold the success of their adult children provides parents with an important role in relation to their children and also helps them to feel as if they are able to contribute to their children's ongoing development. The benefit for adult children is the realization that parents are there to support and assist them when needed. Parental scaffolding also sends the important message to children that parents are interested in their well-being and want to help them toward the achievement of their goals.

Thinking Critically

Do you know of a situation involving unmarried young parents where their parents have stepped in to scaffold the parenting efforts of those young parents? If so, in what ways do you think those young parents benefit from the scaffolding efforts of their parents?

The Scaffolding of Childrearing Efforts by Parental Partners. Finally, the vital role that parental partners play in supporting young parents' childrearing efforts has been well documented. An important aspect of scaffolding seen in two-parent families is emotional support of each other's parenting efforts. In addition to emotional support, there are numerous practical opportunities for sustaining each other's childrearing efforts in the typical family. Examples of practical help that support childrearing efforts include taking turns getting up with a crying baby, participating in the bathing of the children,

Anthony Magnacca/Merill.

In this scene, the father and mother are working together to sustain each other's childrearing efforts.

preparing meals for the family, taking the children to school, entertaining the children by playing with them, and helping the children with their homework. When parents work together to provide for the needs of their children, the effectiveness of each parent's childrearing efforts is promoted. Furthermore, there is evidence that many couples today expect to work cooperatively in the care of their children. For example, in a study of new fathers, Fox, Bruce, and Combs-Orme (2000) found that new fathers held high expectations of participation in the caregiving of their infants. The fathers in their study also expressed a high degree of confidence in their ability to care for their newborns.

Thinking Critically

Have you observed a young couple at home with their young child or children? If so, what examples of scaffolding of each other's childrearing efforts were you able to discern between those two parents?

THE INFLUENCE OF PARENTS ON THEIR CHILDREN'S ASSUMPTION OF ADULT SOCIAL ROLES

We will now consider the effect of parental socialization patterns on the social roles that individuals assume during early adulthood. We will consider as well the ways in which young adults and their parents influence the development of each other's social roles through a process known as parallel development.

The Selection of Adult Gender Roles

At some point after leaving home, the majority of young adults enter into domestic partnerships wherein they must make joint decisions with their spouses or partners regarding the division of household labor. In these choices, we see the influence of gender socialization processes as they occur in the family context. To provide an understanding of parental influences on young adults' adoption of gender roles, Cunningham (2001) conducted a study that compared the relative influence of parental characteristics assessed at different points in young adults' upbringing. The findings from this study provided evidence of the importance of parental modeling of household task division and attitudes about gender in the formation of young adults' gender role beliefs.

Among the most significant of the findings in this study was the strong impact of the mothers' gender role attitudes during the early years on the young adults' views regarding the ideal division of household labor. Cunningham's (2001) findings also demonstrated that the parental division of labor during their midadolescence had a significant effect on young adults' interpretation of the way that household tasks should be divided between women and men. Specifically, the higher levels of participation in housework by their fathers were associated with young adults' greater support for men's participation in stereotypically female housework. Based on these findings, Cunningham concluded that fathers' participation in household tasks during the adolescent years, when children are likely to be responsible for a greater proportion of the domestic labor, plays an important behavioral role in leading their children to support household task sharing.

Thinking Critically

It might not have occurred to you that the degree to which fathers were involved in sharing household tasks during their adolescent years is related to the values that young adults have regarding the gender division of household tasks. Consider the sharing of household tasks that you observed during your own adolescence, in your own or another household. Are you able to see a link between your own gender role attitudes and those earlier observations?

The Parallel Development of the Social Roles of Young Adults and Their Parents

Although parents influence the development of the social roles that their children assume during young adulthood, the roles of young adults and their parents continue to be redefined in relation to each other's. Parents and their young adult children exert a strong influence on each other's role development through a process that contributes to their **parallel development.** To achieve parallel development with their parents, young adults must develop **filial maturity.** Blenkner (1965) introduced the concept of filial maturity to describe an adult's capability of responding to the needs of the parent, which represents a move away from egocentrism and a step toward the development of a more mature adult role. Forcefully rejecting the notion of role reversal, Blenkner emphasized that mature sons or daughters do not take on a parental role in relation to their parents but rather they assume a filial role, which involves the ability to be depended on by their parents.

Dimensions of Filial Maturity. Two dimensions are essential to the development of filial maturity: **parental distancing** and **parental comprehending.** Distancing is necessary in the parent and adult–child relationship to allow each party a certain level of independence from one another, and comprehending serves to keep the parent and adult child close to each other. Development in each of these dimensions requires the ability to balance the two forces (Nydegger & Mitteness, 1991). In the following discussion, we will examine the concepts of distancing and comprehending from the perspective of the role of the adult child.

Parental Distancing. A critical task for personal development during young adulthood is to distance oneself from one's parents and establish one's separate identity as an adult. As one begins the process of separating from one's parents, however, it is important to simultaneously take the first step toward development in the filial role (being responsive to the needs of one's parents). The challenge, therefore, is to achieve emotional emancipation while remaining engaged as a son or daughter. Establishing a psychological distance from their parents is a necessary step for young adults to take in order to be able to see both themselves and their parents more objectively. Acquiring a level of objectivity in relation to their parents allows young adults to perceive their parents as persons, apart from the parental role (Nydegger & Mitteness, 1991).

Although parental distancing is a normal and beneficial process, the course of emotional weaning is likely to be slow and painful for parents as well as their adult children (Erikson, 1963). The initial phase of parental distancing is triggered by the physical separation from parents typical of early adulthood in industrialized countries. This period of adjustment is likely to be characterized by elevated criticism and reduced contact (Nydegger & Mitteness, 1991), and it is important to examine the processes underlying these interactions. Transitions such as physical separations from parents can be stressful because they challenge attachment bonds between family members. Therefore, open communication and the processing of emotions are crucial when family members change. The expression of emotions fosters the renegotiation of bonds and the clarification of family members' needs and concerns (Dankoski, 2001).

Reconnecting Phase. The separation phase wherein young adults temporarily withdraw from their parents is generally followed by a stage of renewed acquaintance. The emancipation that occurs during the withdrawal phase tempers young adults' egocentrism, thereby helping them to see their parents more realistically during the phase of renewed acquaintance. The more realistic perception of the parent, which occurs in the **reconnecting phase** of the parent–child relationship, is typically accompanied by a greater appreciation of the parent as an individual. A second outcome of young adults' distancing and renegotiated relationships with their parents is their improving ability to perceive themselves in the adult child role, from the viewpoint of what their parents need from them (Nydegger & Mitteness, 1991).

A concern of young adults that emerges during the emancipation stage and continues during the stage of renegotiated relationships with parents is the issue of privacy. It is, therefore, important to devise a family etiquette to handle the delicate balance between the parents' interest in knowing what is going on in their adult children's lives and their adult children's right to privacy (Nydegger & Mitteness, 1988). Just as there are hindrances to parental distancing, there are factors that serve to promote the level of distancing necessary for the development of mature relationships between adult children and their parents. Interviews of young adults and their parents have suggested that demonstrating maturity in other adult roles promotes young adults' self-confidence, which in turn encourages parental distancing. Another factor that has been suggested as important in the promotion of parental distancing is the maturity of the parents themselves (Nydegger & Mitteness, 1991).

Thinking Critically

What is an example of family etiquette that you and your parents have worked out (or are currently in the process of working out) to handle the delicate balance between your parents' interest in knowing what is going on in your life and your right to privacy?

Parental Comprehending. There is much emphasis on the need of parents to understand their children and this is an appropriate focus of parent–child relationships when children are developing toward adulthood. When children become young adults, however, they develop filial maturity, which includes the capability of comprehending their parents. As might be expected, the ability to comprehend one's own parents requires considerable objectivity. The development of the ability to comprehend their parents brings adult children to the place whereby they realize that their parents had their own existence prior to assuming the role of parent and continue to exist as individuals outside their parental role (Nydegger & Mitteness, 1991).

The development of the ability to comprehend one's own parents not only lags behind parental distancing but also is a slower process. Most adults can remember a time when they began to really understand their parents (typically in their early 20s). They usually realize that their understanding of their parents was a gradual process that occurred as they themselves began to take on the adult roles held by their parents—those of spouse, parent, and worker. A positive outcome of young adults' development of the capability of comprehending their parents is the reduction of conflict with parents. The comprehension of mothers happens earlier than does the comprehension of fathers. The level of comprehension of fathers is not expected to be achieved during early adulthood but instead is anticipated to occur during the 40s. Although, for many adults, comprehension of their fathers does not occur until their fathers are very old and may not take place until after their fathers' deaths (Nydegger & Mitteness, 1991).

Thinking Critically

Can you identify the ways in which you distanced yourself from your parents as you became a young adult? Are you currently in the process of comprehending your parents? If so, what have you discovered that helps you to appreciate your parents as individuals?

YOUNG ADULTHOOD AND PARENT–CHILD RELATIONSHIPS: A FAMILY SYSTEMS PERSPECTIVE

So far we have discussed the various ways in which the parent–child relationships of young adults impact the emotional, social, and cognitive development of young adults. We considered as well the influence of parents on the development of young adults' social roles and the parallel development of the roles of parents and children in relation to each other. We will now examine the ways in which the relationships of young adults and their parents alter the family system in which they occur by viewing that family from the perspective of Family Systems Theory. According to Family Systems Theory, which was discussed in Chapter 1, each family member's behavior affects the behavior of all other family members. Furthermore, all individuals in a family work together to maintain the stability of the family system in the face of change. The changes that require adjustment of expectations, roles, and behaviors of family members include the arrival or departure of any family member, the experience of a family crisis, and the ongoing developmental changes of family members (Steinberg & Steinberg, 1994).

When Young Adults Establish Separate Residences

According to Family Systems Theory, whenever young adults leave home, a disruption occurs in the family system. This disruption requires all family members, including the departing member, to adapt to a change in the family system (Steinberg & Steinberg, 1994). A common disruption of the family occurs when young adults leave home to go to college. As young adults move out of the homes they lived in with their parents, a number of changes occur in their parent–child relationships that necessitate that both generations readjust their expectations of each other and modify their roles in relation to each other. Furthermore, there are different degrees of leaving home. For college students in the United States, even though they *live* in college residences they typically still *go home* for holidays, many weekends, and the summer. When college students go home, they often are surprised and/or disappointed to discover that their rooms have been taken over by younger siblings or that younger siblings have achieved a status in the family hierarchy that they (the college student) held prior to leaving home. Similarly, parents of young adult college students are frequently taken aback by their children's new independence. For example, parents might expect their college-age children to observe an earlier curfew when home for weekends and holidays than those that young adults adhere to while away at college. The following example is a reaction of a college student to a suggested change in the parental household after that student had been living away from home for 2 years while attending a state university.

> My Mom wanted to turn my room into a sewing room and I said "no way—that is my room." I know she will have sewing things all over the place and I won't feel like it's my room anymore. I told her that I am not ready to give up my room. (Unpublished interview of a 20-year-old college student)

The Changes That Occur in Parent–Child Relationships When Members Are Added to the Family System

Not only do family roles and expectations change when young adults leave their parents' home, the rules and roles are further modified when young adults enter into committed relationships of marriage or other partnerships and/or when they have children. The integration of each of these new family members into the existing family system triggers a further shift in family roles (Steinberg & Steinberg, 1994).

Thinking Critically

In what ways have you observed that roles, rules, and other alterations in the household changed after you went away to college?

Parents-in-Law and Children-in-Law. Parents of newlywed young adults take on the roles of mothers-in-law and fathers-in-law, and their children's spouses assume the roles of daughters-in-law and sons-in-law. The challenge for parents when children-in-law enter into the family system is that the previous relationships they had with their adult children require alterations to support their children's allegiance to their spouses or partners. Helping the partners or spouses of adult children feel welcome in the family requires an understanding that these individuals have come from family systems with roles, expectations, and boundaries that differ from those of their new family (Steinberg & Steinberg, 1994).

From the perspectives of both parents-in-law and children-in-law, there will be times when family members feel that "This is not the way we did things in our family." These discoveries will sometimes be pleasant surprises and at times will be disappointing. The degree to which family members are sufficiently open minded and flexible to incorporate the needs of old and new family members makes a difference in the level of satisfaction experienced by all members of the expanded family system. Successful assimilation of new family members into an existing family system requires that all members receive encouragement to openly discuss their feelings and expectations. A positive integration of new family members into the existing family system is more likely to occur in families that respect the feelings of all family members. Furthermore, a willingness of family members to alter expectations to ensure that all members' needs are met is a positive step toward family cohesiveness (Steinberg & Steinberg, 1994).

When Young Adult Children Enter Gay or Lesbian Unions. Whereas the unions of most young adults are supported by their parents, young adults who are gay and lesbian do not typically have the support of their parents for their partnerships. In their study of the intergenerational relationships of gay men and lesbian women, LaSala (2002) found that the majority of these young adults experience parental disapproval, which might interfere with their union if both of the partners fail to prioritize the needs of the partner relationship over the parent relationship. The disappointment expressed in the following comment of a gay man discussing his partner's parents demonstrates the effect of parental disapproval on the lives of that couple: "Anytime he wants to go to see them, which is frequent . . . we have this whole conversation about whether I should go or shouldn't go. . . . If they were accepting, there would be no friction" (p. 331).

Although failure to prioritize the needs of the partner relationship often occurs, most gay men and lesbian women defend the partnership boundaries against intergenerational pressures (LaSala, 2002). An example of the way in which young adults in gay or lesbian unions defend their partnerships in the face of parental disapproval is illustrated in the comment of another gay man: "I respect her right to feel that way about my homosexuality. I recognize that her experiences are different from mine. I can validate her feelings and not buy into them. Just because my mother does not want to see me in a gay relationship does not mean I'm going to leave the one I'm in" (p. 332). Another way that gay men and lesbian women maintain intergenerational boundaries is by distancing themselves from their disapproving parents, as seen in the next comment: "My parents' religious objections don't affect the relationship. I don't see them very much" (p. 332).

Whereas both gay men and lesbian women who are in committed relationships typically experience moderate to strong parental disapproval of their homosexual unions, there are gender differences in the relationships these young adults have with their parents. Lesbian women experience less parental disapproval of their homosexual lifestyle than do gay men, and compared with gay men they are able to identify parental support for themselves even when parents are not supportive of their lifestyles (LaSala, 2002). The following statement reflects the value a lesbian woman places on the relationship she has with a parent who does not support her homosexual lifestyle: "It's positive, my parental relationship, because she comes over and we have dinner together and talk. . . . If I couldn't talk with my mother, I would feel closed off, and that would affect me and my relationship" (p. 332).

Even though gay men and lesbian women are frequently able to identify support for themselves, when parents disapprove of their partnerships the lack of parental support makes these relationships more challenging. One of the ways that young adults in these situations tend to cope with these challenges is by avoidance strategies designed to keep the peace. Either they do not discuss their sexuality with their parents or they hide negative comments from their partners. The next statement is an example of such a strategy, which is more likely to be used by lesbian women than by gay men: "When my father says something homophobic or ignorant, I jump in quick to correct it. I don't tell my partner because I don't want her to be hurt. She really needs my parents so much in light of her own parents' rejection" (p. 332).

Although most parents of gay men and lesbian women do not fully support their children's homosexual lifestyle, there are parents who demonstrate support of their young adult children's unions with their partners (LaSala, 2002). The benefit of this support in the lives of these individuals is demonstrated in the following statement of a young lesbian woman. "My parents being fully invested in my relationship has a positive effect. It lets me be fully present because my family is very close and important to me. I wouldn't be successful in a relationship without their support" (p. 332).

The Ways in Which the Arrival of Children Alters the Family System. The arrival of children changes the family system of young adults and their parents. The primary impact of the birth or adoption of children, though, is on the members of the family system wherein those children reside. For new parents, they are suddenly placed in the largely expanded roles of *mother* and *father* and this important transition requires significant adaptations (Cox, Paley, Burchinal, & Payne, 1999). These novel role positions contribute to alterations of their roles as members of a couple, and the strains accompanying the arrival of children often result in the lowest level of marital satisfaction of any point in their relationship. This is particularly true for women, who (as discussed in Chapter 3) tend to be less satisfied with their partners in the months after birth or adoption (Kluwer et al., 2002).

As explained in Chapter 3, the most likely reason for young mothers' greater dissatisfaction with their partners or spouses following the advent of parenthood is that new mothers usually take on more child care and related household responsibilities than do new fathers. Even when both parents are employed outside the home and work similar hours, young mothers typically spend more time taking care of the children and doing housework than do young fathers (Kluwer et al., 2002). On the other hand, not all new parents experience a decline in satisfaction with their relationship or with each other. Indeed, some individuals experience greater satisfaction with their relationship during the years that they are most involved in childrearing. This is particularly true for young parents who are able to have an egalitarian relationship while rearing their young children. In these relationships, young parents are able to work out a collaborative approach to child care and household responsibilities based on (a) shared parenting goals, (b) the willingness to acknowledge each parents' contribution to the well-being of their family, and (c) an attitude of flexibility. These dimensions of shared parenting enhance couples' marital satisfaction as well as their sense of competency as parents (Ehrenberg, Gearing-Small, & Hunter, 2001).

Barbara Schwartz/Merill.

Working mothers and fathers who share household responsibilities and child care experience greater satisfaction with their relationship.

COMBINING WORK AND PARENTAL ROLES

During the same time that young adults are adapting to their roles as parents and redefining their couple relationship to include parental responsibilities, most young adults are engaged as well in aligning family and work responsibilities. The fundamental problem for parents when both of them work outside the home is being able to coordinate family and work obligations. **Role overload** occurs when the demands of work and family roles result in a person feeling strained and overwhelmed. Research has documented the negative effects of role overload on family relationships (Erdwins, Buffardi, & Casper, 2001). Moving beyond the problems associated with role overload, however, recent evidence has provided a more positive scenario of families in which both fathers and mothers are working. First, women who are simultaneously carrying out the roles of wife, mother, and employee do not necessarily suffer role overload. Second, role overload is less common in dual-worker families than is **role buffering.** In many dual-income families, both parents act in many ways to buffer the impact of stress associated with performing the dual roles of parent and paid worker. Moreover, these young adults who are able to balance parental and vocational roles are healthier, happier, and more successful in their combined roles than are parents who function well in only one of these roles (Hochschild, 1997). Furthermore, there is evidence that during the early years, mothers and fathers both tend to increase sensitivity to their young children over time (Mills-Koonce et al. 2002).

SUMMARY

- In this chapter, we have explored the relationships of young adults and their parents as well as young adults and their children in diverse circumstances and in varied cultures within the United States and throughout the world.
- We examined the parent–child relationship from the perspective of the impact of this relationship on the emotional, social, and cognitive development of young adults.
- Also discussed in this chapter were the ways in which the alterations in the lives of young adults impact the family system.

KEY TERMS

- connectiveness
- dialectical reasoning
- empty nest
- filial duty
- filial maturity
- full nest
- generativity achievement
- individuation
- intimacy achievement
- parallel development
- parental comprehending
- parental distancing
- reconnecting phase
- role buffering
- role overload
- scaffolding

USEFUL WEB SITES

Understanding Families as Systems

http://www.Psychologicalscience.org/pdf/Cox.pdf

This site contains a theoretical article titled *Understanding Families as Systems.* The authors of this article discuss recent research that has emerged from theoretical and conceptual models that use a systems metaphor for understanding families. These ideas are useful for examining continuity and discontinuity in adult adaptation and family functioning.

The Launching Years

http://www.newhorizons.org/lifelong/adolescence/Kastner.htm

The article at this site, titled *The Launching Years: No Time to Stop Parenting,* describes the complicated and vastly overlooked transitional period for young adults and their parents. Problems that newly launched adult children have adjusting to their newly independent status are addressed in this article.

The College Years

http://www.georgetown.edu

In the search box, type in "The College Years: Challenges for Students and Parents."

This newsletter points out the exciting opportunities as well as the stressful challenges for young adults and their parents during the college years, which are viewed as a major transition period for both parties. Recommendations are provided for ways in which parents can assist their children who are college students during the transition from home to college. Challenges that occur during freshman, sophomore, junior, and senior year are also addressed.

The Interface of Work and Family

http://www.labour.hrdc-drhc.gc.caworklife/vcswlb-eretyp/p010202.ffm

This site contains the results of a survey of working Canadian parents who reported on problems with the interface of work and family. Challenges related to role overload, role interference, and specific challenges associated with achieving a work-family balance are reported.

Middle Age and Older Parenthood and Grandparenthood

Objectives

After completing of this chapter, you should be able to

- Explain the ways in which parent–child relationships between middle and older adults provide opportunities for the ongoing development of generativity.
- Demonstrate an understanding of how the normative transitions of their adult children contribute to greater satisfaction in these relationships for middle-aged parents.
- Identify the nonnormative transitions of adulthood and middle age, and explain why these nonnormative transitions negatively impact parent–child relationships.
- Compare the role of grandparent in traditional cultures to the role of grandparent in Western cultures, with special attention to cultural variations within the United States.
- Identify some of the unique challenges faced by custodial grandparents.
- Identify some of the factors that increase the likelihood that adult children will provide care for their aging parents.
- Explain the factors that contribute to the quality of relationships between aging adults and their adult children.
- Demonstrate an understanding of some of the challenges associated with providing care for elderly parents, including how the expectations of adult children and their parents sometimes differ in these situations.
- Discuss the changes that occur in adults' family interaction patterns following parental death.
- Identify the types of legacies that older parents leave for their children and grandchildren upon their death.

The psychological and social development of middle-aged and older adults is affected by the relationships in which they participate with their parents, children, and grandchildren. Furthermore, these relationships influence the continuing growth and development of the family systems in which they take place. In the upcoming discussion, we will take a look at middle age and elderly parenthood and grandparenthood in diverse cultures within the United States as well as in cultures throughout the world. We also will consider the influence of varied life circumstances (such as divorce, remarriage, retirement, and widowhood) on these relationships.

PARENTHOOD AND THE SOCIAL–EMOTIONAL DEVELOPMENT OF MIDDLE-AGED ADULTS

The development of a sense of generativity has its beginnings during early adulthood when young adults become parents. During middle age, most people become grandparents, and the relationships grandparents develop with their grandchildren contribute to further development of a sense of generativity. As we will see in the upcoming discussions, whether middle-aged adults experience a sense of continued development of generativity versus a sense of stagnation is influenced by a number of transitions that happen in their lives and in the lives of their adult children.

The Impact of Adult Children's Social Status Transitions

Beginning when their children are in early adulthood, the relationships of middle-aged adults and their children are altered along a series of social status transitions. **Social status transitions** refer to those changes in an individual's life that modify that person's social role. Normative social status transitions occur as young adults graduate from college, enter a career, get married, or have children. Nonnormative social status transitions result from experiences such as getting divorced or losing one's job. Normative transitions of adult children contribute to increased intergenerational closeness and contact (Mottran & Hortacsu, 2005). Adult children's nonnormative transitions, on the other hand, tend to negatively affect parent and adult–child relationships (LaSala, 2002).

The Positive Impact of Normative Transitions. When adult children go off to college, begin careers, get married, and have children, parent–child relationships generally improve. The positive change that occurs in intergenerational relations when adult children experience normative transitions has been attributed to two factors. First, such transitions verify that the adult child is conforming to social norms in terms of maturational development. Second, the transitions themselves increase the number of adult social roles that adult children share with their parents (Suitor, Pillemer,

Keeton, & Robison, 1994). For example, in a study of mothers and daughters, Mottran and Hortacsu (2005) found that a shared sense of femaleness increased and was reinforced by daughters' experience of wife and mother roles, which resulted in greater empathy for mothers.

The Consequences of Nonnormative Status Transitions. Whereas adult children's normative status transitions generally enhance affectionate ties between middle-aged parents and their adult children, nonnormative status transitions frequently have a detrimental affect on these relations. Parents tend to have strong developmental expectations for their children. They hope that their children will mature into functioning adults and become important parental supports. Furthermore, parents often feel they cannot carry on with their own lives until their children have made these important transitions. Children who have not established their own households or become independent of their parents serve as a reminder that parents have not achieved their goal of socializing their children to become independent, capable adults. In addition to violating parental expectations, many nonnormative transitions of adult children increase adult children's demands on their parents, and these unanticipated burdens tend to have a negative impact on parent–child relations. Studies that document the effect of adult children's job loss support this argument. Parent–child relationships often become strained when sons lose their jobs and adult children's unemployment has been found to be one of the main factors in parental conflict when generations share a home (Clarke, Preston, & Raskin, 1999).

The Impact of Middle-Aged Parents' Social Status Transitions

As their young adult children are making the normative transitions into their adult roles and sometimes undergoing nonnormative transitions, middle-aged parents are experiencing transitions in their own lives. The transitions in the lives of both generations affect their relationships with each other. A universal normative social status transition of middle age occurs when parents become grandparents and this transition generally has a positive impact on both middle-aged persons and their adult children. Nonnormative transitions, such as divorce and remarriage, on the other hand, present a variety of challenges for adult children.

The Normative Transition into Grandparenthood. Even though the birth or adoption of the first grandchild marks the move into the role of grandparent, most individuals have more than one grandchild and the arrival of each grandchild alters the grandparent role. Becoming a grandparent is a welcome role shift for most individuals and provides the opportunity for the acquisition of new roles. Many grandparents perceive the role of grandparent as easier, and more gratifying, than the role of parent, affording them pleasure and gratification without requiring them to take on the major responsibility for the care and socialization of the children. Furthermore, Reitzes and Mutran (2004) found that men and women tend to feel more positive about their grandparent identities in comparision to their other adult identities.

One of the reasons that contemporary grandparents derive such a high level of satisfaction from the role of grandparent is likely to be that they bring more energy and financial resources to the grandparent role than did grandparents a generation ago. Today's grandparents are more youthful, more involved, and have more money to spend on their grandchildren than a generation ago, when 47 was the average lifespan.

Although first-time grandparents are typically younger today (Paul, 2002), that is not the case when adult children delay parenthood. In these situations, their parents become grandparents at a later age. It is important to keep in mind, however, that the recent increase in longevity is associated with individuals remaining healthy and active over a longer span of their lives. For older active adults, their roles as grandparents remain a vital aspect of their lives and they are able to maintain close ties to their adult children as well as to their grandchildren. In addition to improved health and more active lifestyles among older grandparents, other factors that impact intergenerational relationships are stable finances and early retirement, which have made geographic mobility possible for retirees. The geographical mobility of older persons is especially relevant for their relationships with their adult children and grandchildren because the research shows that the primary reason for a residential move among older persons is to be near their adult children (Giarrusso, Silverstein, & Bengston, 1996).

Middle-Aged Parents' Nonnormative Transitions. Serious illness, death, divorce, remarriage, and second-generation fatherhood represent social status transitions in the lives of middle-aged adults that might negatively impact their relationships with their adult children. These nonnormative transitions present challenges for adult children and require a higher level of adjustment than do predictable normative transitions.

Parental divorce and remarriage. The most consistent finding is that divorce of middle-aged parents adversely affects parent–child relationships (Kaufman & Uhlenberg, 1998). Furthermore, there are gender differences in the impact of middle-aged parents' divorce on their adult children. The findings of Shapiro (2003) showed that divorced older fathers are more likely than stably married older fathers to experience a decline in regular contact with at least one adult child. In contrast, divorced older mothers are more likely than married older mothers to experience an increase in contact with an adult child. Shapiro's findings also showed that the possibility of a mother having little or no contact with an adult child is slightly increased by divorce. Divorce and remarriage also alters the financial support that these parents provide for their adult children. For example, Pezzin and Schone (1999) revealed that divorce has a negative effect on intergenerational transfers, especially for middle-aged fathers, and that remarriage further reduces the level of financial assistance that these parents provide for their adult children. These authors also observed that parents engage in lower levels of transfers with stepchildren relative to biological children, and that remarried parents are more sensitive to the needs of biological children than to the needs of stepchildren.

This second-generation father faces the challenge of expanding his paternal role to include parenting a young child while also being the parent of adult children.

Second-generation fathers. Not only are relationships between middle-aged fathers and their adult children likely to be strained following the older parents' divorce and/or remarriage, these relationships are further altered in cases when older fathers have more children. Although the population of middle-aged, **second-generation fathers** is growing, only a few researchers have studied the relationships between these fathers and their adult children. According to this research, most men who become "refathers" are not doing so because they have discovered a need to father late in life. Instead, most of these fathers love their wives or partners who want to have children, like the idea of having more children, and have more time to spend with children than they had when their adult children were younger. Because there is often a generation difference between second-generation fathers and their wives or partners, these fathers are usually learning how to parent all over again. When rearing their first set of children, they often have been part of the old male model of the father as the disciplinarian and financial provider and are typically grateful to have a second chance to parent (Cleaver, 1999).

Although second-generation fathers are given the opportunity to adapt their fatherhood role according to the contemporary model of the involved father, observation of their father's new role might contribute to resentment by their older children. Possibilities of tension between second-generation fathers and their adult children center around three issues: (a) seeing their fathers spend more leisure time with their younger siblings than they had experienced as children, (b) concern about the division of family financial resources, and (c) not being as free to rely on their fathers' assistance with their own children. The adult children of second-generation fathers might interpret their father's greater involvement with their younger siblings as evidence that their fathers have a greater affection for their younger siblings. What older siblings are witnessing, however, is an example of an alteration in the fatherhood role across the two generations. "Refatherhood" is an example of the way in which the parenthood role changes from one generation to the next and is influenced by social and societal changes (Cleaver, 1999).

THE RELATIONSHIPS OF OLDER PARENTS AND THEIR MIDDLE-AGED CHILDREN

We will now change the focus from middle-aged adults and their children to middle-aged adults and their older parents. In distinguishing middle-aged parents from older parents, it is important to keep in mind that some of these older parents might be considered elderly, whereas some might be viewed as merely older. In the past, it was easier to distinguish between older persons and middle-aged individuals. People who had reached their 60s were thought to be old. Today, due to better health, an increase in longevity, and variation in lifestyles among older persons, these distinctions are less clear. The majority of older persons in the United States (approximately 80%) have living children, and many of these older individuals (the oldest old—about 10%) have children who are 65 or older. As will become clear in the upcoming discussions, older persons and their children have relationships that vary in terms of residential proximity, frequency of interaction, mutual aid, feelings of affection, and beliefs regarding filial duty and obligation.

PARENT–CHILD RELATIONSHIPS AND THE SOCIAL–EMOTIONAL DEVELOPMENT OF OLDER PERSONS

The quality of the relationships that elderly individuals have with their children and grandchildren contributes to the development of the older person's sense of integrity versus despair (Erikson, Erikson, & Kivnick, 1986). According to Erikson (1968), during old age, individuals reexamine their lives and make judgments regarding whether they have accomplished the things they had hoped for in their work as well as in their personal relationships. If their interpretation of their lives is a positive one, they incorporate a **sense of integrity.** If they look back with regrets, they develop a **sense of despair.** Because parent–child relations play such an integral role in the life of an individual, the development of a sense of integrity or a sense of despair is linked to whether or not their children have turned out as parents had hoped they would. The attainment of a sense of integrity is related as well to whether parents have been able to maintain satisfactory relations with their children over the years. Both older men and older women evaluate their life histories in terms of the social networks of which they have been a part but there is a gender difference in these life reviews. In their remembered past, feeling as if they have had a social influence on others is more highly valued for men, whereas for women **social anchorage** (maintaining connections to others) is seen as more important (McCamish-Svenson, Samuelsson, & Hagberg, 1999).

The Transitions of Elderly Parents and Their Middle-Aged Children

We will now explore the ways in which the transitions experienced by older persons and their middle-aged children affect their relationships with each other. We also will examine the impact on older persons' lives when their middle-aged children do not make the expected transition into independent living.

The Normative Transitions of Older Parents. The two primary normative transitions of older adults that affect their relationships with their middle-aged children are retirement and widowhood. In the case of retirement, the support required by older parents from their children in coping with retirement is minimal. Moreover, the adjustment made by the family following the older parent's retirement is likely to be increased family participation by the retiree. Although the retirement of older parents is associated with increased family participation, a number of factors influence the degree to which retired parents interact with their adult children. These include the geographic distance between parents and children, the gender of the retired person, and the presence or absence of grandchildren. For those children living within 10 miles, their mothers' retirement is associated with fewer visits and their fathers' retirement is associated with more visits. In contrast, for children living more than 10 miles away, mothers increase and fathers decrease their visits. Interestingly, retired mothers are more likely to visit their children who have children living in the household, whereas retired fathers are more likely to visit their childless children (Szinovacz & Davey, 2002).

In the case of parental widowhood, Norton and Van Houtven (2006) found that renegotiation of parent–child roles resulted in daughters providing increasingly more care for parents. Although there is more care from adult children to their aging parents following widowhood, the findings of these researchers demonstrated that adult children who help their aging parents with activities are likely to receive some amount of financial compensation from their parents. Thus, assistance to older parents is typically reciprocated by support from older parents. The intergenerational exchange of support was also demonstrated by Grundy (2005) who analyzed the exchange of support between Third Age parents (aged 55–75) and their adult children and found that between two-thirds and three-fourths of parents in this age group were involved in some sort of mutual exchange with at least one of their children. Furthermore, more older parents were providers than recipients of help. Parental characteristics associated with the greater likelihood of providing assistance to adult children included higher income, home ownership, and being married or widowed rather than divorced. Receiving help from children was positively related to parental age or disability.

Older Parents' Adjustment to Their Children's Transitions. In addition to the effects of transitions associated with aging such as retirement and the death of a spouse or partner, older adults also are affected by the transitions in their children's lives, for instance, their children's career changes and geographic locations. The normative transitions in the lives of middle-aged children generally do not strain the relations between older parents and their children. The nonnormative transitions of middle-aged adults, on the other hand, tend to burden older parents. When older parents are troubled by the nonnormative transitions of their middle-aged children, there are likely to be difficulties in the parent–child relationship.

The Impact of Middle-Aged Children's Stressful Life Circumstances. Stressful life circumstances and prolonged dependency are two primary problems that middle-aged adults encounter that tend to negatively affect their older parents' psychological adjustment and have a harmful effect on the relationships they have with their aging parents. For example, Pillemer and Suitor (1991) found that parents of adult children who have mental or physical impairments, substance abuse, or stress-related problems experience more depression than do parents whose children do not have these problems. Another factor that detrimentally impacts the psychological adjustment of older parents is when their adult children fail to become emotionally and economically independent. The morale of older parents suffers if their middle-aged children's problems necessitate older parents continuing to provide them with high levels of care and support. Thus, to the extent that the problems of middle-aged adults lead to their continued or increased dependency on their older parents, the quality of these intergenerational relationships tends to decline and the psychological well-being of older parents might be compromised (Clarke et al., 1999; Gibson, 2002).

Thinking Critically

Consider the relationships your grandparents have with their children, including your own parents, and see if you can identify the normative and nonnormative transitions that have altered or currently impact these relationships.

GRANDPARENTHOOD, PERSONHOOD, AND THE LIFE COURSE

Earlier in the chapter we discussed the ways in which becoming a grandparent represents a social status transition that typically occurs during middle adulthood and alters the relationship between middle-aged parents and their adult children. We now will explore the ways in which participation in the role of grandparent affects the lives of middle-aged and older individuals, their children, and their grandchildren.

Grandparenthood and Older Adults' Psychological Development

According to Erikson et al. (1986), grandparenthood offers many individuals a "second chance" at generativity because it provides the possibility of caring for the newest generation more vigorously and less ambivalently than they did with their own children. With grandchildren, elders might participate in any number of ways of guiding and maintaining these children. By taking children for the weekend, for example, grandparents are caring for their grandchildren as well as their children. Furthermore, the distance of the next generation frequently allows those grandparents who had difficulty with parenthood to experience feelings of pride in their grandchildren that they might not have experienced with their children. Finally, participation in the role of grandparent contributes to the psychological development of older adults based on the inclusion of this experience in the older adult's life review. Kivnick (1982) identified five distinct dimensions of meaning that grandparenthood brings to the life review process: (a) role centrality, (b) valued eldership, (c) immortality through clan, (d) reinvolvement with personal past, and (e) indulgence.

The Greater Number and Various Roles of Grandparents Today

Today, an unprecedented number of people in American society are grandparents, and with the increase of grandparents has been a parallel boost in the variety of ways in which the grandparent role has come to be defined. Thinking of grandparents in terms of the stereotype of persons with a common lifestyle who have few roles outside their role as grandparent is very difficult to maintain. Although we still see grandparents at home baking cookies for their grandchildren, we also encounter them on the jogging track and the hiking trail, watch them perform as rock stars, and are likely to be working for them in the corporations that they head. Not only do we have difficulty identifying grandparents by the roles they play in society, we also are unable to pin them down in terms of a life stage because they range in age from 40 to 110!

The Cultural Role of Grandparent. In addition to variations in age and lifestyle of grandparents, there are cultural differences in the roles grandparents play in relation to their grandchildren. These roles differ according to the degree to which there is a cultural norm of independence (found in individualistic cultures) or of interdependence (seen in collectivistic cultures). Because traditional cultures value family interdependence, the lives of grandparents in these cultures are more integrated into the daily lives of grandchildren, and grandparents are expected to play a central role in the upbringing of grandchildren. In cultures characterized by large, extended families and a reverence for elders, grandparents are likely to live with their adult children and grandchildren and to be part of the social support system of the family. An illustration of the integration of grandparents into the social support system of ethnic minority families in the United States is found in the central role that elders play in the Latino American culture. In this culture, older adults are twice as likely to influence childrearing, family decision making, and advising in comparison to their African American or European American peers. In contrast to the role of grandparents in traditional cultures, grandparents in individualistic cultures are not expected to play a primary role in the socialization of grandchildren. Moreover, the role of grandparent in Western societies is less clear than the

Michal Heron/PH College.

The role of grandparent in ethnic minority families in the United States is typically integrated into the social support system of the family.

role in traditional cultures. In contrast to the role of the grandparent in ethnic minority cultures, European American grandparents are more likely to take on roles in relation to their grandchildren whereby they maintain close relationships with their grandchildren while living independently from the parent–child household (Burnett, 1999).

The Contributions of Grandparents. Despite cultural and social differences in the expectations associated with the grandparent role, grandparents everywhere make valuable contributions to the lives of their grandchildren. One of the most important types of support provided by grandparents is that they help their families by just being there. Their presence in the lives of their children and grandchildren provides symbols of longevity and continuity and having grandparents who are available increases feelings of security in younger generations. Another important role served by grandparents is that of family historian. The evolution of the family is passed down from generation to generation by the stories told by grandparents and great-grandparents. Grandparents also sometimes serve as mentors and role models to their grandchildren (Giarrusso, Silverstein, & Bengston, 1996). Another type of support provided by grandparents is that they fulfill the role of crisis managers in the family. As noted earlier, when crises such as divorce, death, or prolonged unemployment occur, older parents often provide substantial assistance to their children and grandchildren. Moreover, many grandparents assume the role of custodial parents when neither of their grandchildren's parents is able to fulfill that responsibility (Gibson, 2002). Finally, although much of the research has focused on the role of the grandmother, both grandmothers and grandfathers play an important role in the lives of their grandchildren Roberto, Allen, and Blieszner (2001). An example of the closeness between a grandfather and his grandson is exemplified in the following quote:

> *"I asked [Grandson] one time, I said '[Grandson], who's your best friend?' I didn't have any idea what he was going to say. He said 'Granddad, you are my best friend in the whole wide world.' You know, so that's a special relationship."* (p. 417, Roberto et al., 2001).

Thinking Critically

If you have (or had) grandparents, or older adults in your life who fulfilled the role of grandparent, see if you can identify the various roles that these individuals have played or are currently playing in your life.

OLDER ADULT CAREGIVERS OF THEIR GRANDCHILDREN

We will now turn our attention to the ways in which intergenerational relations are altered in situations when older parents become the caregivers of their grandchildren. As noted in Chapter 3, the number of grandparents who are assuming the role of primary caregivers of their grandchildren has substantially increased in the United States. Although there has been an increase in grandparent-headed households, there are ethnic differences in the prevalence of these households. African Americans are three times as likely and Latino Americans twice as likely as other grandparents to be providing custodial care for their grandchildren. The **skipped-generation caregiving** by grandparents in these ethnic groups does not reflect less parental responsibility among African American and Latino American parents in comparison to parents in other ethnic groups but rather an integration of cultural norms with social forces. There has been a recent increase in the United States of children who are cared for by nonbiological parents and many of these children are growing up in foster care or adoptive families (Roche, 2000). Rather than watch their grandchildren being placed in foster care or adoption, when their adult children are unable or unwilling to provide the care they need, African American and Latino American grandparents are likely to step into the vacated parental role. The role of grandparents as primary caregivers of their grandchildren is a culturally congruent social role in these communities for a couple of reasons. First, it fits with the African American and Latino American commitment of assisting family members by providing a safety net for children. Second, kinship care in African American and Latino American families is an acceptable response to family member loss and separation.

Challenges Faced by Custodial Grandparents. Although the role of primary care grandparent is on the rise in the United States, caring for one's grandchildren is not as simple as transferring residences. To better understand the challenges faced by second-generation grandparents, Gibson (2002) interviewed a number of these grandparents to determine their concerns about their grandchildren and adult children. One of the findings from the study was that, after assuming their role of primary care grandparent, these older adults became aware of previously unknown problems faced by their grandchildren. These problems included a lack of age-appropriate skills, low self-esteem, developmental delays, sexualized behaviors, and hyperactive behavior. As they became aware of their grandchildren's troubles, these grandparents began to realize that their grandchildren behaved differently than did their parents at similar ages.

The following quote exemplifies a custodial grandmother's reaction to her residential grandchildren's behaviors: "M. was so hyper and he was so angry . . . and he broke everything. I mean he fought constantly. He would just . . . he had a foul mouth that was hard for me to get used to" (p. 6). The next quote demonstrates a grandmother's worries regarding her grandchildren's low self-esteem: ". . . I'm trying to work on the children's self-esteem. . . . They are missing a lot of things, and I want them to be proud of who they are and what they can do" (p. 6). The comments of the grandparents in Gibson's study demonstrated that as their awareness increased, they were often surprised at their grandchildren's idiosyncrasies. For instance, one grandmother remarked: "M. will not wear a shirt with buttons on it. . . . So I don't press the issue. If I buy, I buy a shirt that goes over his head. . . . Friends give me a lot of things . . . so I either give those shirts to someone else or save them 'til the next child grows into them (Gibson, 2002, p. 7).

Besides the adjustments related to the direct care of their grandchildren, skipped-generation parents are often burdened with worries about their children who are parents of the children in their care. For example, Gibson found expressions of disappointment related to their children's present and past behaviors and attitudes. These disappointments centered around three primary themes: parenting skills, parenting attitudes, and irresponsible behavior. "She's always complaining either she's ill or she just doesn't feel good when she has the children. But she can always go out on Thursdays and Fridays. She's just . . . I don't know . . . she always said, 'Well, I just shouldn't have had those kids.' Well, since you have, you're supposed to love them and give them all you can. You're supposed to be devoted to them" (p. 6). Another grandparent's remark expresses her lack of understanding of the attitude of the parent: "I couldn't understand how she could not want to be a part of her baby's life. I couldn't understand it because she wasn't raised that way" (p. 6).

Gibson found that chief among the concerns of these custodial grandparents was ensuring the safety of their grandchildren by keeping them out of foster care and monitoring interactions between them and their parents. For some of the custodial grandparents, there were no concerns regarding grandchildren safety when interacting with their parents. When there were concerns, the grandparents reacted by supervising the interactions between the parents and the grandchildren and by placing limits on these interactions. Examples of ways in which primary care grandparents put themselves between their grandchildren and the parents in these situations are exemplified in the following statements. In referring to her daughter, one mother said "She couldn't stay here and disrupt the kids. If she wanted to stay, long as she was attempting to help herself, or like, get a job, but she could not bother the kids" (p. 8). In the next comment, it is evident that the grandmother's role in protecting her grandchild has taken its toll on her relationship with her son who is the child's father: "I feel like we're [grandmother and parent] not as close as we used to be because like I said, now that he's out [prison] and out of trouble, he wants to come in and [exert authority] and I have my own set of rules" (p. 8, brackets added by author).

THE IMPORTANCE AND QUALITY OF INTERGENERATIONAL RELATIONSHIPS

So far we have considered the relationships of older adults and their children in terms of transitions, life stresses, and altered roles, including the assumption of the grandparent role. We will now take a look at the able elderly in the family context, including the importance and quality of these intergenerational relationships.

Measures of Relationship Quality

The quality of the relationships of older parents and their children are reflected in (a) how close they live to one another, (b) the frequency of their interactions with each other, (c) the degree to which they provide mutual aid to one another, and (d) the closeness or strength of feelings between them.

Residential Proximity. One indicator of the importance of the relationships of middle-aged children and their older parents is the effect of these relationships on where people live. In regard to residential proximity, it is clear that older persons prefer to live near their children. The majority of older adults have children who live less than an hour away. Even for elderly parents and grown children who do not live in close proximity to each other, their relationships with each other are typically close. Surprisingly, geographic distance does not seem to detrimentally affect these close ties. Technological advances over the years such as cheaper telephone rates, the availability of electronic mail, and increased air travel allow frequent contact between parents and children who reside at a distance (Fingerman, 2001).

Frequency of Interaction. Not only are older persons inclined to live near their children, but also interaction rates between older persons and their children tend to be high. Several status factors influence the frequency of these interactions. First, the gender of each party plays an important role in the interaction patterns of older adults and their children. Women's intergenerational ties tend to be characterized by greater intimacy than men's intergenerational ties. Therefore, mothers and daughters are likely to experience greater intimacy in comparison to fathers and sons. The marital status of older parents is another factor that influences intergenerational relationships. Married older women interact less with their children than do those who are widowed or divorced (Fingerman, 2001).

Mutual Aid. The crucial dimension of the relationship between adult children and their older parents is mutual aid. Mutual aid flows in both directions and is multidimensional, consisting of services such as child care and/or housework, information and advice, as well as money and gifts. Although the stereotypical view of dependency is that older parents are dependent on their children, research findings have demonstrated that older parents are primarily donors who provide substantial aid to their middle-aged adult children. Furthermore, the level of assistance that older parents make available to their children is directly proportional to parents' perceptions of their children's level of need. For example, elderly parents provide much of the care of adult children who are developmentally disabled or mentally impaired and not living in institutions (Kelly & Kropf, 1995).

Degree of Closeness. Whereas proximity, interaction frequency, and mutual aid are significant indicators of the quality of relationships between middle-aged adults and their older parents, qualitative aspects of the relationship, such as the degree of closeness or strength of feelings might be even more revealing. Intimacy between aging parents and their offspring are marked by two features: (a) recognition of the other person as an individual with strengths and weaknesses, and (b) a deep concern for the other party's well-being. The acceptance of each other's weaknesses and foibles allows adult children and their aging parents to achieve a closeness that was not available to them in their earlier relationship. Unlike other intimate relationships, such as those between romantic partners, the increased closeness of aging parents and their offspring does not typically include a greater sharing of problems. As off-

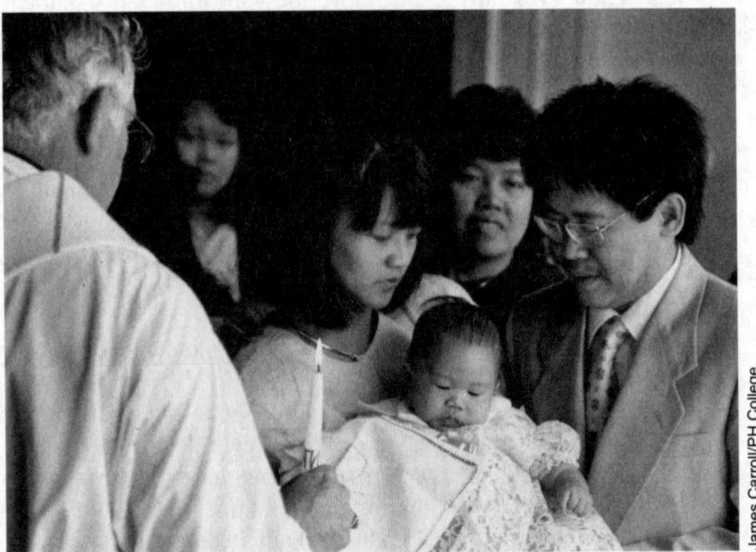

The intergenerational dynamics of families are played out in many activities shared by older persons, their adult children, and their grandchildren.

spring pass through early and middle adulthood, each party realizes the other has different needs and limitations requiring a new kind of distance. The type of mutual respect that marks the relationships of older parents and their adult children influences parents to cease trying to direct their children's lives and influences children to seek to protect their parents from worry (Fingerman, 2001).

Thinking Critically

Consider your parents, in terms of their relationships with their own parents (your grandparents). How would you assess the importance of these relationships for both generations?

Factors Influencing Relationship Quality

Three social structural positions play an important role in determining the quality of parent–child relationships during later life: age, gender, and ethnicity. Age generally has a positive influence on intergenerational relationships. As adults grow older, they experience less conflict and greater closeness in the relationships they have with their children as well as with their parents (Fingerman, 2001). In addition to age, the gender of both the older parents and their middle-aged children impacts their intergenerational relations. There are more affectionate ties between mother and daughter than any other combination and less affectionate ties between son and father than any other combination. Both sons and daughters report greater closeness to their mothers than to their fathers, and both mothers and fathers report greater closeness to their daughters than to their sons (Rossi & Rossi, 1990). An important gender role that contributes to relationship quality across the generations is that of **kinkeeper.** The kinkeepers of an extended family are typically middle-aged older women who tend to provide the key connections between families. Kinkeepers gather the family together for celebrations and keep family members in touch with each other. Kinkeeping appears to be a mechanism for the achievement of social anchorage that has been linked to the realization of a sense of generativity for women (McCamish-Svenson et al., 1999).

Thinking Critically

In considering the extended family relationships (including older parents and/or grandparents) of your family (or someone' else's family), can you identify the kinkeepers of the family? What are some of the behaviors of the kinkeepers that promote family closeness?

Ethnicity and Relationship Quality. The relationship quality of older parents and their adult children is clearly influenced by the culture in which these relationships are played out. For example, cultural beliefs influence whether or not middle-aged and older parents will live in the same household. In individualist cultures, such as the majority cultures of the United States, Britain, and Canada, middle-aged persons and their elderly parents are not expected to live together. In collectivist cultures such as India, South America, and much of Asia and Africa, it is anticipated that older persons will live with their middle-aged children. For instance, expectations that adult children will care for their elderly parents in Thailand result in the common arrangement that at least one adult child lives in the same household or close by, thereby providing a minimum level of social support (Gardiner, Mutter, & Kosmitzki, 1998). Within the United States, African American, Latino American, and Asian American middle-aged parents are more likely to have their parents living with them in comparison to European American middle-aged parents (Phua, Kaufman, & Park, 2001).

Time Usage and the Quality of Intergenerational Relationships

Previous discussions have provided evidence of the strength of the relationships between middle-aged and older parents, which extends to their involvement in the lives of their grandchildren. Further evidence of the strength of these relationships is seen in the ways in which older parents, their children, and their grandchildren spend their time together, by participating in leisure activities. Intergenerational leisure and recreation provide meaning for all family members, contribute to continued family development, and serve as a platform for the rehearsal of family dynamics. Leisure activities provide meaning for intergenerational relationships in various ways. Leisure serves as a stage on which aspects of a family's history are replayed (such as rituals associated with family holidays or family vacations). Leisure activities in the form of rituals also support alterations in family composition or roles (such as celebrations of birth, adoption, marriage, or graduation). As celebrations of these family events, leisure activities have the potential for promoting family harmony and cohesion. Finally, leisure activities of older parents, their children, and their grandchildren provide some illumination of the family dynamics across generations. For example, whether family members are engaged in putting together a family celebration, traveling together, or simply deciding which restaurant to go to for dinner, action, interaction, and transaction are all occurring. In the course of sharing ideas, opinions, and feelings, a shared reality develops.

Thinking Critically

What are the leisurely activities in your family that involve your parents and your grandparents? What benefits do you think these activities provide for family members of various ages?

ALTERATIONS IN THE ROLES OF ADULT CHILDREN AND THEIR AGING PARENTS

As older parents continue to advance in age, the relationships they have with their children undergo continuing adaptation. The adaptation of middle-aged children to the needs of their aging parents is observed in the gradual filial role development of these individuals. The notion of gradual filial role development is that adult children of aging parents become increasingly aware of their parents' failing health or diminished functional ability. The term "filial role" derives from the Chinese term **filial piety** which, in general terms, means to take care of one's parents, including showing love, respect, and support, displaying courtesy, wisely advising one's parents, and concealing their mistakes (Nydegger & Mitteness, 1991). Based on this model, Cicirelli (2000) conducted a study to determine the ways in which filial role development plays out in the lives of adult children of aging parents. Findings of that study were that adult children progress through several predictable stages that parallel their parents' aging process. In the first stage of filial role development, adult children show high levels of *concern for their parents health*. Interestingly, this concern is not tied to indicators of the parents' health status; instead, concern with parents' health seems to be a pervasive aspect of the relationships that adults have with their aging parents. The second stage identified in the study was *urging,* which refers to a situation in which adult children see their parents' physical health worsening and attempt to influence their parents to take action to improve their health. At a still later stage in filial role development, termed *action,* adult children observe that their parents' functional mobility, maintenance of daily activities, and everyday problem solving are deteriorating. At that point, they take direct action to assist their parents in dealing with their health problems. During the action phase, there are clear manifestations of health problems such that the adult children actually observe their parents

James Carroll/PH College.

Many middle-aged daughters or daughters-in-law take on the role of caregiver for elderly parents when those parents become ill or frail.

having difficulty. This later stage of filial role development is not related to the existence of various chronic conditions and symptoms, but only to the later stages of such conditions, when the parent's functional abilities are affected. The alteration in the filial role that occurs at the action phase is as if the adult child were saying:

> *I recognize that you are getting older and I am beginning to keep an eye on you and give you sympathy when you have some complaints; when your health complaints become stronger, I urge you to do something to deal with your problems; however, only when I can actually observe that you are having real difficulties in daily functioning, will I step in and actively help you with your health problems and daily functioning.* (Cicirelli, 2000, p. 170).

When Older Parents Become Chronically Ill and/or Frail

As previously discussed, adult children typically become aware of their older parents' failing health and increasing difficulty in everyday functioning. This awareness is expressed in concern for the well-being of the older parent. If parents' health or frailty leads to the necessity of assistance with daily living, adult children often intervene to be certain that their parents receive the care they need. In these situations, many adult children provide direct care for their parents but frequently expect their aging parents to reciprocate with deference. When older persons do not defer to their children who provide care, intergenerational relations often become strained, and adult children are likely to set limits on their caregiving. Furthermore, there are differences in the caregiving dynamics of older parents and their adult children that are related to whether or not the older parent has individualistic or collectivistic values. Older persons with individualistic values emphasize personal independence, whereas those who embrace collectivist values have a history of working together for the welfare of the entire family. Individualist parents expect to maintain their power base of autonomy and self-determination as long as they are healthy. If their health fails, however, they often experience a sudden and dramatic decline in their personal autonomy when their children intervene in order to ensure that their parents are receiving proper care. The loss of parental power that coincides with children's well-intended intervention frequently leads individualistic older parents to resist and resent children's assistance (Pyke, 1999). Consider the following real-life example of Maryanne, an only child, and her memory-impaired, 89-year-old mother, Betsy, who have a friendly but distant relationship. After neighbors notified Maryanne that her mother's lights had been turned off because she was not paying the utility bills, Maryanne and her husband moved her mother out of her house and into a residential facility. This action led to resentment from her mother who complained that they had forced this decision on her. The elderly mother's assessment of the situation is shown in the following quote:

> *"They're trying to live my life for me, and I still feel capable of taking care of myself. They decided I was too old to live alone. . . . I grant you, there are some things that I'm glad not to be doing anymore, but I'd like to have given them up myself instead of having them taken away from me"* (p. 664, Pike, 1999).

The daughter's explanation for why she moved her mother is reflected in the following quote:

> *"I felt like I had to. She wanted to be in control, but she was no longer really able to, and she still won't admit she's not able to be in control. So I [feel] a lot of guilt. . . . I feel like she'll probably think I'm taking everything away from her, that I've taken control"* (p. 665, Pyke, 1999).

Whereas individualist parents sometimes resent their children taking over their affairs, even when they are unable to do so, parents with collectivist beliefs are less likely to think that their adult children should mind their own business. Adult children of aging collectivist parents are usually permitted to participate in (and direct) the decisions of their aging parents and their involvement in their parents' affairs is less often a source of disagreement. Furthermore, although collectivist adult children are allowed to interfere in their parents' lives, their parents carefully refrain from interfering in the lives of their middle-aged children. This arrangement reflects middle-aged children's greater power in these families. This also clarifies why children and grandchildren in collectivist families frequently describe their aging members as especially understanding and easy going. The following is a description of an 88-year-old, memory-impaired mother, by her 60-year-old daughter, Abby, who lives with and cares for her: "*Whatever I do, she's quiet; she's more passive than most mothers, ... She's very non-interfering .*" Abby sometimes yells at her adult sons and her mother and her sons argue back, but *"my mother doesn't argue. . . . She says nothing"* (p 665, Pyke, 1999).

Thinking Critically

Based on the differences between collectivist and individualistic older parents, which type of older parent do you think you will be? Also, do you have older grandparents or great grandparents that need assistance from their adult children? If so, are you able to determine whether these older family members have individualistic or collectivistic values?

The Challenges Associated with Providing Care for Elderly Parents

We will now consider varying aspects related to providing care for aging parents. As you will see, characteristics of aging parents as well as of their middle-aged (or older) children influence who takes on the role of providing care for elderly parents. The personalities of both generations also influence the dynamics between them.

Who Are the Caregivers of Elderly Parents? First, it is important to emphasize that not all older persons require assistance with the tasks of daily living. Second, older persons are more likely to be in a role whereby they are coming to the aid of their adult children, rather than receiving assistance from them (Kelly & Kropf, 1995).

Third, when elderly parents become frail or suffer from disabilities, their children do not necessarily take on the caregiver role. In the United States, the first choice related to the care provision of their parents by the majority of adults is to provide no care. The second choice of adults faced with their parents' need for care is to designate one child as the caregiver. The third choice for parental care is for siblings to share the responsibilities related to the care of an elderly parent. Furthermore, whether a child takes on the caregiver role or shares parental care with siblings is affected by a number of child and parent characteristics (Checkovich & Stern, 2002).

Child Characteristics That Influence Decisions Regarding Parental Care. Characteristics of the child that influence whether or not that person will become a caregiver of an aging parent include geographic location, employment, age, and gender. The further children live from their parents the less likely they are to provide care, although modern technologies as simple as the telephone and cheaper and faster forms of travel have made it increasingly possible for children to provide some form of long-term care from a considerable distance. Another influence of whether or not children provide direct care for their parents is related to their work responsibilities. Less care is devoted to parental care by children who work. The age of the children is another factor that impacts the decision of whether or not they will assume the caregiver role, with older children less likely to be in that role than younger children. The link between older children's decreased likelihood of becoming caregivers might reflect situations in which frailty or disability is more common among the oldest of the elderly population whose oldest children are likely to be elderly themselves. Finally, all things being equal, women provide considerably more care of aging parents than do men. Both daughters and daughters-in-law are more likely to assume the role of caregiver of older parents than are sons or sons-in-law (Checkovich & Stern, 2002).

Child Versus Spousal Care. In the United States, women are more likely than are men to take on the responsibilities of caring for their aging parents, but spouses more frequently become caregivers than do adult children. Because women typically outlive their husbands, older fathers who become ill, frail, or disabled, typically have wives who provide the care they require. Older women who become ill, frail, or disabled, however, are more likely to be widows. Therefore, older fathers who require assistance with the tasks of daily living are likely to be cared for by their wives, and older mothers in that same situation are more likely to be cared for by their daughters or daughters-in-law (Checkovich & Stern, 2002). Finally, the "sandwich" generation has been conceptualized as middle-aged adult children who are simultaneously involved in the raising of their dependent children and providing care for their frail, elderly parents. In reality, such a combination of dependency is very unusual. Actually, those adults who become caregivers of their aging parents are usually in late mid-life or early old age and typically do not have dependent children. There are exceptions, of course, when caregivers of older parents have adult children who continue to be partly dependent on their parents (Grundy & Henretta, 2006). Moreover, with the increase of grandparents caring for their grandchildren (Roche, 2000), it is likely that many of these older adults might be faced with the need to also provide care for their aging parents.

Parental Characteristics That Influence Decisions Regarding Parental Care. The characteristics of parents that influence whether or not they will be cared for by their children include marital status, level of education, the number of children they have and the presence or absence of a disability. Married parents are less likely to receive direct care from their children than are parents who are not married, which reflects the tendency of spouses to take on the role of caregiver for their spouses who are ill or disabled. More educated parents also are less likely to have children in the role of caregivers because each year of parental education decreases the amount of long-term care provided by children.

The relation between parental education and decreased care by children might reflect the link between education and income. Parents with more education typically have higher incomes and are, therefore, better able to provide for their own care by funding in-home care, opting to pay for institutionalized services, or living in a retirement community that offers appropriate services. Finally, the level of parental need as well as the presence of children to meet these needs affect the decisions that children make related to parental care. That children consider parental need in making caregiving decisions is reflected in findings that parents with disabilities receive more assistance from children than do parents without disabilities. When there are several children in the family that can divide the caregiver responsibilities among themselves, those children are more likely to provide direct care for their parents. In this situation, less care is provided by each individual child but more total care is received by the parents in comparison to families where there are fewer children (Checkovich & Stern, 2002).

Reactions of Caregivers to the Demands of Caring for Elderly Parents. The literature confirms that the care of elderly parents has negative effects on the caregivers, who show more financial, physical, and emotional strains than do noncaregivers. Also, caring for one's elderly parents is not a homogeneous experience but varies according to gender and residential status. Because women provide more intensive personal care than do men, they tend to experience more problems and strains related to caregiving than do men (Braus, 1998; Clyburn, Stones, & Hadjistavropoulos, 2000).

The Stresses of Caregivers. One example of the effects of stress on caregivers of their parents was shown by Braus (1998), who documented that family caregivers often must juggle work responsibilities and stretch their finances while dealing with the additional stress of caring for an elderly parent. Braus found that these caregivers benefit from informal supports provided by family and friends and that they are most in need of the kind of support that allows them to catch up on needed rest. Another example of the stresses associated with providing care for a parent was provided by Clyburn et al. (2000) who studied the stresses incurred by family caregivers of persons with Alzheimers' disease. These researchers found that a higher frequency of disturbing behaviors exhibited by the family member in their care, combined with low informal help from family and friends, was related to a higher burden for the caregiver. Furthermore, caregivers of family members exhibiting more disturbing behaviors and functional limitations received less informal help from family and friends.

Adaptation to the Role of Caregiver. Although the stresses related to assumption of the role of caregiver of one's parents has received much research attention, it is important to emphasize that the coping behaviors of these caregivers varies. For example, many caregivers report that being in the caregiver role provides personal meaning for them. Noonan, Tennstedt, and Rebelsky (1996) interviewed caregivers of elderly family members in an attempt to discern the meaning of the experience on a personal level. The results of these interviews revealed several common ways in which caregivers were able to find meaning in their caregiver roles, including: (a) gratification and satisfaction with the caregiver role, (b) a sense of family responsibility/reciprocity, (c) the friendship and company that caregiving offered, and (d) a commitment to doing what needs to be done. Less common themes that emerged from this investigation were having the ability to express a caring personality, experiencing personal growth, and having an improved relationship with the elderly parent.

Interventions That Support and Provide Relief for Caregivers. As noted in the foregoing discussion, being in the caregiver role potentially contributes to the caregiver's personal development. Nevertheless, the responsibilities associated with this role sometimes detrimentally impact the psychological well-being of the caregiver and the relationships of older parents and their children. Whether assuming the role of caregiver of one's parents has a positive or negative impact on individual development and intergenerational relationships depends on whether or not caregivers receive the necessary support to effectively carry out their caregiver responsibilities. As noted by Braus (1998), caregivers of aging parents greatly benefit from support from other family members and friends.

Thinking Critically

Were you surprised to learn that the experience of caring for one's parents might, despite the stresses involved, contribute to the development of a caregiver's coping strategies? In what ways do you think that the development of coping strategies associated with caring for one's parents might influence the ongoing development of the adult child?

THE DEATH OF AN OLDER PARENT

Most research on the effects of parental death has been concerned with the impact of a parent's death on the lives of minor children. Actually, the death of a parent is much more likely to occur when one is an adult than when one is a child. Even though adults are not as dependent on their parents as are children, the loss of a parent during adulthood is a significant loss due to the importance of the parent–child relationship at any age. Relationships with parents have unique symbolic importance for adult children because of special aspects of the parent–child bond that set it apart from other types of kinship relations. Parents socialize the person during childhood and help shape the person's definition of self. Furthermore, the parental influence continues to be important throughout adulthood because social interaction patterns learned during childhood remain central to adult children's lives. As emphasized throughout this chapter, older parents and their middle-aged children typically remain in frequent contact with each other, share many values and attitudes, engage in mutual exchanges of support and services, and experience high levels of positive sentiment from one another (Umberson & Chen, 1994).

Changes in Family Interaction Patterns Following Parental Death

An example of the impact of parental death on the family interactions of adults can be observed in the changes in communication patterns between adult siblings following the death of a parent. Generally, the death of a parent negatively impacts the relationships adults have with their siblings. One of the roles that older parents (particularly mothers) play in their relationships with their adult children is that of kinkeeper. As noted in previous chapters, kinkeepers are responsible for getting families together for family social occasions, promoting cooperation among family members, and sharing news about family members' well-being. Although siblings typically rally following the death of a parent who has served as kinkeeper, after the initial period of grieving there tends to be a decline in sibling closeness and in some families a reactivation of childhood power struggles. Persons who have experienced the death of at least one parent are more likely to report that they do not get along with at least one sibling in comparison to persons with two living parents (Fuller-Thomson, 2000).

Thinking Critically

In your experience or awareness of the death of an older person (such as a grandparent), what have you observed regarding the effect of that family member's death on the relationships of his or her adult children?

The Legacy That Parents Leave for Their Adult Children and Their Grandchildren

Parents care for the well-being of their children throughout their lives and toward the end of life, they anticipate the impact of their life and death on their adult children and consider the legacy that they will leave for them. Leaving a legacy for one's children and grandchildren consists of three distinct but overlapping categories, including biological legacy, material legacy, and a legacy of values. Findings of Hunter and Rowles (2005) showed that aging parents identify with at least one form of legacy and the majority expressed all three types, with the legacy of values viewed as the most important form of legacy. Not only do aging parents typically contemplate the legacy they will leave for their children, there is evidence that the bond between parents and their children continue after the death of the parent. For example, in a study of bonds with living versus deceased parents, Shmotkin (1999) found that bond intensity for parents was not diminished by parental death. These findings suggest that the affective bonds of adult children toward their parents transcend parental death and mourning. An illustration of the legacy of a deceased parent, as well as the enduring bond between deceased parents and their children, is illustrated in the following statement from a woman whose father had died more than a decade earlier. This statement was in response to the question, "What do you consider to be the legacy your father left for you?"

> *The legacy my father left for me was his model of a way to live my own life. He was loving, kind, and fair to everyone. He didn't consider anyone better or beneath him but treated everyone as an equal. He also had integrity and was his own person, guided by his own moral compass. If I could pass those characteristics to my own children, that would be the greatest gift I could give them.*

SUMMARY

- In this chapter, we contemplated the ways in which the psychological and social development of middle-aged and older adults is influenced by their relationships with their parents, their children, and their grandchildren.
- We also considered the ways in which these relationships impact the family systems in which they occur. To gain a broad understanding of these interactions, we explored multigenerational relationships in diverse cultures within the United States as well as in cultures throughout the world.
- We found that considerable variability exists in the level of interdependence, living arrangements, and roles of older adults in relation to their adult children and grandchildren. Despite the diversity in intergenerational relationships, we have seen evidence that parent–child–grandchild relationships have a high priority in the lives of middle-aged and older adults in all walks of life.
- The intergenerational relationships examined in this chapter suggest that older adults experience continued parental imperatives that are rooted in the adult child's continued need for security and the older parent's enduring desire to protect the welfare of continuing generations of family.
- The significance of the parent–child bond was further exemplified by a discussion of the impact of parental death, which included an emphasis on the legacies that deceased parents leave for their children and grandchildren.

KEY TERMS

- filial piety
- kinkeeper
- second-generation fathers
- sense of despair
- sense of integrity
- skipped generation caregiving
- social anchorage
- social status transitions

USEFUL WEB SITES

The Iowa State University website
http://www.extension.iastate.edu/homefamily/aging/acap.htm

Information related to aging, including caregiving and financial planning is provided here. Topics also include lifetime relationships, tools for talking, strengthening later-life relationships, organizing records and documents, and talking about legal decisions in later life.

The Texas Cooperative Extension website
http://www.fcs.tamu.edu/families/aging/elder_care/index.php

This is an excellent site for obtaining information related to building positive relationships between adult children and their aging parents. Information is also available for older parents to help them build satisfactory relationships with their adult children. Among the issues addressed are attachment, conflict, filial maturity, and knowledge of parents' aging process.

Another useful resource for children of aging parents is the Mayo Clinic website
http://www.Mayoclinic.com.

This site provides answers to questions that adult children frequently have regarding their aging parents' health. An example of information found at this site is the article *"Aging Parents: Five Warning Signs of Health Problems."* This site also offers a free weekly newsletter and provides links to where to find other useful information, such as home health services, long-term care for parents, and home safety.

The Canadian Mental Health Association
http://www.cmha.ca/bins/index.asp

Information found here focuses on a variety of ways to promote mental health for aging persons and their adult children, including how to maintain quality in family relationships. There is also information related to adults providing caregiving for aging parents, and ways in which parent caregivers can take care of themselves. Referrals to other resources for additional help is also available.

Parenting Children with Special Needs

Objectives

After completing this chapter, you should be able to

- Apply child-first language when referring to children with exceptionalities.
- Describe the paradox of emotions that parents of children with impairments typically experience.
- Describe the social interactions of families who have children with autism.
- Identify the primary social problems experienced by children with ADHD and children with learning disabilities.
- Describe the challenges of parents who have children with physical impairments and discuss ways in which to assist these parents.
- Provide suggestions for helping parents of children with physical impairments meet the needs of their children.
- Discuss the unique challenges confronted by parents of children who have hearing impairments, including the decision that must be made early on and the differences in parenting a child who is deaf for parents who are also deaf in comparison to hearing parents.
- Identify the concerns that parents have for their children who are blind and provide recommendations for these parents regarding how to enhance their children's development.
- List the characteristics of "gifted families," identify the ways in which having a child who is gifted sometimes negatively affects family relationships, and describe positive ways for parents to interact with their gifted children.
- Describe the impact that a child's chronic illness has on family relationships and the home environment.

- Identify the unique challenges faced by low-income families of children who are chronically ill.
- Discuss ways parents might help their children cope with being ill, including coping with hospitalizations.

In this chapter, we will examine the lives of parents and their children who have exceptionalities or chronic illnesses. We will consider the changes that occur in the lives of parents who assume the role of caregivers for their children whose special needs require specialized care. We will also focus on the ways in which family interactions are impacted by the needs of children with various exceptionalities or chronic illnesses. Throughout all these discussions, recommendations will be provided for improving the lives of children with special needs and the parents who care for them.

PARENTING CHILDREN WHO HAVE EXCEPTIONALITIES

Whenever the development of a child deviates from the expected norm, that child is considered to be **exceptional**. Exceptionalities are classified either as **impairments** or as giftedness depending on the nature of the exceptionality. Children with impairments have physical, psychological, mental, intellectual, or medical conditions that make it difficult for them to learn and/or behave according to normal expectations. Children identified as **gifted** deviate from the norm in that their talents and/or academic capabilities exceed normal expectations. Children, whose developmental progress places them outside the realm of normal expectations, whether impaired or gifted, require special attention from parents, educators, and other professionals in order to realize their developmental capabilities (Chan, 2002).

The purpose of the following discussion is not to address all the exceptionalities of children with which parents contend, but rather to provide an overview of some of the common experiences of parents and their children with exceptionalities. The exceptionalities discussed in this chapter include mental and physical impairments, autism, attention deficit/hyperactivity disorder (ADHD), conduct disorders, learning disabilities (LDs), chronic illness, and giftedness. Although the parent–child relations associated with each of these exceptionalities will be presented separately, some children have a combination of exceptionalities such as mental and physical impairments, and parents of these children face multiple challenges. Furthermore, even though the needs of children with different exceptionalities vary, most children with exceptionalities need higher levels of understanding and patience from their parents, and many require specialized care. Thus, children with various exceptionalities challenge parents to gain an understanding of their special needs and to develop specific skills for caring for them. These parents also must learn to work with the professionals who provide specialized services for their children.

The Importance of Child-First Language

The first thing that parents should be aware of in addressing the specialized needs of their children who have exceptionalities is the importance of seeing the child first and the exceptionality second. Rehabilitation professionals have been strongly encouraged to adopt **person-first language** that focuses on the person rather than the exceptionality. This perspective helps parents of children who have impairments to understand the whole child. The adoption of person-first language also assists parents in focusing on the things a child *can do* or is able to learn, rather than the things a child has difficulty in achieving or cannot do. For parents of children who are gifted, seeing the child first helps them to appreciate that, although their child has special gifts and talents, that child also has needs and abilities that fall within the normal range. Perceiving the child before the exceptionality is reflected in the terminology that a parent uses (and teaches others to use) in referring to their child. Terminology that places the child before the exceptionality consists of language like *the child who is blind* rather than *the blind child* and the *child who has a mental impairment* rather than *a mentally impaired child* (Lynch, Thuli, & Groombridge, 1994).

Parental Reactions to Having a Child With a Disability

Parents of children with disabilities experience difficult feelings whether they are aware of their children's impairments from the beginning or slowly become aware that their children are not developing as expected. On learning of their child's impairment, parental adjustment is required to accept the reality of having a child who has a disability. Some feelings that are common during this adjustment stage include grief over the loss of the child parents expected to have, feeling guilty about their disappointment, and being resentful of the time and energy that caring for their child will require (see Figure 11.1). Although the reactions to learning that their child has a disability are initially negative, parents typically face up to the challenges connected with that role. In their acceptance of their role as parents of exceptional children, parents undergo tremendous development as they gain knowledge of the skills necessary to meet their children's special needs. Furthermore, parents typically report that their children with special needs have a positive impact on their families. For example, in a recent study, Taunt (2002) asked questions about perceptions and experiences of families of children with developmental disabilities. One of the questions that parents were asked was what effects their child with disabilities had on them, the child's siblings, and extended family members. In their responses, these parents reported a range of positive perceptions and experiences for themselves as well as for other family members. Furthermore, most of these parents said that they had positive perceptions of the future for their child and their family.

1. A feeling of devastation, of being overwhelmed, and of being traumatized
2. Feelings of shock, denial, numbness, and disbelief
3. Feelings of confusion when attempting to cope
4. Feelings of a sense of loss of the "hoped for child"
5. Feelings of grief similar to those experienced at the death of a loved one
6. Feelings that future hopes are challenged or destroyed
7. Feelings of guilt, responsibility, and shame
8. Strong feelings of anger toward the medical staff involved with the child
9. Feelings of what-if's, such as what if the child dies
10. Lowered self-esteem and parental efficacy as providers and protectors
11. Strained marital and family relations
12. Disruption in family routines

FIGURE 11.1 Typical Reactions of Parents to the Birth of a Child With a Disability
Source: Adapted from Barnett, D., Clements, M., Kaplan-Estrin, M., & Fialka, J. (2003). Building new dreams: Supporting parents' adaptation to their child with special needs. *Infants and Young Children, 16(3)*, 184.

THE ROLE OF PARENTS WHOSE CHILDREN HAVE EXCEPTIONALITES

As they undertake the growth required to become skilled parents of exceptional children, parents typically report that the role brings joy and satisfaction in addition to the obvious adjustments. The road from disappointment and self-blame to joy and acceptance, however, is not an easy one. These parents must (a) learn to manage internal opposing forces between loving the child as he or she is and wanting to erase the disability, (b) deal with the child's incurability while pursuing solutions, and (c) maintain hopefulness for their child's future while being given negative messages and battling their own fears. Due to their conflicting emotions, much effort is required in the development of their parental role. In addition to learning to provide the care their children require, these parents must find a way to develop hopeful life trajectories for themselves and their children. Despite the effort involved, there is evidence that these parents are able to meet the challenges they encounter (Larson, 1998; Vacca, 2006). Furthermore, parents who are primary caregivers for a child with a disability typically identify positive aspects of being in that role. For example, Berg-Weger, McGartland, and Tebb (2001) found that caregiving of children with exceptionalities can be a rewarding experience. Positive experiences associated with this caregiver role were also reported by Schwartz (2003), who found that parents reported a sense of gratification related to being able to fulfill their parental duties and also from leaning about themselves. Some of these parents described caring for their child with a disability as a commitment that gave their life content and meaning.

Factors That Contribute to Parental Gratification. Both child and parent characteristics, as well as the parental level of emotional strain, have been linked to gratification from caregiving. Interestingly, younger and more disadvantaged parents (unemployed or bad health) who care for their children with disabilities report more satisfaction in that role than do older, more advantaged parents. For disadvantaged mothers, for example, caring for their children with special needs becomes a career and contributes to a sense of self-actualization. Moreover, it is possible that learning to cope with difficult situations contribute to these parents becoming increasingly aware of their inner resources. Parents with lower levels of emotional stress also experience more gratification from carrying out the responsibilities related to the caregiving role. In contrast, parents who experience emotional strains (guilt, shame, sadness, anger, and stress) report less gratification in their caregiver role (Schwartz, 2003).

Parental Advocates for Their Children with Exceptionalities

Although all parents work with professionals to meet the varied educational and health needs of their children, parents of children who have exceptionalities work with more professionals due to their children's need for greater assistance. In the United States, all children with exceptionalities are entitled to receive assistive services, and their parents have the opportunity and challenge of working with professionals to determine which services best meet their children's needs. The **Individuals with Disabilities Education Act (IDEA)**, a law that has been in effect since 1975, was reauthorized by Congress in 2004. The IDEA is based on six basic guidelines, which include the right to (a) a free and appropriate public education, (b) appropriate evaluations, (c) an Individual Education Program (IEP), (d) be educated in the Least Restrictive Environment (LRE), (e) parent and student participation, and (f) procedural due process (Anderson, 2007). Guidelines for parent–teacher collaboration, to assist them in achieving the mutual goal of assisting children with special needs, are shown in Figure 11.2.

Although the guidelines of IDEA are consistent from state to state, each state is charged with insuring that the process they use is consistent with the federal law. The role of parents in this process is to advocate for the needs of their children. As their children's advocates, parents of children with special needs are true partners in their children's education experiences. Being advocates for their children, however, is sometimes challenging or even intimidating. Furthermore, some parents in that position are shy, some speak a different language, and some feel that they are not equal to the professionals on the team. Even though some parents might not realize it, every time they stand up for their children's rights or speak up for their needs, they model an essential skill of advocacy. Parents are equal to the professionals in those meetings in that the professionals are qualified by virtue of their specialized education and parents are qualified by virtue of their role as their children's designated advocates. Furthermore,

1. It is important for parents to encourage their children to make choices, set priorities, and make decisions regarding everyday activities such as what to wear, which foods to eat for snacks, after school activities, and so on.
2. Parents should inform their children of the consequences of their choices. For example, "If you choose fruit or cheese for snacks, you will be making a healthy choice."
3. Children with disabilities benefit when their parents help them to identify interests, strengths, and needs. For children with severe disabilities, parents may infer preferences or interests based on observation of their behavior.
4. It is helpful if parents explain to their children that a goal is something to be achieved, and that barriers sometimes get in the way of achieving goals. Then, parents can help their children so they can overcome the barriers by learning something new, or changing something in the environment.
5. If parents teach their children how to use logical problem solving, their children can participate in discussions regarding ways to solve the obstacles they confront. Children might also lead problem-solving discussions.
6. It is essential that parents and professionals place children at the center of goal setting, action planning, and progress monitoring activities. Even if children require extensive support to complete these activities, this approach lets the child decide on the course of action and allows them to monitor their own progress.
7. Parents and professionals need to support a child's need to rethink a goal when progress is slow or minimal. In this case the child, parent, and other involved professionals might adjust or rework the action plan if the child still wants to pursue the goal.
8. At the end of the process, parents should be sure to ask their children how they feel about the goals and what they have learned.

FIGURE 11.2 A Model for Parent–Teacher Collaboration

Source: Adapted from "A Model for Parent-Teacher Collaboration in Young Children with Disabilities," by S. H. Lee, 2006, *Teaching Exceptional Children, 38(3),* pp. 36–41.

when their children observe how effectively their parents express needs and opinions during IEP meetings, they learn a valuable skill that will be important for their future, when they must advocate for themselves (Anderson, 2007).

The Distinction Between Needs and Services. In considering ways in which to advocate for their children with special needs, it is important for parents to understand that a service is not a need. According to Luker and Luker (2007), parents frequently ask professionals how they can obtain specific services for their children with statements such as "My son/daughter needs an aide, more occupational therapy, a smaller class, and so on." When parents state their requests in this fashion, they run the risk of being told that a school will not provide a service. The problem with this approach is that needs are being confused with services. When preparing for IEP meetings, parents might keep in mind that special education is a needs-driven service delivery system. A need, simply stated, is a problem that requires that an action be taken, either by the child or another person helping the child. If parents are able to explain their child's problem, they and the professionals working with them are better prepared to work on resolving the problem, and there might be a variety of ways in which the problem might be approached. For example, a parent might say that a child needs to have friends. Based on being made aware of that need, the IEP team is better able to follow through with services to help the child meet that need. Before providing services, however, they need to determine which services would best meet the need of that particular child. For example, they might explore whether the child lacks social skills, receives segregated educational services, has intensive personal care needs that make scheduling social activities difficult, or lacks access to general community interactive experiences.

What This Means for Professionals. Parents of children with exceptionalities need to understand that it is always appropriate to advocate for their children the best that they can, even if they make mistakes. For parents who are interested in advocating more effectively it is helpful if they learn about the system and the process of special education. Community Parent Resource Centers, for example, offer free workshops about special education law and parent advocacy. Also, communication skills are an important part of advocacy. Useful communication tips include self-awareness, including recognition of one's own communication attitude (for example understanding one's level of receptiveness), listening as well as talking, and asking questions (especially of the person most likely to have the information or expertise the parent needs). Ultimately, parental advocacy is all about making sure children receive the services and education to which they are entitled. Furthermore, parents' valuable perspectives can help the IEP team make decisions that will benefit those children now and in the future (Anderson, 2007).

Thinking Critically

Were you surprised to learn about the types of skills that parents of exceptional children need to develop in order to effectively advocate for their children? If you were a parent in an IEP meeting, acting as an advocate for your child(ren), what questions would you ask?

PARENTING CHALLENGES RELATED TO SPECIFIC CHILD EXCEPTIONALITIES

In the upcoming discussions, we will focus on parenting challenges related to caring for children with specific exceptionalities. As you will see, many of these challenges are common for all parents, a number of them are similar for parents of children with varying exceptionalities, and some of them are specific to a child's particular exceptionality. We will begin by discussing the lives of families that have a child who is mentally impaired. We will then focus on the challenges related to parents and their children with autism. Next, we will examine the lives of families of children who have activity or conduct disorders. After that, we will consider the family relationships of children with learning disorders.

Parenting Children with Mental Impairments

A child with a **mental impairment** is a slow learner in all, or almost all, intellectual pursuits. In young children, mental impairment is frequently labeled as **pervasive developmental delay** to allow for the possibility that the child will catch up to normal, age-appropriate development. Pervasive developmental delay is characterized by patterns of impediment in the development of communicative, social, and cognitive skills that arise in the first year of life. A common challenge for parents of a child with cognitive deficits is changes in sibling relationships when there are younger siblings in the family that developmentally overtake that child. For example, a 3-year-old child with a mental impairment, who still wets the bed, is likely to object to wearing diapers at night "like the baby." Parents of children with mental impairments report also that they experience stress and difficulties in coping with many of the everyday situations related to caring for their children. Although parents of children with mental impairments encounter different challenges, a primary concern for most of these parents is the treatment and education of their children (Bower & Hayes, 1998).

The Alignment of Parental Care to the Special Needs of Children with Mental Impairments. An important first step in matching parental care to the special needs of a child who is mentally impaired comes with the recognition, and acceptance, of the child's impairment. When parents initially fail to recognize that their child has a mental impairment, they might regard that child as fussy, disinterested, or unresponsive and react by being punitive or less spontaneous toward the child. In contrast, when parents are aware of their child's mental impairment from the beginning, they have an advantage in that they are more prepared to respond to their child in appropriate ways (Volkmar, Cook, & Pomeroy, 1999). Furthermore, parents' professional involvement in their children's education and other treatment contributes to higher levels of functional progress for their children. Unfortunately, not all parents believe that professional intervention can help their children who have mental impairments. In a study of the attitudes of mothers of children with developmental delays, Smith, Oliver, and Boyce (2000) found that the extent to which the parent views the child's condition as controllable or noncontrollable is related to (a) the type and amount of treatment the parent seeks and implements, and (b) the level of parental involvement with the child. For example, parents in the study who believed that their child(ren)'s improvement was controllable were more responsive to their child(ren) and more involved in their child(ren)'s treatment.

Parenting the Child Who Is Autistic

Children with autism have impairments in social interaction, language as used in social interaction, and/or symbolic or imaginative play. Although there are variations, characteristics of children with **autism** include some combination of those listed in Figure 11.3. Due to their cognitive deficits, children with autism experience a prolonged infant–toddler stage that creates practical problems related to teaching self-help behaviors and managing difficult behavior. As a result, living with a child who is autistic is not easy, and the combination and severity of their child's behavior and communication deficits presents these parents with unique challenges (Dunn, Burbine, & Bowers, 2001; Volkmar et al., 1999). Furthermore, because children with autism typically appear normal, strangers might not realize that a child with autism has a disability and might blame the child's parents when the child publicly displays aggressive or bizarre behavior. Additionally, parents and other family members frequently become aware that the child shows precocity in memory, artistic tendencies, or mathematical skills, which sometimes leads

1. The inability to relate to other people in an ordinary manner, including an absence of social smiling, a preference for interaction with objects rather than people, and the absence of distress when a parent leaves the room.
2. Language deficits, including mutism, echolalia, noncommunicative speech, pronoun reversals, and immature grammar.
3. Sensory impairment characterized by over- or under-responding to noise, touch, and visual stimuli.
4. Abnormal affect, including extreme or no fear reactions, tantrums, and uncontrolled giggling and crying.
5. Self-stimulation, including spinning self and objects, repetitive hand movements, rocking, humming, and so on.
6. Inappropriate play, including self-stimulation.
7. Extreme resistance to environmental changes, food, everyday schedule, familiar routes, and so on.

FIGURE 11.3 Characteristics of Children with Autism

Source: Adapted from "Behavioral Assessment and Curriculum Development," in R. Koegel, A. Rincover, and A. Egel (Eds.), *Educating and Understanding Autistic Children* (pp. 1–32), by J. Johnson and R. Koegel, 1982, San Diego, CA: College-Hill Press.

to unrealistic expectations for the child. These idealistic hopes contribute to feelings of disappointment or blame as parents are consistently confronted by their child's lack of progress. A further challenge for parents is that children with autism typically show little affection, instead appearing aloof. Their parents, therefore, receive little reinforcement from these children for the care they provide them. For all these reasons, parents whose children are autistic endure more stress than do parents of children with other disabilities. The strain experienced by these parents comes from dealing with the difficult behaviors of their children as well as from the reactions of others to them and their children. In response to these challenges, families with a child who has autism often become socially isolated, and the more stress that is experienced the more socially isolated these families become (Dunn et al., 2001).

Assistance for Parents of Children with Autism. Although children with autism will inevitably have a significant effect on their families, the nature and extent of that effect can be guided by awareness and sensitivity on the part of friends and professionals. For example, social support has been found to be an important moderator of parental stress. Practitioners would, for that reason, be well advised to facilitate social support for these parents. In addition to needing social support, securing appropriate direct services for their child with autism is a high-priority need for parents, and a goal that will typically override all other family considerations. Finding suitable educational, residential, and treatment programs is of such urgency that parents have observed that, until they had identified an appropriate school or program for their child with autism, they were unable to adequately address their own needs and the needs of their other family members (Dunn et al., 2001).

Parenting Children with Activity/Conduct Disorders and Children with Learning Disabilities

Although attention deficit disorders, learning disabilities, and conduct disorders are distinctive exceptionalities, children with these exceptionalities all face some similar challenges. Because their exceptionalities are invisible, parents and other adults frequently react negatively toward them and/or hold them responsible for behaviors that are beyond their control. Moreover, there are high incidents of co-occurrence for these exceptionalities. For instance, about half the children with attention deficits with hyperactive disorder (AD/HD) also have a learning disability. Furthermore, conduct problems and hyperactivity/attention problems frequently occur together.

Parenting Children with Attention Deficit/Hyperactivity Disorder. Children with **attention deficit/hyperactivity disorder (ADHD)** have difficulty in focusing their attention, are easily distracted, display impulsive behavior, have trouble waiting their turn when playing games with other children, and tend to begin but not finish numerous activities (American Psychiatric Association, 1994). They also are unable to remain seated or calm for periods of time that are perceived as normal for other children their age. These children are also at risk for problems in relationships with parents, teachers, siblings, and peers. The primary social problem experienced by highly active children is that others perceive them in negative ways (Cunningham & Boyle, 2002; Podolski, 2001). Due to their difficulty in sitting still, paying attention, and following instructions, children with ADHD are typically placed in special education classrooms. They also are frequently prescribed stimulant medication that is often effective for helping them manage their behavior (Thiruchelvam, Charach, & Schachar, 2001).

The reactions of parents and other adults to children with ADHD. Whether the negative behaviors associated with children who are highly active are qualities directly attributable to their high activity levels is debatable. Researchers have suggested that the undesirable traits credited to children who are highly active are related to the unconstructive responses of their parents and other adults who lack an understanding of the special needs of these children. For instance, their mothers and fathers tend to be directive, intrusive, and authoritarian. These parents also tend to get into power struggles with their children and appear to be hostile and unresponsive to their children's needs and interests (Cunningham & Boyle, 2002; Harrison & Sofronoff, 2002; Podolski, 2001). One of the reasons that parents are likely to react negatively toward their children with ADHD is that these parents have higher levels of stress and depression than do other parents (Harrison & Sofronoff, 2002). Another explanation is that parents of children with exceptionalities are more likely to hold their children responsible for their problem behaviors when the exceptionality is characterized as a behavioral excess (Chavira, Lopez, & Blacher, 2000). When parents have higher levels of stress and depression and also hold their children responsible for problem behaviors, they tend to respond to unwanted behaviors with controlling negative suggestions and decreased positive or preventive suggestions. Furthermore, parents respond more negatively to their sons who have ADHD in comparison to their daughters with ADHD. For example, it has been shown that mothers of girls with ADHD give more rewards for positive behavior than do mothers of boys with ADHD (Cunningham & Boyle, 2002).

What This Means for Professionals. Although parents of children with ADHD might be expected to be challenged by their children's higher than usual activity levels, it is important that they not develop a pattern of disapproving responses. Consistent pessimistic responses to children contribute to a negative cycle of parent–child interactions and to less positive developmental progress for children. Thus, it is helpful when parents of children with ADHD consciously work on ways to prevent the development of negative parent–child interactions. One approach for helping parents to interact more positively with their children with ADHD is suggested by the findings of Podolski (2001). In a study of parents of

1. Spend at least 15 minutes per day doing what the child would like to do such as playing a game or reading a story.
2. Do not express disapproval of the child's behavior unless some extreme behavior occurs.
3. Establish daily routines that place highly active children in an active role and allow their high energy levels to be put to constructive use.
4. Assist highly active children to create order in their lives by providing structure, including:
   a. Places for books, toys, and clothes that the child can easily access (such as child-level hooks for coats and hats), and
   b. Regular times for meals, snacks, playtime, bathtime, and bedtime.

FIGURE 11.4 Developing Positive Interactions with Children who are Highly Active.
Source: Adapted from *Attention Deficit Hyperactivity Disorder: A Handbook for Diagnosis and Treatment*, by R. A. Barkley, 1990, New York: Guilford Press.

children with ADHD, Podolski found that parental coping through the use of reframing (thinking about problems as challenges that could be overcome) is related to higher satisfaction in the parental role for both mothers and fathers of children with ADHD. Recognizing that parents, who have developed a harmful interaction pattern with their highly active children, might need assistance in establishing harmonious relationships with them, Barkley (1990) developed specific guidelines designed to interrupt the negative cycle of parent–child interactions. These guidelines, outlined in Figure 11.4, reflect the need for highly active children to (a) have positive interactions with their parents, (b) be engaged in carrying out constructive activities, and (c) have structure in their daily routines to increase the predictability in their lives.

Parenting Children with Learning Disabilities. As prevously mentioned, about half of the children with attention deficit hyperactivity disorder (AD/HD) also have a learning disability. In general, a child with a **learning disability** (LD) has at least a normal intelligence level but falls markedly behind in a specific area of learning. A learning disability is part of a larger diagnosis of underachievement, which might represent a number of different areas, including difficulty in perceiving, processing, storing, and understanding information. The problems that children with LDs experience are compounded by the difficulties they encounter in their social relations. In comparison to children without learning disabilities, they have fewer and less stable friendships, and the friends they have are likely to also have LDs, or to be younger. With regard to friendship quality, children with LDs have higher levels of conflict, lower levels of validation, and more problems with relationship repair in comparison to children without LDs. Two of the reasons that children with LDs have trouble in

This father is reading with his son and encouraging his son's efforts to read on his own, both of which are very helpful for children with learning disabilities.

social relations are that, in comparison to children without LDs, they have more difficulty in the accurate perception of social cues (Sprouse, Hall, Webster, & Bolen, 1998). Findings by Bradlow, Kraus, and Hayes (2003) have demonstrated that children with LDs also have greater difficulty perceiving sentences when there is background noise.

Children with learning disabilities at home and at school. Even though professionals recommend that parents of children with LDs provide a supportive environment for their children, the reality is that the home environments of these children are typically less, rather than more, supportive. Parents of children with LDs tend to establish a more rigid home environment, wherein they demand more achievement from their children with LDs, while expecting less personal growth. Moreover, the interpersonal relationships in these families tend to be more conflicted than relationships in other families (Sprouse et al., 1998). Children with LDs also frequently encounter demanding contexts in school, because they must expend considerable energy attending to and accomplishing schoolwork that is much easier for their peers. The distractibility and impulsivity exhibited by these children might stem from fatigue, or reflect their disappointment with themselves in trying to master tasks that are difficult for them to perform.

What This Means for Professionals. Parents and professionals should be aware that children with LDs are at risk for developing low self-esteem. Because other individuals tend to be annoyed by their behavior and respond to it disapprovingly, this sets up a negative cycle with playmates, teachers, and parents. Hence, children with LDs need the encouragement of their parents to persevere in difficult situations. Through parental encouragement, these children develop higher self-esteem, and a positive self-esteem could be an important factor in motivating them to persevere when confronted with difficult tasks (Jerome, Fujiki, Brinton, & James, 2002). Although children with LDs encounter more challenges in making and keeping friends, improvement in social skills has been found to enhance their friendships (Wiener & Schneider, 2002). It is also important for their parents to understand the difficulty that their children face in reading social cues and understanding conversation when there is background noise. These parents might be encouraged to be more patient when their children have difficulty in picking up social cues. Also, these parents can help their children to better understand what is being said if they limit background noise when they are speaking with their children (for example, turning down the television or stereo).

Thinking Critically

If you were speaking to a group of parents whose children had either LD or ADHD, what would you say to them about the common needs of their children? Also, how would you address the importance of promoting the self-esteem of these children?

Children with Conduct Problems and Their Parents. Children with **conduct disorders** have repetitive and persistent patterns of behaviors that violate societal norms or rules, such as acts of aggression to people and/or animals, and/or the destruction of property. As noted earlier, conduct problems in children and hyperactivity/attention problems frequently occur together, although most children show decreasing frequencies of both problems as a function of age. For children whose conduct problems do not decrease with age, there is a risk of later serious antisocial behavior (Nagin & Trembley, 2001). Whether children develop conduct problems, as well as whether these problems decrease with age, have been linked to several family and parental characteristics. Brophy and Dunn (2002), who studied mothers of "hard to manage" children, found that these mothers were less involved with their children and less focused on their children's activities in comparison to mothers of children who did not have conduct disorders. These mothers also tended to use more frequent negative control toward their children. The link between negative control (punitive discipline) and child conduct disorders was also noted by Shaw, Lacourse, and Nagin (2005). These researchers also identified a number of other factors associated with child conduct disorders, including low maternal education, overcrowding in the home, and teenage parenthood. Maternal depression has also been consistently linked with child behavior problems (Shaw, Bell, & Gilliam, 2000). Another contributor to children's development of conduct disorders is exposure to violence between their parents, which is a common experience for large numbers of children, because approximately 15.5 million children are exposed to interparent physical violence annually (McDonald, Jouriles, & Ramisetty-Mikler, 2006). Furthermore, approximately one-third of the children who are brought to women's domestic abuse shelters exhibit conduct disorders (Ware et al., 2001).

Help for children with conduct disorders and their parents. Although children with conduct disorders need specialized care, many of them would also benefit from intervention designed to help their parents in (a) eliminating interpersonal violence, and (b) learning to use effective child management skills. With this goal in mind, an intervention known as Project SUPPORT was developed by McDonald (2006) to help battered women make the transition from women's shelters to homes away from their abusive partners. This intervention approach included two primary components: (a) providing practical and emotional support to these mothers as they made this transition, and (b) teaching them to put into practice a set of child management and nurturing skills that have been shown to be effective in the treatment of children's conduct problems. The results of this intervention was a dramatic reduction in mothers' use of aggressive childrearing methods and a corresponding reduction in their children's conduct problems.

What This Means for Professionals. The previous discussion of the difficulties faced by children with conduct disorders suggests that they are in need of professional intervention. It is equally important, though, to consider how dependent these children's behavior problems are on the family environments in which they are living and interacting. As suggested by Gardner (1994), the promotion of "harmonious cycles" of family interaction might hold the promise for helping children with conduct disorders to have better social relationships and more satisfactory lives.

Thinking Critically

After learning about the family lives of children with conduct disorders, what would you (as a professional) recommend to parents of these children?

Parenting Children with Physical Impairments

Children with **physical impairments** have congenital birth defects, diseases such as cerebral palsy or muscular dystrophy, or have been involved in accidents that have caused them to have impaired motor control. Due to their functional limitations, these children receive a wide variety of rehabilitation services. The mobilization of family resources to allow parents to arrange for medical attention, work with rehabilitation teams, and assist their children with daily living, however, is often accomplished by diverting resources from other purposes. Consequently, physical impairments of children are frequently associated with a variety of potentially negative outcomes in families, including increased time spent on child care and housework, decreased maternal employment (Lukemeyer, Meyers, & Smeeding, 2000), and increased financial strain. Furthermore, stressors affecting one family member have repercussions for other family members (Rogers & Hogan, 2003). Although these children receive an array of services, the caregiver and other family members are typically in need of social support.

Meeting the Needs of Parents and Their Children with Physical Impairments. Melissa Crisp (2001), an active teenager with cerebral palsy, provides several guidelines for parents to remember when interacting with and guiding their children with physical impairments. First, she advises parents to "let go a little," emphasizing that, in addition to a need to experience their parents' love, all children need to experience as normal a childhood as possible. According to Melissa, having a normal childhood means being involved in after-school activities, doing household chores, going to slumber parties, attending camp, participating in adapted sports, and, yes, even dating. Another guideline that Melissa has for parents of children with physical disabilities is to "remember the importance of mobility" for a child with an ambulatory limitation. To ensure the greatest level of mobility, Melissa emphasizes how critical it is for parents to select the appropriate mobility device (wheelchair, scooter, crutches, etc.). Melissa also suggests that parents of children with physical disabilities "take it easy" by practicing patience. She points out that absolutely nothing is more frustrating to the child with a disability than when parents become agitated because that child cannot perform a task with the speed and accuracy of a child who does not have a disability.

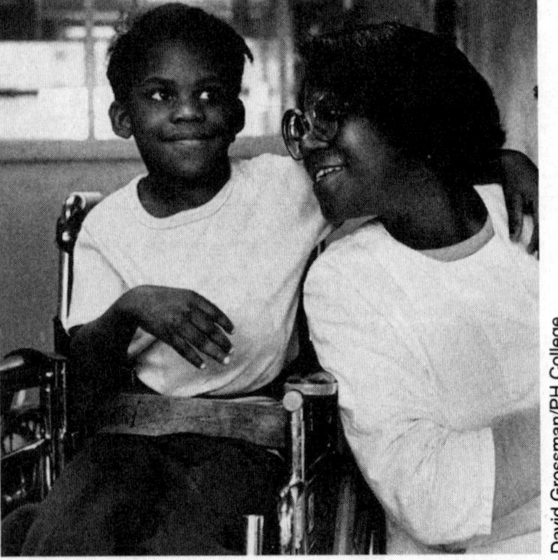

Being the parent of a child with a physical impairment requires providing the child with needed assistance while simultaneously recognizing and promoting the child's capabilities.

David Grossman/PH College.

The next piece of advice Melissa offers parents of children with physical impairments is to "teach their children and themselves about the disability." She points out that people with disabilities are typically willing to discuss the challenges they face. Through talking with other individuals with impairments, as well as with parents of children with disabilities, parents are better prepared to teach their children about what it means to have exceptionalities. Still another recommendation that Melissa has for parents is to work to "increase public awareness" of what it means to have an impairment. She calls attention to the fact that many people do not understand how to react to individuals with disabilities and frequently feel uncomfortable or embarrassed by their own curiosity. Melissa suggests that by speaking openly about their child's physical challenges, welcoming questions, and if possible using humor, parents can put others more at ease. According to Melissa, talking candidly about a child's special needs not only helps others gain a better understanding of the child's exceptionality but also shows children with obvious disabilities how to deal with strangers' questions.

Thinking Critically

What do you think qualifies Melissa as an expert in how to parent a child with a physical impairment? What insights do you think she can offer parents that others cannot?

The Selection of Standers for Children with Physical Disabilities. In the preceding discussion, Melissa emphasized that parents should pay particular attention to the choice of a mobility device for their children with physical disabilities. According to Warner (2007), with the exception of a wheelchair, there is no type of assistive technology that is more helpful to children and adults with physical impairment needs than a standing device. A **stander** is an alternative position device for an individual with a physical disability, which supports the person in a standing position. Even for children with physical disabilities who can stand and walk, many of them struggle to hold themselves up and usually do so with very poor posture. Because many different kinds of standers exist, and trying to find the best stander to meet a child's specific needs can be confusing, Warner recommends that parents consult different therapists who interact with their child. After determining the type of stander that their child needs, parents then need to seek out a supplier who is willing to work with them and their child's therapist to do trials of different types of standers. Because parents are able to see how comfortable the child is while they are in the stander and how quickly they become fatigued, it is important that they be involved in the selection process.

Social Support for Families: The Role of Grandparents. Although many families who have children with physical impairments do not have the level of support that they need, many others benefit from assistance from the child's grandparents. The role of grandmothers in these families is especially important because they tend to provide emotional support for family members. In recognition of the centrality of grandparents in families of children with physical impairments, Findler (2000) recommends that social workers, and other professionals working with these families, recognize grandparents among other service providers. For example, they might offer both parents and grandparents joint workshops designed to facilitate caregiving skills with children who have physical disabilities.

Parenting Children Who Have Sensory Impairments

We will now turn our attention to the lives of parents and their children who have profound sensory impairments. The descriptors of *blind* and *deaf* and of *visual* and *auditory impairment* will all be used in the upcoming discussions in recognition of the lack of agreement regarding the use of these terms.

Parents and Their Children Who Are Visually Impaired. A review of the research literature, focused on families with children who are visually impaired, shows that the experience of caring for a child who is blind is frequently stressful and can be challenging as well as threatening to family members. In a study of parents of children with visual impairments, Leyser and Heinze (2001) asked parents about the particular concerns they had that were related to their child's blindness. The primary concern voiced by these parents was anxiety regarding their child's future. Their apprehension regarding the future of their child with a visual impairment focused on uneasiness regarding the child's independence and ability to achieve, concerns related to their child's self-esteem, and worries about their child's future job opportunities. Another major concern, expressed by parents of a child with a visual impairment, was questions regarding their ability to provide for the needs of their child. Other concerns of these parents were finances, adequate services, and the effects of their child's disability on their other children.

Enhancing the development of children who are visually impaired. Although parents of children who are blind have a number of concerns about their children's future, and their ability to provide appropriate care for their children, there are a number of ways these parents might enhance their children's development. Mary Zabelski (2001), President of the National Association for Parents of Children with Visual Impairments (NAPVI), and a parent of a grown child who is blind, offers a number of recommendations regarding ways in which to encourage self-esteem in children who are visually impaired. Her first recommendation is that children with visual impairments be given opportunities to help others. Zabelski points out that most people want to help individuals who are blind and that children who are blind also need to have opportunities to help others. Zabelski shared a story about when her daughter brought her guide dog to a grade school where several other children who were blind could meet her and her dog. In that visit, her daughter demonstrated how she used her dog to assist her in daily tasks, explaining that first she had to be a

Scott Cunningham/Merrill.

The independence enjoyed by this child, who has a visual impairment, is crucial to the child's well-being.

good cane user. By her demonstration, Zabelski's daughter was able to provide other children with hope for their future and a belief in their ability to be independent.

Besides providing their children with opportunities to help other people, Zabelski emphasized the importance of parents giving children domestic responsibilities (such as putting toys away, walking the dog with parents, and setting the table) at a very early age. She stressed that a child's ability to perform small domestic chores might represent a critical step toward independence in later years. She, therefore, cautioned parents not to feel sorry for their children and not to always do everything for them because that attitude lowers the child's feelings of self-worth. Based on her belief that all children need structure and discipline, Zabelski advised parents to let their children with visual impairments know that they are expected to behave according to the rules of the family, just like their brothers and sisters. She pointed out that when parents have expectations of their child who is visually impaired that are similar to those they have for their other children, they show confidence in all their children. Finally, Zabelski suggested that when children with visual impairments are provided opportunities to demonstrate their capabilities in various areas, these incremental successes build on each other, leading to self-assurance and self-esteem.

Parenting Children Who Are Hearing Impaired. Of all the areas of childhood disability, deafness is probably the most confusing and controversial because the ability to speak is so closely connected in our minds with thought, communication, and intelligence. For children whose lack of hearing begins at a very early age, their most serious problem is not their hearing loss but rather their challenge to develop an adequate communication system. Furthermore, the means of communication chosen can profoundly affect almost every area of the child's life, including the hopes and expectations for the child, selection of educational and recreational programs, and how best to include the child in family communication.

The challenges for parents of children who have hearing impairments. Parents who have lived their entire lives using language are initially handicapped in their attempts to understand their child who is deaf. On the other hand, parents who are deaf themselves are better able to understand their child who is deaf and to teach that child valuable communication skills. In families where the parents are deaf, the vast majority of these parents communicate with each other and their children primarily in sign language. In contrast to parents who are deaf, fewer hearing parents use sign language with their child who is deaf and very few of those do so from the time of diagnosis. Because the majority of parents of children who are deaf are members of the hearing world, the decision regarding whether or not to learn to use and to teach sign language to their child must be addressed very early. There are differing beliefs regarding whether the child who is deaf should be taught sign language or be expected to learn to lip read and speak, but the reality is that not all individuals who are deaf can readily learn to lip read. On the other hand, studies have shown that children who are deaf learn sign language as easily as hearing children learn spoken language. Furthermore, sign language is more easily mastered during the first years of the child's life, which represents the critical period of language development (Berger, 2001).

Suggestions for working with professionals. There are several specific suggestions for ways in which parents of children who are deaf might work with professionals. First, for children who are deaf or hard of hearing, early intervention has

Whether verbal or manual, effective parent–child communication contributes to more satisfactory parent–child relationships.

Barbara Schwartz/Merrill.

been shown to be important for their development of language and literacy (Calderon, 2000; Yoshinago-Itano, 2003). Second, in working with professionals, the information that parents provide regarding their children and their goals for their children helps these professionals to better serve their families. According to Sebald and Luckner (2007), parents of children who are deaf should expect to answer the following questions from teachers and other professionals working with their children: *What does your child like to do for fun? What is stressful to your son or daughter? At what age does your child want to graduate from high school?* Third, parents will need to develop skills for effective collaboration with their children's service providers. Through effective collaboration, parents and professionals are able to help their children with hearing impairments to live more independent lives and also to think about the future they want to create for themselves. For example, parents of adolescents with hearing impairments should consider their responses to questions that relate to their children's plans after graduating from high school. These parents might be asked questions regarding whether their children will need help in finding colleges that provide assistance for students who are deaf or if their children will require assistance in acquiring employment. In addition to questions related to future college attendance and/or employment, parents might be asked questions related to their adolescent children's goal of living independently. Examples of this line of questioning might include questions such as, *When your children are young adults, what will they do with their free time and how will they get to work, school, or other places around town?*

Ways in which professionals might assist parents of children with hearing impairments. There are a number of ways in which professionals might assist parents to better advocate for their children. In a study of families with children who were deaf, Luckner and Velaski (2004) asked them a variety of questions related to their experiences with professionals and what advice they have for professionals working with families who have a child who is deaf. The three most common responses from these parents were *"Be patient with the child and the parent." "Know that you may not always agree with the parents on the choices they make for their child but be supportive and understanding." "Encourage us, help us understand, but don't judge us"* (p. 330).

Thinking Critically

The exceptionality of the child does not necessarily represent a handicap. A child might feel handicapped, however, if others respond negatively toward the child based on the child's exceptionality. What are some parental attitudes and behaviors that prevent a child's exceptionality from becoming handicapping?

Parenting Children Who are Gifted

Unlike other exceptionalities that reflect some aspect of disability, giftedness is not generally considered to be a disability but rather a welcome exceptionality. Children are identified as gifted when they have demonstrated exceptional abilities and/or have shown themselves to be capable of high academic performance. In comparison to the past, when high scores on intelligence tests were the measure of giftedness, today giftedness is viewed as representing a number of abilities. Thus, children identified as gifted these days demonstrate higher than average performance in such areas as general intellectual ability, specific academic aptitude, creative thinking, leadership ability, and talent in visual and performing arts (Chan, 2002). Not only is giftedness generally welcomed, there is evidence that parents might play an important role in the promotion of giftedness in their children. In numerous studies, the families of children who have been identified as gifted have been found to have certain characteristics in common. By and large, the profile of "gifted families" epitomizes the self-actualizing family system. In families wherein at least one child participates in a gifted education program, the following family interactions have been documented: (a) mutually supportive relationships, (b) appropriate degrees of closeness, (c) flexibility, and (d) open expression of thoughts and feelings. Parental perceptions of their child as gifted (whether or not the child has been formally identified) also has been found to be associated with positive labeling of the child, taking pride in the child's accomplishments, better parent–child communication patterns, and more intimacy in the parent–child relationship (Moon & Hall, 1998).

The Challenges of Parenting a Child Who Is Gifted. Having a child who is gifted is typically a source of pride for parents but the presence of a gifted child sometimes has a negative impact on family relations. First, making the child who is gifted the focus of parental attention can lead to inappropriate comparisons between that child and the other children in the family. Second, because highly intelligent children often demonstrate advanced reasoning abilities, parents might find themselves treating their children who are gifted as more mature than these children actually are. When this happens, role distinctions between children and adults become blurred and an imbalance of power is likely to occur in the family. In this situation, parents relinquish control of family interactions in the direction of the child's ideas and decisions (Moon & Hall, 1998). Discovering that their child is gifted also sometimes contributes to parents experiencing an exaggerated sense of responsibility to "do right by" their child. The exaggerated sense of responsibility on the part of these parents includes fears regarding their adequacy to raise the child or feelings of guilt that they are neglecting their child's development. To the degree that parents experience feelings of inadequacy in meeting the developmental needs of their children who are gifted, family interactions might be adversely affected. To compensate for their feelings of inadequacy, parents sometimes place excessive performance demands on themselves as well as on their children. This approach to parenting a child who is gifted not only negatively affects the child but also contributes to psychological problems for the entire family.

Recommendations for Parents. In recognition that early life experiences can powerfully influence children's early attitudes toward learning and later educational achievement, Sankar-DeLeeuw (2007) conducted a case study of the lives of five gifted kindergarten children. In this study, parents provided specific guidelines regarding the rearing of their young-gifted children. In general, these parents saw their parental role as facilitators of their children's growth. They expressed the belief that they should provide stimulating intellectual experiences appropriate for their children's developmental level. They also saw themselves as advocates for, and personally involved with, the education of their children. Listed below are the guidelines collectively produced by these parents, which according to Sankar-DeLeeuw are applicable to parents of all children.

1. Discover, not charter, your child's identity.
2. Listen to your child's own thoughts, feelings, joys, sorrows, hopes, and fears.
3. Encourage responsibility by offering choice.
4. Allow your child to independently do things, without assistance.
5. Support friendships.
6. Be patient.
7. Be a good role model (including providing for rich language expression and life-long learning.)
8. Read, both to your child and also on your own.
9. Discuss and debate daily news, songs, and books.
10. Mediate television viewing (p. 98).

In addition to generating guidelines for rearing their children, the parents in the Sankar-DeLeeuw study provided a variety of reading material to their children, including picture books, songs, poetry, fiction, fantasy, folktales, jokes, magazines, nonfiction, fables, and newspapers. Additionally, some of the parents read materials with their children that their children could read independently. While reading to their children, these parents compared story content to their children's own knowledge with questions such as, *"Does it make sense?"* Additionally, they focused on reading for meaning versus identifying letters or words.

Thinking Critically

Consider the contrasting lives of children with conduct disorders and children who are gifted. Based on the previous discussions related to the lives of children with those two exceptionalities, do you think children with conduct disorders could have turned out to be gifted if they had been socialized in a more positive environment? On the other hand, do you think that children who are gifted might have become children with conduct disorders if they had been exposed to interpersonal violence and a preponderance of family negativity?

PARENTING CHILDREN WITH CHRONIC ILLNESSES

A number of chronic illnesses are generally associated with children: spina bifida, cystic fibrosis, and sickle-cell anemia. Children are sometimes born with, or develop shortly thereafter, a number of other diseases, such as leukemia, cancer, diabetes, kidney disease, and heart disease. In recent years, there has been an increase in children who are born with fetal alcohol syndrome, are addicted to drugs, and/or are HIV-positive. These chronic illnesses that result from prenatal exposure to alcohol, drugs, or the HIV virus present novel and challenging problems for their parents or caregivers—many of whom are adoptive or foster parents.

Coping with a Child's Chronic Illness

All parents must learn to cope with childhood illnesses, including making efforts to help their children feel better, getting medical attention for their children, and coaxing them to take their medicine. Having a child who is sick also impacts parental employment because a parent typically takes time off from work to stay home with that child. For parents who are coping with a child's chronic illness, however, all these challenges are compounded. For example, children with chronic illnesses require more medical intervention, including more frequent hospitalizations. Also, parental caregivers of children with chronic illnesses have higher levels of stress than do other parents. Furthermore, their relationships with other family members (including their other children) are often altered to allow for parents to provide more care

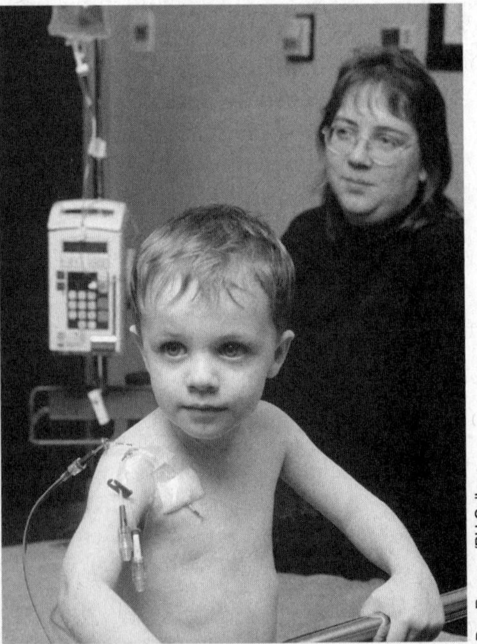

Children who experience the stresses of chronic illness need extra support from their parents or guardians.

Roy Ramsey/PH College.

for the child with a chronic illness. Low-income families have additional stressors related to financial hardships that make it difficult for these parents to meet medical costs and provide specialized care. For all these reasons, families with children with chronic illnesses require higher levels of support in comparison to other families.

Helping Children Who Are Chronically Ill to Cope with Hospitalization

One of the ways to help parents cope with the challenges related to their children's chronic illness is to assist them in their efforts to help their children cope with being ill. Children who are chronically ill require more care within the household as well as more medical assistance outside the household in comparison to healthy children. Because frequent hospitalization is often necessary to keep these children alive, the medical treatment and periods of recuperation (in the hospital as well as at home) are stressful on the child as well as the parent. Children's reactions to the stresses of chronic illness depend a great deal on the ways in which their parents respond to their special needs. One of the difficulties associated with periods of hospitalization is a great deal of waiting and subsequent boredom, which is experienced by both children and their parents. Furthermore, it is not only the physical or emotional pain that must be endured by children who are ill but also the lack of activity. Healthy, active children are able to gain attention from adults and entertain themselves in ways that are difficult or impossible for sick children. In recognition of their children's emotional needs, parents might use times of waiting to read or sing to their children, play games with them, tell them stories or jokes, or inform them about what is happening in the family and the neighborhood. Parents might also provide play materials or books that match their children's interests, energy level, and ability to concentrate. As trying and difficult as recuperation times can be for children as well as for their parents, these are also times that parents and children often become closer because they have the time together that they might not have otherwise taken (Fine, 1991).

The Effects of a Child's Chronic Illness on Family Relationships

Having a child who has been diagnosed with a life-threatening illness is one of the most difficult experiences parents might have, and caring for a child with a chronic illness presents parents with a number of challenges (Best, Streisand, Catania, & Kazak, 2001). Caring for a child who is chronically ill evokes an intense emotional interdependence with the child and involves a range of tasks, including brokering information for the child and gaining the child's cooperation with treatment. When faced with a severe or life-threatening illness, everyday concerns about the child's diet or management of the child's behavior take on a new significance and are likely to contribute to heightened parental stress. The parental caregiver role also tends to compromise the parent's ability to function in other roles, including the role of parent to the other children in the family. Thus, the stress of a child's chronic illness alters the relationships parents have with the child that is ill, as well as the relationships they have with each other, and with their other children (Young, Dixon-Woods,

Findlay, & Henry, 2002). Furthermore, caring for a child with a chronic illness increases parental vulnerability to depression and marital discord. The degree to which family relationships are impacted are related to the length of time that the child is ill, the degree of medical involvement, and the interruption of normal family activities (Lavee, 2005).

The Unique Challenges of Low-Income Families with Children Who Are Chronically Ill. When families care for children with chronic illnesses, they incur significant expenses that are directly related to providing care for their children. Children with chronic illnesses frequently need special medical care, therapeutic services, and a longer period of care, as well as specialized care. All of these expenses create an especially heavy burden for low-income families. A primary expense for these families is lost employment, especially for low-income mothers, because they cannot afford to pay for specialized child care while they work. The lost wages of these parents represent a substantial burden for their families (Lukemeyer et al., 2000).

Assistance for Families with Children Who Are Chronically Ill

Because parents of children with chronic illnesses often experience stress and face challenges related to functioning in their other family roles, Wamboldt and Wamboldt (2000) suggested that these parents are likely to benefit from social support. Assistance for these parents is especially important because they play a key role in facilitating their children's medical treatment. There are also lessons to be learned from the research by Lavee (2005), who found that stable and strong relationships that are based on mutual support enhance the parents' emotional well-being under stressful situations. These findings indicate that family practitioners need to attend not only to the parents' psychological responses to their child's illness, but to the parents' marital relationship as well. It is thus recommended that family health practitioners, other family members, and friends provide support to parents not only shortly after a diagnosis is made, which is typically a time of major stress, but also over a prolonged period of time, when these parents often find that both their internal and external resources are depleted.

Assistance for Low-Income Families. Low-income families of children who are chronically ill need both social support as well as financial assistance. Temporary Assistance for Needy Families (TANF) and public insurance coverage are two primary avenues to obtaining financial assistance for low-income families with children who are chronically ill. Types of public health insurance include Medicaid, state-based insurance programs such as those resulting from the State Child Health Insurance, and other public programs offering assistance, such as the Indian Health Service (Wise, Wampler, Chavkin, & Romero, 2002). Although low-income families whose children have chronic illnesses are more dependent on financial assistance than other low-income families, many of these parents provide exemplary care for their children. For example, Koenig and Chesla (2004) interviewed asthma management among low-income Latino and African American parents and found that, although they held differing beliefs regarding how best to respond to their children, they were clearly effective caregivers. These mothers managed their children's asthma using management styles that reflected their own personal beliefs. For example, some mothers tended to believe that their child's survival depended primarily on them while others relied more on medical professionals. Furthermore, many mothers in this study used a prevention approach in dealing with their children's asthma. The following quote is from a mother whose management style reflects her belief that she is primarily responsible for her child's survival:

> I'm thinking, "What if he has an asthma attack and dies in his sleep or I don't hear him wheezing and I can't help him," but I, I'm a very light sleeper now. I use to could just, I would sleep hard I couldn't hear anything in my sleep. But now I'm a very light sleeper. Cause I always want to hear" (p. 63).

A mother's prevention approach for dealing with her child's asthma is illustrated in the following quote:

> In raising a kid with asthma, it's a little bit different because you have to be very clean. . . . around certain people, . . . "Can you please not smoke or can you blow your smoke the other way?" Or, "Don't touch her if you have dirty hands." Or if a kid's sick, "Please don't let your kid touch her, I'm not trying to sound rude but she's a very sick child with asthma" (p. 64).

SUMMARY

- In this chapter, we examined the lives of parents and their children with special needs related to exceptionalities or chronic illnesses. We learned that these parents must develop specialized skills for caring for their children, while simultaneously working with professionals who are involved in their children's lives.
- We also considered the ways in which the lives of parents are changed as they take on the role of caregivers of their children who have special needs.
- Finally, we learned that having a child with special needs in the family affects family interactions and that these families typically need varied kinds of support.

KEY TERMS

- attention deficit/hyperactivity disorder
- autism
- conduct disorders
- exceptional
- gifted
- impairment
- Individuals with Disabilities Education Act (IDEA)
- learning disability
- mental impairment
- person-first language
- pervasive developmental delay
- physical impairments
- stander

USEFUL WEB SITES

For children who are deaf or their parents, a variety of resources are offered by NTID and RIT

http://www.ntid.rit.edu/prospective/outreach/php

The NTID was created 40 years ago by the U.S. government in response to a growing need for technology-focused career options for young people who are deaf. After setting aside funding for that purpose, NTID identified Rochester Institute of Technology as its host university, because this univesity was widely known for its technical education and cooperative work experience program for students. Furthermore, Rochester, NY, home to the Rochester School for the Deaf, already had a sizable population of deaf persons. Descriptions of the multiple ways in which NTID provides accommodations for students who are deaf or hard or hearing are provided at this website; for example, inclusive classrooms, tuition reduction, career preparation for students, and training programs for prospective employers to show how to integrate an employee who is deaf or hard-of-hearing into the workplace.

For families with disability, The Beach Center on Disability

http:// www.beachcenter.org

The Beach Center's site is an excellent site to find research. Another feature of this site is that families have posted their real-life stories describing how a particular disability issue or need has played out at the family level. The stories link the families to relevant research. This site has discussion boards, blogs, free newsletters, event calendars, and legal updates.

For parents of children who are gifted, this is a useful site

http://www.gifted-children.com

This is a monthly, online newsletter for the parents and teachers of gifted children. The annual subscription is just $10—and given the amount of information available, it seems well worth the price. To get an idea of this enormous site, check out the free links, available to everyone (they carry an asterisk). The creator is Arthur Lipper, who publishes *Gifted Children Monthly*. For subscribers only are: "Chat Rooms," "Parents' Ideas," "Research Papers," "Links," "Teachers' Sharing," and "Ask the Expert."

For families of children who are gifted, another excellent site is BRITESPARKS

http://www.britesparks.com

This virtual community was created in Australia. It contains information and interesting links about children who are gifted ranging from toddlers to teens. The creator is Beth Crothers from Queensland, Australia. Don't miss the "Toddlers" and "Kids" links for fun and educational sites for children who are gifted, and the "Librarians' Tools" page within the "Education" link. "Gifted Canada" is a similar site, with a different perspective, http://www3.telus.net/giftedcanada.

For parents of children with chronic illnesses, The National Association of Children's Hospitals has an excellent site

http://www.childrenshospitals.net

This site provides information regarding child advocacy, clinical care, public policy, and short relevant informational notices, such as caring for the whole child.

Parents of children with chronic illnesses might also want to check out the information about Camp Kaleidoscope, a summer camp for children with chronic illnesses, sponsored by Duke University's health system

http://www.dukehealth1.org/childrens_services/campk.asp

Camp Kaleidoscope's web site describes the summer camp and provides comprehensive information to parents who are interested in allowing their children to take advantage of this opportunity.

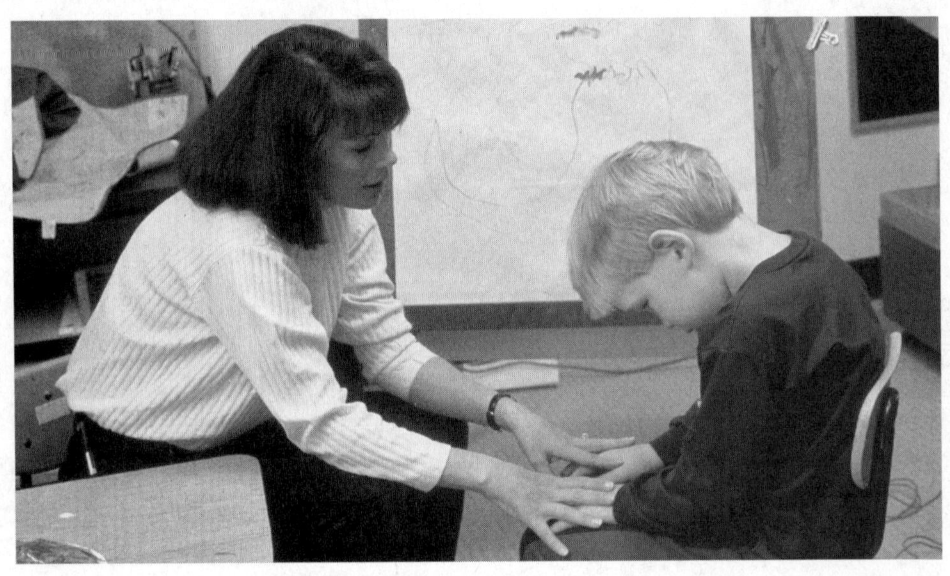

Families at Risk and Families Coping with the Death of a Family Member

Objectives

After completing this chapter, you should be able to

- Describe the history of child maltreatment in the United States, and the prevalence of child abuse and neglect at the present time.
- Identify the factors related to parental maltreatment of children.
- Explain the impact of parental maltreatment on the lives of children.
- Demonstrate an understanding of various interventions designed to interrupt the cycle of child maltreatment.
- Discuss the impact of interparental violence on the lives of children.
- Show an understanding of ways in which to interrupt the cycle of domestic abuse.
- Explain the ways in which parental alcoholism affects parenting skills, such as the nurturing of children and the monitoring of their whereabouts.
- Describe the ways in which the dynamics in families with an alcoholic parent differ from families that are not touched by alcoholism.
- Discuss the four typical roles of children in alcoholic families, including the characteristic behaviors and needs of children in these roles.
- Explain the ways in which the understanding of death corresponds to children's stages of cognitive development.
- Describe the feelings and behaviors of children who are grieving the death of a parent or sibling.
- Describe ways in which parents and other adults might assist children in coping with the death of a family member.

- Demonstrate an understanding of the feelings associated with parental loss of a child through death.
- Provide examples of ways in which to support parents who are grieving the death of a child.

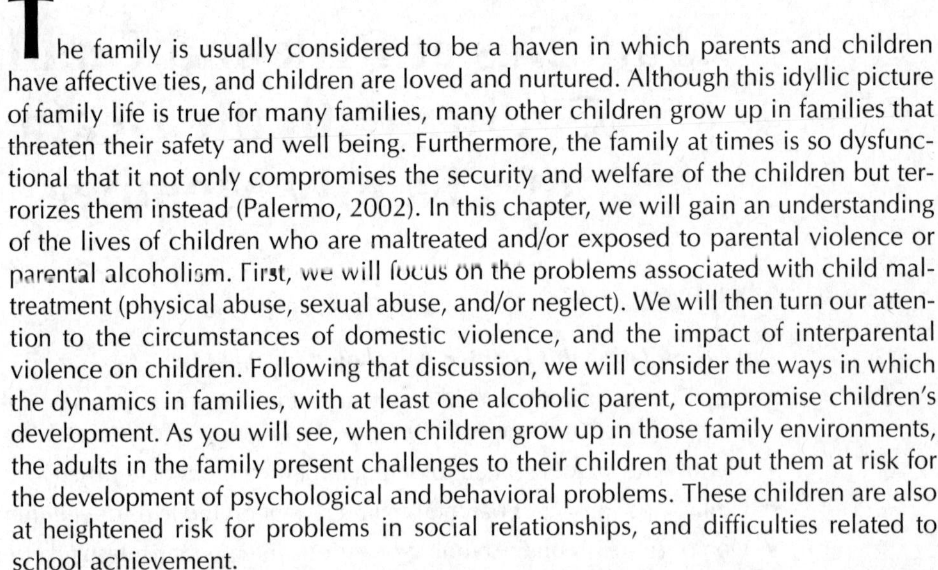

The family is usually considered to be a haven in which parents and children have affective ties, and children are loved and nurtured. Although this idyllic picture of family life is true for many families, many other children grow up in families that threaten their safety and well being. Furthermore, the family at times is so dysfunctional that it not only compromises the security and welfare of the children but terrorizes them instead (Palermo, 2002). In this chapter, we will gain an understanding of the lives of children who are maltreated and/or exposed to parental violence or parental alcoholism. First, we will focus on the problems associated with child maltreatment (physical abuse, sexual abuse, and/or neglect). We will then turn our attention to the circumstances of domestic violence, and the impact of interparental violence on children. Following that discussion, we will consider the ways in which the dynamics in families, with at least one alcoholic parent, compromise children's development. As you will see, when children grow up in those family environments, the adults in the family present challenges to their children that put them at risk for the development of psychological and behavioral problems. These children are also at heightened risk for problems in social relationships, and difficulties related to school achievement.

Following the discussions related to families at risk, we will examine the lives of parents and children who are dealing with the untimely death a family member. As you probably recall, we discussed the impact of an elderly parent's death in Chapter 10. In contrast to that earlier discussion, the coverage of death in the family in this chapter focuses on the untimely death of a parent, sibling, or child. Included in this discussion are recommendations for assisting children to deal with the death of a parent or sibling and suggestions for helping parents to contend with the death of a child.

CHILD MALTREATMENT

When parents (or other persons who are responsible for children's welfare) inflict nonaccidental physical injury on children under the age of 18, that act is legally defined as **physical abuse** and is prohibited by law in all states within the United States. When parents (or other persons responsible for the child's well being) engage in sexual activity with children under the age of 18, that act is legally defined as **sexual abuse** and is prohibited also by state law. When parents (or other designated caregivers) fail to provide children with basic care and protection, those persons can be held legally accountable for **child neglect**.

The History of Child Maltreatment in the United States

Child maltreatment has been a common occurrence for many centuries, but the public objection to child maltreatment in the United States is a relatively new phenomenon. In the past, it was believed that "child discipline" needed to be maintained even if "harsh corporal punishment had to be used" (Radbill, 1974). The first scientific documentation in the literature of the harmful effects of child abuse did not occur in the United States until 1962, with the publication of a revolutionary article by Kempe, Silverman, Steele, Droegenueller, and Silver, who coined the phrase, "the battered child syndrome." According to Kempe and colleagues, the **battered child** is a child who has sustained serious physical injury from an adult caregiver. The authors of this article noted that child battering is frequently undiagnosed and mishandled by professionals, due to a hesitancy to report such violence to the authorities. The public reaction to the article was extraordinary and child abuse soon became a topic that was openly discussed in the research literature as well as in the media (Newberger, 1991).

Several years after the publication of the article by Kempe and colleagues, the first documented use of the phrase "**family violence**" to refer to violent acts of family members against each other, and the effects of these actions on children, was in an article entitled "*Youth, Violence, and the Nature of Family Life*" by Havens (1972). Havens suggested that, due to the increasing awareness of child abuse within the family, medical and health professionals should stop idealizing family life and accept the fact that some parents intentionally injure and sometimes kill their children. The work of Kempe and colleagues in the 1960s, and Havens in the 1970s, led to laws in the United States that were designed to protect children from violence. These publications also led to mandatory reporting laws for mental health and other professionals who work with children (such as doctors, teachers and counselors). Subsequently, the identification of other types of childhood maltreatment (neglect, sexual abuse, and the witnessing of maternal battering) has received considerable attention (Edwards, Holden, & Felitti, 2003; Margolin & Gordis, 2000).

Child Maltreatment Today

Despite the growing awareness of child abuse and neglect within the family, as well as the passage of laws to protect children from maltreatment, many children continue to be abused and/or neglected today. The number of reported, and substantiated, cases of child maltreatment in the United States has been almost 1 million per year since 1993 (U.S. Department of Health and Human Services, 2003). A number of factors have been linked with family violence, including the intergenerational transmission of abuse, parental substance abuse, and certain characteristics of both parents and children.

The Intergenerational Transmission of Family Violence. A great deal of research has emphasized the relation between having experienced or witnessed abuse during childhood and subsequent violence toward children during adulthood. Specifically, adults are predicted to replicate the aggressive behaviors of their parents. Recent research also shows that childhood abuse significantly increases parents' risk for abusing their own children (Heyman & Slep, 2002; Pears & Capaldi, 2001). As noted by Heyman and Slep, however, the cycle of violence is hardly a sealed fate. The most typical outcome for both men and women who were abused as children is to be non-violent in their adult families. Thus, the link between previous childhood abuse and the maltreatment of one's own children is not that simple. For many individuals, their experience of being abused as children is counter-balanced by professional counseling and/or support from a partner. Accordingly, it is more appropriate to consider previous childhood abuse as a risk factor for future parental abuse, instead of stigmatizing parents based on their own early childhood victimization. For example, Bifulco, Moran, and Ball (2002) found that mothers' own childhood neglect or abuse contributed to their higher levels of vulnerability, and chronic or recurrent depression. These researchers emphasized that these mothers' vulnerability and depression put them more at risk for abusing or neglecting their children. They emphasized, however, that by providing intervention services designed to decrease the vulnerability and depression levels of women who were abused as children, professionals are likely to benefit these mothers as well as their children.

Parental Alcoholism or Drug Abuse. One of the ways in which researchers have been able to determine the relation between child maltreatment and alcoholism or drug abuse has been to examine the lives of children who have been removed from their parental homes and placed in foster care. One such study, conducted by Haapasalo (2000), found that many of the children in foster care were removed from homes where they were abused and/or neglected by alcoholic or drug-addicted parents. The link between parental maltreatment and alcoholic dependence was also demonstrated by Fals-Stewart, Kelley, and Fincham (2004), who found that both mothers' and fathers' alcohol dependency is related to psychological and physical abuse of their children.

Parental Age. The age of a parent is another factor that has been associated with child abuse and neglect. The research linking parental age and child abuse has consistently shown that adolescent mothers are more likely to abuse their children than are older mothers. The increased risk for child abuse among teenaged parents is probably due to the effects of poverty and limited education. In Chapter 3, we learned that teenagers who become parents are typically already disadvantaged youth, whose low educational achievement and poverty precede rather than stem from early parenthood (Sawhill, 2000). These conditions, undoubtedly, present considerable challenges for these young parents, and increase the likelihood that they will abuse their children. Not only are these young parents more likely to abuse their infants and young children but they are also more likely to abuse their children when they and their children grow older. As a case in point, Kinard (2003) found that mothers of school-age children had a greater tendency to abuse their children if they had become parents during their teenage years. As noted by

Kinard, these younger child bearers were unable to overcome the social and economic deficits associated with early childbearing which placed them at greater risk for child maltreatment.

Other Parental Characteristics. In addition to parental age, a number of other parental attributes are common among parents who abuse their children. These include (a) a tendency toward role reversal (whereby the parent depends on the child to gratify certain needs), (b) parental impulse control problems (learned from being exposed to family violence during childhood), (c) low self-esteem, (d) defensiveness (that aims to defend one's low self-esteem), (e) the propensity to blame others for their problems (which is seen when a parent scapegoats a child), and (f) parenting attitudes that devalue children (Jackson, Thompson, & Christiansen, 1999). Abusive parents also tend to have inappropriate developmental expectations of their children, which leads them to misjudge normal child behaviors. For example, abusive mothers find infant crying more aversive than do nonabusive mothers (Azar, 1997). Another characteristic of abusive parents is that they tend to show less parental acceptance of their children (Krishnakuman & Buehler, 2000). Finally, there is evidence that abusive parents have not developed the skills to discuss stressful circumstances, examine options or actions, and come up with effective ways for solving family problems. For instance, Cantos, Neale, and O'Leary (1997) found that mothers who physically abuse their children have a general lack of coping skills.

Child Characteristics. A primary characteristic of children that puts them at greater risk for being abused is their age. Physical abuse and neglect falls most heavily on children under age 6, and the greatest risk of abuse occurs during the first year of life when children are the most vulnerable (Berger, 2005). The most common type of infant abuse is **shaken baby syndrome**, which consists of shaking a crying baby. This practice is extremely dangerous, and often contributes to infant death as a result of head trauma (Biron & Sherton, 2005). Although the highest rates of abuse are perpetrated against the youngest children, high numbers of older children and adolescents are also abused. Furthermore, in homes where parents are involved in domestic violence, adolescents are at particularly high risk of physical abuse. Unfortunately, there is a perception that adolescents do not need protection from parental abuse because their physical injuries are not as severe as are those of younger children. Also, negative societal attitudes toward adolescents contribute to beliefs that they are to blame for their own abuse (Rossman & Rosenberg, 2000).

Risk Factors Related to Parental Sexual Abuse. A number of risk factors have been found to be specifically associated with the sexual abuse of children, including interparental violence, family isolation, and residential mobility. The presence of a stepfather in the home, maternal and paternal drug use, psychological problems, and a prior history of sexual abuse have also been found to be related to child sexual abuse (Bailey & McCloskey, 2005).

Thinking Critically

Let's take a moment to consider what you have learned so far regarding the parental characteristics that increase the likelihood of child abuse. Were you surprised by any of these characteristics? Do you think you could develop a program or workshop to prevent some incidents of child abuse based solely on what you have learned so far?

THE IMPACT OF MALTREATMENT ON CHILDREN'S LIVES

At every stage of development, parents' abilities to respond to their children's needs, and to guide and support them as they negotiate developmental tasks, is essential for children's healthy development. Experiencing child abuse and/or neglect has been associated with a full range of problems for children, including disturbances in the attachment process, difficulties in adjusting to the school environment, and poor academic performance.

The Impact of Abuse or Neglect on Parent–Child Attachment. Parents of securely attached children nurture, comfort, and protect them, thereby promoting their sense of security, trust, and self-esteem. Moreover, secure attachments assist children in the establishment of self-identity and self-worth. Children who have been neglected and/or abused, rather than nurtured, comforted, and protected, however, typically do not develop the sense of security, trust, and self-esteem associated with secure attachment. Instead, they are likely to develop insecure attachments that interfere with their ability to trust others (Weinfield, Sroufe, & Egeland, 2000). Because these children are without important sources of protection and support, they often learn to rely on themselves, to approach an abusive parent only after having assessed the parent's mood, or attempt to find other sources of emotional support (Wolfe, Scott, & Wekerle, 2001).

The Link Between Maltreatment and Lower School Achievement. Even at a very young age, children who have been maltreated have trouble adapting to their child care and preschool environments. Children who have suffered from any form of maltreatment demonstrate more cognitive deficits as they get older and are considered to be more at risk for school failure and school drop-out than are their nonmaltreated peers. The neglect of children is particularly detrimental to those children's ability to achieve in school. In comparison to other groups of maltreated children, those who have experienced parental neglect have been found to have the poorest academic achievement (Kinard, 2001).

The Association Between Maltreatment and The At-Risk Behaviors of Adolescents. In addition to the psychological consequences of abuse, such as anxiety, depression, and suicidal behavior, parental abuse also intensifies adolescents' risk-taking and escape behaviors, for example running away from home, drug use, premature sexual behavior, truancy, and violent and nonviolent delinquency (Wolfe et al., 2001).

Thinking Critically

Given the negative consequences of parental abuse and neglect, what interventions do you think would be beneficial to provide for children who have been maltreated, to help them to overcome the trauma they have experienced?

Interventions for Parents Who Abuse or Neglect Their Children

Because children who are maltreated are at high risk for the development of psychological, social, and cognitive impairments (Gibson, 2002; Shaw, Lewis, Loeb, Rosado & Rodriquez, 2001), it is critical to understand the steps that can be taken to prevent or interrupt the cycle of child maltreatment. Based on their previous experiences and present life circumstances, parents who are at risk for abusing their children are in need of informal and formal intervention. The first step toward intervention for potentially abusive or neglectful parents typically comes from informal support systems. Informal support from family members, friends, and community members, in the form of respite child-care, transportation, or financial assistance, might relieve the stress of parents and in so doing reduce the possibility of child maltreatment. Second, formal community supports, such as family therapy, food, and clothing, can go a long way toward mediating the stresses experienced by parents who are at risk for child maltreatment. Third, programs that teach basic parenting skills are particularly helpful in reducing child maltreatment.

In situations in which child maltreatment has been reported and substantiated, parents and children frequently become involved with protective service agencies. In these circumstances, parents are given a service plan to assist them in developing nonabusive relationships with their children. DePanfelis and Zuravin (2002) found that those parents who attended the services outlined in their service plan (such as parenting classes) were much less likely to abuse their children. Based on these findings, they concluded that actively engaging families in a helping alliance and encouraging them to accept and receive services might help reduce the likelihood of further maltreatment.

Thinking Critically

Why do you suppose that actively engaging families in a helping alliance, and encouraging them to accept services, helps reduce their likelihood of child maltreatment?

Help for Children Who Have Been Maltreated

Relatives, the wider community, foster parents, and adoptive parents play a vital role in providing maltreated children with the safety, dedication, and nurturance they need to recover from their traumas. Having at least one adult in their lives who nurtures them and provides for their basic needs helps maltreated children to develop resiliency in the face of risk. These supportive adults might be extended family members, such as grandparents; nonfamily foster parents; or in cases in which parental rights are severed, adoptee parents (Lowenthal, 1999). These alternative caregivers frequently encounter immense challenges as they attempt to gain the trust of children who have been traumatized. Not only do maltreated children have lower levels of trust, they frequently exhibit challenging behaviors, and/or a lack of basic skills that reflect the maltreatment they have received (Gibson, 2002). Furthermore, even though these children have experienced abuse and neglect at the hand of their parents, they typically suffer feelings of grief related to (a) separation from the only parents they have ever known, (b) the loss of a familiar environment, and (c) the loss of a number of established and ongoing relationships with other family members, friends, and teachers. Additionally, foster parents might have difficulty understanding the child's feelings of grief associated with their separation from abusive or neglectful parents, especially given that foster parents are providing a safer and more nurturing environment than the one from which the child was removed. In order to provide these children with the social support they need, however, it is important for foster parents and other service providers to acknowledge and support the grief these children experience (Edelstein & Burge, 2001).

Children's Behaviors Related to Separation from Their Parents. For adults, it is easier to recognize grief if children display sadness or withdraw from social relationships. They might have difficulty understanding that many foster children tend to express their feelings of loss and grief through acting out behaviors toward the most available adult target—the foster parent. It is helpful if foster parents are able to recognize the various problems associated with foster children's feelings of grief. For example, feelings of anxiety and wishes to search for their parents or

This sad and bewildered child is waiting to be placed with a foster family. Like many other children, she is being removed from their parents due to child abuse or neglect.

previous caregivers might interfere with foster children's ability to settle into their new home. Furthermore, it is not unusual for children who are being placed in an unfamiliar environment to have problems in their sleeping, elimination, and eating patterns. Troubles in paying attention and remembering things they are told are other common problems for children during this adjustment phase (Edelstein & Burge, 2001). Leathers (2003) also found that foster children experience conflicting allegiances to foster families and biological parents. The anxieties related to conflicting loyalties are typically triggered by visits with biological parents. The suggestion of Leathers is that the anxieties experienced by foster children might be somewhat alleviated by interventions designed to reduce loyalty conflicts.

The Honeymoon Phase. A further confusing aspect of the grief of children in foster placement is that initially foster parents, and their foster children, experience a "**honeymoon phase**," during which time the children are on their best behavior. Then, several weeks or months after a child has seemingly adjusted to the new environment, that child might suddenly begin to display behavior problems (a testing of the limits) or emotional withdrawal. This behavior is often distressing to their foster or adoptive parents who are prepared to give emotionally, but who encounter an emotional void instead. Consequently, the child's inability to respond emotionally to the foster or adoptive parents who are caring for them sometimes elicits unexpected anger from those parents (Edelstein & Burge, 2001).

Thinking Critically

Imagine yourself at any point in your childhood and try to picture a typical day from that period of your life. Think about the home in which you lived, the people with whom you shared your home, the neighborhood in which you played, and the school you attended. Then, imagine the feelings you might have had if strangers had come into your home and told you to pack up only what you could put in a paper bag. After being told you could no longer live with the only parents you had known, you began to try to put your life together again in a new home, with a new family, in an unfamiliar neighborhood, and at a strange school. In that situation, how do you think you might have felt and behaved? Now, consider how a child in foster care might feel in these circumstances.

CHILDREN'S EXPOSURE TO INTERPARENTAL VIOLENCE

Children's development is compromised not only when they are abused and neglected but also when they are exposed to acts of violence between parents or other family members. Approximately 15.5 million American children live in dual-parent households in which intimate partner violence has occurred within the past year. Furthermore, approximately 7 million of these children live in households in which severe partner violence (beat up, choked, burned, threatened, or used a knife or gun) has recently occurred (McDonald et al., 2006). The most common form of family violence is spousal abuse. Today's household, though, often consists of persons who might not be related to each other (such as a parent's romantic partner) and the witnessing of violence between those members of the household is traumatizing for children as well (Kashani & Allan, 1998). The picture of interparental violence looks like this. Women are more likely to be the victims of spousal or partner battering. Both the batterer and the victim are more likely to be young, and the abuser also is likely to be a substance abuser (Coker, Smith, & McKeown, 2000). Parental unemployment (particularly the unemployment of fathers) is also frequently linked to violence among family members. For instance, women who are battered are more likely to have spouses who are unemployed than are women who are not battered (McClosky, Treviso & Scionti, 2002).

Fathers, or domestic partners, who batter their mothers are viewed by the children in the household as unpredictable and frightening, and these mothers often are distracted by basic issues of safety and survival for themselves and their children (Margolin & Gordis, 2000). Not surprisingly, parents involved in interparental violence frequently have poor parenting skills. For instance, Krisknakumar and Buehler (2000) found a negative relationship between marital conflict/discord and parental warmth. According to these researchers, hostility and conflict in one family system, the marital relationship, negatively influences another family system, in this case, the parent–child relationship. Finally, domestic violence itself promotes a negative view of the child for both the batterers as well as the victims. The negative perceptions of the child, in turn, increase the risk of child abuse for both parents. Thus, violent interactions between parents have negative spillover effects on other family relationships (Brody, Arias, & Fincham, 1996; McGuigan, Vuchinich, 2000).

The Impact of Interparental Violence on Children's Development

Children who are exposed to domestic abuse are at risk for a number of developmental problems, including physical symptoms (such as headaches or stomach aches), and **post-traumatic stress disorder (PTSD)**. A PTSD is a debilitating condition that often follows a terrifying physical or emotional event, which causes the person to have persistent, frightening thoughts and memories of the ordeal. Furthermore, the impact of interpersonal violence differs according to children's ages. Although a common belief is that infants and young children are not impacted by interparental violence due to their inability to fully comprehend violent episodes, their distress can be discerned by their behaviors. For instance, mothers victimized by domestic violence have reported that their infants exhibit trauma symptoms (Bogat, DeJonghe, Levendosky, von Eye, & Davidson, 2006), and also show more distress related to conflict in comparison to infants living in homes where domestic abuse is not present (DeJonghe, Bogat, Levendosky, von Eye, & Davidson, 2005). Other changes that have been observed in the behaviors of these infants and children include irritability, sleep disturbances, emotional distress, fears of being alone, and regression in toileting behavior and language (Margolin & Gordis, 2000). For school-aged children and adolescents, exposure to interparental violence compromises their ability to regulate emotions, show empathy, and attend to increasingly complex cognitive material. Children who consistently witness interparental violence also are likely to have cognitive consequences and peer relationship problems. These difficulties make it exceedingly challenging for these children to accomplish the developmental tasks of achieving in school and establishing positive relationships with their peers (DeJonghe et al., 2005).

Interrupting the Cycle of Domestic Violence

In Chapter 11, we learned about the prevalence of significant conduct problems among children brought to women's shelters (Ware et al., 2001). We also learned that Project Support, developed by McDonald (2006) has been effective in helping many women who had been battered not to return to their battering partners, and also to develop less aggressive parenting patterns. In addition to providing services for adult victims of domestic violence, it is important to protect children from domestic violence and actively advocate for ways to reduce violence in families. To that end, Jaffe, Baker, and Cunningham's (2005) edited book, *Protecting Children from Domestic Violence: Strategies for Community Intervention*, provides up-to-date information about how best to respond to domestic violence. This book, which emerged from the International Conference on Children Exposed to Domestic Violence that was held in London, Ontario in 2001, represents the views of a number of scholars regarding ways that professionals and policy makers might work together to make families safer for children.

The recommendations of the contributors to the Jaffe et al. book are as follows: The paper by Edleson emphasized the need to refer battered women and their children to community services. In order to determine which services are needed, it was recommended that a broad range of assessments and services be developed that involve child welfare professionals. In another paper, Davis emphasized the need to provide a treatment program for male batterers. While supporting the emphasis on community services, Graham-Bermann and Halabu pointed out that intervention programs need to be culturally relevant. These authors noted, for example, that it is important to deliver public broadcast messages about domestic violence in different languages and involve community leaders in helping to challenge views that tend to play down the scope of the problem of domestic violence. In another paper, Hardesty and Campbell recommended the need for safety planning strategies for both women and children. Finally, Jaffe et al. outlined specific steps that might be taken by communities, service providers, and policy makers. They emphasized the benefits of reaching out to families from diverse cultural backgrounds, involving fathers, and (most importantly) engaging communities. As noted by these authors, "children are best insulated from the effects of exposure to violence when their mothers can live safely and their fathers can function without violence" (p. 221).

THE IMPACT OF PARENTAL ALCOHOLISM ON CHILDREN

As is the case for child maltreatment and interparental violence, many children's lives are negatively impacted by their parents' **alcoholism**, which is the most frequent form of substance abuse found among parents. As noted by Brown and Lewis (1999), growing up with an alcoholic parent is both a common and unique experience. The uniqueness of the experience is that the family with an alcoholic parent has different dynamics than a family where parental alcoholism is not present. On the other hand, the dynamics within alcoholic families are similar and the roles that children assume in order to adapt to that family system are predictable. The following discussion focuses on the family relations, family roles, and developmental outcomes of children who grow up in homes where at least one parent is an alcoholic. Treatment programs for parents with alcoholism are described as well. As you will learn, the dynamics in families where a parent is an alcoholic sets the family apart from other families. These dynamics include disrupted family routines and rituals, compromised parenting behaviors, a heightened risk for harsh punishment, and a greater likelihood of child maltreatment and/or interparental violence.

Unpredictable or Disrupted Family Routines and Rituals

Family rituals include traditions developed to celebrate culturally defined occasions as well as more individualistic family traditions and anniversaries. Family rituals also incorporate daily interaction patterns, such as mealtime and bedtime rituals. Daily routines and rituals serve an important function in families, especially families with young children, because they provide stability, structure, and predictability to everyday life. By engaging in routines and rituals, children learn the rules, roles, and values that govern their family life. Family rituals also strengthen family identity by establishing the roles and belongingness of family members. Unfortunately, family rituals are often interrupted in families with an alcoholic parent, who is more likely to be the father than the mother because men are three times more likely than women to drink at harmful levels (Zajdow, 2002). In the case of paternal alcoholism, most mothers try to compensate for the fathers' failure to sustain parental roles and responsibilities during episodes of drinking and hangovers. Furthermore, the degree to which these mothers manage to maintain routines and rituals determine to a large extent how much the father's drinking influences the lives of the children in the family. For example, maintaining family rituals and routines has been related to better adjustment in children of alcohol-abusing parents during childhood (Haugland, 2005).

Although most mothers who are married to men who are alcoholics make efforts to maintain family rituals and routines when their spouses are intoxicated. Fiese, Tomcho, Douglas, Poltrock, and Backer (2002) discovered that not all mothers assume this moderating role. They found that some mothers react to their spouses' alcoholism by withdrawing psychologically, or directing their frustration or irritability toward the children during periods of paternal drinking. Furthermore, even though men are three times more likely to be alcoholics than are women, many families are also impacted by the mother's drinking problem. When mothers abuse alcohol, their excessive drinking goes undetected longer than does fathers' alcohol abuse because (a) men are more likely than are women to drink in public places, and (b) female heavy drinkers are more likely to live with heavy-drinking partners. In families where only the mother has a problem with alcoholism, fathers are likely to make attempts to uphold family routines. For example, Brown and Lewis (1999) described how the recovery of an alcoholic wife was organized by her spouse who not only maintained family routines, but also joined Al-Anon and encouraged his adult children to do the same. In this family, the father and children were well on the road to recovery before the Mom stopped drinking.

Compromised Parenting Behaviors

In addition to disrupted family routines and rituals, problem drinking by parents negatively impacts a number of important parenting skills. For example, parents who are alcoholics show (a) inconsistency or unpredictability in parenting behaviors, (b) poorer monitoring of children's behaviors, (c) lower levels of parental nurturing and emotional availability, (d) a greater likelihood to use harsh punishment, and (e) a higher tolerance for adolescent drinking and other substance abuse.

Inconsistency or Unpredictability in Parenting Behaviors. While intoxicated, some parents become more (or less) accepting of their child's failure to perform household tasks, do their homework, and act responsibly in a number of other ways. It has been determined that such inconsistency in parenting might undermine a child's sense of order, control, and stability in the family relationship, thereby reducing feelings of self-esteem and perceptions of self-competence (Windle, 1996).

A Decrease in Parental Monitoring. Parental problem drinking also leads to a decrease in parental monitoring, which places children at greater risk for involvement in antisocial behavior. For example, the research literature has consistently shown that lower levels of parental monitoring are associated with higher levels of adolescent alcohol and other drug use, as well as other delinquent behavior (Jacobson & Crockett, 2000).

Less Emotional Availability and Poorer Judgment in Discipline. In comparison to other parents, those who abuse alcohol are less emotionally available to their children as a result of drinking-related consequences, including hangovers, irritability, and negative mood states. Alcoholic parents also tend to exercise poorer judgment in disciplining their children, and might become less inhibited and overly aggressive (Whipple et al., 1995). Moreover, although alcoholism is not always associated with family violence, it is a common contributor to child abuse and neglect (Fels-Stewart, Kelley, & Fincham, 2004; Haapsalo, 2000).

The Parentification of Children. Another way in which parenting behaviors are compromised in families with an alchoholic parent is by the tendency of alcoholic parents to parentify their children. **Parentification** is a construct defined by Boszormanyi-Nagy and Spark (1981) to describe the distortion of the parent–child relationship in such a way that the child is often placed in the role of the parent. Parentified children might be enlisted to care for their parents' physical, emotional, or even financial needs. Temporary parentification is considered to be normal at times, and might even be associated with responsibility, competence, or autonomy in children. For example, the taking on of parental responsibilities by children is a natural arrangement in large families, single-parent families, and families in which both parents work. Parentification is considered problematic, though, when parents are excessively and chronically dependent on their children for nurturance (Kelley, French, & Bountress, 2007). According to Burnett, Jones, Bliwise, and Ross (2006), when parents drink and children feel frightened and helpless, these children might assume caretaking behaviors in relation to the parent in order to bring a sense of control to otherwise uncontrollable circumstances. Even though parentification might be a mutually agreed upon situation, it robs children of their childhood and of the care and protection of their parents.

Greater Tolerance of Adolescent Drinking and Other Substance Abuse. Parents who are problem drinkers not only model alcohol abuse but are more likely than other parents to show a greater tolerance for adolescent drinking and substance use, thereby providing implicit approval for their children's substance use (Hill & Yuan, 1999; Hopfer, Stallings, Hewitt, & Crowley, 2003). Also, the parental use of tobacco, alcohol, and other drugs increases the likelihood that their adolescent children will also use these substances (Epstein, Williams, Botvin, 2002; Unger & Chen, 1999). The way in which parents' alcoholism contributes to their children's substance usage might be explained by social learning theory. For instance, parents who model such behaviors encourage imitation by their children. Furthermore, children who believe that drug use is normative are more likely to perceive social reinforcement for such behavior, and are more inclined to smoke or drink themselves (Unger & Chen, 1999).

The Dynamics and Roles in Families with Alcoholic Parents

Based on the previous discussion, it is easy to see that parental alcohol abuse places a strain on family relations, which in turn impacts children's development of healthy family roles. In that family, all members are typically engaged in a conspiracy of silence regarding the issue of alcoholism. Although everyone in the family is generally aware that a parent drinks too much, one of the main rules in the alcoholic family is to behave as if the problem does not exist. In these families, children are typically exposed to a high level of stress while simultaneously receiving the consistent message that they are not to acknowledge the predicament the family is in, or talk about their feelings (Black, 2005).

The Roles of Family Members. According to Family Systems Theory, both parents and children assume certain roles that help them to adapt to the dynamics of their particular family system. Whenever individuals in a family are expected to consistently suppress their feelings, however, interactions between family members are constrained and family members take on more restrictive roles. The roles of family members in an alcoholic family reflect the ways in which each person adapts to living in a dysfunctional family system. For children in that family, these constrained roles limit their development of other aspects of their personalities. Furthermore, parents in alcoholic families tend to see children in terms of their role positions rather than in relation to their feelings or developmental potential. Finally, even though the roles are developed to help these children cope with a dysfunctional family system, these roles tend to persist into adulthood.

The roles assumed by parents and children in an alcoholic family were carefully detailed by Wegscheider (1989) and include the (a) **alcoholic** parent, (b) **codependent** spouse or partner, (c) family scapegoat, (d) family hero, (e) family mascot or clown, and (f) lost child. These family roles are played out in a recent videorecording by Claudia Black (2005), which is used by counselors in working with families affected by parental alcoholism.

The Alcoholic Parent and Codependent Spouse. The primary role of the alcoholic parent consists of behaviors focused on obtaining and using alcohol. As a codependent, the spouse of an alcoholic typically spends a great deal of energy trying to control the drinking of the alcoholic spouse while simultaneously enabling that person to continue drinking, by covering up or denying the problem. (Black, 2005).

The family scapegoat. The **scapegoat** in a family with an alcoholic parent is viewed as a troublemaker, whose visible traits include hostility, defiance, and sullenness. These behaviors are designed to draw attention away from the real problem, and direct negative attention toward the scapegoat. Instead of admitting that there is a problem in the family system, such as parental alcoholism, family members are encouraged to blame the scapegoat for the family's difficulties. The child who has the role of scapegoat might also learn to exhibit problem behaviors in order to disrupt the fighting between parents, who must then stop fighting to deal with the child's problems.

The family hero. The **family hero** in this family is super responsible, an overachiever, typically does what is right, and needs everyone's approval. Often the oldest child, or in traditional families the first boy, the family hero provides family members with a sense of self-worth. In their denial that there exists a problem in the family, parents point to the family hero as an example of their parenting effectiveness and a symbol of family normalcy. Although the child in the role of family hero appears to have it all together, what others do not see is a child who has low self-esteem, and feels okay only when accomplishing a goal. Furthermore, the family hero is overly needy of attention, because this child typically lacks the ability to provide self-reinforcement.

The family mascot or family clown. The **family mascot** or **family clown** is considered to be especially cute, and will usually do anything for a laugh or to gain attention. What the child in this role represents to the family, and why they play along, is comic relief, fun, and humor. From the perspective of others, the family clown is having a great time and sees life from a fun, laughable point of view. The hidden feelings of the family mascot that are not revealed are low self-esteem, terror, and loneliness. Whereas the hero child's acceptance in the family is associated with personal achievements, the family clown's recognition in the family is tied to the ability to keep everyone laughing.

The lost child. Another role that is common in dysfunctional families is that of the **lost child**, who is usually quiet, and generally ignored. The lost child is a loner and a daydreamer who engages in solitary play, and is withdrawn from other family members. The benefit the lost child provides for the dysfunctional family system is relief, because this child does not cause any problem or inconvenience. By and large, lost children have been given the message that parents do not want to have to worry about them. While on the surface the lost child appears to be independent and content to spend time alone, the reality is that the child feels unimportant, hurt, and abandoned. The lost child also feels defeated in efforts to gain attention, and the behavior of the lost child reflects the feelings of having given up.

Adult Children of Alcoholic Parents

Because growing up a dysfunctional family contributes to the development of roles that help children adapt to a dysfunctional way of life, **adult children of**

alcoholics have not typically developed roles that cultivate their ability to achieve happiness and fulfillment in the adult world. On the other hand, adults who grew up in alcoholic families often benefit from caring relationships and professional help. Being able to recognize the adult behaviors and needs associated with each of the childhood roles helps family members, friends, and therapists to better understand the feelings and behaviors of adult children of alcoholics. Figure 12.1 describes both the behaviors and needs of these adult children.

The Family Scapegoat

Behaviors

Tends to keep people at a distance
Works hard to hide the hurt inside
Elicits anger from employers and family
Is likely to abuse chemicals
Might become involved with the law

Needs

Support of feelings
Acceptance from others
Challenge of inappropriate behavior
To be listened to
To accept responsibility for own behavior
To learn appropriate expressions of anger
To get in touch with a range of inner feelings

The Family Hero

Behaviors

Ties self-worth to accomplishments
Tends toward "workaholism"
Is too serious and rigid to enjoy self and others
Continuously seeks approval
Has expectations of self and others that are unrealistic
Takes on leadership roles
Might be emotionally or chemically dependent

Needs

To become tolerant of mistakes of self and others
To learn to play
To learn to take risks and be vulnerable
To learn to accept self
To learn to express feelings

Continued

The Family Mascot

Behaviors

Appears cheerful and witty
Is entertaining
Experiences sense of impending doom
Might have an eating disorder
Has sense of obligation to others

Needs

Physical touch
To be asked for input
To be taken seriously
To learn to laugh on the inside as well
To develop alternative ways of interacting with others

The Lost Child

Behaviors

Concerns regarding being boring
Is afraid to take risks, fear of being hurt
Suffers from stress-related problems (e.g., anxiety attacks, asthma)
Is quiet, aloof, isolated, passive (feels helpless)
Experiences difficulty in making decisions/takes whatever comes
Might have an eating disorder

Needs

Invitation to join in group discussion or activity
Encouragement and reward for efforts
To consider self needs
To learn to accept/receive from others
To let others be responsible for their lives and mistakes

FIGURE 12.1 Behaviors and Needs of Adult Children of Alcoholic Parents
Source: Adapted from Wegscheider (1989).

FAMILIES IN RECOVERY

There are various pathways for recovery from addiction to alcohol or other substances. One of the most successful treatment approaches is Alcoholics Anonymous (AA) or Narcotics Anonymous (NA), and their closely affiliated organizations of Al-Anon and Nar-Anon, that are designed to support family members of persons with substance abuse. There are also residential treatment centers, where the parent who is addicted to alcohol or other substances might go for a period of time to start on the road to recovery. Many of these centers have an increasing emphasis on the involvement of the entire family in the treatment of substance abuse. There are also treatment centers for mothers with addiction that are designed to accommodate these mothers as well as their children.

Alcoholics Anonymous/Narcotics Anonymous

Alcoholics Anonymous (AA) is a voluntary worldwide fellowship of men and women who meet together to attain and maintain sobriety. There are no dues or fees for AA membership; the only requirement for membership is a desire to stop drinking. Alcoholics Anonymous is a total abstinence program, where members stay away from one drink one day at a time and sobriety is maintained the through the sharing of experience, strength, and hope, and through the suggested Twelve Steps for recovery from alcoholism (Alcoholics Anonymous World Services, 2007). **Narcotics Anonymous (NA)** operates under the same principles and guidelines as Alcoholics Anonymous but instead of focusing on helping their members to attain and maintain sobriety, their goal is to help their members stay clean from drugs. Like Alcoholics Anonymous, Narcotics Anonymous is a voluntary worldwide fellowship. Its membership is open to all drug addicts, regardless of the particular drug or combination of drugs used (Narcotics Anonymous World Services, 2005).

Al-Anon and Nar-Anon Family Groups

Al-Anon and **Nar-Anon** Family Groups are worldwide fellowships for family members or others affected by someone else's alcoholism or drug addiction. Similar to Alcoholics Anonymous and Narcotics Anonymous, both groups offer help to members through the sharing of experience, strength, and hope. Both of these family groups also use a Twelve-Step program, which is designed to help members recover from the effects of living with an addicted relative or friend. The only requirement for membership and attendance at these meetings is that the individual has a friend or relative with alcoholism (for Al-Anon), or a problem with drugs or drug addiction (for Nar-Anon). Sometimes individuals attend Al-Anon or Nar-Anon because a family member or friend is in AA or NA, but individuals often join these groups on their own to help them deal with living with a family member with alcoholism or problems with drugs.

An Example of a Family-Centered Treatment Center

With the increased emphasis on the involvement of the entire family in the treatment of parental substance abuse, a number of treatment centers provide comprehensive family services. The Nurturing Program for Families in Substance Abuse and Recovery is an example of this effort. This program, which is a modification of *The Nurturing Program for Parents of Children Birth to Five Years Old* by Stephen Bavolek (2000), was developed by the Coalition on Addiction, Pregnancy and Parenting at the Center for Substance Abuse Prevention. The program focuses on the improvement of parenting skills, the promotion of child development, and the enhancement of parent–child relationships, with the goal of improving treatment outcomes and reducing the risk of relapse. Another goal of the program is to decrease child neglect and abuse. The program consists of 18 different 90-minute sessions, all of which focus on the goals just described (Moore & Finkelstein, 2001). The goals of each session are described in Figure 12.2.

Session 1. Growth and Trust: During this session, participants explore themes and tasks of human development, with emphasis on the interrelated development of recovery and of parenting.

Session 2. Feelings: Through the use of games and art, participants in this session explore a number of ways in which to identify and express feelings. A particular emphasis in this session is on helping children to identify and express their feelings.

Session 3. Self-Esteem: In this third session, information is presented that focuses on the building blocks of self-esteem for both parents and children. Participants work in small group tasks that emphasize ways of promoting children's self-esteem.

Sessions 4–7. Making Connections: This theme, which emphasizes the importance of communication, continues for four sessions, and includes the following topics: "Communication," "Confrontation and Problem-Solving," "Body Talk," and "What Babies Teach Us."

Sessions 8–11. Building Structure: For four more sessions, participants deal with the development of family structure. The topics covered in these sessions include: "Managing Stress," "Setting Boundaries," "Schedules and Routines," and "Safety and Protecting Children."

Session 12. Guiding Children's Behavior: The belief that parents guide and teach, rather than manage, their children is explored in this session which focuses on the issue of parental encouragement. Specific tools of teaching, such as self-calming and redirection, are discussed in this session.

Session 13. Knowing Our Values: In this session, participants consider the ways in which the behaviors of preschool children reflect their development of a sense of purpose. Participants also explore their own values and work on their ability to describe those values.

Session 14. Recovery–Love and Loss: During this session, the losses that have been experienced by parents and children as a result of substance abuse are explored. The process of grieving is also described and discussed, as well as ways of supporting adults and children in grief.

Session 15. Having Fun: In this final session, the importance of incorporating play and fun in recovery and family life is explored. An emphasis on cultural traditions, games, and stories are incorporated into the focus of play and fun.

FIGURE 12.2 The Nurturing Program for Families in Substance Abuse and Recovery
Source: Adapted from Moore & Finkelstein (2001).

Treatment for Mothers with Accommodations for Children

The responsibilities associated with parenting often limit women's efforts to seek treatment for alcoholism or other substance abuse problems (McMahon, Winkel, Suchman, & Luthar, 2002). When women enter substance abuse programs that do not allow them to take their children with them, they have difficulty focusing on treatment. Also, mothers who enter substance abuse programs without their children are more likely than men to be stigmatized because mothers tend to be the primary caregivers of children. For example, in many subcultures, the placement of children outside the home or ethnic community is considered a violation of ethnic traditions that focus on the role of the family and motherhood (Hardesty & Black, 1999). Separation from their children during substance abuse treatment also frequently contributes to a mother's feelings of inadequacy associated with the inability to fulfill the parental role (Metsch et al., 2001). For all these reasons, women who seek treatment tend to seek programs that do not require them to be separated from their children. In recognition of these issues, programs designed specifically for women with children attempt to preserve family stability by offering family residence and child care (Knight & Wallace, 2003).

In-Home Continuing Care for Families Affected by Substance Abuse

Whether parents who are recovering from alcohol or drugs go to treatment centers or stay at home, there is typically a need for a continuing care program designed to assist the substance-affected family. In their 2001 article, Gruber, Fleetwood, and Herring described an intervention approach, known as the Bridges Program, that combines substance abuse recovery work with family preservation services. Thus, in addition to helping the individuals avoid the use of alcohol or other drugs, services are also directed toward helping them to recover their roles within their families. For this aspect of their recovery, parents are assisted in gaining the education and skills they need for effective parenting, supportive family involvement, and the avoidance of drugs. The program, described in Figure 12.3, focuses on helping substance

Domain 1. Individual Actions and Cognitions: This domain of the program addresses behaviors and thinking patterns of the substance abusing parent that represent aspects of functioning that are necessary for engaging in a lifestyle not dependent on alcohol or drug use.

Domain 2. Individual Recovery Actions: This domain emphasizes the behavioral changes that substance abusing parents must integrate into their daily lives in order to achieve and maintain sobriety.

Domain 3. Family Actions and Cognitions: This domain addresses the behaviors and thinking patterns of the substance abuser's family that represent aspects of family functioning that are necessary to providing the support and structure the recovering substance abuser needs in order to be able to engage in a lifestyle not dependent on alcohol or drug use.

Domain 4. Family Recovery Actions: These are the actions that the families of substance abusers need to take to help them understand substance abuse and assist the substance abuser to achieve and maintain sobriety.

FIGURE 12.3 The Bridges Program for Helping Substance Abusers and Their Families Prevent Relapses

Source: Adapted from Gruber, Fleetwood, & Herring (2001).

abusers and their families prevent relapses by addressing four domains of recovery needs: 1. Individual Actions and Cognitions, 2. Individual Recovery Actions, 3. Family Actions and Cognitions, and 4. Family Recovery Actions.

COPING WITH THE UNTIMELY DEATH OF A FAMILY MEMBER

We will now turn our attention to the challenges family members face when they are confronted with the untimely death of a family member. We begin by exploring the ways in which children cope with feelings of loss and grief following the death of a parent or sibling. We will then consider the feelings of loss and grief of adults who lose a child through death.

The Death of a Parent During Childhood or Adolescence

The loss of a parent during childhood or adolescence represents a profound psychological insult that threatens a person's social and emotional development (e.g., Dowdney, 2000; Lin, Sandler, Ayers, Wokchik, & Luecken, 2004). According to Perry (2001), a child experiences the most distress following a death when the child is close to and dependent on the one from whom that child is separated. It is normal for children and adolescents to experience a sense of unreality or numbness as they are faced with the pain of separation from the parent. Although children at

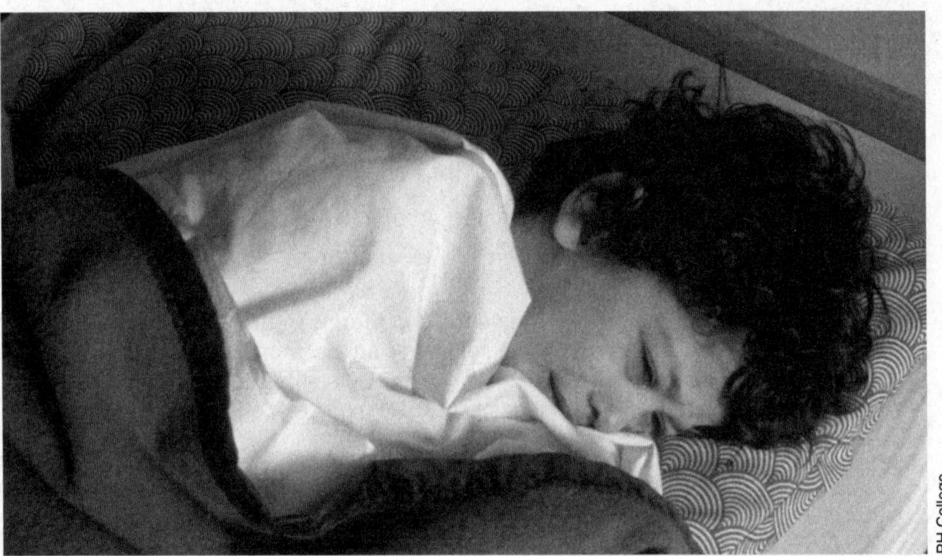

PH College.

Although young children do not understand the concept of death and might have difficulty expressing their feelings in words, their facial expressions, body language, and behavior all reflect their sadness and grief.

every age experience profound sadness and grief following the death of a parent, they have different conceptions of death than do adults. Furthermore, young children have difficulty in comprehending what death means. The lack of understanding regarding death is illustrated in the following comment of a 5-year-old child whose parent has died, "When is my mommy coming home from heaven? I've been waiting and waiting." (Perry, 2001, p. 22). For infants and toddlers, parental death is equated with parental separation and preschoolers do not understand that death is permanent. Thus, young children are not only saddened by the loss of a family member but are at a disadvantage when they attempt to understand why a parent has disappeared from their lives. Although older children and adolescents have a clearer understanding about death, they nevertheless struggle to come to grips with the loss of a parent. As children move beyond the initial feelings of grief, disorganization is common because familiar routines, habits, and roles become disrupted. Mourning children must confront the reality of facing life without the presence and support of the deceased parent. Eventually, a period of reorganization or recovery occurs and even though the sadness is still felt, its intensity is somewhat diminished. With the passing of time, most children and adolescents who have experienced the death of a parent find that they carry that parent with them in numerous memories (Perry, 2001). Thus, the strength of the parent–child relationship endures even beyond the life of the parent.

The Death of a Sibling During Childhood or Adolescence

Siblings are a part of one's past, present, and future. They form strong attachments to one another, have a shared history together, and expect their relationship to continue into adulthood and old age. Furthermore, the sibling relationship impacts a child or adolescent's personality development, because siblings are a central part of everyday family experience and social adjustment (Horsley & Patterson, 2006). Siblings are important sources of companionship and affection and also serve as confidants for one another. Thus, like the death of a parent, the childhood experience of a sibling's death is a rare event with profound and enduring effects on surviving children and adolescents. The childhood loss of a sibling through death is a painful and traumatic loss, which is complicated by the fact that children and adolescents are at high risk for failing to grieve that loss. When children are not permitted to mourn, they are not assisted in the grief work that could help them to maintain their personal attachment to their deceased sibling (Worden, Davies, & McCown, 1999). An example of the lack of support for mourning the death of a sibling is shown in the following statement from a 14-year-old girl whose older brother had died as a result of committing suicide.

> I had just talked with him the night before and had trouble believing that my wonderful brother was gone forever from my life. I was completely devastated and my parents were beside themselves with grief. I realized that they were too deep in their own grief to be available to comfort me. On two separate occasions, when relatives saw me crying, they reprimanded me, telling me to stop crying because it would further upset my parents (Anonymous).

The adult in this scene understands that grieving children need to be comforted.

Anne Vega/Merrill.

Help for Grieving Children and Adolescents

A number of circumstances have been found to affect children's and adolescents' adjustment to a family member's death. First of all, they need to be able to express their grief and receive comfort from surviving parents and/or other adults. Also, children and adolescents need help as they struggle to adapt to the many changes that occur in the family system during a time of grief and confusion (Raveis, Siegel, & Karus, 1999). One of the main reasons that people typically do not talk about death to children and adolescents is that they sometimes consider the topic taboo and are afraid that discussing a loved one's death with them will increase their feelings of sadness. It is helpful, though, when adults are willing to talk with children and adolescents about the feelings they are having, because they do not benefit from admonitions to "not think about it" or "put it out of their minds." In discussing the death of a family member with a child or adolescent, it is important to attempt to get a sense of what they are thinking about the loss they have experienced and to try to find out how they view death in general (Perry, 2001). Furthermore, grieving children and adolescents need to be given information about the circumstances of a family member's death (according to the child's ability to understand). In providing that type of information, adults should keep in mind that they might need to repeat the same information time and again because children have difficulty processing information in the midst of a stressful experience. Additionally, it is helpful for grieving children and adolescents when adults avoid the tendency to do most of the talking. After inviting a child or adolescent to talk about feelings related to their loss, the adult should let the child or adolescent take the lead as to when, how long, and how much is discussed (Perry, 2001). Finally, surviving parents or other adults should (a) exercise caution in making decisions related to the deceased parent or sibling (e.g., about disposal of possessions of the deceased), and (b) proceed carefully in making further changes in the family during the days, weeks, and months following a family member's death (e.g., changing residences).

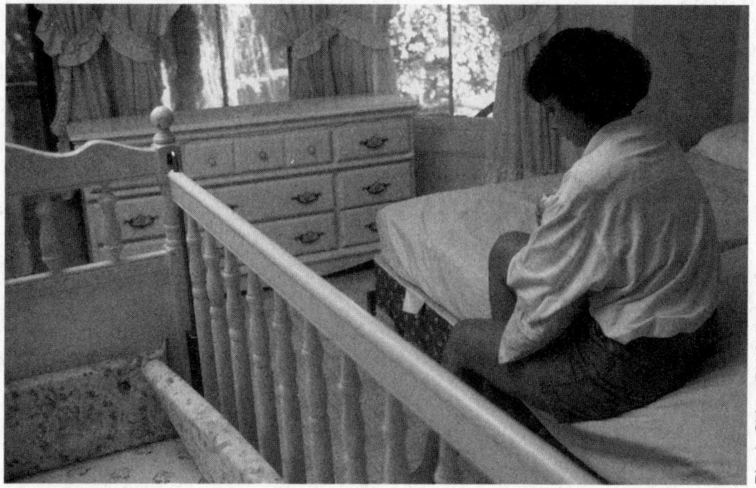
Rhoda Sidney/PH College.

There is no greater loss than the death of one's child, and bereaved parents need the support of family members and friends.

Thinking Critically

Two related problems are associated with talking with children or adolescents about the death of a family member. First, adults frequently do not talk with children or adolescents about the experience of death. Second, those who talk with them about death tend to talk too much. Why do you suppose these two approaches are so common and how do you think they are related?

The Grief of Parents When a Child Dies

The death of a child is a devastating life experience and disbelief that one's offspring has died before oneself is a common response regardless of the age of the child or the cause of the death. A child's death causes parents intense personal suffering and affects family reorganization and reintegration into community life. Furthermore, despite the cause of death and irrespective of whether accountability and blame are established, parents typically feel responsible for their children's deaths because the role of the parent is to protect the child and contribute to the child's continued growth and development (Murphy, Johnson, Gupta, & Das, 1998). When their child dies, the grief that parents feel encompasses their lives in a variety of ways, including every aspect of day-to-day living. To be able to move through the necessary period of mourning, adults who have lost a child through death must make their way through a maze of grief. During the grief process, many parents feel trapped in the labyrinth of overwhelming sadness. The feeling of being unable to escape the pain associated with the death of their child contributes to various reactions. Some bereaved parents tend to panic and run in all directions in an attempt to return to a normal life, whereas others are inclined to sit and wait for the hurting to subside. Over time, the grief related to the death of one's child subsides but the life of an adult who has lost a child through death is forever altered. According to the results of a study of bereaved parents by Wheeler (2001), for a majority of parents, the death of the child precipitates a crisis of meaning and initiates a search for meaning which involves both cognitive mastery and renewed purpose. A large proportion of parents believe that their lives following the death of the child have a different meaning than before their child's death. Their findings suggest that the process of meaning making is a significant aspect of readjustment for bereaved parents.

Helping Parents Cope with the Death of a Child

Each bereaved parent must make a tremendous endeavor to get through the grief associated with the death of a child but this effort is more effective when it occurs within the framework of supportive people. Even though family members and friends would like to help parents who are grieving the loss of a child, they often feel helpless and unsure about what to say or do in that situation. Several guidelines have been suggested by Chin-Yee (1990) for assisting parents in dealing with the death of a child, including (a) understanding a parent's unique response to death, (b) reinforcing the child's identity, (c) expecting to deal with a bereaved parent's anger, and (d) providing support for the other children.

Understanding a Parent's Unique Response to Death. The first step in assisting grieving parents is to understand that one person's way of coping with the death of a child cannot be compared to someone else's. People tend to deal with loss based on how their family of origin coped with loss. The most helpful approach others can take to assist grieving parents is to allow them the freedom to express their grief according to their individual way of coping.

Reinforce the Child's Identity. A second suggestion for helping bereaved parents to deal with the loss of a child is to reinforce that child's identity by encouraging parents to talk about the events surrounding their child's birth, life, and death. It is beneficial as well for family members and friends to always refer to the baby or child by name and to call parents *mother* or *father* and the siblings' *brother* and/or *sister*.

Expect to Deal with a Bereaved Parent's Anger. It is not unusual for parents who have lost a child through death to have feelings of anger, and family members and friends sometimes bear the brunt of that fury. Parents whose child has died are simply lashing out at the world and those people just happened to get in the way. Persons who are providing support to sorrowful parents should realize that anger is a natural expression of anguish when one's child has died.

Provide Support for Their Other Children. An important, but often overlooked, step in helping bereaved parents who have other children is to talk to those children about the death of their sibling. When talking to these children, it is valuable to reassure them that, although their parents are very sad, they still love their children, will continue to take care of them, and will be available to talk with and play with them soon.

SUMMARY

- In this chapter, we examined a variety of circumstances that place children at risk for not realizing their developmental potential.
- First, we discussed the problems of child maltreatment, and the difficulties confronted by children living in those families. That presentation focused on the ways in which maltreatment places children at risk for the development of social and psychological problems. Recommendations were provided for disrupting the cycle of child maltreatment and increasing resiliency in children who have experienced abuse or neglect.
- We then considered the ways in which children's lives are impacted when they are exposed to acts of violence between parents or other adults in the household. Recommendations for the interruption of violence were included in that discussion.
- Next, we considered the problems encountered by children growing up in alcoholic families. That discussion focused on (a) the ways in which alcohol abuse affects parenting skills, (b) an examination of the roles that children take on in alcoholic families, and (c) the effects of parental alcoholism on adult children.
- A focus on the recovery of parents with alcoholism or drug addition emphasized various options. Services for children of parents with alcoholism or other addictions were also explored.
- Then we turned our attention to the impact on the lives of both parents and children who experience the untimely death of a family member.
- We learned that the death of a parent during childhood or adolescence is especially challenging. A part of that discussion included ways in which to support children and adolescence as they grieve that loss.
- We also considered the difficulties parents face who must cope with the death of a child. Included in that discussion were various suggestions for helping parents as they grieve the loss of their child.

KEY TERMS

- adult child of an alcoholic
- Al-Anon
- alcoholic
- Alcoholics Anonymous
- battered child
- child neglect
- child maltreatment
- codependent
- domestic violence
- dysfunctional family
- family hero
- family mascot or clown
- family rituals
- family scapegoat
- family violence
- honeymoon phase
- lost child
- Narcotics Anonymous
- Nar-Anon
- parentification of children
- physical abuse
- post-traumatic stress disorder (PTSD)
- scapegoat
- shaken baby syndrome
- sexual abuse

USEFUL WEB SITES

Prevent Child Abuse America, at
http://www.preventchildabuse.org

Awareness, education, and hope are provided for people involved in the effort to prevent the abuse and neglect of children. Working with their various chapters, they provide leadership to promote and implement prevention efforts at both the national and local levels. With the help of their state chapters, and many other concerned individuals, they emphasize the valuing of children, strengthening of families, and engagement of communities nationwide.

At Keep Kids Healthy
http://www.Keepkidshealthy.com

This site is a pediatrician's guide to health and safety, which has a link to child abuse. This link contains information related to various types of child abuse. There are also recommendations from pediatricians regarding how to prevent child abuse. For example, there is information from Dr. Ianelli, a pediatrician and author of a book for first time fathers, who explains how to calm a crying baby.

The National Domestic Violence Hotline, at
http://www.ndvh.org

Here is probably one of the most important websites for assisting victims of domestic violence. The 24-hour hotline (1-800-799-SAFE (7233) OR 1-800-787-3224) provides help to domestic victims from all 50 states, and translation is available. The stated belief of that organization is that every caller deserves to be treated with dignity and respect, and every family deserves to live in a world free from violence. The view that safe homes and safe families are the foundation of a safe society is a guiding principle of that organization.

Another excellent website that focuses on domestic violence is the Medline Plus site at

http://www.nlm.nih.gov/medlineplus/domesticviolence.html

This site provides useful articles such as "Domestic Violence, Protecting Yourself and Your Children" (in both English and Spanish) by the American Academy of Physicians. Information is also provided at this site regarding symptoms of domestic violence, with questions such as "Are you being abused?

The Al-Anon Family Groups at

http://www.al-anon.alateen.org

A fellowship of relatives and friends of alcoholics share their experience, strength, and hope in order to solve their common problems. The shared philosophy of these family groups is that alcoholism is a family illness and by changing attitudes, families of alcoholics can be helped. The only goal of these organizations is to help recovering families of alcoholics.

The Kidshealth website at

http://www.kidshealth.org/teen/your_mind/families/coping_alcoholic.html

Information is found here for teens regarding coping with an alcoholic parent. Answers are provided at this site for common questions, such as "Why does my parent drink?" or "Why can't my parent stop drinking."

The Kidshealth website, at

http://www.kidshealth.org.nz/index.php/ps_pagename/contentpage/pi_id/26

Information related to the ways in which children at different ages grieve, and suggestions for helping children cope with grief can be investigated on this site. In addition to a variety of other topics, this site addresses the needs of children bereaved by the death of a parent. Topics include communicating with your grieving child and where to go for more information/support.

Another excellent site that focuses on the needs of grieving family members is at

http://serendip.brynmawr.edu/sci_cult/mentalhealth/disaster.html.

This site, which is provided by The Parent Education Program at Bryn Mawr, has topics such as suggestions for families dealing with grief and loss, and helping children cope. This site also offers suggestions for activities and books for grieving families.

Appendix

Four Nationally Recognized Parenting Programs

All states and communities have various parent education initiatives, designed to meet both general and specific parenting needs, and many of these programs are exemplary. A listing of these programs would be exhaustive and it would be difficult to assess their quality. Selecting some of these programs for inclusion in this appendix, even if very high in quality, would have resulted in the exclusion of other equally high-quality programs. For these reasons, the parenting programs described in this appendix include only nationally recognized programs. All of these programs have parenting goals that align with the democratic philosophy of childrearing, which has been consistently emphasized in this book.

THE ACTIVE PARENTING PROGRAM

This parenting program, which was developed by Michael Popkin, is video-based so that workshop participants are able to view scenes that demonstrate how the skills they are learning might be effectively used. The use of videos is combined with activities and discussions in all versions of this program. The goal of the program is to assist parents in raising responsible and cooperative children. The skills taught to parents in the program are nonviolent and emphasize the encouragement of children. This program can be presented in three different ways: (a) as a video and discussion program, in which the presenter teaches the entire program as a 3-session class, 90 minutes each; (b) as a video library, which can be used for in-home visits or made available for parents to check out and view themselves; and (c) as a lunch-and-learn program, which can be offered in three short (30–40 minute) parenting classes. The three most popular versions of this program are listed below:

1, 2, 3, 4 Parents—This version of Active Parenting is for parents of children aged 1 to 4, available in English as well as Spanish, and presented in three sessions. In *Session* 1, the focus is on the special job of parenting, the ages and stages of development, how the participants will parent, building the bond between the parent and child and activities to try at home. In *Session 2,* parents share and tell, are taught how to use nonviolent discipline skills, are provided tips for avoiding accidents and problems, and learn the A-C-T of parents. Parents also learn about rules in this session. The topics presented in *Session 3* include choices and consequences, the power of encouragement, and the importance of caring for the caregiver.

Active Parenting Now is an updated version of the basic skills-building program for parents who have children between 5 to 12 years of age. This program is presented in six 2-hour sessions and includes the following: *Session 1* focuses on styles of parenting, mutual respect and how to get it, methods of choice, drugs, sexuality, and violence, and caring for the caregiver. *Session 2* emphasizes emotional intelligence, handling problems, active communication, and the think-feel-do cycle. In *Session 3,* parents learn about teaching responsibility, effective nonviolent discipline, "I Messages," and logical consequences. The topics of *Session 4* include why children misbehave, the four goals of misbehavior, and stimulating independence. In *Session 5,* discussions include success and failure cycles, the BANK Method of Encouragement, and stimulating independence. In *Session 6,* participants discuss parents' influencing events and family meetings.

Active Parenting of Teens. This program is for parents of adolescents between the ages of 13 and 19 years of age and is also taught in six 2-hour sessions. In this program, the following topics are addressed: In *Session 1,* discussions include current teen issues, styles of parenting, drugs, sexuality, and violence: the problem. In *Session 2,* participants focus on building courage and self-esteem, and discuss drugs, sexuality, and violence: the "think-feel-do" cycle. The topics of *Session 3* include problem-solving, five goals of teen behavior, problem-prevention talks, drugs, sexuality, and violence. In *Session 4,* parents learn about respectful discipline skills, mutual respect, and discuss drugs, sexuality, and violence, including stages of drug use. The focus of *Session 5* is effective communication skills, avoidant communication skills, drugs, sexuality, violence, and communication. In the final meeting, *Session 6,* the topics include family talks, family council meetings, drugs, sexuality, and violence: active problem solving.

THE NURTURING PARENTING PROGRAMS

These parenting programs represent an evidence-based family-centered initiative to teach parents nurturing parenting skills as an alternative to abusive and/or neglectful childrearing practices. These programs target families at risk for abuse or neglect of children birth to 18 years old. They can be offered in a group setting, a home setting, or in a combination of home and group settings. The philosophy of these programs is nonviolent parenting, the development of empathy, self-worth, self-awareness, empowerment, appropriate family roles, and age-appropriate developmental expectations. The parents and children in these parenting classes learn how to play games, sing songs, and have fun as a family. To meet the specific needs of families, the following programs have been designed according to the levels of prevention, including prevention programs, intervention programs, and treatment programs. Nurturing Programs are also offered to parents according to their children's developmental ages and for families dealing with specific issues. Many programs are designed for specific family situations, five of which are described below:

The Nurturing Program for Parents and Their Infants, Toddlers and Preschoolers—In this 48-session, home-based, or 24-session group-based program, parents learn how to recognize and understand feelings, how to provide infant and child massage, how to establish nurturing parent routines, alternatives to hitting, child development, and ways to promote their children's self-esteem and self-concept.

The Nurturing Program for Parents and Their School-Age Children, 5–11 Years—In this 15-session, group-based program, parents and children are assisted in increasing their empathy. Parents also learn nurturing ways to encourage appropriate behaviors, and ways to build self-concept and self-esteem.

The Nurturing Programs for Parents and Adolescents—In this 12-session group-based program, parents and adolescents learn how to use nurturing communication strategies, how to recognize each other's needs, how to understand the developmental stage of adolescence, and ways in which to build their own personal power, self-esteem, and self-concept.

The Nurturing Program for Teen Parents and Their Children—In this 50-session, home-based or 26-session group-based program, adolescent parents learn about children's brain development, infant and child massage, developmental milestones, how to have fun with their children, nurturing parenting routines, and ways in which they might help their children to build self-esteem and self-concept.

The Nurturing Program for Parents and Their Children with Health Challenges

This parenting program was designed to provide support for families as they deal with the unexpected challenges of parenting a child who is born or is diagnosed with a life-altering illness. In these sessions, family members explore their hopes and fears, develop effective parenting strategies, learn valuable communication skills, develop strategies for facing challenges, and learn to identify opportunities for celebration. The primary goal of this program is to establish a foundation of cooperation for families that will carry them through difficult times and create opportunities for growth as they face their various challenges.

THE PARENTING NOW PROGRAM

This parenting program, which is a division of the national Zero to Three initiative, is a group-based positive parenting curriculum based on best practices principles. The target audience for this program is highly stressed parents of young children (birth to 8). This program has two distinct curricula, both of which offer the same content, adapted according to the goals of that curriculum. This content includes group-based parent education, positive parenting principles and skill building, an opportunity to build social support for families, individual modules for each parent education session, videos spotlighting segments of the curriculum, parent booklets, a parent educator guide, and a group-based program to complement home-visiting programs, such as parents as teachers. The two curricula are as follows:

Making Parenting a Pleasure (MPAP)—This curriculum is designed for highly stressed families, with children from birth to 8 years of age, and those parents meet together in a group. This program is adaptable for specific populations, such as adolescent parents, parents who have been mandated by the court to attend parenting classes, and parents with developmental disabilities. Spanish adaptation is also available.

Parenting the First Three Years (P:F3Y)—This curriculum is for the general population and offers developmental information specific to the age of the children whose parents are attending the program. These groups include families with same-age children, either infants, 1-year-olds, or 2-year olds. Families can participate for 3 years and organizations can offer all three of the series: *Incredible Infants, Wonderful Ones, and Terrific Twos,* or they can offer just one of the three.

THE SYSTEMATIC TRAINING FOR EFFECTIVE PARENTING PROGRAM

This program, which was developed by Don Dinkmeyer and Gary McKay, is one of the most widely used parenting programs in the United States. There are three versions of the program, and each of the versions is designed to be taught as a class that meets for seven sessions. One-day seminars can also be taught and various segments of the program can be taught in 1-hour parent or lunch-and-learn meetings. All versions of the program teach positive approaches to understanding and guiding children, including The Goals of Child Misbehavior, The Goal to be Imperfect, Effective Listening, Effective Discipline, Problem Solving, Natural and Logical Consequences, and Encouragement. Additionally, leaders of each of the three program versions teach parenting skills and strategies designed specifically for parents of young children, parents of school-age children, or parents of teenagers. Brief descriptions of the contents of each of these programs are listed as follows:

Early Childhood STEP—This program is for parents of children under 6 years of age. In addition to the basic skills previously mentioned, this program also emphasizes understanding young children, understanding young children's behavior, building self-esteem in the early years, communicating with young children, helping young children learn to cooperate, effective discipline, and nurturing emotional and social development.

STEP–Systematic Training for Effective Parenting—For Parents of Children 6 to 12 Years Old—In this program, in addition to learning positive approaches for guiding children, participants also focus on understanding themselves and their children, understanding beliefs and feelings, and encouraging their children and themselves. They also learn to listen to and talk with their children, to help their children learn to cooperate, how to discipline that makes sense, and how to choose their parenting approach.

STEP/Teen – For Parents of Children 13–19—In this program, parents learn the basic skills previously described, and also learn to better understand themselves and their teenage children. They are taught ways in which to change their responses to their teenagers, how to communicate respect and encouragement, ways to encourage cooperation and solving problems, and how to use consequences and build responsibility. Finally, there are discussions called "Deciding What to Do, Parts I and II," that help parents to synthesize what they have learned.

Glossary

Absorbent mind. The view of Montesorri regarding the process by which young children learn at a rapid pace due to their minds unconsciously soaking up information from the environment.

Abstract thought. A Piagetian concept regarding the type of reasoning that occurs during adolescence, which is not limited by reality but allows for possibility.

Active listening. A communication strategy that consists of a verbal response containing no actual message of the parent, but rather a mirroring back of the child's previous message.

Adult children of alcoholics. Because growing up in an alcoholic family contributes to the development of roles that help children adapt to a dysfunctional way of life, these adults have not typically developed roles that cultivate their ability to achieve happiness and fulfillment in the adult world.

Affective synchrony. The matched emotional states of parents and their children, especially noticeable between caregiver parents and their infants and small children.

Al-Anon. A worldwide fellowship for family members or others affected by someone else's alcoholism.

Alcoholic. Persons whose use of alcohol is excessive and whose drinking creates problems in their social relationships and/or careers.

Alcoholics Anonymous. A voluntary worldwide fellowship of men and women who meet together to attain and maintain sobriety.

Amae. A cultural value in Japan that emphasizes close, affectionate mother–child relationships as the foundation for parenting.

Anorexia Nervosa. This condition, found mostly among adolescent girls, is basically intentional starvation, which is related to a distorted body image and serious health problems.

Atmosphere of psychological safety. When parents create an environment and relationship with their children, based on unconditional love, that promotes children's self-esteem.

Attention deficit/hyperactivity disorder (ADHD). A condition that causes children to have difficulty focusing their attention, become easily distracted, display impulsive behavior, have trouble waiting their turn, and begin but not finish numerous activities.

Authoritarian parenting. An approach to childrearing in which parents are strict and harsh and are also less nurturing and responsive to their children.

Authoritative parenting. Parents who use this childrearing approach are demanding but also nurturing and communicative with their children.

Autism. A developmental disorder, characterized by impaired communication, excessive rigidity, and emotional detachment.

Autocratic parenting. At the beginning of the 20th century, this was the prevailing belief guiding early American childrearing. Parents who used this approach told their children what to do and expected them to respond accordingly, without expressing their opinions regarding parental demands.

Battered child. A child who has sustained serious physical injury from a parent or adult caregiver.

Bicultural identity. Adolescents with a bicultural identity have pride in their ethnic heritage and also value their membership in the mainstream culture.

Bulimia Nervosa. A health problem found mostly among adolescent girls and characterized by binge eating and purging.

Bullying. Repeated, systematic efforts to inflict harm through physical, verbal, or social attack.

Centration. A Piagetian concept that defines the preschool child's tendency to focus on one feature or perspective at a time.

Child neglect. When parents fail to provide children with basic care and protection.

Chronosystem. This latest addition to Bronfenbrenner's ecological model highlights the influence of time on the various interacting systems that affect a person's development.

Codependent. In an alcoholic family, the codependent is typically the spouse or partner of the alcoholic. The codependent spends a great deal of energy trying to control the drinking of the alcoholic spouse, while simultaneously enabling that person to continue drinking, by covering up or denying the problem.

Collectivist cultural beliefs. Cultural beliefs that place a high value on cooperation, mutual respect, maintaining harmonious relationships, and contributing to the well-being of the family and community.

Colostrum. A thick, high-caloric fluid secreted by the woman's breast at the birth of her baby, which has many benefits for the newborn.

Communalism. A common value in traditional families and communities that emphasizes group (family and community) cooperation and the success of the group rather than the success of the individual.

Communication roadblocks. Parental responses that make a child feel as if the parent has not heard what the child is saying, is not interested in hearing the child, does not understand what is being said, or does not care about the child's feelings.

Comothers. Refers to the roles of two lesbian women, who are the parents of a child or children.

Conduct disorders. Children with these disorders have repetitive and persistent patterns of behaviors that violate societal norms or rules, such as acts of aggression to people and/or animals, and/or the destruction of property.

Connectiveness. Emotional ties to parents, family members, or other individuals.

Conserve. This Piagetian concept reflects the ability to understand that the quantity of matter (such as clay) does not change when the shape changes, or that the volume of water remains the same if it is poured from a short, squat glass to a tall, narrow glass.

Contingency. Refers to the relation between a behavior and the events that follow the behavior.

Contingent responsiveness. A parenting interaction that allows children and infants to be actively engaged in the roles of elicitor as well as receiver of parental attention.

Cultural congruence. Refers to similar behaviors, beliefs, and values, as well as shared language, and overall appearance between two or more individuals.

Culture. A culture consists of a variety of customs, religions, family traditions, and economic practices.

Democratic parenting. According to this parenting approach, although parents and children are not equal in terms of responsibility or privilege, both have equal worth. The attitude of equal worth is played out in valuing the needs and desires of each family member.

Dialectical reasoning. A type of reasoning that recognizes and tolerates ambiguities and contradictions in many life dilemmas. Basically, this reasoning is based on an understanding that there are no easy answers to many of life's dilemmas.

Egalitarian relationship. Relationships based on the principle of equality of partners. In these families, household responsibilities are generally shared.

Egocentric thought. An excessive reliance on one's own point of view, coupled with a corresponding inability to be objective.

Empty Nest. The term used to describe the home from which young adults are launched into independent living.

Enuresis. Any instance of involuntary urination by a child over 3 years of age, usually seen in bedwetting.

Ethnic identity foreclosure. Occurs when adolescents identify either with their ethnic group or the majority culture without sufficient exploration of the values of the other culture.

Exceptional. Whenever the development of a child deviates from the expected norm, that child is considered to be exceptional. Exceptionalities are classified either as impairments or giftedness depending on the nature of the exceptionality.

Extended family. Members of the extended family include relatives, other than parents and children, such as grandparents, aunts, uncles, and cousins.

Familism. The constellation of beliefs that define the roles and expectations of family members in relation to the needs of the entire family group, as opposed to the needs of the individual.

Family hero. In an alcoholic family, the child who is a super responsible overachiever, typically does what is right, and needs everyone's approval. The family hero provides family members with a sense of self-worth.

Family mascot or clown. The child in an alcoholic family who is considered to be especially cute, and will usually do anything for a laugh or to gain attention. What the child in that role represents to the family, and why they play along, is comic relief, fun, and humor.

Family rituals. Traditions developed to celebrate culturally defined occasions as well as more individualistic family traditions and anniversaries. Family rituals also incorporate daily interaction patterns, such as mealtime and bedtime rituals.

Family scapegoat. In an alcoholic family, this child is viewed as the troublemaker, whose visible traits include hostility, defiance, and sullenness. These behaviors are designed to draw attention away from the real problem, and direct negative attention toward the scapegoat.

Family structure. The way in which a family is constructed and how family members are connected.

Family violence. Violent acts of family members against each other and the effects of these actions on children.

Fast mapping. A process by which preschool children learn new words, usually from only hearing them once, at a rapid rate of about 10 to 20 new words per day.

Filial duty. The belief, which is found in many cultures throughout the world, that adults have a duty to work and provide financial support for their parents.

Filial maturity. The term used to describe the capability of adults to engage in behaviors and attitudes that respect the needs of their parents.

Filial piety. In general terms, this means to take care of one's parents, including showing love, respect and support, displaying courtesy, wisely advising one's parents, and concealing their mistakes.

Fine motor skill development. Involves the development of the ability to use and coordinate smaller muscles, such as those in the fingers and hands.

Four goals of misbehavior. According to Driekurs, children often misbehave to achieve one of four goals of misbehavior: to gain attention or power, seek revenge, or show a display of inadequacy.

Four pluses and a wish. A parenting technique for motivating children's cooperation, which requires a parent to smile, use relaxed body language, say the child's name, and pay a compliment to the child, before making a request.

Full nest. Describes the household in which young adults are residing with their parents.

Gayby boom. Greater access to donor insemination in the past two decades has resulted in what has been termed a "**gayby boom**" among North American and European lesbian women.

Generativity achievement. Represents the development of the ability of adults to contribute to the well-being of others, which is primarily achieved through work or parenthood.

Gifted. A child who deviates from the norm in that the child's talents and/or academic capabilities exceed normal expectations.

Grandfamily. A relatively new term, which refers to families in which grandparents are raising their grandchildren. In the past several decades, there has been a dramatic upsurge in the number of these households.

Gross motor skill development. The development of the large muscle groups that are involved in the movement of the body, arms, and legs.

Guided participation. A process by which the parent engages the child in joint activities and guides the child's participation by providing instruction, as well as direct involvement.

Honeymoon phase. The phase during which foster parents, and their foster children, experience few problems, and during which time the children are on their best behavior.

House of self. According to Dorothy Briggs, the child's house of self is constructed by the words, body language, and treatment by important others in their environment, particularly parents.

Identity achievement. The identity status of young persons who have established a clear and definite sense of who they are, and where they fit in their particular culture. These young persons have made definite personal, occupational, and ideological choices, after first exploring a number of possibilities.

Identity diffusion. The identity status characterized by individuals not questioning who they are, not exploring available paths of identity formation, and not committing to possible choices.

Identity foreclosure. The identity status in which persons have committed to personal, occupational, or ideological choices, without having first experimented with a range of possibilities.

I-message. A statement used to express the problem owner's feelings regarding the other person's undesirable behavior. *I* messages are not blameful; hence, they are not *you* messages.

Imitation. A type of learning wherein children observe the behavior of others and use that as a reference for their own behaviors.

Impairment. Refers to the condition of an individual who has physical, psychological, mental, intellectual, or medical conditions that make it difficult for that person to learn and/or behave according to normal expectations.

Indifferent parenting style. An approach to childrearing in which parents seem uninvolved or uninterested in their child's development.

Individualistic cultural values. Cultural values that prioritize independence, individual freedoms, and individual achievements.

Individuals with Disabilities Education Act (IDEA). This is a law that has been in effect since 1975, and was reauthorized by Congress in 2004. The IDEA is based on six basic guidelines, which include the right to (a) a free and appropriate public education, (b) appropriate evaluations, (c) an Individual Education Program (IEP), (d) be educated in the Least Restrictive Environment (LRE), (e) parent and student participation, and (f) procedural due process.

Individuation. Refers to the process that occurs during early adulthood, when individuals explore a differentiated sense of self, which is typically achieved without severing emotional ties with parents.

Induction. A parenting strategy that reduces undesirable behavior in children by increasing their awareness of the likely consequences of their actions for themselves as well as others.

Indulgent parenting style. An excessively permissive childrearing pattern that emphasizes high responsiveness and low demandedness.

Intent participation. A type of learning especially valued and emphasized in communities where children have access to learning from informal community involvement. In these communities, young children observe and listen with intent concentration and initiative, and their future collaborative participation is expected when they are ready.

Iron-deficiency anemia. A health condition, often seen during preschool, that is caused when there is too little iron in the diet, or there is poor absorption of iron within the body.

Joint attention. When two or more individuals are reading together, working a puzzle together, or participating in any other activity that requires the attention of both individuals, these individuals are engaged in joint attention.

Kangaroo care. The traditional cultural practice of holding infants skin to skin, which is used in many infant intensive care units to promote the survival of at-risk babies.

Kinkeepers. Individuals in an extended family who are responsible for getting families together for family social occasions, promoting cooperation among family members, and sharing news about family members' well-being.

Learning disability. Part of a larger diagnosis of underachievement, which might represent a number of different areas, including difficulty in perceiving, processing, storing, and understanding information.

Linguistic turn taking. A verbal dialogue in which two or more speakers leave a brief pause when speaking in order to allow time for the other person/s to respond.

Logical consequence. A strategy that a parent might use to provide a consequence for a child's misbehavior that is logically related to that behavior.

Lost child. The child in an alcoholic family who is quiet and generally ignored. The lost child is a loner, and a daydreamer, who engages in solitary play, and is withdrawn from other family members. The benefit the lost child provides for the alcoholic family system is relief, because this child does not cause any problem or inconvenience.

Mental impairment. The condition of a child who is a slow learner in almost all intellectual pursuits.

Modeling. Parental modeling is a process of observational learning in which the behavior of the parent serves as an example for similar behaviors of the child.

Mutual gazing. Parents and infants spending equally large amounts of time gazing at each other's faces.

Nar-Anon. A voluntary worldwide fellowship group for family members or others affected by someone else's drug addiction.

Narcotics Anonymous. A voluntary worldwide fellowship of men and women who meet together to help each other stay clean from drugs.

Natural consequences. An outcome that naturally occurs as the result of a behavior, such as slipping and falling down on an icy sidewalk.

No-lose method of conflict resolution. A democratic approach to the resolution of parent–child conflict in which both parents and children win.

Overregularization. A tendency of preschool children to apply regular rules of English to words that have an exception.

Parallel development. The process by which the roles of young adults and their parents continue to be redefined in relation to each other.

Parent–child coregulation. Represents the sharing of social power between parents and their children, which is a common behavior between parents and their school-age children.

Parent–infant synchrony. The ability of both the parent and infant to accurately read and respond to cues provided by the other person.

Parental comprehending. The ability of young adults to realize that their parents had an existence prior to assuming the role of parent and that their parents continue to exist as individuals outside their parental role.

Parental demandedness. The demands that parents make on their children including maturity demands, behavioral monitoring, and the delivery of consequences for inappropriate behavior. By and large, demandedness is the degree to which parents expect and demand responsible behavior from their children.

Parental distancing. A critical task for personal development whereby young adults distance themselves from their parents and establish a separate identity as an adult.

Parental responsiveness. The degree to which parents respond to the child's needs in an accepting, supportive manner. It also refers to the extent to which parents foster their children's development by being attuned to them and supportive of their needs.

Parentese. Form of adult-to-infant speech that is higher pitched; has more low-to-high fluctuations; has simpler, more concrete vocabulary; and its sentence length is shorter than normal speech.

Parentification. The distortion of the parent–child relationship in such a way that the child is often placed in the role of the parent. Parentified children might be enlisted to care for their parents' physical, emotional, or even financial needs.

Perceived mattering. One's sense of mattering consists of the psychological tendency to evaluate the self as significant to specific other people.

Permissive parenting style. An approach to childrearing in which parents are noncontrolling and nondemanding, but highly responsive to their children.

Person-first language. Language that emphasizes the importance of seeing the child first and the exceptionality second. Rehabilitation professionals have been strongly encouraged to adopt person-first language that focuses on the person rather than the exceptionality.

Personal boundaries. Young children learn about their limitations as well as what they may and may not do when they make errors in judgment, fail to accomplish certain goals, and when boundaries are crossed that lead to disapproval from parents.

Pervasive developmental delay. A label given to a young child with a mental impairment to allow for the possibility that the child will catch up to normal, age-appropriate development.

Physical abuse. Occurs when parents inflict nonaccidental physical injury on children under the age of 18.

Physical impairment. An impairment that affects the ability to move or to coordinate and control movement when performing tasks.

Poisonous pedagogy. A term used by Alice Miller to describe the authoritarian parenting style. Miller charges that the authoritarian parenting approach robs children of their human spirit, and inhibits their normal emotional development.

Posttraumatic stress disorder (PTSD). A debilitating condition that often follows a terrifying physical or emotional event, which causes the person to have persistent, frightening thoughts and memories of the ordeal.

Praise. Messages parents send to their children that emphasize the parent's feelings as opposed to the child's feelings.

Preconcepts. Represent children's first symbolic concepts, which are not as complete or logical as those of older children and adults.

Preoperational thought. Occurs during the preschool years, when children are able to think at a symbolic level, but their thoughts are not yet logical.

Problem ownership. The ability to sort out who has the problem when a problem has arisen in a parent–child relationship.

Psychosocial crisis. The crises that emerge at each developmental level. According to Erikson, the quality of the parent–child relationship impacts the individual's ability to resolve psychosocial crises related to each stage of development.

Quest for identity. The developmental quest of adolescents, who are searching for answers to questions about who they are, and who they are becoming. This quest involves the exploration of a range of possible selves.

Racial socialization. A type of child socialization that includes providing a home that is rich in racial culture, and socializing children to be proud of their racial heritage. Racial socialization is believed to act as a buffer against negative racial messages in the environment.

Recognition reflex. According to Dreikurs, a child who is misbehaving might sometimes be made aware of the goal of the misbehavior. When that occurs, the child has a recognition reflex.

Reconnecting phase. During young adulthood, after adult children have undergone a phase of distancing themselves from their parents, they experience a reconnecting phase during which time they have a more realistic perception of the parent. This phase is typically accompanied by a greater appreciation of the parent as an individual.

Reinforcement. Any consequence that strengthens a particular behavior, thereby increasing the likelihood that that behavior will be repeated.

Religiosity. In the case of parent–child relationships, refers to whether and how often parents provide religion to children at home (prayers at meals, family devotions), how much the family's social activities include the church and its members, and whether religious beliefs affect the way parents interact with their children.

Reverse-order sentences. A sentence in which the order of the action required is reversed by the use of words such as *after, if,* or *when* These type of sentences are not understood by young children who understand actions in the sequence in which they are presented. An example of a reverse-order sentence is "You can have a cookie after you wash your hands."

Role buffering. Process by which both parents in a household act in many ways to buffer the impact of stress associated with performing the dual roles of parent and paid worker.

Role overload. Occurs most often in dual-worker families with young children, and describes the ways in which the demands related to the work role and the demands of the parental role result in a parent feeling strained and overwhelmed.

Scaffolding. Term used to describe the supportive strategies parents use to guide their children in solving cognitive tasks.

Second-generation fathers. Fathers of adult children who also have younger children with a second wife or partner.

Secure attachment. An affectionate tie that develops when a child's caregiver is emotionally and physically available to the child.

Self-esteem. Refers to the judgments that children make regarding their own worth, and the feelings associated with these judgments.

Self-regulation. Children's development of control over their own bodies.

Self-reliance. The ability of a child to behave in ways that are considered by parents and other caregivers to be acceptable.

Sense of industry. According to Erikson, the development of a sense of industry is related to school-age children's drive to become competent or skilled in the activities valued by their parents and other significant adults in their culture. Based on their level of success in mastering these skills or competencies, school-age children judge themselves as competent or incompetent, productive or failing.

Sense of initiative. An Eriksonian concept that reflects the preschool child's striving to become increasingly more independent, which is reflected in their making and carrying out multifaceted plans.

Sense of integrity vs. sense of despair. According to Erikson, during old age, individuals re-examine their lives and make judgments regarding whether they have accomplished the things they had hoped for in their work as well as in their personal relationships. If their interpretation of their lives is a positive one, they incorporate a sense of integrity. If they look back with regrets, they develop a sense of despair.

Sense of guilt. According to Erikson, preschool children's feelings about their behaviors that parents, or other adults, label as wrong or bad.

Sense of trust vs. mistrust. Erikson's terms for the psychosocial crisis of infancy, during which time the infant learns whether the world is safe and predictable (trust) or unsafe and unpredictable (mistrust).

Sensitive period of development. A genetically determined timetable during which certain developmental changes occur when normal environmental conditions are present, such as the development of infant attachment, or the early development of language.

Sensorimotor intelligence. A Piagetian perspective that infants think exclusively with their senses and motor skills during this stage of development.

Sexual abuse. When a parent, or other person responsible for the child's well-being, engages in sexual activity with a child under the age of 18.

Sexual orientation identity. Involves the personal acknowledgment of one's sexual orientation as well as the public presentation and recognition of one's sexual orientation.

Shaken baby syndrome. Refers to a trauma experienced by an infant as a result of being shaken, usually by a parent, in an effort to keep the baby from crying. The trauma resulting from being shaken might result in brain damage or death.

Skipped generation caregiving. Refers to the custodial care that many grandparents provide for their grandchildren in grandparent-headed households.

Social anchorage. Both older men and older women evaluate their life histories in terms of the social networks of which they have been a part. In their remembered past, social anchorage (maintaining relationships and connections to others) is seen as important, especially for women.

Social coordination of movement. This ability, which develops during the preschool years, reflects the ability of children to coordinate the movements of their own bodies with the movements of other people. Being able to change directions while running in anticipation of another child's movement in a game of *tag* reflects the young child's development of social coordination of movement.

Social referencing. Refers to the behavior of infants and toddlers when they continuously check their parent's gaze or facial expressions as well as verbal responses of pleasure or displeasure to guide their behavior.

Social status transitions. Beginning when their children are in early adulthood, the relationships of middle-aged adults and their children are altered along a series of social status transitions. These transitions modify those persons' social roles.

Society. People who live and interact with each other because they share a common geographical area.

Socioeconomic status (SES). Refers to social status, which includes educational level, income level, and occupational status.

Stander. An alternative position device, for an individual with a physical disability, that supports the person in a standing position.

Surrogate parents. Persons who have stepped into the parental role to ensure that children have homes in which to live and caring adults to guide and protect them.

Symbolic thinking. A thought process that involves the use of words, gestures, pictures, or actions to represent ideas, things, or behaviors.

Tag-team parenting. A type of child-rearing that takes place in some dual-earner families, in which parents partake in nonoverlapping shift patterns of employment to allow for one parent to care for the children at all times.

Teratogens. Agents and conditions, including malnutrition, viruses, drugs, chemicals, and stressors, that can interfere with prenatal development and contribute to birth defects or death.

Theory of mind. An understanding of human mental processes, such as trying to understand a playmate's anger or determining when a sibling will be generous, that develops during the preschool years.

Traditional cultures. Cultural groups that do not share the characteristics of the majority culture.

Traditional parenting style. An approach to childrearing, usually found in traditional cultures, that emphasizes high responsiveness and a type of demandingness that does not encourage discussion or debate.

Unsafe communities. Communities with high levels of violence, crime, and drug activity. In these neighborhoods, parents and children are directly and indirectly exposed to robberies, physical assaults, and murders.

Vicarious reinforcement. The basic premise of Social Learning Theory, that children do not have to be directly reinforced or punished to learn a behavior. Instead, children learn through two interrelated strategies: imitation and modeling.

the West. Includes majority cultures in the United States, Canada, Western Europe, Australia, and New Zealand.

References

Abel, M. (1997). Low birth weight and interactions between traditional risk factors. *The Journal of Genetic Psychology, 158*, 443–456.

Ainsworth, M. D. S. (1967). *Infancy in Uganda: Infant care and the growth of love.* Baltimore: Johns Hopkins University Press.

Ainsworth, M. D. S. (1973). The development of infant–mother attachment. In B. M. Caldwell & H. N. Ricciutti (Eds.), *Review of child development research: Vol. 3. Child development and social policy* (pp. 1–94). Chicago: University of Chicago Press.

Ainsworth, M. D. S., & Bell, S. M. (1969). Some contemporary patterns of mother–infant interaction in the feeding situation. In A. Ambrose (Ed.), *Stimulation in early childhood.* London & New York: Academic Press.

Ainsworth, M. D. S., Blehar, M. C., Waters, E., & Wall, S. (1978). *Patterns of attachment.* Hillsdale, NJ: Erlbaum.

Alcoholics Anonymous World Services (2007). *Information on A.A.* Available at: http://www.Alcoholics-anonymous.org/en_information_aa.cfm

Allen, J., & Land, P. (1999). Attachment in adolescence. In J. Cassidy & P. R. Shaver (Eds.), *Handbook of attachment: Theory, research and clinical applications* (pp. 319–335). New York: Guilford.

Allen, S., & Crago, M. (1996). Early passive acquisition in Inuktitut. *Journal of Child Language, 23*, 129–155.

Allès-Jardel, M., Fourdrinier, C., Roux, A., & Schneider, B. H. (2002). Parents' structuring of children's daily lives in relation to the quality and stability of children's friendships. *International Journal of Psychology, 37*, 65–73.

Amato, P. R. (2000). Diversity within single-parent families. In D. H. Demo, K. R. Allen, & M. A. Fine (Eds.), *The handbook of family diversity* (pp. 149–172). New York: Oxford University Press.

Amato, P. R., & Gilbreth, J. (1999). Nonresident fathers and children's well-being: A meta-analysis. *Journal of Marriage and the Famiily, 61*, 557–573.

Amato, P. R., & Sobolewski, P. R. (2003). Effects of divorce and marital discord on adult children's psychological well-being. *Sage Urban Studies Abstracts, 31*(1), 3–133.

American Psychiatric Association. (1994). *Diagnostic and statistical manual of mental disorders* (4th ed.). Washington, DC: Author.

Anderson, C. (2007). The Individuals with Disabilities Education Improvement Act of 2004. *Exceptional Parent, 37*(3), 94–96.

Ansbaugh, R., & Peck, S. (1998). Treatment of sleep problems in a toddler: A replication of the faded bedtime with response cost protocol. *Journal of Applied Behavior Analysis, 31*, 127–129.

Ariel, J. (2001). Therapy with lesbian and gay parents and their children. *Journal of Marital and Family Therapy, 26*(4), 421–432.

Aries, P. (1962). *Centuries of childhood: A social history of family life* (R. Baldick, Trans.). New York: Knopf. (Original work published 1960)

Arlin, P. K. (1975). Cognitive development in adulthood: A fifth stage? *Developmental Psychology, 11*, 602–606.

Arnett, J. J. (1999). Adolescent storm and stress reconsidered. *American Psychologist, 54*, 317–326.

Arnett, J. J. (2004). *Adolescence and emerging adulthood: A cultural approach* (2nd ed.). Upper Saddle River, NJ: Prentice Hall.

Arnett, J. J. (2007). *Adolescence and emerging adulthood: A cultural approach* (3rd ed.). Upper Saddle River, NJ: Prentice Hall.

Arroyo, C. G., & Zigler, E. (1995). Racial identity, academic achievement, and the psychological well-being of economically disadvantaged adolescents. *Journal of Personality and Social Psychology, 69*, 903–914.

Aunola, K., Stattin, H., & Nurmi, J. E. (2000). Parenting styles and adolescents' achievement strategies. *Journal of Adolescence, 23*, 205–222.

Azar S. T. (1997). A cognitive-behavioral approach to understanding and treating parents who physically abuse their children. In D. A. Wolfe, R. J. McMahon, & R. D. Peters (Eds.), *Child abuse: New directions in prevention and treatment across the lifespan* (pp. 79–101). Thousand Oaks, CA: Sage.

Bailey, C. T., & Boykin, A. W. (2001) The role of task variability and home contextual factors in the academic performance and task motivation of African American elementary school children. *The Journal of Negro Education, 70*(1–2), 84–95.

Bailey, J., & McCloskey, L. (2005). Pathways to adolescent substance use among sexually abused girls. *Journal of Abnormal Child Psychology, 33*(1), 39–53.

Bakel, H. J., & Riksen-Walvaren, J. M. (2002). Quality of parent-infant attachment as reflected in infant interactive behavior during instructional tasks. *The Journal of Child Psychology and Psychiatry and Allied Disciplines, 43*(3), 387–394.

Baker, A. J. L., McKay, M. M., Lynn, C. J., Hans Schlange, L. H., & Auville, A. (2003). Recidivism at a shelter for adolescents: First-time versus repeat runaways. *Social Work Research, 27*(2), 84–93.

Baker, J. (2000). Immunization and the American way: Childhood vaccines. *American Journal of Public Health, 90*, 199–207.

Baldry, A. C. (2003). Bullying in schools and exposure to domestic violence. *Child Abuse and Neglect, 27*(7), 713–732.

Baldwin, A. L., Baldwin, C., & Cole, R. E. (1990). Stress-resistant families and stress-resistant children. In J. Rolf, A. Masten, D. Cicchetti, K. Neuchtherlin, & S. Weintraub (Eds.), *Risk and protective factors in the development of psychopathology* (pp. 257–280). Cambridge, UK: Cambridge University Press.

Baldwin, D. A. (2000). Interpersonal understanding fuels knowledge acquisition. *Current Directions in Psychological Science, 9*, 40–45.

Ball, H., Hooker, E., & Kelly, E. (1999). Where will the baby sleep? Attitudes and practice of new and experienced parents regarding cosleeping with their newborn infants. *American Anthropologist, 101*, 143–151.

Bandura, A. (1977) *Social learning theory*. Upper Saddle River, NJ: Prentice Hall.

Bandura, A. (1986). *Social foundations of thought and action: A social cognitive theory.* Upper Saddle River, NJ: Prentice Hall.

Bandura, A., & Walters, R. (1963). *Social learning and personality development.* New York: Holt, Rinehart, & Wilson.

Bar-Haim, Y., Sutton, D. B., & Fox, N. (2000). Stability and change of attachment at 14, 24, and 58 months of age: Behavior, representation, and life events. *The Journal of Child Psychology and Psychiatry and Allied Disciplines, 41*, 381–388.

Barkley, R. A. (1990). *Attention deficit hyperactivity disorder: A handbook for diagnosis and treatment.* New York: Guilford Press.

Barnes, G. M., Welte, J. W., & Hoffman, J. H. (2005). Shared predictors of youthful gambling, substance abuse, and delinquency. *Journal of the Society of Psychologists in Addictive Behaviors, 19*(2), 165–174.

Barnett, D., Kidwell, S., & Leung, K-H. (1998). Parenting and preschooler attachment among low-income urban African American families. *Child Development, 69*, 1657–1671.

Barnett, M., Quackenbush, S., & Sinisi, C. (1996). Factors affecting children's, adolescents', and young adults' perceptions of parental discipline. *Journal of Genetic Psychology, 157*, 411–424.

Barrett, A. E., Turner, R. J. (2005). Family structure and mental health: The mediating effects of socioeconomic status, family process, and social status. *Journal of Health and Social Behavior, 46*(2), 156–169.

Bassett, M. T., & Perl, S. (2004). Editor's Choice: Obesity: The public health challenge of our time. *American Journal of Public Health, 94*(9), 1477.

Bates, J. E., Viken, R. J., Alexander, D. B., Beyers, J., & Stockton, L. (2002). Sleep and adjustment in preschool children: Sleep diary reports by mothers relate to behavior reports by teachers. *Child Development, 73*(1), *62–74*.

Baum, A. C., Crase, S. J., & Crase, K. L. (2001). Influences on the decision to become or not to become a foster parent. *Families in Society, 82,* 202–213.

Baumrind, D. (1967). Child care practices anteceding three patterns of preschool behavior. *Genetic Psychology Monographs, 75,* 43–88.

Baumrind, D. (1968). Authoritarian vs. authoritative parental control. *Adolescence, 3,* 255–272.

Baumrind, D. (1971). Current patterns of parental authority. *Developmental Psychology Monographs, 4*(1, Pt. 2), 1–103.

Baumrind, D. (1987). A developmental perspective on adolescent risk taking in contemporary America. In C. E. Irwin, Jr. (Ed.), *Adolescent social behavior and health. New Directions for Child Development, 37,* 93–125.

Baumrind, D. (1991a). Effective parenting during the early adolescent transition. In P. A. Cowen & E. M. Hetherington (Eds.), *Advances in family research* (Vol. 2, Family Transitions, pp. 111–163). Hillsdale, NJ: Erlbaum.

Baumrind, D. (1991b). The influence of parenting style on adolescent competence and substance abuse. *Journal of Early Adolescence, 11,* 56–95.

Baumrind, D. (1996). The discipline controversy revisited. *Family Relations, 45,* 405–414.

Beatty, V. (2000). A Dad's diary of labor and delivery. *Baby Talk, 65,* 32–34.

Bednar, D. E., & Fisher, T. D. (2003). Peer referencing in adolescent decision making as a function of perceived parenting style. *Adolescence, 38,* 607–621.

Beevar, D. A., & Beevar, R. J. (1988). *Family therapy: A systemic integration.* Boston: Allyn & Bacon.

Belle, D., Doucet, J. H., Miller, J., & Tan, J. (2000). Who is rich? Who is happy? *American Psychologist, 55*(10), 1160–1161.

Bempechat, J., Graham, S., & Jimenez, N. (1999). The socialization of achievement in poor and minority students: A comparative study. *Journal of Cross-Cultural Psychology, 30,* 139–159.

Benedikt, R., Wertheim, E. H., & Love, A. (1998). Eating disorders and weight-loss attempts in female adolescents and their mothers. *Journal of Youth and Adolescence, 27,* 43–57.

Berger, C. (2001). Infant mortality: A reflection of the quality of health, *Health and Social Work, 26*(4), 277–282.

Berger, K. S. (2005). *The developing person through the life span* (6th ed.). New York: Worth.

Berger, R. (2000). Gay stepfamilies: A triple stigmatized group. *Families in Society, 81,* 504–516.

Berghold, K. M., Lock, J. (2002). Assessing guilt in adolescents with anorexia nervosa. *American Journal of Psychotherapy, 56*(3), 378–390.

Berg-Weger, M., McGartland, D. R., & Tebb, S. S. (2001). Strengths-based practice with family caregivers of the chronically ill: Qualitative insights. *Families in Society, 82,* 263–272.

Best, M., Stresisant, R., Catania, L., & Kazak, A. E. (2001). Parental distress during pediatric leukemia and post-traumatic stress symptoms (PTSS) after treatment ends. *Journal of Pediatric Psychology, 26,* 299–307.

Bhattacharya, G. (2000). The school adjustment of South Asian immigrant children in the United States, *Adolescence, 35*(137), 77–85.

Bhattacharya, J., DeLeire, T., & Haider, S. (2003). Research and practice—Heat or eat? Cold weather shocks and nutrition in poor American families. *American Journal of Public Health, 93*(7), 1149–54.

Bifulco, A., Moran, P. M., & Ball, C. (2002). Childhood adversity, parental vulnerability and disorder: Examining intergenerational transmission of abuse. *The Journal of Child Psychology and Psychiatry and Allied Disciplines, 43*(8), 1075–1086.

Bigner, J. J. (1998). *Parent–child relations: An introduction to parenting* (5th ed.). Upper Saddle River, NJ: Prentice Hall.

Biron, D., & Shelton, D. (2005). Perpetrator accounts in infant abusive head trauma brought about by a shaking event. *Child Abuse and Neglect, 29*(12), 1347–1358.

Black, B., & Logan, A. (1995). Links between communication patterns in mother–child, father–child, and child–peer interactions. *Child Development, 66,* 255–270.

Blenkner, M. (1965). Social work and family in later life, with some thoughts on filial maturity.

In E. Shanas & G. Streib (Eds.), *Social structure and the family: Generational relations* (pp. 46–59). Upper Saddle River, NJ: Prentice Hall.

Bluestone, C., & Tamis-LeMonda, C. S. (1999). Parenting—Correlates of parenting styles in predominantly working class and middle-class African-American mothers. *Journal of Marriage and the Family, 61*(4), 881–894.

Bogat, G. A., Dejonghe, E., Levendosky, A. A., Davidson, W. S., & von Eye, A. (2006). Trauma symptoms among infants exposed to intimate partner violence. *Child Abuse and Neglect, 30*(2), 109–127.

Bogenschneider, K., Wu, M., Raffaelli, M., & Tsay, J. C. (1998). Parent influences on adolescent peer orientation and substance abuse: The interface of parenting practices and values. *Child Development, 69*, 1672–1688.

Bower, A., & Hayes, A. (1998). Mothering in families with and without a child with disability. *International Journal of Disability, Development, and Education, 45*, 313–322.

Bowlby, J. (1951). Maternal care and mental health. *Bulletin of the World Health Organization, 3*, 355–534.

Bowlby, J. (1958). The nature of the child's tie to his mother. *International Journal of Psychoanalysis, 39*, 350–373.

Bowlby, J. (1969). *Attachment and loss, Vol. 1. Attachment.* New York: Basic Books.

Boykin, A. W., & Allen, B. A. (2000). Beyond Deficit and Difference: Psychosocial integrity in developmental research. In C. C. Yeakey & E. W. Gordon (Eds.), *Producing knowledge, pursuing understanding.* JAI Press.

Boykin, A. W., & Cunningham, R. (2001). The effects of movement expressions in story content and learning content on the anological reasoning performance of African American children. *Journal of Negro Education, 70*(1–2), 72–83.

Boyle, M., & Morris, D. (1999). *Community nutrition in action: An entrepreneurial approach* (2nd ed.). Belmont, CA: Wadsworth.

Bradlow, A. R., Kraus, N. & Hayes, E. (2003). Speaking clearly for children with learning disabilities: Sentence perception in noise. *Journal of Speech, Language, and Hearing Research, 46*(1), 80–97.

Brand, H., Crous, B., & Hanekom, J. (1990). Perceived parental inconsistency as a factor in the emotional development of behavior-disordered children. *Psychological Reports, 66*, 620–622.

Brandstadter, J. (1998). Action perspectives on human development. In W. Damon & R. Lerner (Eds.), *Handbook of child psychology, Vol. 1: Theoretical models of human development* (5th ed., pp. 941–973). New York: Wiley.

Braus, P. (1998). When the helpers need a hand. *American Demographics, 20*, 66–72.

Bray, J., & Kelly, J. (1998). *Stepfamilies: Love, marriage and parenting in the first decade.* New York: Broadway Books.

Brenner, V., & Fox, R. A. (1999). An empirically derived classification of parenting practices. *The Journal of Genetic Psychology, 160*(3), 343–356.

Briggs, D. (1975). *Your child's self-esteem: The key to his life.* New York: Doubleday.

Brill, A. (1938). *The basic writings of Sigmund Freud.* New York: The Modern Library.

Britton, L. (1992). *Montessori, play and learn: A parent's guide to purposeful play from two to six.* New York: Crown.

Brody, G. H., Arias, I., & Fincham, F. D. (1996). Linking marital and child attributions to family processes and parent-child relationships. *Journal of Family Psychology, 10*, 408–421.

Brody, G. H., Ge, X., & Conger, R. (2001). The influence of neighborhood disadvantage, collective socialization, and parenting on African American children's affiliation with deviant peers. *Child Development, 72*, 1231–1246.

Brody, G. H., Stoneman, Z., Flor, D., & McCrary, C. (1997). Religion's role in organizing family relationships: Family processes in rural, two-parent African-American families. *Developmental Psychology, 32*, 696–706.

Bronfenbrenner, U. (1979). *The ecology of human development.* Cambridge, UK: Cambridge University Press.

Bronfenbrenner, U. (1989). Ecological systems theory. In R. Vasta (Ed.), *Annals of child development* (Vol. 6). Greenwich, CT: JAI Press.

Brophy, G. (2000). Social work treatment of sleep disturbance in a 5-year-old boy: A single case evaluation. *Research in Social Work Practice, 10*, 748–758.

Brophy, M., & Dunn, J. (2002). What did mummy say? Dyadic interaction between young "hard to manage" children and their mothers. *Journal of Abnormal Child Psychology, 20*(2), 103–115.

Brown, S. L. (2006). Family structure transitions and adolescent well being. *Demography, 43*(3), 447–461.

Brown, S. L., & Lewis, V. (1999). *The alcoholic family in recovery: A developmental model.* New York: The Guilford Press.

Bruer, J. (1999). *The myth of the first three years: A new understanding of early brain development and lifelong learning.* New York: Free Press.

Bryce, J. C., Boshi-Pinto, K., Shibaya, R. E., Black, R. E. (2005). WHO estimates of the causes of death in children, *Lancet, 364*(9465), 1147–1152.

Bullock, K. (2004). The changing roles of grandparents in rurual families. *Families in Society, 85,* 45–54.

Burbach, A. D., Fox, R. A., & Nicholson, B. C. (2004). Challenging behaviors in young children: The father's role. *Journal of Genetic Psychology, 165*(2), 169–183.

Burnett, D. (1999). Social relationships of Latino grandparent caregivers: A role theory perspective. *Gerontologist, 39,* 49–58.

Burnett, G., Jones, R., Bliwise, N., & Ross. (2006). Family unpredictability, parental alcoholism, and the development of parentification. *American Journal of Family Therapy, 34*(3), 181–189.

Butler, R. (1998). Age trends in the use of social and temporal comparison for self-evaluation: Examination of a novel developmental hypothesis. *Child Development, 69,* 1054–1073.

Bynner J. (2000). Social change and the sequencing of developmental transitions. In L. Crockett & R. Silbereisen (Eds.), *Negotiating adolescence in times of social change* (pp. 89–110). Cambridge: Cambridge University Press.

Calderon, R. (2000). Parental involvement in deaf children's educational programs as a predictor of child's language, early reading, and social-emotional development. *Journal of Deaf Studies and Deaf Education, 5*(2), 140–155.

Cantos, A. L., Neale, J. M., & O'Leary, K. D. (1997). Assessment of coping strategies of child-abusing mothers. *Child Abuse and Neglect, 21,* 631–636.

Caputo, R. K. (2004). Parent religiosity, family processes, and adolescent outcomes. *Families in Society, 85*(4), 495–510.

Carton, M., & Dominguez, M. (1997). The relationship between self-actualization and parenting style. *Journal of Social Behavior and Personality, 12,* 1093–1100.

Ceballo, R. & McLoyd, V. C. (2002). Social support & parenting in poor, dangerous neighborhoods. *Child Development, 73*(4), 1310-1321.

Ceci, S. J. (2006). *Urie Bronfenbrenner (1917–2005). American Psychologist, 61*(2), 173–174.

Ceron-Mireles, P., Harlow, S., & Sanchez-Carrillo, C. (1996). The risk of prematurity and small-for gestational-age birth in Mexico City: The effects of working conditions and antenatal leave. *American Journal of Public Health, 86,* 825–831.

Chan, D. (2002). Perceptions of giftedness and self-concept among junior secondary students in Hong Kong. *Journal of Youth and Adolescence, 31,* 243–252.

Chan, R., Raboy, B., & Patterson, C. (1998). Division of labor among lesbian and heterosexual parents. *Journal of Family Psychology, 12*(3), 402–419.

Chao, R. K. (1994). Beyond parental control and authoritarian parenting styles: Understanding Chinese parenting through the cultural notion of training. *Child Development, 65,* 1111–1119.

Chao, R. (2001). Extending research on the consequences of parenting style for Chinese Americans and European Americans. *Child Development, 72,* 1832–1843.

Chapman, M., & McBride, M. (1995). The education of reason: Conflict and its role in intellectual development. In C. Shantz & W. Hartup (Eds.), *Conflict in child and adolescent development* (pp. 36–69). Cambridge, UK: Cambridge University Press.

Chase-Lansdale, P. L., Mott, F. L., & Brooks-Gunn, J. (1991). Children of the national longitudinal study of youth: A unique research opportunity. *Developmental Psychology, 27,* 918–931.

Chavira, V., Lopez, S., & Blacher, J. (2000). Latina mothers' attributions, emotions, and reactions to the problem behaviors of their children with developmental disabilities. *The Journal of Child Psychology and Psychiatry and Allied Disciplines, 41,* 245–252.

Checkovich, T., & Stern, S. (2002). Shared caregiving responsibilities of adult siblings with elderly parents. *The Journal of Human Resources, 37,* 441–478.

Cherlin, A. J., Scabini E., & Rossi, G. (1997). Still in the nest: Delayed home leaving in Europe and the United States. *Journal of Family Issues, 18,* 572–575.

Chin-Yee, F. (1990). Through the maze: Grief counseling through the childbearing cycle. *International Journal of Childbirth Education, 5,* 31–32.

Chirkov, V., & Ryan, R. (2001). Parent and teacher autonomy-support in Russian and U.S. adolescents: Common effects on well-being and academic achievement. *Journal of Cross-Cultural Psychology, 32,* 618–635.

Cicirelli, V. G. (2000). An examination of the trajectory of the adult child's caregiving for an elderly parent. *Family Relations, 49*(2), 169–175.

Clark, R., Novak, J., & Dupree, D. (2002). Relationships of perceived parenting practices to anger regulation and coping strategies in African-American adolescents. *Journal of Adolescence, 25,* 373–384.

Clarke-Stewart, K. A., & Hayward, C. (1996). Advantages of father custody and contact for the psychological well being of school-age children. *Journal of Applied Developmental Psychology, 17,* 239–270.

Cleaver, J. Y. (1999). Good old Dad. *American Demographics, 32,* 58–62.

Cleverley, J., & Phillips, D. (1986). *Visions of childhood: Influential models from Locke to Spock* (Rev. ed). New York: Teachers College Press.

Clyburn, L., Stones, M., & Hadjistavropoulos, T. (2000). Predicting caregiving burden and depression in Alzheimer's disease. *Journals of Gerontology, Series B: Psychological Sciences and Social Sciences, 55B,* S2–S13.

Cohen, D. (1979). *J. B. Watson: The founder of behaviorism.* London: Routledge & Kegan Paul.

Cohen, P. N. & Casper, L. M. (2002). In whose home? Multigenerational families in the United States, 1998–2000. *Sociological Perspectives, 45*(1), 1–20.

Coker, A. L., Smith, P. H., McKeown, R. E., & King, M. J. (2000). Injury and violence—Frequency and correlates of intimate partner violence by type: physical, sexual, and psychosocial battering. *American Journal of Public Health, 90*(4), 553–560.

Colarossi, L. G., & Eccles, J. S. (2000). A prospective study of adolescents' peer supports, gender differences, and the influence of parental relationships. *Journal of Youth and Adolescence, 29*(6), 661–678.

Coleman, M., Ganong, L., & Fine, L. (2000). Reinvestigating marriage: Another decade of progress. *Journal of Marriage and the Family, 62,* 1288–1307.

Coley, R. L., & Chase-Lansdale, P. L. (1999). Adolescent pregnancy and parenthood: Recent evidence and future directions. *American Psychologist, 53*(2), 152–166.

Conley, D., & Bennett, N. (2001). Birth weight and income: Interactions across generations. *Journal of Health and Social Behavior, 42,* 450–465.

Cooney, T. M., & Mortimer, J. T. (1999). Family structure differences in the timing of leaving home. Exploring mediating factors. *Society for Research in Adolescence, 9*(4), 367–377.

Cornell, S. (2001). Governor responds as CT grapples with teen pregnancy. *Fairfield Journal, 4,* 8.

Cox, M., Paley, B., & Burchinal, M. (1999). Marital perceptions and interactions across the transition to parenthood. *Journal of Marriage and the Family, 61*(3), 611–625.

Crespo, C. J., Smit, E., Troiano, R. P., Bartlett, S. J., Macera, C. A., & Andersen, R. E. (2001). Television watching, energy intake, and obesity in U.S. children: results from the third National Health and Nutrition Examination Survey, 1988–1994. *Archives of Pediatric Adolescent Medicine, 155,* 360–365.

Crisp, M. (2001, April). Growing up with a disability: What children with disabilities need from parents. *Exceptional Parent,* 74–78.

Cuffe, S. P., McKeown, R. E., & Addy, C. L. (2005). Family and psychosocial risk factors in a longitudinal epidemiological study of adolescents. *Journal of the American Academy of Child and Adolescent Psychology, 44*(2), 121–130.

Cullen, K. W., Ash, D. M., & Warneke, C. (2002). Intake of soft drinks, fruit-flavored beverages, and fruits and vegetables by children in grades 4 through 6. *American Journal of Public Health, 92*(9), 1475–1478.

Cunningham, C., & Boyle, M. (2002). Preschoolers at risk for attention-deficit hyperactivity disorder and oppositional defiant disorder: Family, parenting, and behavioral correlates. *Journal of Abnormal Child Psychology, 30*, 555–569.

Cunningham, M. (2001). The influence of parental attitudes and behaviors on children's attitudes toward gender and household labor in early adulthood. *Journal of Marriage and the Family, 63*, 111–122.

Dalton, W. T. III, Frick-Horbury, D., & Kitzmann, K. M. (2006). Young adults' retrospective reports of parenting by mothers and fathers: Associations with current relationship quality. *The Journal of General Psychology, 133*(1), 5–18.

Daly, D. I., & Dowd, T. P. (1992). Characteristics of effective, harm-free environments for children in out-of-home care. *Child Welfare, 71*, 487–496.

Daniluk, J. C., & Hurtig-Mitchell, J. (2003). Themes of hope and healing: Infertile couples experiences of adoption. *Journal of Counseling and Development, 81*(4), 389–399.

Dankoski, M. (2001). Pulling on the heart strings: An emotionally focused approach to family life cycle transitions. *Journal of Marriage and Family Therapy, 27*, 177–187.

Davidson, A. (1999). Beestings, *The Oxford Companion to Food,* Oxford: Oxford University Press, 69.

Davis A. A. (2002). Younger and older African American adolescent mothers' relationships with their mothers and female peers. *Journal of Adolescent Research, 17*, 491–508.

Deater-Deckard, K. (2000). Parenting and child behavioral adjustment in early childhood: A qualitative genetic approach to studying family processes. *Child Development, 71*, 458–484.

DeBellis, M. D. (2001). Developmental traumatology: The psychobiological development of maltreated children and its implication for research, treatment, and policy. *Development and Psychopathology, 13*, 539–564.

Dejonghe, E. S., Bogat, G. A., Levendosky, A. A., von Eye, A., & Davidson, W. S. (2005). Infant exposure to domestic violence predicts heightened sensitivity to verbal conflict. *Infant Mental Health Journal, 26*(3), 268–281.

Delsing, M., Oud, J., & Bruyn, E. (2003). Family relationships: Intergenerational perspectives—Current and recollected perceptions of family relationships: The social relations model applied to members of three generations. *Journal of Family Psychology, 17*(4), 445–459.

Delva, J., Wallace, J. M., & O'Malley, P. M. (2005). The epidemiology of alcohol, marijuana, and cocaine use among Mexican American, Puerto Rican, Cuban American, and other Latin American eighth grade students in the United States. *American Journal of Public Health, 95*(4), 696–702.

Demaray, M. K. & Malecki, C. K. (2003). Perceptions of the priority and importance of social support by students classified or victims, bullies, and bully/victims in an urban middle school. *School Psychology Review, 32*, 471–489.

DeMier, R., Hynan, M., & Hatfield, R. (2002). A measurement model of perinatal stressors: Identifying risk for postnatal emotional distress in mothers of high-risk infants. *Journal of Clinical Psychology, 56*, 89–100.

DePanfelis, D., & Zuravin, S. (2002). The effect of services on the recurrence of child maltreatment. *Child Abuse and Neglect, 26*, 187–205.

Dietz, T. (2000). Disciplining children: Characteristics associated with the use of corporal punishment. *Child Abuse and Neglect, 24*(12), 1529–1542.

Dietz, W. (1999). Barriers to the treatment of childhood obesity: A call to action. *Journal of Pediatrics, 134*, 535–536.

DiFilippo, J. M., & Overholser, J. C. (2000). Suicidal ideation in adolescent psychiatric inpatients as associated with depression and attachment relationships. *Journal of Clinical Child Psychology, 29*, 155–166.

Dinkmeyer, D., & McKay, G. (1989). *Systematic training for effective parenting: The parent's handbook* (3rd ed.). Circle Pines, MN: American Guidance Services.

Dori, G., & Overholser, J. C. (1999). Depression, hopelessness, and self-esteem: Accounting for suicidality in adolescent psychiatric inpatients. *Suicide and Life-Threatening Behavior, 29*, 309–318.

Douvan, E., & Adelson, J. (1966). *The adolescent experience.* New York: Wiley.

Dowdney, L. (2000). Childhood bereavement following parental death. *The Journal of Child Psychology and Psychiatry and Allied Disciplines, 41*(7), 819–830.

Doyle, K. W., Wolchik, S. A., Dawson-McClure, S. R., & Sandler, I. N. (2003). Positive events as a stress buffer for children and adolescents in families in transition. *Journal of Clinical Child and Adolescent Psychology, 32*(4), 536–545.

Dreikurs, R. (1972). *Discipline without tears.* New York: Hawthorne.

Dreikurs, R., & Grey, L. (1968). *A new approach to discipline: Logical consequences.* New York: Hawthorne Books.

Dreikurs, R., & Grey, L. (1970). *A parent's guide to child discipline.* New York: Hawthorne.

Dreikurs, R., & Soltz, V. (1964). *Children: The challenge.* New York: Duell, Sloan, & Pearce.

Dunn, M., Burbine, T., & Bowers, C. (2001). Moderators of stress in parents of children with autism. *Community Mental Health Journal, 37,* 39–52.

Dunne, G. (2000). Opting into motherhood: Lesbians blurring the boundaries and redefining the meaning of parenting and kinship. *Journal of Gender and Society, 14*(1), 11–35.

Edelstein, S., & Burge, D. (2001). Helping foster parents cope with separation, loss, and grief. *Child Welfare, 80,* 5–25.

Edwards, C., & Liu, W-L. (2002). Parenting toddlers. In M. Bornstein (Ed.), *Handbook of parenting* (2nd ed., pp. 45–71). Mahwah, NJ: Erlbaum.

Edwards, O. W. (2003). Living with Grandma: A grandfamily study. *Psychological International, 24*(2), 204–217.

Edwards, V. J., Holden, G. W., & Velitti, V. J. (2003). Relationships between multiple forms of childhood maltreatment and adult mental health in community respondents: Results from the adverse childhood experiences study. *The American Journal of Psychiatry, 160*(8), 1453–1460.

Eggebeen, D. (2005). Cohabitation and exchanges of support. *Social Forces, 83*(3), 1097–1110.

Ehrenberg, M. F., Gearing-Small, M., & Hunter, M. A. (2001). Childcare task division and shared parenting attitudes in dual-earner families with young children. *Family Relations, 50*(2), 143–153.

Elkind, D. (1976). Child development and education: Piagetian perspective. New York: Oxford University Press.

Elkind, D. (2003). The overbooked child: Are we pushing our kids too hard? *Psychology Today, 36,* 64–70.

Elkin, F., & Handel, G. (1989). *The child and society: The process of socialization* (5th ed.). New York: Random House.

Engels, R. C., Finkenauer, C., & Meeus, W. (2001). Parental attachment and adolescents' social adjustment: The associations with social skills and relational competence. *Journal of Counseling Psychology, 48*(4), 428–439.

Ennett, S. T. , Bailey, S. L., & Federman, E. B. (1999). Social network characteristics associated with risky behaviors among runaway and homeless youth. *Journal of Health and Social Behavior, 40*(1), 51–65.

Epstein, J. A., Williams, C., & Botvin, G. J. (2002). How universal are social influences to drink and problem behaviors for alcohol use? A test comparing urban African-American and Caribbean American adolescents. *Addictive Behaviors, 27*(1), 75–86.

Erdwins, C., Buffardi, L., & Casper, W. (2001). The relationship of women's role strain to social support, role satisfaction, and self-efficacy. *Family Relations, 50,* 230–238.

Erera, P., & Fredrickson, K. (1999). Lesbian stepfamilies: A unique family structure. *Families in Society: The Journal of Contemporary Human Services, 80,* 263–270.

Erera-Weatherly, P. (1996). On becoming a stepparent: Factors associated with the adoption of alternative stepparenting styles. *Journal of Divorce and Remarriage, 25,* 155–174.

Erikson, E. (1963). *Childhood and society.* New York: Norton.

Erikson, E. H. (1968). *Identity, Youth and Crisis.* New York: Norton.

Erikson, E. H. (1982). *The life cycle completed: A review.* New York: Norton.

Erikson, E. H., Erikson, J., & Kivnick, H. (1986). *Vital involvement in old age.* New York: Norton.

Erkut, S., Szalacha, L. A., & Coll, C. G. (2005). A framework for studying minority youths' transitions to fatherhood: The case of Puerto Rican adolescents. *Adolescence, 40,* 709–727.

Ernst, M., Moolchan, E., & Robinson, M. (2001). Behavioral and neural consequence of prenatal exposure to nicotine. *Journal of the American Academy of Child and Adolescent Psychiatry, 40,* 630–641.

Eskenazi, B., Stapleton, A., Kharrazi, M., & Chee, W-Y. (1999). Associations between maternal decaffeinated and caffeinated coffee consumption and fetal growth and gestational duration. *Epidemiology, 10,* 242–249.

Fabes, R. A., Leonard, S. A., & Kupanoff, K. (2001). Parental coping with children's negative emotions: relations with children's emotional and social responding. *Child Development, 72*(3), 907–920.

Fabricius, W. V. (2003). Listening to children of divorce: New fidings that diverge from Wallerstein, Lewis, and Blakeslee (2003). *Family Relations, 52*(4), 385–396.

Facio, A., & Batistuta, M. (1998). Latins, Catholics, and from the far south: Argentenian adolescents and their parents. *Journal of Adolescence, 21*, 49–67.

Fagot, B. (1997). Attachment, parenting, and peer interactions of toddler children. *Developmental Psychology, 33*, 489–499.

Fals-Stewart, W., Kelley, M. L., & Fincham, F. D. (2004). Emotional and behavioral problems of children living with drug-abusing fathers: Comparisons with children living with alcohol-abusing and non-substance abusing fathers. *Journal of Family Psychology, 18*(2), 319–330.

Farmer, E. M. Z., Burns, B. J., Chapman, M. V., Phillips, S. D., Angold A., & Costello E. J. (2001). Use of mental health services by youth in contact with social services, *Social Service Review*, 75, 605–624.

Feldman, R., Greenbaum, C., & Yirmiya, N. (1999). Mother–infant affect synchrony as an antecedent of the emergence of self-control. *Developmental Psychology, 35*, 3–19.

Feldman, R., Weller, A. S., & Fidelman, L. (2003). Testing a family intervention hypothesis: The contribution of mother-infant skin-to-skin contact (kangaroo care) to family interaction, proximity, and touch. *Journal of Family Psychology, 17*(1), 94–107.

Feldman, R., Weller, A. S., & Sirota, L. (2002). Skin-to-skin contact (kangaroo care) promotes self-regulation in premature infants: Sleep–wake cyclicity, arousal modulation, and sustained exploration. *Developmental Psychology, 38*, 194–207.

Fernandez, C., & Antonio, J. (1997). Youth residential independence and autonomy: A comparative study. *Journal of Family Issues, 18*, 576–607.

Fiese, B. H., Tomcho, T. J., & Douglas, M. (2002). A review of 50 years of research on naturally occurring family routines and rituals: cause for celebration. *Journal of Family Psychology, 16*(4), 381–390.

Findler, L. S. (2000). The role of grandparents in the social support system of mothers of children with a physical disability. *Families in Society, 81*(4), 370–381.

Fine, M. (1991). The handicapped child and the family: Implications for professionals, in M. Fine (Ed.), *Collaboration with parents of exceptional children* (pp. 3–24). Brandon, VT: Clinical Psychology.

Fingerman, K. (2001). A distant closeness: Intimacy between parents and their children in later life. *Gerontology, 25*, 26–33.

Finnegan, R. A., Hodges, E. V., & Perry, D. G. (1998). Personality processes and individual differences—victimization by peers: association with children's reports of mother-child interaction. *Journal of Personality & Social Psychology, 75*(4), 1076–1087.

Fishman, C. (1999). The smorgasbord generation. *American Demographics, 21*, 54–60.

Flowers, P., & Buston, K. (2001). "I was terrified of being different." Exploring gay men's accounts of growing up in a heterosexual society. *Journal of Adolescence, 24*, 51–65.

Floyd, F., Stein, T., & Harter, K. (1999). Gay, lesbian, and bisexual youths: Separation–individuation, parental attitudes, identity consolidation, and well-being. *Journal of Youth and Adolescence, 28*, 719–739.

Fox, G. L., Bruce, C., & Combs-Orme, T. (2000). Parenting expectations and concerns of fathers and mothers of newborn infants. *Family Relations, 49*(2), 123–131.

Fox, R. A., Platz, D. L., & Bentley, K. S. (1995). Maternal factors related to parenting practices, developmental expectations, and perceptions of child behavior problems. *Journal of Genetic Psychology, 156*, 431–447.

Fredrickson, K. (1999). Family caregiving responsibilities among lesbian and gay men. *Social and Work, 44*, 142–155.

Freeman, H. S., & Brown, B. B. (2001). Primary attachment to parents and peers during adolescence: Differences by attachment style. *Journal of Youth and Adolescence, 30*(6), 653–674.

Freeman, H. S., & Newland, L. A. (2002). Family transitions during the adolescent transition: Implications for parenting. *Adolescence, 37*, 457–475.

Freud, A. (1946). *The ego and the mechanisms of defense.* New York: International Universities Press.

Freud, S. (1931/1961). *Civilization and its discontents* (J. Strachey, Trans.). New York: Norton. (Original work published 1931)

Froebel, F. (1909). *Friedrich Froebel: Pedogogies of the kindergarten, or his ideas concerning play and playthings of the child* (Josephine Jarvis, Trans.). New York: Appleton. (Original work published 1895)

Fuligni, A. J., Tseng, V., & Lam, M. (1999). Attitudes toward family obligations among American adolescents with Asian, Latin American and European backgrounds. *Child Development, 70,* 1030–1044.

Fulkerson, J. A., Strauss, J., Newmark-Sztainer, D., Story, M., & Boutelle, K. (2007). Brief reports—Correlates of psychosocial well-being among overweight adolescents: The role of family. *Journal of Counseling and Clinical Psychology, 75*(1), 181–187.

Fuller-Thomson, E. (2000). Loss of the kin-keepers: Sibling conflict following parental death. *Omega, 40,* 547–559.

Fuller-Thomson, E., & Minkler, M. (2001). American grandparents providing extensive child care to their grandchildren: Prevalence and profile. *Gerontologist, 41,* 201–209.

Fuller-Thomson, E., Minkler, M., & Driver, D. (1997). A profile of grandparents raising grandchildren in the United States. *The Gerontologist, 37,* 406–415.

Furr, L. (1998). Fathers' characteristics and their children's scores on college entrance exams. *Adolescence, 33*(131), 533–542.

Gable, S., & Lutz, S. (2000). Household, parent and child contributions to childhood obesity. *Family Relations, 49*(3), 293–300.

Galinsky, E. (1987). *The six stages of parenthood.* Boston: Addison-Wesley.

Gandini, L. (1995). Fundamentals of the Reggio Emilia approach to early childhood education. *Young Children, 49*(1), 4–8.

Ganong, L., Coleman, M., & Fine, M. (1999). Stepparents' affinity-seeking and affinity-maintaining strategies with stepchildren. *Journal of Family Issues, 20,* 299–327.

Garey, A. (1995). Constructing motherhood on the night shift: Working mothers as stay-at-home moms. *Qualitative Sociology, 18,* 415–437.

Gardiner, H. W., Mutter, J. D., & Kosmitzki, C. (1998). *Lives across cultures: Cross-cultural human development.* Boston: Allyn & Bacon.

Garfinkle, I., McLanahan, S., Tienda, M., & Brooks-Gunn, J. (2000). Fragile families and welfare reform. *Children and Youth Services, 23*(3), 453–457.

Garg, R., Levin, E. U., & Kauppi, C. (2005). Parenting style and academic achievement for East Indian and Canadian adolescents. *Journal of Comparative Family Studies, 35*(4), 653–661.

Gartrell, N., Banks, A., Reed, N. , Hamilton, J., Rodas, C., & Deck, A. (2000). The national lesbian family study: 3. Interviews with mothers of five-year-olds. *American Journal of Orthopsychiatry, 70*(4), 542–549.

Gartrell, N., Hamilton, J., Banks, A., Mosbacher, D., Reed, N., Sparks, C., & Bishop, H. (1996). The national lesbian family study: 1. Interviews with prospective mothers. *American Journal of Orthopsychiatry, 66,* 272–281.

Gershoff, E. T. (2002). Corporal punishment by parents and associated child behavior and experiences: A meta-analytic and theoretical review. *Psychological Bulletin, 128,* 539–579.

Giarrusso, R., Feng, D., & Silverstein, M. (2001). Grandparent and grandchild affection and consensus: cross-generational and cross-ethnic comparisons. *Journal of Family Issues, 22*(4), 456–477.

Giarrusso, R., Silverstein, M., & Bengston, V. L. (1996). Family complexity and the grandparent role. *Generations, 20,* 17–23.

Gibson, P. (2002). Caregiving role affects family relationships of African American grandmothers as new mothers again: A phenomenological perspective. *Journal of Marital and Family Therapy, 28,* 341–353.

Gindes, M. (1998). The psychological effects of relocation for children of divorce. *Journal of the American Academy of Matrimonial Lawyers, 15,* 115–148.

Goduka, N. I., & Kunnie, J. E. (2004). *Indigenous peoples' wisdom and power: Affirming our knowledge through narratives.* Hampshire, UK: Ashgate.

Goldhaber, D. (2000). *Theories of human development.* Mountain View, CA: Mayfield.

Goldscheider, F. (1997). Recent changes in U.S. young adult living arrangements in comparative perspective. *Journal of Family Issues, 18,* 709–724.

Goldscheider, F., & Goldscheider, C. (1999). *The changing transition to adulthood: Leaving and returning home.* Thousand Oaks, CA: Sage.

Golish, T. D. (2003). Stepfamily communication strengths: Understanding the ties that bind. *Human Communication Research, 29*(1), 41–80.

Golombok, S., Perry, B. B., Murray, A., & Burton, A. (2003). Children with lesbian parents. *Developmental Psychology, 39*(1), 20–33.

Gonzales, N. A., Pitts, S. C., Hill, N. E., & Roosa, M. W. (2000). A mediational model of the impact of interparental conflict on child adjustment in a multiethnic, low-income sample. *Journal of Family Psychology, 14,* 365–379.

Goodman, C., & Silverstein, M. (2002). Grandmothers raising grandchildren: Family structure and well being in culturally diverse families. *Gerontologist, 42*(5), 676–689.

Goodman, E. (1999). The role of socioeconomic status gradients in explaining differences in U.S. adolescents' health. *American Journal of Public Health, 89,* 1522–1528.

Goodman, E., Slap, G. B., & Huang, B. (2003). Adolescent health—The public health impact of socioeconomic status on adolescent depression and obesity. *American Journal of Public Health, 93*(11), 1844–1851.

Gopnik, A., Meltzoff, A., & Kuhl, P. (1999). *The scientist in the crib: Minds, brains, and how children learn.* New York: Morrow.

Gordon, T. (1975). *P.E.T.: Parent effectiveness training.* New York: New American Library.

Gordon-Larsen, P., McMurray, R. G., & Popkin, B. M. (1999). Adolescent physical activity and inactivity vary by ethnicity: the National Longitudinal Study of Adolescent Health. *Journal of Pediatrics, 6,* 266–275.

Gorman-Smith, D., Tolan, P. H., Henry, D. B., & Florsheim, P. (2000). Patterns of family functioning and adolescent outcomes among urban African American and Mexican American families. *Journal of Family Psychology, 14*(3), 436–457.

Gray, S. (2006). The relationship between phonological memory, receptive vocabulary, and fast mapping in young children with specific language impairment. *Journal of Speech, Hearing, and Research, 49*(5), 955–969.

Green, C., & Chalip, L. (1997). Enduring involvement in youth soccer: The socialization of parent and child. *Journal of Leisure Research, 29,* 61–77.

Gregory, A., & O'Connor, T. (2002). Sleep problems in childhood: A longitudinal study of developmental change and association with behavioral problems. *Journal of the American Academy of Child and Adolescent Psychiatry, 41,* 964–971.

Grossman, N. S., & Okum, B. F. (2003). Family psychology and family law introduction to the special issue. *Journal of Family Psychology, 17*(2), *163–168.*

Gruber, K. J., Fleetwood, T. W., & Herring, M. W. (2001). In-home continuing care services for substance-affected families: The Bridges Program. *Social Work, 46*(3), 267–277.

Grundy, E. (2005). Reciprocity in relationships: socioeconomic and health influences on intergenerational exchanges between Third Age parents and their adult children in Great Britain. *The British Journal of Sociology, 56*(2), 233–255.

Grundy, E., & Henretta, J. (2006). Between elderly parents and adult children: A new look at the intergenerational care by the 'sandwich generation.' *Aging and Society, 26,* 707–722.

Grusec, J., & Goodnow, J. (1994). Impact of parental discipline on the child's internalization of values: A reconceptualization of current points of view. *Developmental Psychology, 30,* 4–19.

Grusec, J., Hastings, P., & Mammone, N. (1994). Parenting cognitions and relationship schemes. In J. Smetana (Ed.), *Beliefs about parenting: Origins and developmental implications* (pp. 5–19). San Francisco: Jossey-Bass.

Grych, J. H., Harold, G. T., & Miles, C. J. (2003). A prospective investigation of appraisals as mediators of the link between interparental conflict and child adjustment. *Child Development, 74,* 1176–1193.

Gunnoe, M., Hetherington, E., & Reiss, D. (1999). Parental religiosity, parenting style, and adolescent responsibility. *Journal of Early Adolescence, 19,* 199–225.

Haapasalo, J. (2000). Young offenders' experience of child protection services. *Journal of Youth and Adolescence, 29*(3), 355–371.

Haas, J. S., Lee, L. B., & Kaplan, C. P. (2003). The association of race, socioeconomic status, and health insurance status with the prevalence of overweight among children and adolescents.

American Journal of Public Health, 93(12), 2105–2110.

Hack, M. Flannery, D. J., Schluchter, M., Carter, L., Borawski, E., & Klein, N. (2002). Outcomes in young adulthood of very low birthweight infants. *New England Journal of Medicine, 346*(3), 149–157.

Hack, M., Klein, N. K., & Taylor, H. G. (1995). Long-term developmental outcomes of low birth weight infants. *The Future of Children, 5,* 176–197.

Hagan, J., & McCarthy, B. (1997). *Mean streets: Youth crime and homelessness.* Cambridge, UK: Cambridge University Press.

Hagopian, L. P., Wilson, D. M., & Wilder, D. A. (2001). Assessment and treatment of problem behaviors maintained by escape from attention and access to tangible items. *Journal of Applied Behavior, 34*(2), 229–232.

Hall, G. S. (1904). *Adolescence: Its psychology and its relation to physiology, anthropology, sociology, sex, crime, religion, and education* (Vols. 1 & 2). Upper Saddle River, NJ: Prentice Hall.

Hall, G. S. (1965). *Health, growth, and heredity: G. Stanley Hall on Natural Education,* Edited and with an Introduction and Notes, by Charles Strickland and Charles Burgess. New York: Teachers College Press.

Hamner, T., & Turner, P. (2001). *Parenting in contemporary society.* Boston: Allyn & Bacon.

Hanish, L. D., & Tolan, P. H. (2001). Family change and family process—Patterns of change in family-based aggression prevention, *Journal of Marital and Family Therapy, 27*(2), 213–226.

Hardesty, M., & Black, T. (1999). Mothering through addiction: A survival strategy among Puerto Rican addicts. *Qualitative Health Research, 9*(5), 602–619.

Hare, J. (1994). Concerns and issues faced by families headed by a lesbian couple. *Families in Society, 75,* 27–35.

Harrison, C., & Sofronoff, K. (2002). ADHD and parental psychological distress: Role of demographics, child behavioral characteristics, and parental cognitions. *Journal of the American Academy of Child and Adolescent Psychiatry, 41,* 703–711.

Hart, B., & Risley, T. (1995). *Meaningful differences in the everyday experience of young American children.* Baltimore: Brooks.

Hart, C. H., Newell, L. D., & Olsen, S. F. (2003). Parenting skills and social communication competence in childhood. In J. O. Greene & B. R. Burleson (Eds.), *Handbook of communication and social interlined skills.* (pp. 753–797).

Harter, S. (1998). The development of self-representations. In W. Damon & N. Eisenberg (Eds.), *Handbook of child psychology: Vol. 3. Social, emotional, and personality development* (pp. 553–618). New York: Wiley.

Harter, S. (1999). *The construction of the self: A developmental perspective.* New York: Guilford Press.

Hartman, C. A., Lessem, J. M., Hopfer, C. J., Crowley, T. J., & Stallings, M. C. (2006). The family transmission of adolescent alcohol abuse and dependence. *Journal of Studies on Alcohol, 67*(5), 657–664.

Harwood, R., Leyendecker, B., Carlson, V., Ascensio, M., & Miller, A. (2002). Parenting among Latino families in the U.S. In Marc H. Bornstein (Ed.), *Handbook of parenting, Vol. 4: Social conditions and applied parenting* (2d ed.) (pp. 21–46). Mahwah, NJ: Erlbaum.

Hattery, A. (2001). *Women, work, and family: Balancing and weaving.* Thousand Oaks, CA: Sage.

Haugland, B. S. W. (2005). Recurrent disruptions of rituals and routines in families with paternal alcohol abuse. *Family Relations, 54*(2), 225–241.

Havens, L. (1972). Youth, violence, and the nature of family life. *Psychiatric Annals, 2,* 18–29.

Heath, P. (1993). Misbehavior and learning. In F. N. Magill & J. Rodriquez (Eds.), *Survey of science: Applied science series (Vol. 1, Survey of social sciences: Psychology Series,* (pp. 1581–1588). Pasadena, CA: Salem Press.

Heath, P., & Camarena, P. (2002). Patterns of depressed affect in early adolescence. *Journal of Early Adolescence, 22,* 256–276.

Heights, R., & Beaty, L. A. (1999). Identity development of homosexual youth and parental and familial influences on the coming out process. *Adolescence, 34,* 597–601.

Hess C. R., Papas M. A., & Black M. M. (2002). Resilience among African American adolescent mothers: Predictors of positive parenting in early infancy. *Journal of Pediatric Psychology, 27,* 619–629.

Hetherington, E. M., & Stanley-Hagen, M. (1999). The adjustment of children with divorced parents: A risk and resiliency perspective. *The Journal of Child Psychology and Psychiatry and Allied Disciplines, 40*(1), 129–140.

Heyman, R. E., & Slep, A. M. S. (2002). Does child abuse and interparental violence lead to adulthood family violence? *Journal of Marriage and the Family, 64*(4), 864–870.

Hill, J., Kondryn, H., & Mackie, L. (2003). Adult psychosocial relationships following cancer: The different roles of sons' and daughters' relationships with their mothers and fathers. *The Journal of Child Psychology and Psychiatry and Allied Disciplines, 44*(5), 752–762.

Hill, S., & Yuan, H. (1999). Family density of alcoholism and onset of adolescent drinking. *Journal of Studies on Alcohol, 60*, 7–17.

Hobbes. (1994). *Leviathan: With selected variants from the Latin edition of 1668*. Edited, and Introduction and Notes by Edward Curley. Indianapolis/Cambridge, MA: Hackett.

Hobson, R. P., Patrick, M. P. H., & Crandell, L. E. (2004). Maternal sensitivity and infant triadic communication. *The Journal of Psychology, Psychiatry, and Allied Disciplines, 45*(3), 470–480.

Hochschild, A. R. (1997). *The time bind: When work becomes home, and home becomes work.* New York: Metropolitan Books.

Hoff-Ginsberg, E., & Tardif, T. (1995). Socioeconomic status and parenting. In M. Bornstein (Ed.), *Handbook of parenting: Biology and ecology of parenting, Vol. 2.* (pp. 211–234). Mahwah, NJ: Erlbaum.

Hofferth, S. L., & Reid, L. (2002). Early childbearing and children's adjustment and behavior over time. Family Planning Perspectives, *34*(1), 41–50.

Hofferth, S. L., Smith, J., & McLoyd, V. C. (2000). Achievement and behavior among children of welfare recipients, welfare leavers, and low-income single mothers. *The Journal of Social Issues, 56*(4), 747–773.

Holmbeck, G. N., Paikoff, R. L., & Brooks-Gunn, J. (1995). Parenting adolescents. In M. H. Bornstein (Ed.), *Handbook of Parenting, Vol. 1. Children and parenting* (pp. 91–118). Mahwah, NJ: Erlbaum.

Hopfer, C. J., Stallings, M. C., Hewitt, J. K., & Crowley, T. J. (2003). Family transmission of marijuana use, abuse, and dependence. *Journal of the American Academy of Child and Adolescent Psychiatry, 42*(7), 834–842.

Horsley, H., & Patterson, T. (2006). The effects of a parent guidance intervention on communication among adolescents who have experienced the sudden death of a sibling. *The American Journal of Family Therapy, 34*, 199–137.

Horwitz , S. M., Balestracci, K. M. B., & Simms, M. D. (2001). Foster care placement improves children's functioning. *Archives of Pediatrics and Adolescent Medicine.* In R. L. Heger & M. Scannapieco (Eds.), *Kinship foster care: Policy practice and research. New York: Oxford University Press, Vol. 155*, 1255–1260.

Hsai, H-C., & Scanzoni, J. (1996). Rethinking the roles of Japanese women. *Journal of Comparative Family Studies, 27*, 309–329.

Hunter, E. G., & Rowles, G. D. (2005). Leaving a legacy: Toward a typology. *Journal of Aging Studies, 19*(3), 327–347.

Hurley, E. A., Boykin, A. W., and Allen, B. A. (2005). Communal versus individual learning of math-estimation task: African American children and the culture of learning contexts. *The Journal of Psychology, 139*(6), 513–527.

Huston, A. C., Duncan, G. J., & McLoyd, V. C. (2005). Impacts on children of a policy to promote employment and reduce poverty for low-income parents: New hope after 5 years. *Developmental Psychology, 41*(6), 902–918.

Hyun, O-K., Lee, W., & Yoo, A-J. (2002). Social support for two generations of new mothers in selected populations in Korea, Hong Kong, and the United States. *Journal of Comparative Family Studies, 33*, 515–527.

Iaupuni, S. M. K., Donoto, K. M., & Thompson-Colon, T. (2005). Counting on kin: social networks, social support and child health status. *Social Forces, 83*, 1137–1164.

Isabella, R., & Belsky, J. (1991). Interactional synchrony and the origins of infant–mother attachment: A replication study. *Child Development, 62*, 373–384.

Isolauri, E., Sutas, Y., Salo, M. K., Isosomppi, R., & Kaila, M. (1998). Elimination diet in cow's milk allergy: Risk for impaired growth in young children. *Journal of Pediatrics, 132*, 1004–1009.

Jackson, L. M., Pancer, S. M., Pratt, M. W., & Hunsberger, B. E. (2000). Great expectations. The relation between expectations, and adjustment during the transition to university. *Journal of Applied Social Psychology, 30*(10), 21–26.

Jackson, S., Bijstra, J., Oostra, L., & Bosnia, H. (1998). Adolescents' perceptions of communication with parents relative to specific aspects of relationships with parents and personal development. *Journal of Adolescence, 21,* 305–322.

Jackson, S., Thompson, R., & Christiansen, E. (1999). Predicting abuse-prone parental attitudes and discipline practices in a nationally representative sample. *Child Abuse and Neglect, 23,* 15–29.

Jacob, T. (1997). Parenting influences on the development of alcohol abuse and dependence. *Alcohol Health and Research World, 32*(3), 204–209.

Jacobson, K. C., & Crockett, L. J. (2000). Parental monitoring and adolescent adjustment: An ecological perspective. *Journal of Research on Adolescence, 10,* 65–98.

Jaffe, J., Beebe, B., Feldstein, S., Crown, C., & Jasnow, M. (2001). Rhythms of dialogue in infancy. *Monographs of the Society for Research in Child Development, 66* (Serial No. 265).

Jaffe, P. G., Baker, L. L., & Cunningham, A. J. (2004). *Protecting children from domestic violence: Strategies for community intervention.* New York: Guilford Press.

James, W. H. (2004). The sexual orientation of men who were brought up in gay or lesbian households. *Journal of Biosocial Science, 36,* 371–374.

Jarrett, R. L., Jefferson, S., & Roach, A. (2000). Family and parenting strategies in unsafe African American neighborhoods. Paper presented at the national Head Start Association Annual Meeting. Washington, D.C.

Jerome, A., Fujiki, M., Brinton, B., & James, S. (2002). Self-esteem in children with specific language impairment. *Journal of Speech, Language and Hearing Research, 45,* 700–714.

Johnson, J. G., Cohen, P., & Kotler, L. (2002). Psychiatric disorders associated with risk for development of eating disorders during adolescence and early adulthood. *Journal of Consulting and Clinical Psychology, 70*(5), 1119–1128.

Jones, D. J., Forehand, R., & Beach, S. R. (2000). Maternal and paternal parenting during adolescence: Forecasting early adult psychosocial adjustment. *Adolescence, 35*(139), 513–530.

Jones, M. (1993). Decline of the American orphanage (1941–1980). *Social Service Review, 67,* 459–480.

Jordyn, M., & Byrd, M. (2003). The relationship between the living arrangements of university students and their identity development. *Adolescence, 38,* 267–278.

Juang, L. P., & Silbereisen, R. K. (1999). Supportive parenting and adolescent adjustment across time in former East and West Germany. *Journal of Adolescence, 22,* 719–736.

Juang, L. P., Silbereisen, R. K., & Weisner, M. (1999). Predictions of leaving home in young adults raised in Germany: A replication of a 1991 study. *Journal of Marriage and the Family, 61*(2), 505–515.

Kagan, J. (1978, August). The parental love trap. *Psychology Today,* 54–61, 91.

Kaiser, J. (2003). How much are human lives and health worth? *Science, 299,* 1836–1837.

Karass, J., VanDeventer, M. C., & Braungart-Reiker, J. M. (2003). Predicting shared parent-child book reading in infancy. *Journal of Family Psychology, 17*(1), 134–146.

Kashani, J., & Allan, W. (1998). *The impact of family violence on children and adolescents.* Thousand Oaks, CA: Sage.

Kaufman, G., & Uhlenberg, P. (1998). Effects of life course transitions on the quality of relationships between adult children and their parents. *Journal of Marriage and the Family, 60,* 924–938.

Keller, T. W., Catalano, R. F., & Hagerty, K. P. (2002). Parent figure transitions and delinquency and drug use among early adolescent children of substance abusers. *American Journal of Drug and Alcohol Abuse, 28*(3), 399–427.

Kelley, M. L., French, A., & Bountress, K. (2007). Parentification and family responsibility in the family of origin of adult children of alcoholics. *Addictive Behaviors, 32*(4), 675–685.

Kelly, T., & Kropf, N. (1995). Stigmatized and perpetual parents: Older parents caring for children with life-long disabilities. *Journal of Gerontological Social Work, 24,* 3–16.

Kempe, C., Silverman, F., Steele, B., Droegenmueller, W., & Silver, H. (1962). The battered child syndrome. *Journal of the American Medical Association, 181*, 17–24.

Keoughan, P., Joanning, H., & Sudak-Allison, J. (2001). Child access and visitation following divorce: A growth area for marriage and family therapy. *The American Journal of Family Therapy, 29*(2), 155–163.

Kermani, H., & Brenner, M. (2000). Maternal scaffolding in the child's zone of proximal development across tasks: Cross-cultural perspectives. *Journal of Research in Childhood Education, 15*, 30–52.

Kerr, D. C., Lopez, N. L., & Olsen, S. L. (2004). Parental discipline and externalizing behavior problems in early childhood: The roles of moral regulation and child gender. *Journal of Abnormal Child Psychology, 34*(4), 369–383.

Kerr, M., Black, M., & Krishnakumar, A. (2000). Failure to thrive, maltreatment and the behavior and development of 6-year-old children from low-income, urban families: A cumulative risk model. *Child Abuse and Neglect, 24*(5), 587–598.

Khaleque, A., & Rohner, R. (2002). Perceived parental acceptance-rejection and psychological adjustment: A meta-analysis of cross-cultural and intrarcultural studies. *Journal of Marriage and the Family, 64*, 54–64.

Khuwaja, S., Selwyn, B. J., & Shah, S. M. (2005). Prevalence and stunting among primary school children in rural areas of southern Pakistan. *Journal of Tropical Pediatrics, 51*(2), 72–77.

Kilgore, K., Snyder, J., & Lentz, C. (2000). The contribution of parental discipline, parental monitoring, and school risk to early onset conduct problems in African American boys and girls. *Developmental Psychology, 36*(6), 835–845.

Kim, D. H., & Schneider, B. (2005). Social capital in action: Alignment of parental support in adolescents' transition to post-secondary education, *Social Forces, 84*(2) 1181–1206.

Kim, E. (2002). The relationship between parental involvement and children's educational achievements in the Korean immigrant family. *Journal of Comparative Family Studies, 33*(4), 529–540.

Kinard, E. (2001). Perceived and actual academic competence in maltreated children. *Child Abuse and Neglect, 25*, 33–45.

Kirkham, C., Harris, S., & Grzybowski, S. (2005). Evidence-based prenatal care: Part II: Third trimester care and prevention of infectious diseases, *American Family Physician, 71*(7), 1307–1321.

Kivnik, H. Q. (1982). *The meaning of grandparenthood.* Ann Arbor, MI: UMI Research.

Kluwer, E., Heesink, J., & van de Vliert, E. (2002). The division of labor in close relationships: An asymmetrical conflict issue. *Personal Relationships, 7*, 263–282.

Knight, D. K., & Wallace G. (2003). Where are the children? An examination of children's living arrangements when mothers enter residential drug treatment. *Journal of Drug Issues, 33*(2), 305–325.

Knoester, C. (2003). Transitions in young adulthood and the relationship between parent and offspring well-being. *Social Forces, 81*(4), 1431–1457.

Kochanski, G., Coy, K. C., & Murray, K. T. (2001). The development of self-regulation in the first four years of life. *Child Development, 72*(4), 1091–1111.

Kochenderfer-Ladd, B. & Wardrop, J. L., (2001). Chronicity and instability of children's peer victimization experiences as predictors of loneliness and social satisfaction trajectories. *Child Development, 42*(1), 134–151.

Koenig, K., & Chesla, C. (2004). Asthma management among low-income Latino and African American families and young children. *Family Relations, 53*(1), 58–67.

Kramer, B. L., & Thompson, E. H. (2002). *Men are caregivers: Theory, research and service implications.* New York: Springer.

Krevans, J., & Gibbs, J. (1996). Parents' use of inductive discipline: Relations to children's empathy and prosocial behavior. *Child Development, 67*, 3263–3277.

Krishnakumar, A. & Buehler, C. (2000). Interparental conflict and parenting behaviors: A meta-analytic review. *Family Relations, 49*(1), 25–44.

Kuersten-Hogan, R. & McHale, J. P. (2000). Stability of emotion talk in families from the toddler to the preschool years. *The Journal of Genetic Psychology, 161*(1), 115–121.

Kuhn, B., Mayfield, J., & Kuhn, R. (1999). Clinical assessment of child and adolescent sleep disturbance. *Journal of Counseling and Development, 77*, 359–368.

Kurdek, L.A. (2001). Differences between heterosexual nonparent couples and gay, lesbian, and heterosexual couples. *Journal of Family Issues, 6*, 727–754.

Laditka, S. B., Laditka, J. N., & Mastanduno, M. P. (2005). Potentially avoidable maternity complications: An indicator of access to prenatal and primary care during pregnancy. *Women and Health, 41*(3), 1–26.

Laible, D., & Thompson, R. (2000). Mother–child discourse, attachment security, shared positive affect, and early conscience development. *Child Development, 71*, 1424–1440.

Landry, S., Smith, K., & Swank, P. (2001). Does early responsive parenting have a special importance for children's development or is consistency across early childhood necessary? *Developmental Psychology, 37*, 387–403.

Lansdale, N. S., & Oropesa, R. S (2001). Father involvement in the lives of mainland Puerto Rican children: Contributions of nonresident, cohabiting, and married fathers. *Social Forces, 79*(3), 945–968.

Lansford, J. E., Chang, L., Dodge, K. A., Malone, P. S., Oburu, P., et al. (2005). Physical discipline and children's adjustment: Cultural normativeness as a moderator. *Child Development, 761*(6), 1234–1246.

Lapsley, D. K., & Edgerton, J. (2002). Separation-Individuation, adult attachment style, and college adjustment. *Journal of Counseling and Development, 80*, 484–492.

Lareau, A. (2002). Invisible immobility: Social class and children in black families and white families. *American Sociology Review, 67*(5), 747–776.

Larson, E. (1998). Reframing the meaning of disability to families: The embrace of paradox. *Social Science and Medicine, 47*, 865–875.

LaSala, M. (2002). Walls and bridges: How coupled gay men and lesbians manage their interrelationships. *Journal of Marriage and the Family, 28*, 327–339.

Laursen, B., Coy, K. C., & Collins, W. A. (1998). Reconsidering changes in parent–child conflict across adolescence: A meta-analysis. *Child Development, 69*, 817–832.

Lavee, Y. (2005). Correlates of change in marital relationships under stress: The case of childhood cancer. *Families in Society, 86*(1), 112–120.

Leach, P. (1997). *Your baby and child: From birth to age 5*. New York: Knopf.

Leadbeater, B. J. & Way, N. (2001). *Growing up fast: Transitions to early adulthood of inner-city adolescent mothers*. Mahwah, NJ: Erlbaum.

Leaper, C., Anderson, K., & Sanders, P. (1998). Moderators of gender effects on parents' talk to their children: A meta-analysis. *Developmental Psychology, 34*, 3–27.

Leathers, S. J. (2003). Parental visiting, conflicting allegiances, and emotional and behavioral problems among foster children. *Family Relations, 52*(1), 53–63.

Lee, Y-R., & Sung, K-T. (1998). Cultural influences on caregiving burden: Cases of Koreans and Americans. *International Journal of Aging and Human Development, 46*, 125–141.

Leitch, M. L. (1998). Contextual issues in teen pregnancy: Refining our scope of inquiry. Comment on L. Blinn-Pike et al., P. M. Camarena et al., R. Solomon, and C. P. Liefield. *Family Relations, 47*, 145–148.

Leonardi, A., Kiosseoglou, G. (2000). The relationship of parental attachment and psychological separation to the psychological functioning of young adults. *The Journal of Social Psychology, 140*(4), 451–464.

Letieca, B. L., & Koblinsky, S. A. (2004). Parenting in violent neighborhoods, African-American fathers share strategies for keeping children safe, *Journal of Family Issues, 25*(6), 715–734.

Levine, J. A., Pollack, H. C., Comfort, M. E. (2001). Academic and behavioral outcomes among the children of young mothers. *Journal of Marriage and the Family, 63*(2), 355–369.

Levine, R., Dixon, S., LeVine, S., Richman, A., Leiderman, P., Herbert K., et al. (1994). *Child care and culture: Lessons from Africa*. New York: Cambridge University Press.

Lewit, E., & Kerrebrock, N. (1998). Child indicators: Dental health. *The Future of Children: Protecting Children from Abuse and Neglect, 8*, 4–22.

Leyser, Y., & Heinze, T. (2001). Perspectives of parents of children who are visually impaired: Implications for the field. *RE:view, 33*, 37–48.

Lieber, E., Nihira, K., & Mink, I. T. (2004). Filial piety, modernization, and the challenges of raising children for Chinese immigrants: Quantitative and qualitative evidence. *Ethos, 32,* 324–347.

Lim, S-L., & Lim, B. K. (2004). Parenting style and child outcomes in Chinese and immigrant Chinese families—current findings and cross-cultural considerations in conceptualization and research. *Marriage and Family Review, 35,* 21–43.

Lin, K. K., Sandler, I. N., Ayers, T. S., Wolchik, S. A., & Luecken, L. J. (2004). Resilience in parentally bereaved children and adolescents seeking preventive services. *Journal of Clinical Child and Adolescent Psychiatry, 33*(4), 673–683.

Lindahl, K., & Malik, N. (1999). Marital conflict, family processes, and boys' externalizing behaviors in Hispanic American and European American families. *Journal of Clinical and Child Psychology, 28,* 12–24.

Liu, Y-L. (2006). Paternal/maternal attachment, peer support, social expectations of peer interaction, and depressive symptoms. *Adolescence, 41,* 705–721.

Love, J., Raikes, H., Paulsell, D., & Kisker, E. (2000). New directions for studying quality in programs for infants and toddlers. In D. Cryer & T. Harms (Eds.), *Infants and toddlers in out-of-home care* (pp. 117–162). Baltimore: Paul H. Brookes.

Lowenthal, B. (1999). Effects of maltreatment and ways to promote children's resiliency. *Childhood Education, 75,* 204–209.

Lubic, R. (1997). A missed opportunity. *Public Health Reports, 112,* 284–287.

Luckner, J. L., & Velaski., A. (2004). Healthy families of children who are deaf. *American Annals of the Deaf, 149*(1), 324–335.

Lukemeyer, A., Meyers, M. K., & Smeeding, T. (2000). Expensive children in poor families: Out-of-pocket expenditures for the care of disabled and chronically ill children in welfare families. *Journal of Marriage and the Family, 62*(2), 399–415.

Luker, C., & Luker, T. (2007). A service is NOT a need. *Exceptional Parent, 27*(2), 31–32.

Lynch, J. (2004). The identity transformation of biological parents in lesbian/gay stepfamilies. *Journal of Homosexuality, 47*(2), 91–118.

Lynch, R., Thuli, K., & Groombridge, L. (1994). Person-first disability language: A pilot analysis of public perceptions. *Journal of Rehabilitation, 60,* 18–22.

Maccoby, E. E., & Martin, J. A. (1983). Socialization in the context of the family: Parent–child interaction. In E. M. Hetherington (Ed.), *Handbook of child psychology, Vol. 4: Socialization, personality and social development* (4th ed., pp. 1–102). New York: Wiley.

Manassis, K., & Young, A. (2001). Adapting a positive reinforcement system to suit child temperament. *Journal of the American Academy of Child and Adolescent Psychiatry, 40*(5), 603–605.

Mantzipoulos, P., & Oh-Hwang, Y. (1998). The relationship of psychosocial maturity to parenting quality and intellectual ability for American and Korean adolescents. *Contemporary Educational Psychology, 23,* 195–206.

Marcia, J. E. (1966). Development and validation of ego identity status. *Journal of Personality and Social Psychology, 3*(5), 551–588.

Marcia, J. E. (1994). The empirical study of ego identity. In A. H. Bosma, T. L. G. Graafsma, H. D. Grotevant, & D. J. de Levita (Eds.), *Identity and development* (pp. 67–81), USA: Sage.

Margolin, G., & Gordis, E. (2000). Effects of family and community violence on children. *Annual Review of Psychology, 51,* 445–479.

Marion, M. (2003). *Guidance of Young Children* (6th ed.). Upper Saddle River, NJ: Prentice Hall.

Markiewicz, D., Doyle, A. B., & Brendgen, M. (2001). The quality of adolescents' friendships: Associations with mothers' interpersonal relationships, attachment to parents and friends, and prosocial behaviors. *Journal of Adolescence, 24,* 429–445.

Marshall, S. K. (2001). Do I matter? Construct validation of adolescents' perceived mattering to parents and friends. *Journal of Adolescence, 24,* 473–490.

Marsiglio, W., Amato, P., Day, R. D., & Lamb, M. E. (2000). Scholarship on fatherhood in the 1990s and beyond. *Journal of Marriage and the Family, 62,* 1173–1191.

Masahiro, Y. (2001). Parasite singles feed on family system. *Japan Quarterly, 48,* 10–16.

Maslow, A. (1970). *Motivation and Personality* (2nd ed.). New York: Harper & Row.

Masten, A., & Coatsworth, J. (1998). The development of competence in favorable and unfavorable environments: Lessons from research on successful children. *American Psychologist, 53,* 205–220.

Matos, P. M., Barbosa, S., De Almeida, H. M., & Costa, M. E. (1999). Parental attachment and identity in Portuguese late adolescents. *Journal of Adolescence, 22,* 805–818.

Mauro, C., & Harris, Y. (2000). The influence of maternal child-rearing attitudes and teaching behaviors on preschoolers' delay of gratification. *The Journal of Genetic Psychology, 161,* 292–306.

McCamish-Svenson, C., Samuelsson, G., & Hagberg, B. (1999). Social relationships and health as predictors of life satisfaction in old age: Results from a Swedish longitudinal study. *International Journal of Aging and Human Development, 40,* 301–324.

McCarty, M., & Ashmead, D. (1999). Visual control of reaching and grabbing in infants. *Developmental Psychology, 35,* 620–631.

McClosky, L., Treviso, M., & Scionti, T. (2002). A comparative study of battered women and their children in Italy and the United States. *Journal of Family Violence, 17,* 53–74.

McDonald, R. (2006). Reducing conduct problems among children brought to women's shelters: Intervention effects 24 months following termination of services. *Journal of Family Psychology, 20*(1), 127–136.

McDonald, R., Jouriles, E. N., & Ramisetty-Mikler, S. (2006). Estimating the number of American children living in partner-violent families. *Journal of Family Psychology, 20*(1), 137–142.

McElwain, N. L., & Booth-LaForce, C. (2006). Maternal sensitivity to infant distress and nondistress as predictors of infant-mother attachment, *Journal of Family Psychology, 20*(2), 247–255.

McGuigon, W. M., Vuchinich, S., & Pratt, C. C. (2000). Violence and the family—Domestic violence, parents' view of their infant, and risk for child abuse. *Journal of Family Psychology, 14*(4), 613–624.

McHale, S., Crouter, A. C., & Tucker, C. J. (2001). Free time activities in middle-childhood: Links with adjustment involving adolescence. *Child Development, 72*(6), 1764–1778.

McLoyd, V. C., & Smith J. (2002). Physical discipline and behavior problems in African American, European American, and Hispanic children. Emotional support as a moderator. *Journal of Marriage and the Family, 64,* 40–53.

McMahon, T. J., Winkel, J. D., Suchman, N. E., & Luthar, S. S. (2002). Drug dependence, parenting responsibilities, and treatment history: Why doesn't mom go for help? *Drug and Alcohol Dependence, 65*(2), 105–114.

McNeil, N. M., Alibali, M. W., & Evans, J. L. (2000). The role of gesture in children's comprehension of spoken language: Now they need it, now they don't. *Journal of Nonverbal Behavior, 24*(2), 131–150.

Meeus, W., Oosterwegel, A., & Collebergh, W. (2002). Parental and peer attachment and identity development in adolescence. *Journal of Adolescence, 25,* 93–106.

Merzenich, M. M. (2001). Cortical plasticity contributing to child development. In J. L. McClelland & R. S. Siegler (Eds.), *Mechanisms of cognitive development: Behavioral and neural perspectives* (pp. 67–95), Mahwah, NJ: Erlbaum.

Metsch, L. R., Wolfe, H. P., Fewell, R., McCoy, C. B., Elwood, W. N., & Wohler-Torres, B. (2001). Treating substance-using women and their children in public housing: Preliminary evaluation findings. *Child Welfare, 80*(2), 199–220.

Meyers, S. A., & Miller, C. (2004). Direct, mediated, moderated, and cumulative relations between neighborhood characteristics and adolescent outcomes. *Adolescence, 39,* 121–144.

Mikkelsen, E. J. (2001). Enuresis and encopresis: Ten years of progress. *Journal of the American Academy of Child and Adolescent Psychiatry, 40*(10), 1146–1158.

Miller, A. (1990). *For your own good: Hidden cruelty in child-rearing and the roots of violence* (H. Hannum & H. Hannum, Trans.). New York: Noonday Press.

Mills-Koonce, W. R., Gariepy, J-L., Propper, S., Sutton, K., Calkins, S., Moore, G., & Cox, M. (2007). Infant and parent factors associated with early maternal sensitivity: A caregiver-attachment systems approach. *Infant Behavior and Development, 30*(1), 114–127.

Minuchin, S. (1974). *Families and family therapy.* Cambridge, MA: Harvard University Press.

Mitchell, V. (1998). The birds, the bees . . . and the sperm bank: How lesbian mothers talk to their children about sex and reproduction. *American Journal of Orthopsychiatry, 68,* 400–409.

Moen, P., & Yu, U. (1999). Having it all: Overall work/life success in two-earner families. In T. Parcel (Ed.), *Research in the sociology of work* (Vol. 7, pp. 109–139). Greenwich, CT: JAI Press.

Moerk, E. (2000). *The guided acquisition of first language skills.* Westport, CT: Ablex.

Monahan, D. (2001). Teen pregnancy prevention outcomes: Implications for social work practice. *Families in Society, 82,* 127–135.

Mondschein, E. R., Adolph, K. E., & Tamis-LeMonda, C. S. (2000). Gender bias in mothers' expectations about infant crawling, *Journal of Experimental Child Psychology, 77,* 304–316.

Moon, S., & Hall, A. (1998). Family therapy with intellectually and creatively gifted children. *Journal of Marital and Family Therapy, 24,* 59–80.

Moore, J., & Finkelstein, N. (2001). Residential substance abuse treatment—parenting services for families affected by substance abuse. *Child Welfare, 80*(2), 221–239.

Moore, S., & Cartwright, C. (2005). Adolescents and young adults' expectations of parental responsibilities in stepfamilies. *Journal of Marriage and the Family, 43*(1/2), 109–128.

Morrisette, P. (1996). Family therapist as consultant in foster care: Expanding the parameters of practice. *The American Journal of Family Therapy, 24,* 55–65.

Morrongiello, B., Fenwick, K., & Chance, G. (1998). Cross-modal learning in newborn infants: Inferences about properties of auditory–visual events. *Infant Behavior and Development, 21,* 543–553.

Mosher, C., Rotolo, T., & Phillips, D. (2004). Minority adolescents and substance abuse use risk/protective factors: A focus on inhalant use. *Adolescence, 39,* 489–502.

Mottran, S. A., & Hortacsu, N. (2005). Adult-daughter, aging mother relationship over the life cycle: The Turkish case. *Journal of Aging Studies, 19*(4), 471–488.

Mounts, N. S. (2002). Parental management of adolescent peer relationships in context: the role of parenting style. *Journal of Family Psychology, 16*(1), 58–69.

Munch, S., & Levick, S. (2001). "I'm special too": Promoting sibling adjustment in the neonatal intensive care unit. *Health and Social Work, 26,* 58–64.

Murphy, S. A., Johnson, C. C., Gupta, K. C., & Das, A. (1998). Broad-spectrum group treatment for parents bereaved by the violent deaths of their 12- to 28-year-old children: A randomized controlled trial. *Death Studies, 22,* 209–235.

Murray, J. A., Terry, D. H., & Vance, J. C. (2000). Effects of a program of intervention on parental distress following infant death. *Death Studies, 24*(4), 275–305.

Nagin, D. S., & Trembley, R. (2001). Analyzing developmental trajectories of distinct but related behaviors: A group-based method. *Psychological Methods, 6,* 18–34.

Nair, H., & Murray, A. D. (2005). Predictors of attachment security in preschool children from intact and divorced families. *The Journal of Genetic Psychology, 166*(3), 245–263.

Nansel, T. R., Craig, W., Overpeck, M. D., Saluja, G., & Ruan, W. J. (2004). Cross-national consistency in the relationship between bullying behaviors and psychosocial adjustments. *Archives of Pediatrics and Adolescent Medicine, 158,* 730–736.

Nansel, T. R., Overpeck, M. D., Pilla, R. S., Ruan, W. J., Simons-Morton, B., & Scheidt, P. (2001). Bullying behaviors among U.S. youth: Prevalence and association with psychosocial adjustment. *JAMA: The Journal of the American Medical Association, 285*(16), 2094–2106.

Narcotics Anonymous World Services (2005). *Information about NA.* Available at: http://www.na.org/

Neitzel, C., & Stright, A. D. (2003). Mothers' scaffolding of children's problem solving: Establishing a foundation of academic self-regulatory competence. *Journal of Family Psychology, 17*(1), 147–159.

Nelson, C. A. (2000). The neurological bases of early intervention. In J. P. Shankoff & P. C. Marshall (Eds.) *Handbook of early childhood interventions (2d ed.),* pp. 207–227.

Nelson, J. (1998). The meaning of crying based on attachment theory. *Clinical Social Work, 26,* 9–22.

Neumann, C. G., Gewa, C., & Bwibo, N. O. (2004). Child Nutrition in Developing Countries. *Pediatric Annals, 33*(10), 658–704.

Neumark-Sztainer, D., Story, M., & Hannan, P. J. (2002). Overweight status and eating patterns among adolescents: Where do youths stand in comparison with Healthy People 2010 Objectives? *Journal of Public Health, 92*(5), 844–851.

Newberger, E. (1991). Child abuse. In M. L. Rosenberg & M. A. Fenley (Eds.), *Violence in America: A public health approach* (pp. 51–78). New York: Oxford University Press.

Nicklas, T. A., Baranowski, T., Baranowski, J. C., & Cullen, K. (2001). Family and child-care provider influences on preschool children's fruit, juice, and vegetable consumption. *Nutrition Reviews, 59*(7), 224–235.

Nickman, S. L., Rosenfeld, A. A., Fine, P., MacIntyre, J. C., Pilowsky, D. J., et al. (2005). Children in adoptive families: Overview and update. *Journal of the American Academy of Child and Adolescent Psychology, 44(10)*, 987–995.

Noonan, A., Tennstedt, S., & Rebelsky, F. (1996). Making the best of it: Themes of meaning among informal caregivers to the elderly. *Journal of Aging Studies, 10*, 313–327.

Norton, E. C., & Van Houtven, C. H. (2006). Intervivos transfers and exchange. *Southern Economic Journal, 73*(1), 157–172.

Nydegger, C., & Mitteness, L. (1991). Fathers and their adult sons and daughters: *Marriage and Family Review, 16*, 3–4.

O'Brien-Caughu, M., O'Campo, P., & Randolph, S. (2002). The influence of racial socialization on the cognitive and behavioral competence of African American preschoolers. *Child Development, 73*, 1611–1625.

O'Connor, B. P. (1995). Identity development and perceived parental behavior as a source of adolescent egocentrism. *Journal of Youth and Adolescence, 24*(2), 205–227.

Offer, D. (1969). *The psychological world of the teenager.* New York: Basic Books.

Owusu-Bempah, J. (1995). Information about the absent parent as a factor in the well-being of children of single-parent families. *International Social Work, 38*, 253–275.

Pancer, S. M., Pratt, M., & Hunsberger, B. (2000). Thinking ahead: Complexity of expectations and the transition to parenthood. *Journal of Personality, 68*(2), 253–280.

Parizkova, J. (1998). Interaction between physical activity and nutrition early in life and the impact on later development. *Nutrition Research Reviews, 11*, 71–90.

Parke, R. D (1996). *Fatherhood.* Cambridge, MA: Harvard University Press.

Paschall, M. J., Ringwalt, C. L., & Flewelling, R. L. (2003). Effects of parenting, father absence, and affiliating with delinquent peers on delinquent behavior among African-American male adolescents. *Adolescence, 38*, 15–34.

Patterson, C. J. (2000). Family relationships of lesbian and gay men. *Journal of Marriage and the Family, 62*(4), 1052–1069.

Paul, P. (2002). Make room for Granddaddy. *American Demographics, 24*(4), 42–45.

Paulson, S. E., Marchant, G. J., & Rothlisberg, B. A. (1998). Early adolescents' perceptions of patterns of parenting, teaching, and school atmosphere: Implications for achievement. *Journal of Early Adolescence, 18*, 5–26.

Pavao, J. M. (1998). *The family of adoption.* Boston: Beacon Press.

Pearce, T. O. (2000). Keeping children healthy: The challenge of preventive care in southeastern Nigeria. *Journal of Comparative Family Studies, 31*(2), 263–279.

Pears, K. C., & Capaldi, D. M. (2001). Intergenerational transmission of abuse: A two-generational prospective study of an at-risk sample. *Child Abuse and Neglect, 25*(11), 1439–1461.

Perina, K. (2003). Young folks at home. *Psychology Today, 36*(5), 5.

Perry, B. (2001). Death and loss: Helping children manage their grief. *Scholastic Early Childhood Today, 15*, 22–23.

Petersen, A. C., Leffert, N., Graham, B., Alwin, J., & Ding, S. (1997). Promoting mental health during the transition into adolescence. In J. Schulenberg, J. Moggs, & K. Hurrelman (Eds.), *Health risks and developmental transitions during adolescence* (pp. 471–497). New York: Cambridge Press.

Pezzin, L. E., & Schone, B. S. (1999). Parental marital disruption and intergenerational transfers. An analysis of lone, elderly parents and their children, *Demography, 36*(3), 287–297.

Phinney, J., Romero, I., & Nava, M. (2001). The role of language, parents, and peers in ethnic identity among adolescents in immigrant families. *Journal of Youth and Adolescence, 30,* 135–153.

Phua, V. C., Kaufman, G., & Park, S. (2001). Strategic adjustments of elderly Asian Americans: Living arrangements and headship. *Journal of Comparative Family Studies, 32,* 263–281.

Piaget, J., & Inhelder, B. (1958). *The growth of logical thinking from childhood to adolescence* (A. Parsona & S. Seagrin, Trans.). New York: Basic Books.

Piaget, J., & Inhelder, B. (1969). *The psychology of the child* (H. Weaver, Trans.). New York: Basic Books.

Pillemer, K., & Suitor, J. J. (1991). "Will I ever escape my child's problems?" Effects of adult children's problems on elderly parents. *Journal of Marriage and the Family, 53,* 585–594.

Planinsec, J. (2002). Relations between the motor and cognitive dimensions of preschool girls and boys. *Perceptual and Motor Skills, 94,* 415–432.

Podolski, C. (2001). Parent stress and coping in relation to child ADHD severity and associated child disruptive behavior problems. *Journal of Clinical Child Psychiatry, 30,* 503–513.

Popkin, M. (1987). *Active parenting: Teaching cooperation, courage, and responsibility.* San Francisco: Perennial Library.

Posada, G., Carbonell, O. A., & Alzate, G. (2004). Through Columbian lenses: Ethnographic and conventional analyses of maternal care and their associations with secure base behavior. *Developmental Psychology, 40*(4), 508–518.

Posada, G., Jacobs, A., & Richmond, M. K. (2004). Maternal caregiving and infant security in two cultures. *Developmental Psychology, 38*(1), 67–78.

Posner, M. I., & Rothbart, M. K. (2000). Developing mechanisms of self-regulation. *Development and Psychopathology, 12,* 427–441.

Pratt, C. (1970). *I learn from children.* New York: Harper & Row.

Presser, H. (1994). Employment schedules among dual-earner spouses and the division of household labor by gender. *American Sociological Review, 59,* 348–364.

Purdie, N., Carroll, A., & Roche, L. Parenting and adolescent self-regulation. *Journal of Adolescence, 27*(6), 663–676.

Purkey, W., Schmidt, J. J., & Benedict, G. C. (1990). *Invitational learning for counseling and development.* Ann Arbor, MI: ERIC Counseling & Personnel Services Clearinghouse.

Radbill, S. (1974). A history of child abuse and infanticide. In R. E. Helfer & C. H. Kempe (Eds.), *The battered child* (2nd ed., pp. 3–21). Chicago: University of Chicago Press.

Ravaja, N., & Keltikangas-Jarvinen, L. (2001). Cloniger's temperament and character dimensions in young adulthood and their relation to characteristics of parental alcohol use and smoking. *Journal of Studies on Alcohol, 62*(1), 98–104.

Raveis, V., Siegel, K., & Karus, D. (1999). Children's psychological distress following the death of a parent. *Journal of Youth and Adolescence, 28,* 165–180.

Reitzes, D., & Mutran, E. J. (2004). Grandparent identity, intergenerational family identity, and well-being. *Journal of Gerontology, Series B: Psychological Sciences and Social Sciences, 59B*(4), S213–S219.

Richardson, S., & McCabe, M. P. (2001). Parental divorce during adolescence and adjustment in early adulthood. *Adolescence, 36,* 467–489.

Richaud de Minzi, M. C. (2006). Loneliness and depression in middle and late childhood: The relationship to attachment and parental styles. *The Journal of Genetic Psychology, 167*(2), 189–210.

Riegel, K. F. (1976). The dialects of human development. *American Psychologist, 31,* 689–700.

Roberto, K. A., Allen, K. R., & Blieszner, R. (2001). Grandfathers' perceptions and expectations with their adult grandchildren. *Journal of Family Issues, 22*(4), 407–426.

Robinson, L. C. (2000). Interpersonal relationship quality in young adulthood: A gender analysis. *Adolescence, 35*(140), 775–784.

Roche, T. (2000). The crisis of foster care. *Time, 156,* 74–82.

Rogers, M. L., & Hogan, D. P. (2003). Family life with children with disabilities. The key role of rehabilitation. *Journal of Marriage and the Family, 65*(4), 818–833.

Rogoff, B. (1990). *Apprenticeship in thinking: Cognitive development in social context.* New York: Oxford University Press.

Rogoff, B., Paradise, R., Arauz, R. M., Correa-Chavez, M., & Angelitto, C. (2003). Firsthand learning through intent participation. *Annual Review of Psychology, 54*, 175–203.

Rosenberg, M., & Guttman, J. (2001). Structural boundaries of single-parent families and children's adjustment. *Journal of Divorce and Remarriage, 36*, 83–98.

Rosenblum, G. D., & Lewis, M. (1999). The relations between body image, physical attractiveness, and body mass in adolescence. *Child Development, 70*, 50–64.

Rosenfeld, A. A., Pilowsky, D. J., Fine, P., Thorpe, M., Fein, E., Simms, M. O., et al. (1997). Foster care: An update. *Journal of American Academy of Child and Adolescent Psychiatry, 36*, 448–457.

Rosenfield, A., & Wise, N. (2000). *The over-scheduled child: How to avoid the hyper-parenting trap.* New York: St. Martin's Press.

Rossi, A., & Rossi, P. (1990). *Of human bonding: Parent–child relations across the life course.* New York: Aldine de Gruyter.

Rossman, B. B., & Rosenberg, M. S. (2000). Maltreated adolescents: Victims caught between childhood and adulthood. *Violence and Abuse Abstracts, 6*(3), 55.

Rothbaum, F., Pott, M., & Azuma, H. (2000). The development of close relationships in Japan and the United States: Paths of symbiotic harmony and generative tensions. *Child Development, 71*, 1121–1142.

Rozie-Battle, J. (2003). Economic support and the dilemma of teen fathers. *Journal of Health and Social Policy, 17*(1), 73–86.

Ruff, C. D., & Keyes, C. L. M. (1995). The structure of psychological well being revisited. *Journal of Personality and Social Psychology, 69*, 719–727.

Sankar-DeLeeuw, N. (2007). Case studies of gifted kindergarten children, Part II: The parents and teachers. *Roeper Review, 29*(2), 93–99.

Sankofa, B. M., Hurley, E. A., Allen, B. A., & Boykin, A. W. (2005). Cultural expression and black students' attitudes toward high achievers. *Journal of Psychology, 139*(3), 247–259.

Sarigiani, P. A., Heath, P. A., & Camarena, P. M. (2003). The significance of parental depressed mood for young adolescents' emotional and family experiences. *Journal of Early Adolescence, 23*(3), 241–267.

Sawhill, I. V. (2000). Welfare reform and reducing teen pregnancy. *Public Interest, 138*, 40–51.

Schwartz, C. (2003). Parents of children with chronic disabilities: The gratification of caregiving. *Families in Society, 84*(4), 576–584.

Schwartz, D. (2000). Subtypes of victims and aggressors in children's peer groups. *Journal of Abnormal Child Psychology, 28*, 181–192.

Sebald, A., & Luckner, J. (2007). Successful partnerships with families of children who are deaf. *Teaching Exceptional Children, 39*(3), 54–60.

Segrin, C., & Nabi, R. (2002). Does television cultivate unrealistic expectations about marriage? *Journal of Communication, 52*(2), 247–263.

Shapiro, A. (2003). Later-life divorce and parent-adult child contact and proximity: A longitudinal analysis. *Journal of Family Issues, 24*(2), 264–285.

Shapiro, J. (1996). Custody and conduct: How the law fails lesbian and gay parents and their children. *Indiana Law Journal, 71*, 623–671.

Shapiro, V. B., Shapiro, J. R., & Parer, I. H. (2001). *Complex adoption and assisted reproductive technology*, New York: Guilford.

Shaw, D. S., Bell, R. Q., & Gilliam, M. (2000). A truly early starter model of antisocial behavior unvisited. *Clinical Child and Family Psychology Review, 3*, 155–172.

Shaw, D. S., Lacourse, E., & Nagin, D. S. (2005). Developmental trajectories of conduct problems and hyperactivity from ages 2 to 10. *Journal of Child Psychology & Psychiatry, 46*(9), 931–942.

Shaw, J., Lewis, J., Loeb, A., Rosado, J., & Rodriquez, R. (2001). A comparison of Hispanic and African-American sexually abused girls and their families. *Child Abuse and Neglect, 25*, 1363–1379.

Shears, J., Summers, J. A., & Boller, K. (2006). Exploring father's roles in low-income families: The influence of intergenerational transmission. *Families in Society, 87*(2), 259–268.

Shek, D. T. L., & Chen, L. K. (1999). Hong Kong Chinese parents' perceptions of the ideal child. *The Journal of Psychology, 133*, 291–302.

Shiono, P., Rauh, V., Park, M., Lederman, S., & Zuskar, D. (1997). Ethnic differences in birthweight: The role of lifestyle and other factors. *American Journal of Public Health, 87*, 787–793.

Shisslak, C. M., & Crago, M. (2001). Risk and protective factors in the development of eating disorders. In J. K. Thompson & L. Smolak (Eds.), *Body image, eating disorders, and obesity in youth:*

Assessment, treatment, and prevention (pp. 103–125). Washington, DC: American Psychological Association.

Shmotkin, D. (1999). Affective bonds of adult children with living versus deceased parents. *Psychology and Aging, 14*(3), 473–484.

Shulman, S., Scharf, M., & Lumer, D. (2001). Parental divorce and young adult children's romantic relationships: resolution of the divorce experience. *American Journal of Orthopsychiatry, 71*(4), 473–480.

Simons, R., Wu, C-I., & Lin, K-H. (2000). A cross-cultural examination of the link between corporal punishment and adolescent antisocial behavior. *Criminology, 38*(1), 47–79.

Singer, J., Fuller, B., & Keiley, M. (1998). Early child care selection: Variation by geographic location, maternal characteristics, and family structure. *Developmental Psychology, 34*(5), 1129–1144.

Skinner, B. F. (1950). Are theories of learning necessary? *Psychological Review, 57*, 193–216.

Skinner, B. F. (1974). *About behaviorism.* New York: Knopf.

Smetana, J., Abernathy, A., & Harris, A. (2000). Adolescent–parent interactions in middle-class African American families: Longitudinal change and contextual variation. *Journal of Family Psychology, 14*, 458–474.

Smith, T. B., Oliver, M. N. I., & Boyce, G. C. (2000). Effect of mothers' locus of control for child improvement in a developmentally delayed sample. *The Journal of Genetic Psychology, 161*(3), 307–313.

Spitz, R. A. (1954). Unhappy and fatal outcomes of emotional deprivation and stress in infancy. In I. Galdston (Ed.), *Beyond the germ theory.* Washington, DC: Health Education Council.

Spock, B. (1946). *The pocket book of baby and child care.* New York: Pocket Books.

Spock, B. (1985). *Baby and child care* (Rev. ed.). New York: Simon & Schuster.

Sprouse, C., Hall, C., Webster, R., & Bolen, L. (1998). Social perception in students with learning disabilities and attention deficit/hyperactivity disorder. *Journal of Nonverbal Behavior, 22*, 125–134.

Stacey, J. & Biblarz, T. J. (2001). (How) does the sexual orientation of parents matter? *American Sociological Review, 66*, 159–183.

Steinbeck, K. (2001). Obesity in children—The importance of physical activity—Proceedings of the Kellogg's Nutrition Symposium 2000, Sydney, Australia, 8 August 2000. *Australian Journal of Nutrition and Dietetics, 58*, 28–32.

Steinberg, L. (1990). Autonomy, conflict, and harmony in the family relationship. In S. Feldman & G. Elliott (Eds.), *At the threshold: The developing adolescent* (pp. 255–276). Cambridge, MA: Harvard University Press.

Steinberg, L. (1996). *Beyond the classroom: Why school reform has failed and what parents need to do.* New York: Simon & Schuster.

Steinberg, L. (2000). We know some things: Parent-adolescent relationships in retrospect and prospect. *Journal of Research on Adolescence, 11*(1), 1–19.

Steinberg, L., & Levine, A. (1997). *You and your adolescent: A parent's guide for ages 10 to 20* (Rev. ed.). New York: Harper-Collins.

Steinberg, L., & Steinberg, W. (1994). *Crossing paths: How your child's adolescence triggers your own crisis.* New York: Simon & Schuster.

Steinhausen, H-C., & Metzke, C. W. (2001). Risk, compensatory vulnerability, and protective factors influencing mental health in adolescence. *Journal of Youth and Adolescence, 30*(3), 259–280.

Stephenson, S. (2001). Street children in Moscow: Using and creating social capital. *Sociological Review, 49*, 530–547.

Stevens, V., Bourdeaudhuij, I., & Oost, P. (2002). Relationship of the family environment to children's involvement in bully/victim problems at school. *Journal of Youth and Adolescence, 31*, 419–428.

Stevenson, H. C. (1995). Relationship of adolescent perceptions of racial socialization to racial identity. *Journal of Black Psychology, 21*, 49–70.

Stewart, S. D. (1999). Nonresident mothers' and fathers' social contact with children. *Journal of Marriage and the Family, 61*, 894–907.

Stice, E., Shaw, H., & Marti, C. N. (2006). A meta-analytic review of obesity prevention programs for children and adolescents: The skinny on interventions that work. *Psychological Bulletin, 132*(5), 667–691.

Sturge-Apple, M. L., Davies, P. T., & Cummings, E. M. (2006). Hostility and withdrawal in marital conflict: Effects on parental emotional unavailability and inconsistent discipline. *Journal of Family Psychology, (20,2),* 227–238.

Suitor, J., Pillemer, K., Keeton, S., & Robison, J. (1994). Aged parents and aging children: Determinants of relationship quality. In R. Blieszner & V. Bedford (Eds.), *Aging and the Family* (pp. 223–242). Westport, CT: Praeger.

Sun, Y. (2003). The well-being of adolescents in households with no biological parents. *Journal of Marriage & Family, 65*(4), 894–909.

Sungthong, R., Mo-suwan, L., & Chongsuvivatwong, V. (2002). Effects of haemoglobin and serum ferretin on cognitive function in school children. *Asia Pacific Journal of Clinical Nutrition, 11*(2), 117–122.

Swann, C. (2006). The foster care crisis: What caused caseloads to grow? *Demography, 43*(2), 309–335.

Synnott, A. (1988). Little angels, little devils: A sociology of children. In G. Handel (Ed.), *Childhood socialization.* New York: Aldine De Gruyter.

Szinovacz, M., & Davey, A. (2002). Retirement effects on parent–adult contacts. *Gerontologist, 41,* 191–200.

Takas, M. (1995). *Grandparents raising grandchildren: A guide to finding help and hope.* New York: Brookdale Foundation.

Talukder, M. (2000). The importance of breastfeeding and strategies to sustain high breastfeeding rates. In Anthony Costello & Dharma Manandhar (Eds.), *Improving newborn health in developing countries.* London: Imperial College Press.

Tanner, E. M., & Finn-Stevenson, M. (2002). Nutrition and brain development: social policy implications. *American Journal of Orthopsychiatry, 72*(2), 182–193.

Tanofsky-Kraff, M., Yanovksi, S. Z., Wilfley, D. E., Maramesh, C., Morgan, C. M., & Yanovski, J. A. (2004). Eating-disordered behaviors, body fat, and psychopathology in overweight and normal weight children. *Journal of Consulting and Clinical Psychology, 72*(1), 53–61.

Taras, H. (2005). Nutrition and student performance in school. *The Journal of School Health. 75*(6), 199–213.

Tarleton, J. L., Hague, R., Mondal, D., Shu, J., Farr, B. M., & Petri, W. A., Jr. (2006). Cognitive effects of diarrhea, malnutrition, and entamoeba histolytica infection on school-age children in Dhaka, Bangladesh. *The American Journal of Tropical Medicine and Hygiene, 74*(3), 475–482.

Taunt, H. (2002). Positive impact of children with developmental disabilities on their families. *Education and Training in Mental Retardation and Developmental Disabilities, 37*(4), 410–420.

Taussig, H. N., Clyman, R. B., & Landsverk, J. (2001). Children who return home from foster care: A 6 year prospective study of behavioral health outcomes in adolescence, In R. L. Hegar & M. Scannapieco (Eds.), *Kinship foster care: Policy, practice, & research, Vol. 108.* New York: Oxford University Press.,

Taylor, R. J., Chatters, L. M., Tucker, M. B., & Lewis, E. (1990). Developments in research on black families: A decade review. *Journal of Marriage and the Family, 52,* 993–1014.

Teller, D. (1997). First glances: The vision of infants. *Investigative Ophthalmology & Visual Science, 38,* 2183–2203.

Thiruchelvam, D., Charach, A., & Schachar, R. (2001). Moderators and mediators of long-term adherence to stimulant treatment in children with ADHD. *Journal of the American Academy of Child and Adolescent Psychiatry, 40,* 922–928.

Tibbs, T., Haire-Joshu, D., Schechtman, K. B., Brownson, R. C., Nanney, M. S., Houston, C., & Auslander, W. (2001). The relationship between parental modeling, eating patterns, and dietary intake among African-American parents. *Journal of the American Dietetic Association, 101*(5), 535–541.

Timpka, T., & Lindqvist, K. (2001). Evidence-based prevention of acute injuries in a WHO Safe Community. *British Journal of Sports Medicine, 35,* 20–27.

Tirone, S., & Pedlar, A. (2005). Leisure, place, and diversity: The experiences of ethnic minority youth. Canadian Ethnic Studies, 37(2), 32–48.

Trawick-Smith, J (2000). *Early childhood development* (2nd ed.). Upper Saddle River, NJ: Prentice Hall.

Triandis, H. C. (1995). *Individualism and collectivism.* Boulder, CO: Westview Press.

Tripp, R. (1970). *The international thesaurus of quotations.* New York: Harper & Row.

Troiano, R., Briefel, R., Carroll, M., & Bialostosky, K. (2000). Energy and fat intakes of children and adolescents in the United States: Data from the national health and nutrition examination surveys. *The American Journal of Clinical Nutrition, 72,* Suppl. 1343S–1353S.

Tse, L. (1999). Finding a place to be: Ethnic identity exploration of Asian Americans. *Adolescence, 34,* 121–138.

Tseng, V. (2004). Family interdependence and academic adjustments in college : Youth from immigrant and U. S.–born families. *Child Development, 75,* 966–983.

Tucker, C. J., McHale, S. M., & Crouter, A. C. (2003). Conflict resolution: Links with adolescents' family relationships and well-being. *Journal of Family Issues, 24*(6), 715–736.

Umberson, D. (1992). Relationships between adult children and their parents: Psychological consequences for both generations. *Journal of Marriage and the Family, 54,* 665–674.

Unger, J. B., & Chen, X. (1999). The role of social networks and media receptivity in predicting age of smoking initiation. *Addictive Behaviors, 24*(3), 371–381.

UNICEF. (1998). *The state of the world's children, 1998.* New York: Oxford University Press.

U.S. Bureau of the Census. (1999). CH-7. Grandchildren living in the home of their grandparents: 1970 to present, Internet release, based on Current Population Reports Series P20-514, "Marital Status and Living Arrangements: March 1998."

U.S. Bureau of the Census. (2000). Statistical Abstracts of the U.S.: 2000: Report No. #69. Children under 18 years old by presence of parents: 1980 to 1998.

U.S. Department of Health and Human Services, (2000). Healthy People 2010! *Understanding and Inspiring Health* (2nd ed.), Washington, D.C.: U.S. Government Printing Office.

U.S. Department of Heatlth and Human Services, Administration on Children Youth and Families (2003). *Child maltreatment (1900–2001).* Washington, DC: U.S. Government Printing Office.

Vacca, J. J. (2006). Parent perceptions of raising a child with a severe disability: Implications for mental health providers. *Best Practices in Mental Health, 2*(1), 59–73.

Valenza, E., Simion, F., & Cassia, V. (1996). Face preference at birth. *Journal of Experimental Psychology. Human Perception and Performance, 22,* 892–903.

Vandell, D., & Bailey, M. (1995). Conflict between siblings. In C. Shantz & W. Hartup (Eds.), *Conflict in child and adolescent development* (pp. 242–269). New York: Cambridge University Press.

Vanfrussen, K. (2003). Family functioning in lesbian families created by donor insemination. *American Journal of Orthopsychiatry, 74*(1), 78–90.

Van Wel, F, & Bogt, T. T., & Raaijmakers, Q. (2002). Changes in the parental bond and well being of adolescents and young people. *Adolescence, 37*(146), 317–335.

Van Wel, F. & Hub Abna, R. (2000). The parental bond and the well being of adolescents and young adults. *Journal of Youth and Adolescence, 29*(3), 307–318.

Variyam, J. N. (2001). Overweight children: Is parental nutrition a factor? *Food Review, 24*(2), 18–22.

Veenema, T. G. (2001). Children's exposure to community violence. *Journal of Nursing Scholarship, 33,* 167–173.

Volkmar, F., Cook, E., & Pomeroy, J. (1999). Practice parameters for the assessment and treatment of children, adolescents, and adults with autism and other pervasive developmental disorders. *Journal of the American Academy of Child and Adolescent Psychiatry, 38,* 32S–54S.

Volling, B. L., McElwain, N. L., & Miller, A. L. (2000). Emotion regulation in context: The jealousy complex between young siblings and its relation with child and family characteristics. *Child Development, 73*(2), 581–600.

Vygotsky, L. (1978). *Mind in society: The development of higher psychological processes.* Cambridge, MA: Harvard University Press.

Waldrup, D., & Weber, J. (2001). From grandparent to caregiver: The stress and satisfaction of raising grandchildren. *Families in Society, 82,* 461–462.

Wallace, L. H., & May, D. C. (2005). The impact of parental attachment and feelings of isolation on adolescent fear of crime at school. *Adolescence 40,* 457–474.

Wallerstein, J., Lewis, J., & Blakeslee, S. (2001). *The unexpected legacy of divorce: A twenty-five year landmark study.* New York: Hyperion Press.

Wamboldt, M. Z., & Wamboldt, F. S. (2000). Role of the family in the onset and outcome of childhood disorders: Selected research findings. *Journal of the American Academy of Child and Adolescent Psychiatry, 39*(10), 1212–1219.

Ware, H. S., Jouriles, E. N., Spiller, L. C., McDonald, R., Swank, P. R., & Norwood, W. D. (2001). Conduct problems among children at battered women's shelters: Prevalence and stability of maternal reports. *Journal of Family Violence, 16,* 291–307.

Warner, M. P. (2007). Standing tall, *Exceptional Parent, 37*(3), 56–57.

Watson, J. B., & Watson, R. (1928). *The psychological care of the infant and child.* New York: Norton.

Weed, K., Keogh, D., & Borkowski, J. G. (2000). Predictors of resiliency in adolescent mothers. *Journal of Applied Developmental Psychology,* 21, 207–231.

Wegscheider, S. (1989). *Another chance: Hope and health for the alcoholic family.* Palo Alto, CA: Science and Behavior Books.

Weinberg, M., & Tronick, E. (1996). Infant affective reactions to the resumption of maternal interaction after the still-face. *Child Development, 67,* 905–914.

Weinberg, M., Tronick, E., & Cohn, J. (1999). Gender differences in emotional expressivity and self-regulation during early infancy. *Developmental Psychology, 35,* 175–188.

Weiner, J., & Schneider, B. H. (2002). A multisource explanation of the friendship patterns of children with and without learning disabilities. *Journal of Abnormal Child Psychology, 30*(2), 127–141.

Weinfield, N., Sroufe, L., & Egeland, B. (2000). Attachment from infancy to early adulthood in a high-risk sample: Continuity, discontinuity, and their correlates. *Child Development, 71,* 695–703.

Wels, F. V., Bogt, T., & Raaijmakers, Q. (2002). Changes in the parental bond and the well-being of adolescents and young adults. *Adolescence, 37,* 317–333.

Wels, F. V., Linnsen, H., & Abma, R. (2000). The paternal bond and the well-being of adolescents and young adults. *Journal of Youth and Adolescence, 29*(3), 307–318.

Wheeler, I. (2001). Parental improvement: The crisis of memory. *Death Studies, 25*(1), 51–66.

Whipple, E. E., Fitzgerald, H. E., & Zucker, R. A. (1995). Parent-child relations in alcoholics and non-alcoholic families. *American Journal of Orthopsychiatry, 65*(1), 153.

Whitaker, R. C., Wright, J. A., Pepe, M. S., Seidel, K. D., & Dietz, W. H. (1997). Predicting obesity in young adulthood from childhood obesity and parental obesity. *New England Journal of Medicine, 337,* 869–873.

Whitelaw, A., & Sleath, K. (1985). Myth of the marsupial mother: Home care of very low birth weight babies in Bogato, Columbia, in T. M. Field (Ed.), *Touch in early development* (pp. 53–65), Mahwah, NJ: Erlbaum, Vol. 2, 1206–1209.

Windle, M. (1996). Effect of parental drinking on adolescents. *Alcohol Health and Research World, 20,* 181–184.

Wise, P. H. , Wampler, N. S., Chavkin, W., & Romero, D. (2002). Chronic illness among poor children enrolled in the temporary assistance for needy families program. *American Journal of Public Health, 92*(9), 1458–1461.

Wolchik, S. A., Wilcox, K. L., Tein, J-Y., & Sandler, L. N. (2000). Maternal acceptance and consistency of discipline as buffers of divorce stressors on children's adjustment problems. *Journal of Abnormal Child Psychology, 28,* 87–102.

Wolfe, D. A., Scott, K., Wekerle, C., & Pittman, A-L. (2001). Child maltreatment: Risk of adjustment problems and dating violence in adolescence. *Journal of the American Academy of Child and Adolescent Psychiatry, 40*(3), 282–290.

Wolke, D., Wood, S., & Stanford, K. (2001). Bullying and victimization of primary school children in England and Germany: Prevalence and school factors. *The British Journal of Psychology, 92*(4), 673–696.

Wong, C. A. (1997, April). What does it mean to be African-American or European-American growing up in a multi-ethnic community? *Paper presented at the biennial meeting of the Society for Research in Child Development,* Washington, DC.

Woodward, A., & Markman, E. (1998). Early word learning. In W. Damon, D. Kuhn, & R. Siegler (Eds.), *Handbook of child psychology, Vol. 2: Cognition, perception and language* (5th ed., pp. 371–420). New York: Wiley.

Worden, J. W., Davies, B., & McCowen, D. (1999). Comparing parent loss with sibling loss. *Death Studies, 23*(1), 1–15.

Wright, D. R., & Fitzpatrick, K. M. (2004). Psychosocial correlates of substance abuse behaviors among African American youth. *Adolescence, 39*, 653–667.

Yoder, K. A., Hoyt, D. R., & Whitbeck, L. B. (1998). Suicide behavior in homeless and runaway adolescents. *Journal of Youth and Adolescence, 27*, 753–772.

Yonkers, K. A., Wisner, K. L., & Stowe, Z. (2004). Management of bipolar disorder during pregnancy and the postpartum period. *The American Journal of Psychiatry, 161*(4), 608–620.

Yoshinga-Itano, C. (2003). From screening to early identification and intervention: Discovering predictors to successful outcomes for children with significant hearing loss. *Journal of Deaf Studies and Deaf Education, 8*(1), 11–30.

Young, B., Dixon-Woods, M., Findlay, M., & Heney, D. (2002). Parenting in a crisis: Conceptualizing mothers of children with cancer. *Social Science and Medicine, 55*, 1835–1847.

Zabelski, M. (2001). Encouraging self-esteem in children: A parent's view. *RE:view, 33*, 99–101.

Zajdow, G. (2002). *Al-Anon narratives: Women, self-stories, and mutual aid.* Westport, CO: Greenwood Press.

Zarit, S., & Eggebeen, D. (1995). Parent–child relationships in adulthood and old age. In M. Bornstein (Ed.), *Handbook of parenting, Vol. 1: Children and parenting* (pp. 119–140). Hillsdale, NJ: Erlbaum.

Zeijl, E., Poel, Y. & Bois-Reymond, M. (2001). The role of parents and peers in leisure activities of young adolescents. *Journal of Leisure Research, 32*(3), 281–302.

Zhou, M. (1997). Growing up in America: The challenge confronting immigrant children and children of immigrants. *Annual Review of Sociology, 23*, 63–95.

Zick, C. D., Bryant, W. K., & Osterbacka, E. (2001). Mothers' employment, parental involvement, and the implication for child outcomes. *Social Science Research, 30*(1), 24–49.

Zimmer-Gembeck, M. J. & Collins, W. A. (2003). Autonomy development during adolescence. In G. Adams & M. Berzonsky (Eds.), *Blackwell handbook of adolescence.* Malden, MA: Blackwell.

Zinsmeister, K. (1996). Divorce's toll on children. *The American Enterprise, 7*, 39–44.

Zajdow. G. (2002). *Al-Anon narratives: women, self stories, and mutual aid.* Greenwood Press: Westport, CO, p. 30.

Author Index

Subject Index